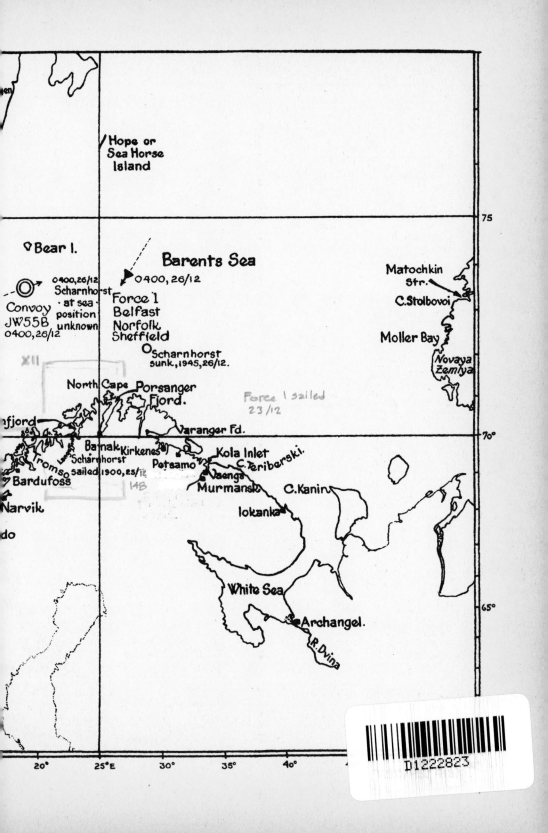

Hope or
Sea Horse
Island

Bear I.

Barents Sea

0400,26/12
Scharnhorst
· at sea ·
position
unknown

0400, 26/12

Matochkin
Str.

C.Stolbovoi

Convoy
JW55B
0400,26/12

Force 1
Belfast
Norfolk
Sheffield

Moller Bay

Novaya
Zemlya

XII

Scharnhorst
sunk,1945,26/12.

North Cape   Porsanger
Fjord.

Force 1 sailed
23/12

fjord

Varanger Fd.

75

70°

Banak
Scharnhorst
Tromso sailed 1900,25/12
Bardufoss
148
Narvik
do

Kirkenes
Petsamo

Kola Inlet
C.Teriberski.

Vaenga
Murmansk

Iokanka

C.Kanin

65°

White Sea

Archangel.

R.Dvina

20°   25°E   30°   35°   40°

SCHARNHORST

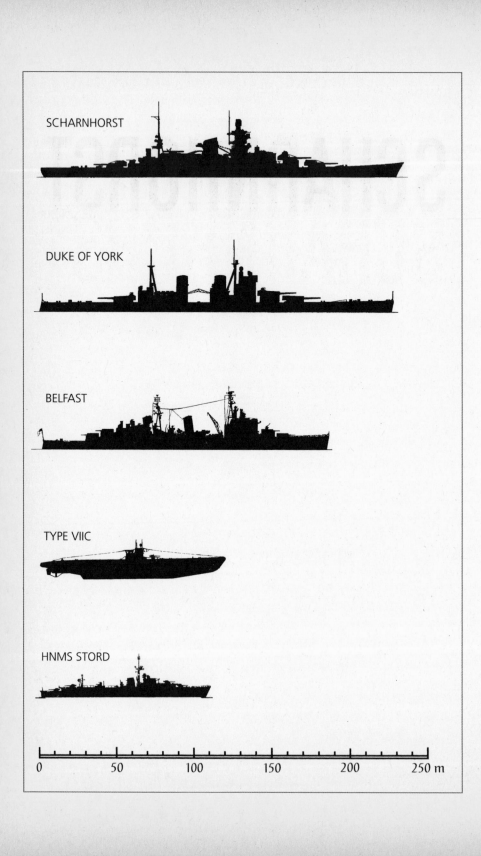

SCHARNHORST

DUKE OF YORK

BELFAST

TYPE VIIC

HNMS STORD

0   50   100   150   200   250 m

SCHARNHORST

ALF R. JACOBSEN

Translated from the Norwegian
by J. Basil Cowlishaw

SUTTON PUBLISHING

First published as *Scharnhorst* in 2001 by H. Aschehoug & Co. (W. Nygaard), Oslo.
First published in English in 2003 by
Sutton Publishing Limited · Phoenix Mill
Thrupp · Stroud · Gloucestershire · GL5 2BU

Translated from the Norwegian by J. Basil Cowlishaw

British Library Cataloguing in Publication Data
A catalogue record for this book is available from the British Library

ISBN 0-7509-3404-2

Typeset in 12.5/16 Garamond 3.
Typesetting and origination by
Sutton Publishing Limited.
Printed and bound in England by
J.H. Haynes & Co. Ltd, Sparkford.

Contents

Foreword

I grew up in the shadow of the Second World War. Admittedly, when I was born – in February 1950 in Hammerfest, the world's northernmost town, not far to the west of the North Cape – the war had been over for nearly five years. But at that time the town had still not been rebuilt after its devastation in the autumn of 1944, and both my parents were still marked by their experiences during five years of war.

Norway was occupied by Nazi Germany in the summer of 1940, the first enemy soldiers making their appearance in Hammerfest in August of that year. They were soon followed by many more, as the town was an important staging-post for the forces being assembled for a joint German-Finnish attack launched on the ice-free port of Murmansk in June 1941, making it an important though little-known sector of the Eastern front.

The first years of occupation were peaceful. Hammerfest was a small town of barely four thousand inhabitants, so the presence of large numbers of enemy troops and naval units demanded a good deal of forbearance and give-and-take on both sides. After a time facilities were improved and the town turned into a supply base. To this end, as early as the autumn of 1940 a large refrigerator ship, the *Hamburg*, was anchored in the harbour. The ship's owners purchased large quantities of Norwegian-caught fish, which were processed and frozen on board. Shortly afterwards a Cuxhaven company, Heinz Lohmann & Co. AG, set up a permanent fish-processing factory in the town, not far from my childhood home. Although the fish was mostly processed by four hundred female workers brought in from the Ukraine, many Norwegians also found employment at the Lohmann factory. One of them was my father, who started work there in 1941. At one time a whole floor of our house was requisitioned as living quarters for two of the factory's managers.

The German presence was further reinforced in January 1943 when Hammerfest became the front-line base of two U-boat flotillas, nos 13 and 14, which operated against convoys carrying supplies through the Barents Sea to

Russia. *U-boot-Stützpunkt Hammerfest* was the *Black Watch*, a 5,000-ton passenger liner which the Germans had commandeered and on board which U-boat crews were given an opportunity to rest and relax after their long and arduous patrols in the Arctic Ocean; it was backed by a cargo ship, the *Admiral Carl Hering*, which provided workshop facilities and kept the U-boats supplied with torpedoes and ammunition. The *Black Watch* was moored behind anti-submarine nets close to the Lohmann wharf and was thus clearly visible from my parents' home.

The end came in the autumn of 1944 when Finland concluded a separate peace with the Soviet Union. Soviet troops broke through the Litza front on the Kola peninsula, which for three years had been the scene of a bloody and more or less static war of position. Forced to establish a new line of defence east of Tromsø, the mountain troops of 20. *Gebirgsarmee* made a rapid retreat. To prevent the Russians from following close on their heels, Hitler ordered their commander, *Generaloberst* Lothar Rendulic, to adopt the same ruthless scorched-earth policy that had been used to such terrible effect in the Soviet Union. In northern Norway the consequences were disastrous, with more than fifty thousand people being forcibly evacuated to regions further south. Every building, along with the infrastructure, was destroyed, being either burned or blown up, and the harbours were mined. By the time the retreat came to an end in February 1945, an area the size of Denmark had been razed. The only building left standing in Hammerfest was the small sepulchral chapel. My mother, father, brother and two sisters were evacuated towards the end of October 1944. All they were able to take with them were two small suitcases; everything else was consumed by the flames.

I grew up in the 1950s, when Hammerfest was still being rebuilt as a centre of Norway's modern fishing and tourism industries. As children, I and my friends played in the ruins of the Lohmann factory, in the demolished bunkers and in what was left of *U-boot-Stützpunkt Hammerfest*. In the long winter evenings I often heard my mother talk about the many dramatic events of the war. She described what it had been like when the Russians and British bombed the German installations and when a German troopship, the *Blenheim*, was torpedoed just outside the approach to the harbour with heavy loss of life. She had seen both the *Tirpitz* and the *Scharnhorst* glide past, shadowy shapes against the mountains to the south.

As a writer and chief editor in the Norwegian Broadcasting Corporation's Television Documentary Department, I set out in the spring of 1999 to search for the wreck of the German battlecruiser *Scharnhorst*, but it was not just with the intention of recreating the Battle of the North Cape, which was fought on

St Stephen's Day, 26 December 1943. I also felt an urgent need to acquire a
deeper understanding of the events that had made the islands and fjords around
Hammerfest and Alta into northern Europe's largest naval base – and had so
strongly affected the lives of my own family.

I discovered that many good books had been written about the battle, but
they were all based on either British or German sources. My advantage was that I
would probably be the first person in a position to draw upon declassified files
and other sources in *all* the countries involved in the chain of events that
concluded with the tragic loss of the *Scharnhorst*, namely Great Britain, Germany
and Norway, as well as, to a lesser extent, the United States and Russia.

The Battle of the North Cape reached its climax after four action-packed
days, starting from the moment convoy JW55B was discovered by a German
aircraft in the Norwegian Sea at about eleven in the morning of Wednesday
22 December 1943; the *Scharnhorst* was sent to the bottom 66 nautical miles
north-east of the North Cape at quarter to eight on the evening of Sunday
26 December. On the German side, in addition to the *Scharnhorst* herself and her
five escorting destroyers of the 4th Destroyer Flotilla, also engaged were various
reconnaissance aircraft and eight U-boats operating from bases in Narvik and
Hammerfest. On the basis of war diaries, reports, letters and interviews with
survivors, I have endeavoured to cover every facet of the action – to convey
something of what it was like for the men battling against wind and wave in the
U-boats and surface vessels, for those carrying out lonely reconnaissance flights
above the endless expanse of storm-lashed ocean and for those who waited at
home, on both sides of the front line. It is the first time such a comprehensive
approach has been adopted. I have also tried to put together the first complete
picture of the intelligence obtained, both through Enigma decrypts and through
the work of the agents in the field. Aided by the new insights afforded into the
Scharnhorst's last moments by our film of her mangled hulk on the sea floor, I
hope that I have succeeded in recounting the story of the German Navy in
northern Norway and the Battle of the North Cape as accurately and realistically
as possible. This book is about one of the greatest naval battles ever fought. But
it is first of all a book about the people involved.

Many people are entitled to a share of the credit for locating, after much hard
work and many frustrating attempts, the wreck of the German battlecruiser in
the autumn of the year 2000. They all helped to make this book possible and all
are mentioned by name, either in the text or in the notes.

I should like at this point to express my thanks to *Bordkameradschaft
Scharnhorst*, in the person of the association's president, Wolfgang Kube, as well

as to the survivors of the ship's sinking and the next-of-kin of the men who were lost, all of whom, in the course of countless long conversations, so freely shared their memories with me. I am especially indebted to Mrs Gertrud Bornmann and Mrs Sigrid Rasmussen, who lost their loved ones in 1943 and 1944 respectively, and who opened their lives to me. I should also like to express my gratitude to the surviving members of *U-716* and other German U-boats who took part in the long, drawn-out and arduous submarine war in the Arctic and who so patiently answered my many questions. The same applies to the British and Norwegian officers and men of the Allied fleet which finally surrounded and defeated the *Scharnhorst* in the fury and darkness of winter off the North Cape.

Allow me also to thank the British television producer Norman Fenton. Over the years he and I spent a great deal of time together in the Barents Sea, from the time we began to search for (and found) the wreck of the British trawler *Gaul*, right up to the time when we did the same with the *Scharnhorst*. It is doubtful whether we would have succeeded had it not been for Norman's experience and unflagging enthusiasm.

At the Bundesarchiv/Militärarchiv in Freiburg I was greatly helped by Helmut Döringhoff, who on our many visits led us to the documents we sought. The same applies to Jürgen Schlemm, a specialist on the U-boat war, who works in close collaboration with Das U-boot-Archiv in Cuxhaven and the amazing website *uboat.net*, and who so generously shared his expertise with me. I also wish to thank my Norwegian editor, Harald Engelstad, for his advice and encouragement in the writing of this book, and my translator, Basil Cowlishaw, who, thanks to his experience as a wireless operator in the wartime Royal Air Force and wide knowledge of the course of the Second World War, made this English-language edition possible. My wife Tove Thorsen Roev, an artist, is responsible for the maps and has been my adviser and, as always, my greatest source of inspiration throughout.

Alf R. Jacobsen
Oslo, Norway
March 2003

I

WESTERN FINNMARK 17, 18   HJELMSØY

SR1 ◉

ROLVSØY

Refsbotn

161, 189   VII, IX.
◉ POINT   Hammerfest
LUCIE
                        SØRØYA   KVALØYA

Lopphavet   Sørøysund   Kvalsund

LOPPA   SEILAND
        SILDA
                        STJERNØY   ◦ Porsa

                        Stjernsund   Vargsund   ◦ Store Lerresfjord

                                Langfjord 35   ◦ Korsfjord
                                                       Skillefjord
                                              35   Leirbotn

Kvænangen   ◦ Alteidet   Kåfjord   VII, IX, 35
        Burfjord   ◦ Alta   266

CHAPTER ONE

Death off the North Cape

THE BARENTS SEA, 19.30, SUNDAY 26 DECEMBER 1943

By this time the starboard side of the ship was already under water. Stoker Helmut Feifer slipped and slithered down the sloping deck until brought up short by an anti-aircraft gun, to which, by a superhuman effort, he managed to cling. He felt an urgent need to pray, but couldn't find the words. The front of his shirt was soaked in blood. He gagged at every breath he took, overcome by the acrid stench of cordite fumes and burning oil. A south-westerly gale had raged all night and throughout the dying day. Battered and bruised, he ached in every joint. His ears were still filled with the cries of the wounded, of the many of his shipmates who had had to be abandoned in passages and sickbays. All about him towered the black waves. The wind, ice-cold, relentless, set him shivering uncontrollably.

Utterly exhausted and in a state of shock as I was, I was tempted to give up. I mentally bade farewell to my mother and father and prepared to die. Then one of my shipmates struggled past and roused me from my stupor. He grabbed hold of me and heaved me out on to the deck. I remained clinging to the gun-mounting until the next wave broke in over the rail. At that moment I released my grip and allowed myself to be swept overboard by the torrent of water, away from the sinking ship.

By then the *Scharnhorst's* death throes had lasted for nearly three hours – since 16.47, when the *Duke of York* and the *Belfast* had fired the first of their star-shells. The end could not be long delayed.

The sea was still running high, despite the deadening effect of a thick covering of oil. It was pitch dark. I shouted and shouted, but no one answered. As my body began to grow numb and stiff with cold, it was brought home to me that, unless a miracle occurred, I didn't have long to live. Suddenly, from the crest of a wave, I saw a life-raft drifting past. I swam towards it. When I crawled aboard, almost at the end of my tether, I heard a voice say, 'He's wounded, he's covered in blood.' I felt a stab of fear. I was afraid they'd throw me back into the sea. I was only twenty and I didn't want to die, so I gasped that it wasn't my blood, it was my friend's.

Feifer was telling the truth. Earlier that evening he had been sitting deep within the bowels of the ship, playing his mouth-organ. Every time the battlecruiser's heavy guns thundered out the whole ship shuddered. But Feifer wasn't worried. He continued to play, one tune following another: *Lili Marlen, Muss I denn, Du schwarze Zigeuner* – carefree, romantic ballads calculated to sustain his shipmates' dreams and yearnings for home. To Feifer, and hundreds of other young sailors like him, the *Scharnhorst* was the ship that couldn't sink – a floating city, an unassailable fortress and the pride of Hitler's Germany. The twenty-one watertight bulkheads were encased in Krupp steel that was in some places 32 centimetres thick. The turbines were capable of developing more than 160,000 horsepower, giving the battlecruiser a maximum speed of 32 knots – faster than any comparable naval vessel in the world. Many people considered the *Scharnhorst* the most graceful warship ever built. To the ship's company and countless other admirers she was, quite simply, invincible. 'I was absolutely convinced that she was unsinkable. I was never the least anxious on that score. I was sure we'd all return home unscathed,' says Feifer.

Even the experienced staff of the British Naval Intelligence Service who interrogated the survivors after the battle remarked on this unshakeable belief.

Contrary to expectations, the survivors, all of whom were ratings, presented a front of tough, courteous security-consciousness and evidence of high morale. . . . *Scharnhorst* seems to have occupied in the affections of the German public a position analogous to that occupied by HMS *Hood* in England before she was sunk. A certain legend had grown up that she was a 'lucky ship' and her men considered themselves the pick of the German Surface Navy and a cut above all their rivals.

It was not until a shell from one of the battleship *Duke of York*'s heavy 14-inch guns penetrated the 'tween deck and burst in the *Scharnhorst*'s number one boiler room that Feifer realized the gravity of the situation. 'All my shipmates were killed instantly – with one exception. He was sitting up against the bulkhead. His clothes caught fire and his hair burst into flame, like a torch. I can't describe how he suffered. I helped to carry him up into C turret and from there to a first-aid station. It was his blood that had stained my shirt.'

In just under three hours the thirteen Allied vessels surrounding the *Scharnhorst* fired more than 2,000 shells and 55 torpedoes at her. By about 19.30 on 26 December 1943 the once-proud battlecruiser had been reduced to a blazing, shattered hulk and was totally defenceless. Some decks looked like abattoirs. The *Interrogation Report* says: 'Survivors described frightful scenes of carnage in some of these compartments, with mangled bodies swilling around in a mixture of blood and sea water while stretcher parties picked their way through the damage with ever-increasing numbers of wounded.'

Despite the destruction, evacuation continued in an orderly fashion until the order came to abandon ship. Ernst Reimann, an artificer from Dresden, was responsible for the hydraulics of the after triple turret. Together with the rest of the gunners, he put on his life-jacket. 'We carried on firing until we ran out of ammunition. The command was then given to load the last shell. We fired, then shut down all the machinery and closed off the hoist leading from the magazine. The list to starboard continued to increase, but we waited calmly. When the order came to abandon ship, one by one we made our way out through the hatch. From there it was only a 10-metre drop into the sea.'

Because of the increasing list, nineteen-year-old signaller Helmut Backhaus from Dortmund was finding it hard to keep his balance on his perch on the observation platform, 38 metres above the deck. He came from a line of Ruhr miners and as a boy had never had anything to do with the sea. His stepfather had been furious when Helmut sought his permission to join the navy, and had refused to give it. But Helmut was not one to take no for an answer. At the age of seventeen he ran away from home and joined the German *Kriegsmarine*. He had been on board when the *Scharnhorst*, accompanied by the *Gneisenau* and *Prinz Eugen*, made her celebrated dash through the English Channel from Brest to the Elbe, and had witnessed attacking British aircraft being shot out of the sky one after another.

Now the boot was on the other foot. The blackness of the night was constantly lit up by the flames belching forth from the muzzles of countless heavy guns. The enemy ships seemed to be everywhere. There was no escape; all that remained was the raging, ice-cold sea beneath him.

The phone rang. It was an artificer friend from my home district. 'Promise me you'll be honest,' he said. 'How serious is it?' I told him to drop everything and prepare to abandon ship. 'You must be mad,' was his reply. He wasn't aware that the *Scharnhorst* was sinking. I tore off my fur-lined jacket and boots and clambered over the bulwark. By the time I got to the enormous searchlight I was already knee-deep in water. A breaking wave lifted me up. I kicked out. I had to get clear, to avoid being sucked down by the sinking ship.

Some distance below where Backhaus had been stationed, on the bridge, where the storm lights had been staved in and the instruments destroyed by shellfire, Petty Officer Wilhelm Gödde heard the Captain issue his last orders:

'All hands on deck! Put on life-jackets! Prepare to jump overboard!' Most of us refused to leave the bridge without the Captain and Admiral Bey. One young seaman said quietly, 'We're staying with you.' The two officers managed to make us leave, one by one. On the deck, all was calm and orderly. There was hardly any shouting. I saw the way the First Officer helped hundreds of men to climb over the rails. The Captain checked our life-jackets once again before he and the Admiral took leave of each other with a handshake. They said to us, 'If any of you get out of this alive, say hello to the folks back home and tell them that we all did our duty to the last.'

Others elected to remain on board. When Günther Sträter left the after 15-cm battery, the deck was strewn with dead and wounded. 'One of the chief petty officers, *Oberstockmeister* Wibbelhof, and his Number Two, Moritz, refused to leave their post. "I'm staying here, where I belong," Wibbelhof said. When we left the turret, he shouted after us: "Long live Germany! Long live the *Führer*!" We answered in similar vein. Then he sat down and calmly lit a cigarette.'

The time was now 19.32. Racing in from the north-west came three British destroyers, *Virago*, *Opportune* and *Musketeer*, heading straight for the doomed giant. At a range of 2,000 metres they fired a total of nineteen torpedoes. These were followed by three more from the cruiser *Jamaica*. Many scored hits, causing the *Scharnhorst* to increase her list to starboard.

A strong gale was still blowing from the south-west, but close to the ships the oil-covered sea was strangely calm. Helmut Backhaus was a strong swimmer. 'I stopped and turned in the water to get my bearings. It was then that I saw the keel and propellers. She had capsized and was going down bow first.

Immediately afterwards there were two violent explosions. It was like an earthquake. The ocean heaved and shuddered.'

To Helmut Feifer, clinging to his life-raft, the hull loomed up in front of him like a black shadow. 'I thought, "*Mensch!* [Man] We've taken one of the British down with us." Even then I hadn't grasped that it was the *Scharnhorst*. I thought it was another ship going down – one *we* had sunk.'

Some distance away Wilhelm Gödde, who was still in the water, could see straight into the *Scharnhorst*'s funnel, which was lying half-submerged. 'It was like looking into a dark tunnel,' he said. The last he heard before the ship rolled over and disappeared beneath the surface of the sea was the sound of the turbines. 'It was a terrible sight, lit up as it was by star-shell and the ghostly white beams of the destroyers' searchlights. Where the searchlights struck the black and blue of the sea, the crests of the waves glittered and gleamed like silver.'

Nineteen-year-old Ordinary Seaman Helmut Boekhoff clung to a wooden grating as he desperately fought to paddle away from the danger area. 'In the light of a star-shell I could see her three propellers still turning. Suddenly she disappeared from sight, only to reappear a moment later. When she went down for a second time, it was for good. I felt the violence of the shock wave as it struck my legs and abdomen; deep down, something had exploded.'

Among those present, the only ones not to see the *Scharnhorst* go down were the men who had vanquished her. When the *Jamaica* completed her torpedo attack at 19.37, the battlecruiser's secondary guns were still firing at irregular intervals. Ten minutes later the *Belfast* closed in at high speed to deliver the *coup de grâce* – but by then all that was left was floating wreckage.

'All that could be seen of *Scharnhorst* was a dull glow through a dense cloud of smoke which the star-shells and searchlights of the surrounding ships could not penetrate. No ship therefore saw the enemy sink, but it seems fairly certain that she sank after a heavy underwater explosion which was heard and felt in several ships about 19.45,' wrote Admiral Bruce Fraser after the engagement.

At the time, however, the situation was far more confused than would appear from the Admiral's report. At 19.51 Fraser signalled all ships to leave the area, '. . . EXCEPT FOR SHIP WITH TORPEDOES AND DESTROYER WITH SEARCHLIGHT'. While Fraser impatiently paced backwards and forwards on the flagship's bridge, the destroyer *Scorpion* picked up thirty survivors; another destroyer rescued a further six. Some twenty minutes later, at 20.16, Fraser was still not certain of how things stood. Accordingly, he wirelessed the *Scorpion*, 'PLEASE CONFIRM SCHARNHORST IS SUNK.' It was not until 20.30 that the *Scorpion* replied, 'SURVIVORS STATE SCHARNHORST HAS SUNK.' Five minutes

later, at 20.35, Fraser signalled the Admiralty in London, '*SCHARNHORST SUNK.*' An hour later the Admiralty replied, 'GRAND. WELL DONE.' Shortly afterwards Fraser gave the order to call off the action and headed at full speed for Murmansk.

Several hundred of those on board went down with the *Scharnhorst*, but a large number – perhaps more than one thousand officers and young ratings – were left to die in the open sea, buffeted by wind and wave. All in all, the German *Kriegsmarine* lost 1,936 men off the North Cape that fateful evening in December. As the German broadcasting service proclaimed a few days later, they 'died a seaman's death in a heroic battle against a superior enemy. The *Scharnhorst* now rests on the field of honour.'

The Battle of the North Cape constituted a turning point in the war in the north. Never again was the German High Seas Fleet a direct threat to the Murmansk convoys. In the event, Hitler's capital ships were to remain inoperative for the rest of the war, while in the Atlantic gunfire was never again to be exchanged between armoured giants of the magnitude of the *Duke of York* and *Scharnhorst*. The era of the battleship was at an end. The Battle of the North Cape brought to a conclusion a process of development that had lasted for a century. When the guns fell silent off the North Cape, a naval epoch came to a close.

Admiral Bruce Fraser delivered his final 'Despatch' one month later. In it he wrote that the *Scharnhorst* 'had definitely sunk in approximate position 72°16'N, 28°41'E', which was about 80 nautical miles north-east of the North Cape.

In naval history this has become one of the most famous spots in the Arctic Ocean, a site spoken of with awe from Labrador to the White Sea, from Reykjavik to Cape Rybachi. It was officially recognized by the British Admiralty and has found its way into a host of textbooks, magazines and works of reference. For me it was destined to prove a source of endless trouble and frustration.

CHAPTER TWO

An Unsuccessful Attempt

THE NORTH CAPE BANK, FRIDAY 24 APRIL 1999

The expedition seemed to be cursed from the start. I should have realized that we were jinxed when we were still moored in Honningsvåg a few days earlier and were busy testing the diving vessel *Risøy*'s sophisticated ROV (Remotely Operated Vehicle). The pictures of the seabed relayed via the control cable to the control room were perfectly clear, but spreading out across the surface of the sea was a thin, rainbow-hued film of oil: hydraulic fluid was seeping out from somewhere. There was clearly a leak, and I should have taken steps to find out where it was. But I was blind – I was too eager to get away. The wind from the night before had died down. The sea was calm and above the Porsanger fjord the Arctic spring sky was a shimmering vault of blue and gold.

'Shall we go?' asked Stein Inge Riise, a diver from Vardø who never said no to the chance of an adventure, and who had built Riise Underwater Engineering into a highly qualified company specializing in risky underwater operations. Forty years old, fair-haired and full of life, he had made an international name for himself when, with the aid of the *Risøy*, a local ferry he had converted, in the autumn of 1997, acting on behalf of Anglia TV, Channel 4 and Norway's NRK, he located the wreck of the British trawler *Gaul* at a depth of 300 metres on the North Cape Bank – a feat the British Ministry of Defence had dismissed as impossible.

Now my partner Norman and I had presented Stein Inge and his crew with a new and equally formidable task. First, by means of the *Risøy*'s ROV, we planned to examine the cables strewn across the seabed around the wreck of the *Gaul*, then to sail for 60 nautical miles eastwards in search of the wreck of the German battlecruiser *Scharnhorst*.

When, late that night, we dropped anchor at the spot where the *Gaul* lay, some 55 nautical miles due north of the North Cape, the weather was still favourable. We were in one of the most unpredictable stretches of ocean in the world, but just now the sea was as calm as a millpond. Bathed in the radiant light of the Midnight Sun, the Barents Sea looked like a sheet of silk.

If the weather was on our side, everything else was against us. We were dogged by a succession of mishaps – electronic and hydraulic problems – which Stein Inge and his crew fought hard to overcome. When the hydraulic cutter broke down, I realized that the cables would have to wait. Now, late on Friday evening, we were making our way eastwards, heading for the position Admiral Bruce Fraser had given as the spot where the *Scharnhorst* had met her doom, the place where the last witnesses, Backhaus, Feifer, Boekhoff and the others, had watched the battlecruiser disappear beneath the waves. Keyed up as we were, we had been on the go, with little sleep, for close on fifty hours. At a depth of 300 metres margins are narrow and the risks correspondingly great – added to which, our troubles had left me with a tight knot in my stomach.

'Relax. I've a hunch we shall find the wreck, provided the position's correct. I can feel it in my bones,' Stein Inge said reassuringly. An incorrigible optimist, he viewed every assignment as a challenge.

'I hope you're right,' I muttered in reply. But I couldn't do anything about the thoughts that continued to revolve in my head. *Was* the position correct? What if we didn't find the wreck? How long could we keep on searching? How long would the good weather last?

The last signal transmitted by the *Scharnhorst* to *Admirals Nordmeer* in Narvik and *Gruppe Nord* in Kiel had been picked up by the British wireless interception service at 19.30 – just before the launching of the last decisive torpedo attack. It read: 'AM STEERING FOR TANAFJORD. POSITION IS SQUARE AC4992. SPEED 20 KNOTS.'

AC4992 was a grid square in the German *Kriegsmarine*'s secret chart of the Barents Sea. It referred to a position of latitude 71°57'N and longitude 28°30'E. According to the battlecruiser's reckoning, when the battle entered its final phase she was thus 15 to 20 nautical miles further south than the British believed her to be. Who was right, Admiral Bruce Fraser on board the *Duke of York*, flagship of the Home Fleet, or *Kapitän-zur-See* Fritz Julius Hintze on board the *Scharnhorst*?

I had chosen to pin my faith on Fraser, whose fix was, I assumed, backed by the navigators of the thirteen Allied vessels. Hintze's men had been stood-to for more than twenty-four hours in extremely harsh weather conditions. They had

had little sleep and had twice been engaged in exchanges of gunfire with British cruisers – on one occasion in the middle of the day, when, in theory, the light should have been at its best. But could the *Scharnhorst*'s navigators have taken an accurate fix under such otherwise unpropitious circumstances? Had they succeeded in accurately pinpointing their ship's position during the almost three-hour-long conclusive phase of the battle?

I doubted it, and all other available data suggested that Admiral Fraser knew what he was about when he reported the position of the sinking as 72°16'N and 28°41'E.

I had meticulously collected and studied fishing charts covering this region ever since April 1977, when, as a newspaper reporter on assignment on board the *Gargia*, I had written:

No fishing is more demanding than trawling in the Barents Sea. For proof you need only look at the muscular arms of the men who fish these waters – and the way those who have been at it for a number of years drink when they are ashore.

I have been long-lining, far out to sea, in January, when darkness reigned for twenty-four hours a day and crews were reeling on their feet after twenty hours without sleep. I have witnessed purse-seine fishing offshore and on the banks further out to sea; and I have taken part in fishing in the confines of the Norwegian fjords. But nothing can compare with trawling. . . . It is not just because of the vast quantities of fish the trawls haul on board. It is also because of the taut, slippery wires, the solid steel of the bobbins and trawl doors, the whine and clang of the winches. Trawling is heavy industry moved out to sea.

I had spent hours in the *Gargia*'s wheelhouse poring over the vessel's old charts, which prompted me to add:

And there are the charts, guides to a wondrous landscape beneath the waves. On these charts, creased and tattered from years of use, the major fishing grounds are thick with the captain's own mysterious markings. There are charts on which are marked the wreck of the *Scharnhorst* and other underwater hazards likely to damage trawls, a jumble of jottings, figures and pencilled lines. These sheets are not mere registers of depths and meridians, the work of the Hydrographic Department; they are also the product and repository of years of hard-won practical experience.

All the charts I had studied told the same story. Precisely where Admiral Fraser reported that the *Scharnhorst* had gone down, due north of the underwater formation known to local fishermen as the Banana, stood an ominous cross: 'Foul bottom! War wreck! Fishing inadvisable.'

By transferring these figures to the *Risøy*'s satellite navigation system we had settled on a rectangular search area, 7,000 metres long by 4,000 metres wide, centred on the position given by Fraser. When the sonar 'fish' was lowered overboard, the echo sounder revealed that the depth ranged from 290 to 310 metres. At a towing speed of 3 knots and with a distance between the lines of 300 metres, it would be possible to cover the whole area by means of the side-scan sonar in the course of some twenty-five to thirty hours.

'Take a break, go and get yourself some sleep,' Stein Inge advised me. 'We'll give you a shout as soon as the wreck comes up on the screen.' I did as he said and went down to the cabin, where I lay watching the waves lap against the porthole, which was almost on the waterline. I couldn't get to sleep. I had thought and dreamed about the wreck of the German battlecruiser ever since, as a small boy in my home town of Hammerfest, I had first heard talk of the big German naval base there whose operations encompassed the whole of western Finnmark and which had made its effect felt on the lives of both my parents' generation and my own.

In those days the county of Finnmark was Europe's last frontier in the north, an outpost standing four-square to the desolate wastes of the Arctic Ocean. But both the war and the years that followed had taught the world that in reality this isolated region was a crossroads, a place where vital strategic and geopolitical interests clashed head-on. A global demarcation line, a hostile frontier, ran through the Barents Sea from the coast of Finnmark in the south to the edge of the polar ice in the north – as the story of the *Scharnhorst* so vividly proved. To me it had become paramount to find the sunken ship. It symbolized the forces that had moulded my childhood, spent there on the shores of the Arctic Ocean. I thirsted after answers to the many puzzles surrounding the loss of this proud ship. What had caused a vessel that was considered to be unsinkable to sink? Why had she lost speed when she was close to escaping and Fraser had called off the hunt? What had caused the last explosions, those that had made the sea itself heave and shudder? What had happened to the close on two thousand men who had gone down with her?

There were other unanswered questions, too. Where did the decisive signals that encouraged the British to set up the perfect ambush come from? From those courageous Norwegian wireless operators who, at risk of their lives, kept the German naval bases under surveillance? Or was it true, as the official British history claimed, that these undercover agents had nothing to do with the matter? If that were so, why, considering the enormous risk involved for them and their loved ones, had they been stationed behind the enemy lines in the first place?

I must have dropped off, because later in the evening I was jolted into wakefulness by a voice saying, 'The wind's getting up. You're wanted on the bridge.'

I knew from the way the *Risøy* was lurching about that all was not well. When I had stretched out on my bunk the waves had been gentle, lulling me to sleep. Now the ship was pitching and tossing with a choppy motion that made it difficult to keep one's balance.

On the bridge the sonar operator had been awake for more than twenty-four hours. He was surrounded by cups black with the dregs of cold coffee and ashtrays filled to overflowing.

I glanced at the rolls of print-outs. 'Found anything?' I asked, though I was already sure of the answer.

'Not a thing, apart from drag marks and pockets of gas. The seabed's as flat as a pancake, you couldn't hide a trawl door here, never mind a battleship.'

My heart in my boots, I studied the lines on the long strips of paper. Some 300 metres below our keel lay the ocean bed, scoured as clean as any dance floor, though scored here and there by the passage of retreating icebergs thousands of years ago. Never had I seen such a desolate expanse of ocean floor: devoid of life, it was nothing but an empty waste.

'No sign at all of a wreck?' I asked.

'No.'

'Nothing to suggest that we might be near the scene of a naval battle either – torpedoes, shellcases, nothing like that?'

'Not so much as a dud.'

'How long can we go on for?'

'Another two hours or so, I'd say, with a bit of luck. There's a gale forecast for later tonight.'

'And how are things to the west?'

'Look out of the window, you'll see for yourself.'

I did. Some distance away to the west I saw the bobbing lights of hundreds of lanterns. It looked as though we were nearing a seaborne city. They were the lights of the international trawler fleet, which was heading for the coast in pursuit of the shoals of cod that were now on their annual migration to new feeding grounds.

'They wouldn't be fishing there if there was a wreck of the size we're looking for on the bottom. They'd keep well away, that's for sure.'

The sea had turned dark-blue. It boded no good. The wind was blowing with unabated force from the north-west, exerting an increasing and irresistible pressure that set the sonar winch in the stern creaking and groaning. Every time an extra-strong gust hit the *Risøy*'s blue-leaded hull, it was like a blow from a steam-hammer. For a fraction of a second the ship stood still, poised, then, pounding heavily, lurched onwards.

'We shall have to bring in the sonar soon,' the operator said. 'There's too much strain on the cables. We can't afford to lose it. There's no point in going on now, anyway.'

We had combed an expanse of ocean more than 25 square kilometres in extent around the position given by Fraser in his official report – and hadn't found a thing. Where the 230-metre-long wreck of the steel colossus we were looking for should have been there was nothing but compacted clay.

All through the night, as the gale continued to rise in fury and the *Risøy* pitched and rolled as she battled her way towards the coast, down in the cabin I clung hard to my bunk. I was feeling sick at heart, worn out and dejected. I had staked everything on realizing my youthful dream: to find the *Scharnhorst* and solve the mysteries that still clung to Hitler's last battlecruiser. And what had I found? Nothing. I had gambled and lost. It wasn't the fault of Stein Inge and his crew, it was just that I had been too optimistic, too naïve and too inexperienced. I had forgotten how infinitely great the Barents Sea really was.

Up top, the waves continued to hurl themselves with undiminished ferocity against the *Risøy*'s superstructure. It was a storm of nearly the same intensity as that which had raged in the same area on 26 December 1943 and turned the *Scharnhorst*'s last voyage into a nightmare. Though sad and dispirited, at the same time I was suffused with a strange feeling of calm. To all intents and purposes the expedition had been a failure; but it had, after all, served to take me to where I had for so long wished to be – the place where that terrible battle had been fought. I was one step nearer to learning the true story. Moreover, I had discovered something important: Admiral Fraser's 'Despatch' had been wrong. The battle had not been fought where the official reports and charts said it had.

While afloat, the *Scharnhorst* had been considered a lucky ship, a naval legend, a ship which time and again had succeeded in slipping away and eluding her pursuers. And even at the end no one had actually seen her sink – apart from the young sailors who were left to fight for their lives in the icy, oil-drenched waters of the Arctic.

And now we knew that no one could say exactly *where* she had sunk, either. The wreck wasn't where it was supposed to be. The *Scharnhorst* had vanished for the last time.

With the coming of morning the North Cape began to loom ever larger to the south-west, a beetling, black, storm-lashed bastion crouched beneath a canopy of torn, ragged clouds. We had failed to find our quarry, but I couldn't just give up. It would be wrong to say that I had found nothing. I had found a purpose. I knew now what I had to do. I had to retrace my steps, return to the original documents and talk to the men who were there. Only they could make my dream come true.

CHAPTER THREE

A Time for Dreams

NORWAY/GERMANY, CHRISTMAS 1943

Many people were waiting, hoping and dreaming as the Christmas of 1943 drew near. In a scenic little community in the district of Alta, in the far north of Norway, twenty-year-old Sigrid Opgård Rasmussen was awaiting the greatest event of all – the birth of her first child. That apart, gloom prevailed. The fourth year of the war had brought nothing but sorrow and disappointments. True, it was whispered that the Germans were in retreat on the Eastern front, but in western Finnmark victory and liberation still seemed a long way off. German troops continued to pour across the county on their way to the trenches and fortifications east of the River Litza. From the fjord local residents could hear the thunder of heavy guns whenever Hitler's admirals set out to test the fleet's armaments.

The thought of the child to which she was about to give birth made Sigrid feel that it was worth while holding on. She felt assured that one day peace would return and real life could be resumed – the life she had dreamed of and planned together with her husband Kalle (Karl).

Sigrid had first met Kalle in the summer of 1942 – a lithe, athletic young man with narrow, sensitive features from which a smile was never far distant. She had walked all the way down from the out-farm in the mountains where she spent her summers, and was feeling hot, sunburned and bursting with energy. When she rounded the corner there he was, sitting on the farmhouse steps, busy tucking into a bowl of sour cream. In some strange way, even then, she sensed his interest, although his real reason for being there was far more mundane. A friend of her brother Halvor, he had only come to buy eggs and

cream, not to see her. Sigrid recalled her mother's refusal to accept payment, claiming that the sum involved was too trifling. She had added, however, that as he was cashier of the municipal Highways Department and his work took him far and wide along the fjords, it would be nice if he could bring a little fish with him next time he called.

All through the autumn Kalle was an increasingly frequent visitor, and on Christmas Eve he was invited to join the family for dinner. What had begun as a vague show of interest had by then evolved into the beginnings of an ardent love affair. It was fun being with Kalle. An accomplished gymnast, he had a ready wit and loved play-acting. His imitations left his audience helpless with laughter. 'I'd never met anyone like him before. He got people going, made them laugh, made them happy.'

April 1943 was the turning point. Sigrid and Kalle started going steady, and before long they were lovers. It had all been so natural: they delighted in each other's company, trusted one another and began to plan a future together. Kalle had a steady job and an assured income, which meant a great deal in those days. When Sigrid found herself pregnant, neither of them was in doubt about the next step. They made their way to Kalle's home town of Vadsø and got married. The date was 7 August, a red-letter day that provided a fitting conclusion to a perfect summer.

We lived at home with my parents as part of the family. All we had for ourselves was a bedroom. That summer and autumn was the best time of my life. In spite of the war and all the trials it brought in its train, we were happy and satisfied with our life together, and in material terms we wanted for nothing. We began to think about our next move. Kalle had already talked to his boss and we were on the lookout for a place of our own.

These halcyon days came to an end in November. Something had happened, and Sigrid feared the worst. It was all so very mysterious. Kalle had begun to spend more and more time with a friend from Vadsø, Torstein Pettersen Råby. Torstein was something of a prankster, but there was more to him than that. Sigrid couldn't quite say why, but for some reason she felt uneasy. The two men increasingly spent their evenings together in the barrack-like hut that served as the Highways Department's office in Kronstad. When Kalle returned home, late at night, he often reeked of cheap spirits. What was going on? Sigrid wondered. Why had her formerly so athletic husband suddenly taken to drink? When she pressed him for an explanation, Kalle was evasive. He was clearly under great strain.

He never said where he was going, not really, when he went out. I found myself anxiously awaiting his return, and I used to go to the window to look for him coming up the road. I oughtn't to have done that really, but I was so on edge that I couldn't help myself. I had a strong suspicion of what the two were up to, but I couldn't be sure. Our marriage suffered because we couldn't be open with one another. I did ask him, but he begged me not to push him. I cried and told him that people had begun to talk about his drinking. 'That's good,' he said. 'That means it's working.'

By now it was only a few weeks till the baby was due; it was expected to be born around the turn of the year. A child born of love and bearing hope for the future, in the event it arrived early in the New Year. But Kalle was away somewhere, together with Torstein. His absence boded ill, and Sigrid was beside herself with worry. The war seemed to have come home to them personally. Twenty years of age, newly wed and with a new-born baby, she felt that her whole future was hanging in the balance.

Some 2,000 kilometres to the south, in the industrial city of Giessen in Hessen, in the heart of Hitler's Third Reich, another young woman was similarly waiting, yearning and hoping. Like Sigrid Opgård Rasmussen, at that time Gertrud Damaski, vivacious and outgoing, was still in the bloom of youth; she was only eighteen. The two girls were completely unaware of each other's existence. All they had in common was their youth – and their fear of what the war might do to their loved ones.

Gertrud came from humble circumstances. Her mother had died young and her father, a waiter, rarely returned home from work until late at night. To earn a living Gertrud had apprenticed herself to a goldsmith, a man who took great pains to teach her how to value, care for and repair watches and jewellery. The war had still not reached Giessen, though bombs continued to rain down over the cities of the Ruhr, some way to the north. Like so many young women, Gertrud wrote letters designed to cheer the hearts of unknown servicemen. That was her contribution to the war effort. One day in the spring of 1943 she was given a field post address by a friend and asked to pen another such 'letter from home'.

The boy to whom I wrote was from Annerod, a village close to Giessen. His name was Heinrich Mulch and he was twenty-one years of age. I didn't know him, and never expected an answer. I only wrote to him to cheer him up. I saw it as my duty.

To Gertrud's surprise, some weeks later the postman delivered an envelope to her home.

'My dear little unknown girl, I have just received your lovely letter, for which I thank you very much. It gave me great pleasure, even though as yet I do not know who you are . . . and if you write again, I promise you an answer.'

I'd no idea of where Heinrich was or what he was doing. Everything was shrouded in secrecy and censorship was very strict. He would have been punished if he'd told me anything like that. But we continued to correspond, often writing to each other several times a week, until, one day, he suddenly turned up outside the goldsmith's shop. My Heinrich had been granted leave.

Gertrud's simple, friendly letter had kindled a flame. The two hit it off from the outset. 'It was as if we had known one another all our lives. That kind of thing happens sometimes. Some people you just take to right away, and that's the way it was with us. It simply happened, all of a sudden.'

Both Heinrich and Gertrud had had a strict upbringing. Because of that their meetings had to be conducted with due decorum – except when they could stroll together in the evenings beside the River Lahn. They held hands, embraced and exchanged stolen kisses.

It was on one of our last evenings together. I asked him where he was stationed.

'That I'm not allowed to say,' he said.

I insisted. 'I *must* know. I have to know where you are.'

He hesitated for a moment, then blurted out, 'Tirpitz'.

I didn't understand what he meant. 'Tirpitz, where's that?' I asked.

'*Tirpitz* is a battleship,' he said. 'It's stationed in the far north. I'm a writer on the Admiral's staff.'

All that autumn passionate letters continued to pass to and fro between Giessen and the Kå fjord in northern Norway. Things were quiet at the naval base. The flagship was undergoing repairs. Many of the men were given leave or sent back to Germany on refresher courses. Heinrich, one of the few of his shipmates to have attended commercial school, applied to a naval college in Frankfurt and was accepted. That was why Gertrud was so happy and full of hope. She could complete her apprenticeship and get a job with a goldsmith in the same city and they would be able to spend the rest of the winter together.

It would be the first winter they had done so since falling in love. Now, all that remained to be settled were a few formalities. The final decision was to be taken early in the New Year. Christmas was fast approaching, but Gertrud was determined to wait until all was officially in order. 'You have given me beauty, trust, love and faith in a wonderful future together. I shall always be devoted to you,' Heinrich had written.

The war continued in mounting fury. To Gertrud it seemed oppressive and meaningless. What kept her going was the thought of Heinrich. The days dragged, but she had long ago learned – knew, in fact, deep within her heart – that love, above all else, was worth waiting for.

II

CHAPTER FOUR

Operation Ostfront

WOLFSSCHANZE, EAST PRUSSIA, 1 JANUARY 1943

Adolf Hitler's rage knew no bounds. His frail body visibly shook. He ranted and raved and hammered the table with his fists. He had celebrated New Year's Eve in a good mood, despite increasingly dismal despatches from Stalingrad, where von Paulus's Sixth Army was nearing annihilation. To the Nazi satraps and top-ranking generals who made their way to Rastenburg to wish their *Führer* a Happy New Year, he elatedly confided that they were in for a pleasant surprise. Early that morning the pocket battleship *Lützow* and the heavy cruiser *Hipper*, together with six destroyers, had attacked a weakly protected convoy 50 nautical miles south of Bear Island. In Hitler's feverish imagination northern Norway was still the place where the outcome of the war would be decided. It was in the north, he believed, that the Allies would open a second front; and it was there that the decisive battle would be fought. It was for this reason that he had personally followed the preparations for Operation *Regenbogen* (Rainbow) and demanded that he be kept abreast of developments.

Hitler's good humour was ascribable to the news of the operation that he had received up to then. As early as 09.36 the commander of the Battle Group, *Vizeadmiral* Oskar Kummetz, reported that he had 'engaged the convoy'. Two hours later he sent a new signal to say that there were no British cruisers in the vicinity of the merchantmen.

The skipper of *U-354*, *Kapitänleutnant* Karl-Heinz Herbschleb, followed the course of the battle through his periscope, as the inky blackness of the Arctic sky was repeatedly rent by the flashes of heavy guns. At 11.45 he wirelessed,

'FROM WHAT I CAN SEE FROM HERE THE BATTLE IS NOW AT ITS HEIGHT. ALL I CAN SEE IS RED.'

At the *Führer*'s headquarters, the *Wolfsschanze* (Wolf's Lair), deep in the East Prussian forests, the only interpretation that could be placed on the two signals was that Kummetz was in the process of destroying the convoy. It augured a resounding victory, a victory Hitler intended to announce to the German people on New Year's Day.

But as the night wore on, Hitler's trepidation grew. The flow of wireless signals had ceased and a curtain of silence seemed to have descended on the Arctic Ocean. The *Kriegsmarine*'s liaison officer, *Vizeadmiral* Theodor Krancke, did his best to reassure his increasingly impatient *Führer*.

'Kummetz has imposed wireless silence in order not to disclose his position,' he said. 'There may be heavy enemy naval units in the area. As soon as he reaches the safety of the coast, we shall have good news.'

But that was not enough to pacify Hitler. Instead of retiring for the night, he paced restlessly to and fro across the floor of his headquarters sanctum. Early the next morning, when Reuters issued a brief bulletin that had just been released by the Admiralty to the effect that the German attack had been beaten off and that the convoy had safely reached Murmansk, Hitler's pent-up fury exploded. He lost no time in venting his rage on the hapless Krancke and demanded an immediate and full explanation. He declared that he no longer had any confidence in his admirals and that everything suggested that they were deliberately withholding the truth from him.

The British report of the outcome of the battle was correct. The *Lützow* and *Hipper* had indeed found the convoy, but Kummetz, hampered by the constraints that governed his dispositions, had acted hesitantly and indecisively. His orders for the operation, which had been approved by Hitler, forbade him to take 'untoward chances' with his cruisers. Moreover, Otto Klüber, the admiral commanding Northern Waters, had reiterated the order, wirelessing while the battle was actually in progress, 'TAKE NO UNNECESSARY RISKS.'

Kummetz was no Nelson and carried out his orders to the letter. When the commander of the British escort vessels, Captain Sherbrooke, gallantly led his inferior force in to attack the two cruisers, Kummetz withdrew under heavy shelling. The British lost the destroyer *Achates* and a minesweeper, the *Bramble*, and several other vessels suffered damage, but the convoy itself escaped. And when the outlying escort, which consisted of the two cruisers *Jamaica* and *Sheffield*, finally reached the scene, the German destroyer *Friedrich Eckholdt* was sent to the bottom and the *Hipper* was almost disabled by a shell that penetrated to her engine-room.

As the morning progressed, Fleet Headquarters in Berlin made several unsuccessful attempts to contact Kummetz. But the teleprinter link to the Kå fjord was out and atmospherics made wireless communication difficult.

By five in the afternoon Hitler could contain himself no longer. He summoned *Vizeadmiral* Krancke and, beside himself with fury, declared that the Navy's big ships were utterly useless. Since the early days of the war, he fumed, they had caused him nothing but worry and disappointment, so much so that they had become a liability and a burden on the war effort. He continued:

I order you without delay to inform the Naval High Command of the following irrevocable decision. The capital ships impose an unwarranted strain on both manpower and matériel. Accordingly they are to be withdrawn from service forthwith and scrapped. Their guns are to be transported ashore and employed for the purpose of coastal defence.

Thunderstruck, Krancke steeled himself to deliver the following reply: 'If that is done, it will be the cheapest victory ever won by the British at sea.'

Six days later Hitler reiterated his injunction to the Commander-in-Chief of the German Navy, *Grossadmiral* Erich Raeder, in a tirade that lasted for an hour and a half. Raeder, then sixty-six years of age, was a highly respected officer who had served Hitler faithfully ever since the dictator's assumption of power in 1933. He was, in fact, the architect of the German nation's modern High Seas Fleet. As such, he had no intention of meekly accepting what he saw as an unjust reprimand and accordingly tendered his resignation. To succeed him he recommended one of the *Kriegsmarine*'s senior career officers, Admiral Carls, or the charismatic commander of the U-boat arm, Karl Dönitz.

Hitler chose Dönitz, and the handover took place on 30 January 1943 – shortly before von Paulus surrendered at Stalingrad. On that day the 51-year-old new Grand Admiral took over Hitler's navy, along with the many perquisites that went with the post. They included an *SS* company to stand guard over his villa in the fashionable Berlin suburb of Dahlem, a donation from the *Führer* of 300,000 Reichsmarks, a Mercedes staff car for his own exclusive use, a personal aircraft and a private set of railway coaches, the *Auerhahn*, which came complete with a comfortably appointed dining-car and sleeping compartment. With his piercing blue eyes and tight lips Dönitz was the very archetype of a Prussian officer, with all that this implied in terms of faith in his *Führer* and unswerving loyalty. As he wrote in his first directive: 'Our lives belong to the State. Our honour resides in doing our duty and in

being prepared to take action. None of us has the right to a private life. The question is one of how the war is to be won. We must pursue this goal in a fanatical spirit of self-sacrifice and with relentless determination.'

The International Military Tribunal at Nuremburg sentenced Dönitz to ten years' imprisonment for his leading role in the Third Reich. Postwar research has resulted in a more finely shaded portrait, however, that of an intelligent, strong-willed and inspiring commander who succeeded in creating and maintaining to the last an intensely loyal U-boat arm despite grievous losses. He was worshipped by the men under his command. Furthermore, while serving his sentence he surprised his captors by his keen sense of humour.

Although Dönitz was one of Hitler's most uncritical supporters, he was not at all afraid to contradict the *Führer* in matters of concern to the Navy. When he visited the *Wolfsschanze* on 26 February 1943, he was well prepared. He strongly opposed Hitler's order to scrap the entire High Seas Fleet.

'The hard-fought battles on the Eastern front make it my duty to deploy the big ships,' he declared. 'It is imperative that the *Scharnhorst* be despatched to northern Norway. There, together with the *Tirpitz*, *Lützow* and six destroyers, she will form the nucleus of a strong battle group.'

Hitler could hardly believe his ears. He had taken a decision that in his eyes was irreversible. He was convinced that the day of the capital ships was over. They had brought him one defeat after another; time and again, because of them, he had been humiliated.

But Dönitz was not to be gainsaid. 'The fighting capacities of the ships concerned were severely curtailed by the demand that they should avoid taking risks,' he declared. 'Their commanders cannot be blamed for that.'

Hitler protested that he had never issued any such political directive. 'On the contrary,' he said, 'I have insisted that the ships should fight, as is being done on the Eastern front, where the Russians are receiving a continual flow of supplies – not least thanks to the last convoy.'

'That is precisely why the ships have to be made use of, instead of being decommissioned,' Dönitz retorted. 'I request permission to despatch the *Scharnhorst* northwards.'

After prolonged discussion Hitler finally gave in – though he made sure that he had the last word.

'And when do you expect to be able to deploy the ships?' he asked.

'In the course of the next three months.'

'And if it turns out to be six months, then you must come to me and admit that I was right.'

The Grand Admiral had won his first victory over Hitler. But it was at a price. From that moment on he was under untold pressure: the big ships would have to be used if he were not to lose face in the eyes of the *Führer*. It was in the nature of a tacit wager between the two. Hitler could well afford to wait, however, while Dönitz had to take action to prove himself correct. Michael Salewski, the chronicler of the *Kriegsmarine*'s High Command, wrote: 'The battleships had been transformed into gigantic toys. But more was at stake: it was a matter of prestige.'

A week or so later, in the afternoon of 6 March 1943, the *Scharnhorst* left her berth in the Bight of Lübeck in the Baltic and set a course for the Kattegat. The atmosphere on board was electric. Almost two years had elapsed since she and her sister ship, the *Gneisenau*, had sought refuge at the naval base in Brest, in Occupied France, after returning from their first foray into the Atlantic. Following their successful dash through the Channel in February 1942 the two ships had lain more or less idle, and the men were weary of lying constantly at anchor – first in Wilhelmshaven, next in Kiel and finally in Gotenhafen.

'Scharnhorst *immer Voran!*' ('*Scharnhorst* ever onwards!') was the cruiser's proud motto – but it was devoid of all meaning unless the ship was actually at sea. Under her legendary and highly popular captain, *Kapitän-zur-See* Kurt Caesar Hoffman, who had commanded the ship throughout the first three years of war, the *Scharnhorst* had chalked up one victory after another. She had been both mined and torpedoed, but on each occasion had carried on regardless. Whereas the *Gneisenau* had sustained severe damage and was destined never again to leave Gotenhafen, the *Scharnhorst* had come through with flying colours and her reputation as a lucky ship had continued to grow.

The two ships had been launched within two months of each other, at Kiel and Wilhelmshaven respectively, in the autumn of 1936 in the presence of Adolf Hitler and senior officers of the Third Reich. They were named after two of Prussia's military heroes, Generals Gerhard Johann von Scharnhorst and August Graf von Gneisenau. Each had a displacement of 26,000 tons, but that was on paper: when fully operational it exceeded 39,000 tons. They were armed with nine 11-inch guns distributed among three triple turrets – Anton and Bruno forward, Caesar aft. Augmented as it was by a further eighty guns of smaller calibre, ranging from 5.9-inch cannon to 20-millimetre anti-aircraft guns, their firepower was formidable. The ships' armour consisted of more than 6,000 tons of Krupp KC Wotan special-quality steel and varied in thickness from 8 to 32 centimetres. Twelve high-pressure boilers generated the steam required to drive the ships' three turbines, each of which developed over

50,000 horsepower. The three bronze propellers were more than 5 metres in diameter. On her proving trials in 1939 the *Scharnhorst* had attained a speed of close on 32 knots.

In November 1939 the twins embarked upon their first joint major sortie. On the 23rd of that month they were cruising south of Iceland when a lookout spotted a plume of smoke on the horizon. *Kapitän-zur-See* Hoffmann personally climbed the foretop and identified the ship as the British armed merchant cruiser *Rawalpindi*, a converted 16,000-ton liner. After an hour's uneven battle the *Rawalpindi*, burning from stem to stern, sank. Despite the heavy sea, the *Scharnhorst* hove to and rescued a number of survivors from two lifeboats. A line from a third lifeboat had just been secured on board when the order was given from the bridge to call off the operation. In an account of the incident Heinrich Bredemeier, the commander of C turret, wrote:

> For some inexplicable reason we were forced to cut the lifeboat loose and leave the scene. The order had to be obeyed. There was nothing we could do – the commander of the flotilla had spoken! Muttering darkly among ourselves we carried out the deck officer's curt order and cut the line. . . . This unaccountable order to abandon the men in the lifeboat was hotly discussed by the embittered sailors while the *Scharnhorst* followed at full speed in the wake of the *Gneisenau*.

The explanation was forthcoming shortly afterwards. The British cruiser *Newcastle* had suddenly put in an appearance close by the sinking *Rawalpindi*. The German flotilla commander, *Vizeadmiral* Marschall, was not prepared to do battle – not even against a lightly armed cruiser; instead, he withdrew. To Bredemeier and the rest of the men this was a foretaste of what Hitler's naval timidity would mean. Against the Royal Navy the *Kriegsmarine* was totally outclassed.

At the outbreak of war the British boasted seventy-three battleships and cruisers, six aircraft-carriers and hundreds of destroyers and smaller vessels, and in time they were also able to draw upon the enormous resources of their American ally. The German surface fleet, on the other hand, comprised a mere sixteen battleships and cruisers and thirty-four destroyers.

Therefore the German admirals were enjoined to caution. It was a matter of the *Führer*'s prestige: they were warned not to take risks whatever the circumstances. Forty-eight hours after the engagement off Iceland, the British Home Fleet ably demonstrated its superiority when it cut off the retreat of the

Scharnhorst and *Gneisenau*. A large force of battleships, cruisers, destroyers and submarines took up station near the Faeroes, and at airfields in Scotland numbers of bombers were alerted, ready for take-off. What saved the two German ships was a violent storm that came sweeping in from the south-east, enabling them to slip undetected through the cordon. On 28 November they dropped anchor in the roads outside Wilhelmshaven. The storm had done a certain amount of damage to the *Scharnhorst*'s armament but, this notwithstanding, a legend had been born: the *Scharnhorst* was a lucky ship, destined to evade every trap set for her.

After a severe winter spent frozen-in in the Baltic, on 9 April 1940 the *Scharnhorst* again found herself in a tight spot, this time off the Lofoten Islands. Together with the *Gneisenau*, she was covering the German landing in Narvik when the two were surprised by the British battlecruiser *Renown* with its 15-inch guns. A running battle ensued between the three ships, a battle hampered by heavy seas and snow showers and lasting for almost two hours. The *Gneisenau* was hit three times, the *Renown* twice; the *Scharnhorst* escaped unscathed, however, despite a series of engine-room breakdowns. Ninety British bombers were despatched to cut off the German ships' retreat, but both managed to slip away and by 12 April they were safely back in Wilhelmshaven. Bredemeier wrote:

From his lofty platform beneath the scorched muzzles of C turret's guns, the 'Old Man' addressed the ship's company the following morning. He reviewed the general war situation and spoke of our losses and of our duties as soldiers. He declared that we had done well in our first serious engagement. All who heard him realized that it hadn't been a matter of luck but of skilled seamanship and the combined efforts of all concerned. What, for example, might not have happened had the engine-room staff not regained control when the battle opened? Then, he said, we wouldn't have been able to avail ourselves of our prime asset, our speed. It is the certainty that all on board are doing their best that welds a ship's company together.

Two months later the two ships were again in action off the Lofotens. At about five o'clock in the afternoon of 7 June they came across the aircraft carrier *Glorious* and her escorting destroyers, *Ardent* and *Acasta*; they were on their way back to England after the failure of the Norwegian campaign. Three hours later all three British ships had been sent to the bottom, with the loss of nearly 1,600 men, including a number of RAF pilots who had been evacuated from the airfield at Bardufoss. The destroyers fought a heroic battle against

overwhelming odds. A torpedo from the *Acasta* struck the *Scharnhorst* near her stern, just below C turret, and in the ensuing explosion 48 seamen lost their lives.

Through a 12-metre-long gash on the starboard side of the ship thousands of tons of water flooded into the after sections. The squadron sought refuge in Trondheim, where temporary repairs were effected. While the ships were in port and when the *Scharnhorst*, hugging the Norwegian coast, limped home fourteen days later, the RAF mounted one attack after another – but in vain. The British submarine *Clyde* was more fortunate, however, torpedoing the *Gneisenau* on the starboard side of her bow. The battlecruiser was forced to return to Trondheim with a gaping hole in her forepart and did not reach her home port until the end of July. Both ships spent the autumn in dry dock. It had been a dramatic baptism of fire. The British had been determined to exact vengeance, sending in wave after wave of aircraft, but both ships survived. The legends about them grew: no matter how hard their opponents tried, Hitler's battlecruisers always managed to escape.

The ships' companies were elated. One of the *Scharnhorst*'s key officers, tall, slim, 35-year-old *Fregattenkapitän* Ernst Dominik, who was in command of the anti-aircraft guns, wrote to his family in Nordheim in July 1940:

I have today been presented with the Iron Cross, First Class. Why and how can be told in a few words. . . . On the way back after three weeks at sea, the moment came that my men and I had been waiting for since 1 September 1939. It was on 21 June, the longest day of the year, which also might well have been our last had we not been so wide awake. . . . The first heavy British combined attack was launched against our ship. It lasted for a full two hours and the British exhibited total contempt for death. We had already survived a number of attacks in Trondheim, but this time they were determined to sink us, no matter what the cost might be! In their fury they dropped about ten tons of bombs on us – without success. Not as much as a splinter struck us. . . . The air battle off Utsira was very hard-fought and proved an unequivocal victory for a German battleship against a veritable hornets' nest of attackers! But God must have been with us on our flak platforms. He was certainly with us at our guns. . . . We soldiers ought not to think about a surprise ending of the war, but I do believe that we are now a good deal closer to a victorious peace.

Early in February 1941 the *Scharnhorst* and *Gneisenau* again brought off a brilliant feat of seamanship, forcing the Denmark Strait between Greenland and

Iceland and breaking out into the North Atlantic. For the next forty-seven days the two ships sailed something like 20,000 nautical miles – from Newfoundland to the Cape Verde Islands and back. When, on 22 March, they finally put into Brest on the west coast of France, they had sunk nineteen merchantmen, totalling some 100,000 tons. Moreover, three tankers had been seized and sent back to Germany with prize crews on board. It was one of the longest and most successful sorties of the war.

However, the longer the *Scharnhorst* and *Gneisenau* remained in Brest, the more hopeless their situation became. They were surrounded by anti-aircraft guns, but found themselves under constant attack from British aircraft, which scored a number of hits.

'The British airfields were only a short distance away. . . . Without warning the planes would sweep in over the town, making for the harbour, and release their bombs before climbing back into the sky at full throttle and vanishing from sight. A few seconds and it was all over. Both the shipyard and the town itself suffered heavy damage,' wrote Bredemeier.

After ten months the German naval chiefs had had enough. On the night of 12 February 1942 the *Scharnhorst*, *Gneisenau* and *Prinz Eugen* slipped their moorings and put to sea. Taking the British completely by surprise, they set a course that would take them straight through the Channel. Escorted by torpedo boats, destroyers and the *Luftwaffe*, the squadron raced past the British defences. When the RAF tumbled to what was happening they made desperate attempts to prevent the escape, but it was too late. Thirty-six hours later the squadron reached Germany without the loss of a single ship.

The Channel dash was a tactical triumph that confirmed the *Scharnhorst*'s reputation as a lucky ship. Twice during her dramatic flight she had been damaged by mines, one of which put her engines completely out of action. She had, in fact, been forced to remain stationary in the water for a whole hour while temporary repairs were effected. Nevertheless, again she had survived. The *Gneisenau* was less fortunate and was compelled to go into dock in Kiel for repairs to the damage she had sustained. In an air raid on the port fourteen days later a bomb penetrated her upper deck and ignited the powder in the magazine of A turret. The explosion and fire thus caused destroyed the whole forward section of the ship. Together with her twin, the *Scharnhorst*, she had successfully ranged the Atlantic for more than two years, but now her career was at an end. She was condemned and ended her days ignominiously as a block-ship in Gotenhafen.

On his triumphal return, Kurt Caesar Hoffman was promoted to *Konter-Admiral* (Rear Admiral) and posted to Holland as Naval Commander-in-Chief.

On 2 April 1942 the *Scharnhorst*'s new captain, *Kapitän-zur-See* Friedrich Hüffmaier, took up his duties. Faced with a critical and supremely confident ship's company, he didn't find things easy and soon earned a reputation as a bit of a bungler. His previous command had been the light cruiser *Köln*. It was rumoured on the lower deck that he owed his promotion not to his seamanship but to influence in Berlin. When the time came to manoeuvre the *Scharnhorst* out into open water, her new captain had to call on a whole fleet of tugs for assistance; there were so many, in fact, that they barely had room to draw alongside. As if that were not enough, after only a short while Hüffmaier managed to run his ship aground at a speed of 26 knots. On another occasion he was forced to put the *Scharnhorst* into dock to have a wire removed from her propellers; and to conclude this chapter of accidents, during an exercise in the Baltic he collided with a U-boat!

But Hüffmaier refused to give up. In the intervals between the *Scharnhorst*'s enforced dockings he carried out a rigorous programme of training that included extensive trials with the ship's two new radar installations.

Tests performed south of the Danish island of Bornholm in January 1943 revealed that the *Scharnhorst*'s forward radar could detect a destroyer at distances of anything from 8 to 13.2 kilometres. The after radar picked up the same target at a distance of 10 to 12 kilometres, while the ship's own warning system (*Funkmessbeobachter*) proved capable of detecting the pulses emitted by enemy radar at the reassuring range of 40 kilometres.

More than a year after her daring dash through the Channel, the *Scharnhorst* eventually turned her bows to the north. By this time both ship and men were fighting fit and ready for whatever lay ahead. Not even the gale that came raging in from the south-west and caught the ship off the Norwegian coast, where Force 10 gusts were registered in the squalls, could dampen their ardour. On 9 March 1943 the *Scharnhorst* reached the safety of the Bogen fjord near Narvik. The first leg of her voyage had been completed without mishap – and the British didn't know she was there.

Dönitz had always taken a fatherly interest in *Vizeadmiral* Oskar Kummetz, who, with his youthful smile and full lips, called to mind an overgrown cherub. Despite having blotted his copybook off Bear Island on New Year's Eve, Kummetz had been permitted to retain his post as Squadron Commander, and was even promoted to full admiral.

On 13 March he again hoisted his flag, this time on board the battleship *Tirpitz*. A week or so later the order was given to put to sea under the cover of a dense sea mist. Shortly before midnight the *Tirpitz* headed out from the Vest fjord, followed by the *Scharnhorst*, *Lützow*, six destroyers and two torpedo-boat destroyers. At four-thirty in the morning of 24 March, beneath overcast skies and with the temperature near zero, the *Scharnhorst* and *Lützow* dropped anchor in the inner reaches of the narrow 45-kilometre-long Lang fjord. The *Tirpitz* and her escort of destroyers carried on to the Kå fjord, another arm of the Alta (Alten) fjord. The new and formidably armed First Battle Group had safely reached its most advanced base, less than 15 hours' sailing from the convoy routes to Murmansk.

Every day, from stations at Banak, Bardufoss and Tromsø, Focke-Wulf Condors and Blohm & Voss flying-boats took off to scour the surrounding ocean; and from their bases in Hammerfest and Narvik U-boats set out to patrol the area south of Bear Island. Western Finnmark had become northern Europe's largest and most important naval base. It had one purpose, which *Grossadmiral* Dönitz in Berlin summed up as follows: 'First and foremost we shall fight. A magnificent feat of arms will vigorously and in style put to shame the *Führer*'s claim that the surface vessels are morally flawed.'

In Oskar Kummetz, who still bore the scars of his Bear Island humiliation, Dönitz had found the perfect tool. To redeem his reputation Kummetz was prepared 'to fight with grotesquely inferior forces and, if necessary, die'.

That, at least, was what Dönitz believed when, towards the end of March 1943, he signed his first directive to the Battle Group. As soon as opportunity offered, the Group was directed to strike a crushing blow at the Arctic convoys, in order to relieve the desperate situation in Russia. The directive was later given a simple but highly significant codename: Operation *Ostfront* (Eastern Front).

CHAPTER FIVE

The Mystery Deepens

OSLO, SPRING 1999

The more I delved into the documents relating to the matter, the more complex the mystery of the *Scharnhorst*'s last hours appeared. I realized with a sinking heart that locating the wreck would be all but impossible.

The first men to set about harvesting the riches of the Barents Sea, and to understand that what the sea gave it would inevitably claim in return, were sixteenth-century whalers. They were followed by sealers and walrus hunters, and, early in the twentieth century, by steel-hulled steam trawlers out to net the seemingly limitless stocks of plaice in the White Sea. They were well-found ships manned by stalwart seamen from Hull, San Sebastián and Fécamp. But stout though both men and ships were, many of them succumbed to the perpetual darkness, drifting ice and unpredictable weather to find an unmarked grave in the depths of the ocean.

The relentless submarine campaigns of two world wars also took their toll. On a fine afternoon on 28 August 1917, for example, the lookout of the Russian steamer *La Marseillaise* spotted the periscope of a U-boat some distance astern. The captain opened fire with the ship's 9-centimetre gun. The hour-long artillery duel that ensued caused the crew to panic and they took to the boats. *La Marseillaise* was carrying 3,500 tons of ammunition destined for Russia and no one wanted to be on board if the U-boat scored a direct hit.

Their adversary proved to be *U-28* in the service of the Imperial German Navy. It was captained by *Kapitänleutnant* Georg Schmidt, who, according to the survivors, was a polite, pale-complexioned and well-shaven man who 'performed his distasteful task like a gentleman'.

Schmidt sent four stokers and a prize crew over to the abandoned steamer, which was ransacked for provisions, among them several cases of champagne and whisky. Although one of the stokers returned very much the worse for drink, brandishing a loaded pistol and declaring that he intended to shoot the entire crew of the U-boat all by himself, Schmidt remained unmoved. He laughed and laughed until finally the man's legs gave way beneath him and he collapsed on to the deck. The lifeboats were given a southerly heading which would take them to the coast, and the men in them eventually reached land safely. Their ship, on the other hand, was towed to join another prize, the steamer *Othello*, where it was blown up by a charge of dynamite.

By that time *U-28* had sunk more than thirty ships, ten of them in the Barents Sea. Five days later another ammunition ship, the *Olive Branch*, fell victim to *U-28*, which brought her up short with a torpedo amidships. The crew took to the two lifeboats while Schmidt drew alongside to give the ship the *coup de grâce*. One of his first shells ignited the cargo. The violent explosion that followed sealed the fate of both the *Olive Branch* and *U-28*. The sunken steamer's shipwrecked crew exacted their revenge on the surviving Germans by leaving them to drown among the wreckage.

One year earlier the British vice-consul in Vardø, Edward Titterington, had reported that 'a chain of U-boats' blocked 'the whole of the Arctic from North Kinn and northwards'.

I studied the positions recorded for the sinkings. All four ships – the *Olive Branch*, *U-28*, *Othello* and *La Marseillaise* – had sunk some 80 to 100 nautical miles north-east of the North Cape, at a latitude of about 72°N and a longitude of between 28° and 30°E – which was precisely the area covered by our own search.

Twenty-five years later, during the Second World War, when Dönitz sent his U-boats back to the Arctic, the bloodbath was resumed. From Bear Island and eastwards to Kildin ship after ship, most of them battered, flaming hulks, had plunged beneath the waves, most notably during the hard-fought battles against the Anglo-American convoys that took place in 1942. The waters off the North Cape were anything but placid and forgiving; on the contrary, they bespoke only cruelty and dire need.

The more reports I read, the more helpless and despondent I felt. The Barents Sea, and in particular the outer lead across the North Cape Bank, 50 to 100 nautical miles from the coast, was a veritable graveyard of ships. The fishing charts of the region were thick with crosses and exclamation marks to indicate hazards of various kinds on the seabed. Many marked places where fishing vessels had lost their gear. There was nothing to indicate precisely what they meant; the markings might stand for any of the countless ships that had foundered in bad weather or been lost to enemy action. The conclusion to be drawn was all too clear: finding the wreck of the *Scharnhorst* would be tantamount to finding a specific ball on a golf course – from a height of 300 metres!

CHAPTER SIX

Empty Days

THE LANG FJORD, SPRING AND SUMMER 1943

Dönitz had promised Hitler that he would mount an all-out offensive against the Russia-bound convoys within three months. However, there was one factor the Grand Admiral had overlooked: he had failed to take into account Britain's First Sea Lord, the ageing Admiral Sir Dudley Pound, and Admiral Sir John Tovey, who was at that time Commander-in-Chief of the Home Fleet. The year before it had been brought brutally home to the two of them exactly what it cost to send merchant ships through the Barents Sea in summer, when night was but a fleeting twilight. In July 1942 convoy PQ17 had been relentlessly harried by German aircraft and U-boats until only twelve of the original thirty-six vessels were left afloat. It was 'sheer bloody murder' to permit ships to sail without an escort beneath a sun that shone for twenty-four hours a day. But that was precisely what had been done. The resultant losses were appalling: 153 Allied seamen were killed and 210 bombers, 430 tanks, 3,350 motor vehicles and 100,000 tons of ammunition lost. Through an MI5 double-agent in Iceland, codenamed Cobweb, Pound and Tovey had warned the Germans that PQ17 was about to sail, the idea being to set a trap for the *Tirpitz*. The plan, Operation Tarantula, was a fiasco, as the Germans didn't take the bait. Thereafter, Pound issued the fateful order for the convoy to disperse when he mistakenly thought that the *Tirpitz* was about to strike at the convoy. He never recovered from the tragedy.

The Germans were now assembling a new and equally strong force in the Kå and Lang fjords – the awe-inspiring 43,000-ton battleship *Tirpitz* with her 15-inch guns, supported by one battlecruiser, one pocket battleship and a flotilla of powerfully armed destroyers and torpedo-boat destroyers. Concurrently the Battle of

the Atlantic was nearing its bloody climax. The British Home Fleet's reserves were strained to the utmost and Pound had no more ships to spare for escort duty in the north. Every available escort vessel was needed to protect the transatlantic convoys.

On 2 March 1943 the twenty-two vessels that made up the eastbound convoy JW53 reached Russian waters without loss. Eight days later the westbound convoy RA53 reached Iceland. Thirty ships, all in ballast, had sailed together from Kola Bay, three falling victim en route to German U-boats. A new and heavily laden convoy, JW54, was scheduled to sail from Scotland on 27 March.

But in the Barents Sea the nights were again rapidly growing shorter, and Pound was alarmed by a series of wireless signals which since January had been passing between Command Headquarters in Kiel and the German naval bases in northern Norway. The British had broken the German ciphers and, with a few hours' delay, were able to read their enemy's wireless traffic. What they learned was disturbing to say the least. Despite its setback off Bear Island on New Year's Eve, the German *Kriegsmarine* was clearly putting together a new task force. On 14 March the British intelligence officers' worst fears were realized: the *Tirpitz*, *Scharnhorst* and *Lützow* were once again concentrated in the north. A renewed attack on the supply route to Russia was evidently in course of preparation.

When the British Defence Committee (Operations) met in London two days later, with Churchill in the chair, Pound had already resolved to hold JW54 back. All convoys to Russia were to be suspended indefinitely. But Churchill was more aggressive than his admirals. Surprised at Pound's decision, he proposed that the convoy should sail as 'bait' to tempt the German force out into the open sea; then, he said, the merchantmen could turn back off Bear Island. He also toyed with the idea of sending along an aircraft-carrier, his reasoning being that the enemy had to be 'teased and kept on edge' even though there was no real justification for risking a carrier.

Admiral Pound was not to be moved, however. 'We have sent twenty-three convoys to Russia under circumstances that did not warrant their sailing,' he said tartly. His decision stood firm, regardless of Churchill's pleas.

Thus when the *Scharnhorst* and the remainder of the striking force anchored in the Lang and Kå fjords in the grey light of 24 March 1943, Dönitz was too late to win his 'bet' with Hitler as the last convoy had already passed. The next was not due until November, when darkness would again enshroud the polar seas; that meant a delay of eight long months. *Admiral* Kummetz had his finger firmly on the trigger, but he had no target in his sights.

In the Lang fjord *Kapitän-zur-See* Friedrich Hüffmaier refused to be put out by the uncertainty attached to the fleet's next move. As senior captain he was responsible for 'gunnery, wireless surveillance and other local counter-intelligence measures, as well as precautions against enemy attack and attempted sabotage', he noted in the entry for 25 March in the war diary.

The *Scharnhorst* had been allotted moorings south of the small community of Sopnes, where the fjord ended in a well-sheltered bay. Opening off to the south-east was the luxuriant Bognelv valley with its dense birchwoods and fertile fields, which kept the local population well supplied with potatoes. On the other side of the fjord lay the Russelv valley; dominated by the almost 1,100-metre-high peak of Russelvtind, it offered protection from the north-west.

It was a beautiful setting, but Hüffmaier was by no means satisfied with the security arrangements. A coastal battery covered the entrance to the fjord, but not an anti-aircraft gun or smoke generator was to be seen.

'The fjord is unprotected against air attack,' Hüffmaier wrote. To make amends he ordered that the *Scharnhorst*'s own guns be manned around the clock and he also stationed a boat close to the inner anti-submarine boom and net beside the Eidsnes light, with orders to open fire in the event of an attack. In addition, armed guards were posted ashore at strategic points to keep a lookout.

When he assembled the ship's company on deck on 29 March, Hüffmaier declared: 'I will do my best to heighten the pleasure of serving [in the Navy], avoid fatigues and build a bridge across a time which, for you, will be a trial.'

Hüffmaier was justified in fearing for the morale of his men if their wait beneath the snowcapped mountains should prove overlong. After all, it was the *Scharnhorst*'s first sortie for more than two years. In Brest the men had lived for ten months in constant fear of attack from the air; it had been a very trying time indeed. But Brest was a town of 80,000 inhabitants, a town amply provided with drinking dens, cinemas and brothels. Moreover, the beaches of Brittany were long and sandy and the sea teemed with lobsters and crayfish. Some of the ship's company were even billeted ashore. Orchestras were formed and theatrical performances put on. The revue *Between St Pauli and Shanghai*, staged at the municipal theatre, had been the highlight of the season. The applause knew no bounds when Hoffmann himself lauded the talent of the performers: 'Such events can only be staged by the men of the *Scharnhorst*!' he declared. By comparison, the months spent in Kiel and Gotenhafen after the ship's breakout through the English Channel had dragged interminably. Some of the men had been posted away. Those who were left consoled themselves with the thought that they were, at any rate, in their own country and thus in a position to visit their families and girlfriends.

Tucked away as they were in the inner recesses of the Lang fjord, life was a different matter altogether. People had lived there since time immemorial.

The climate was mild and dry. Racks of klippfish (sun-dried split cod) lined the beaches, and the area round about was noted for its distinctive traditions of craftsmanship, especially in the field of woodworking. But *Organisation Todt* (OT), the German Building and Construction Organization, had very early on discovered something else about the region. The old cart-track that meandered over Alteidet made the head of the fjord a convenient road junction. For anyone wishing to avoid a long and hazardous voyage around the coast, the Lang fjord was the gateway to southern Norway. With this in mind, OT had joined forces with the Norwegian Highways Department and built a road along the eastern shore of the fjord for transportation of troops to and from the Eastern front. Transit camps had been built en route and the road was also much used by men going on and returning from leave.

This did not alter the fact that the inner reaches of the fjord constituted an isolated outpost, more than 2,000 kilometres from the nearest German town. Not surprisingly, letters in both directions took an age to reach their destination. The few men lucky enough to be granted leave had first to take a bus to Alteidet, whence a troopship, the *Levante*, ran a regular service to Narvik. From there it was a matter of travelling by boat and train via Trondheim to Oslo and thence to Denmark. With luck, a man might manage the trip in two or three weeks! 'If you were an officer you travelled in style, of course, and took a plane, which meant that you were home in a couple of days,' was a complaint often heard among the ordinary sailors.

There were no facilities for normal leisure activities in the inner reaches of the fjord – no cinema, dancehall, café or restaurant. The presence at anchor of the *Scharnhorst*, *Lützow*, several destroyers and a number of auxiliary vessels meant that more than five thousand young men were locked up in the fjord. They constituted a self-contained community of their own. Fresh fish was obtainable locally but other provisions had to be collected from the cargo ship *Dittmarschen*, oil came from the tanker *Jeverland* and water and electric power were provided by the auxiliary vessels *Brenner* and *Harle*.

For twenty-year-old Helmut Feifer it was the first time he had found himself in an anchorage outside Germany. His father was a Polish citizen and worked as a dairy inspector in Wilhelmshaven. He had been proud of his slightly built but bright son, who at the tender age of fourteen had attained the exalted rank of *Gefolgschaftsführer* in the *Hitler-Jugend*, with 120 boys of his own age under his command. By and large this youthful marching and singing army was earmarked for a future in the SS, but Helmut had elected to join the *Kriegsmarine*. He trained as a ship's writer and had been cleared to handle secret orders. When the *Scharnhorst* reached Wilhelmshaven after her dash through the Channel in February

1942, he had arrived ready for active service on board, but before he had time to move into his quarters on the orlop deck, the battlecruiser had left for Kiel; to catch her up, he had to take the train. The months that followed were for Helmut an exciting introduction to life on board an armoured giant with a complement of close on two thousand men. But nothing he had learned prepared him for the trials that lay ahead. At the time he was working in the engine-room typing pool:

> I still remember the Lang fjord as a peaceful and exceptionally beautiful spot. We ratings had no contact with the local population, we kept ourselves to ourselves. In fact, I hardly knew that there were people living on the shores of the fjord until a pal showed me a pair of reindeer-hide moccasins that he had obtained from a mountain Lapp in exchange for a packet of cigarettes. I was very impressed. But the Lang fjord was no more than a stop on the way. It's the Barents Sea that I remember best.

The ship's eighty or so officers and cadets had more freedom of movement, however, and some of them made contacts among the local population, one of whom, Torvald Thomassen, recalls: 'I got some kind of infection in my foot, and our local doctor decided to wait until the inflammation came to a head. I couldn't put any weight on my foot and began to fear the worst. But then a senior officer happened to visit us. He heard about my foot, looked at it and offered to operate. I accepted, he did, and afterwards he treated me for several weeks. My foot began to get better after only a few days.'

At that time Thomassen was only twenty and his childhood home was no more than a stone's throw from the massive mooring posts the Germans had erected on the foreshore at Sopnes. The *Scharnhorst*'s smith helped some of the farmers round about with minor repairs; other people swapped fish for tobacco. The local lads were quite daring: they used to row out to the towering steel giant and ask to be allowed to come aboard. 'It was a great thrill to stand at the rail of a ship like that,' says Kolbjørn Karlstrøm.

All this notwithstanding, for most of the Norwegian population the sight of those menacing, grey-painted warships on their doorstep was an ever-present and intolerable reminder of the Nazis' hated occupation, which was slowly impoverishing both the country and its people. Freedom was a thing of the past: the German presence did not allow anyone to forget that the Norwegians were in thrall, captives in their own country. The local schoolteacher had been shot, probably mistakenly, by a German guard – the matter was never cleared up and no one accepted responsibility. It proved that when it came to the crunch, the

local people were devoid of legal rights. To two local families, the Rødes and the Rapps, having to face, day after day, the sight of the occupiers of their country was especially painful. On 4 December 1942 their doors had been kicked open by German soldiers under the command of *SS-Hauptscharführer* Rudolf Illing. Illing was on the staff of the *Gestapo* in Hammerfest and was married to the daughter of the Nazi sympathizer Jørgen Sivertsen, a clergyman who was later appointed 'bishop' of northern Norway. Anton Røde and Bjørnar Rapp, both of whom were only eighteen at the time, were arrested on suspicion of spying and were badly beaten up. The first from the Lang fjord district to do so, early that summer they had started to report on German naval dispositions to a Resistance group in the next county, Tromsø. But the group had been infiltrated by Henry Oliver Rinnan (an infamous Trondheim-based Norwegian *Gestapo* agent who was executed by firing squad after the war), with the result that more than forty people were arrested in Tromsø and western Finnmark, among them those two young men. In 1943 Røde and Rapp were still incarcerated in wretched circumstances in a prison camp in Tromsø. 'It was a terrible ordeal for our families,' Anton Røde says. 'They didn't know whether they would ever see us again.'

On board the *Scharnhorst* few of the ordinary sailors had any notion of what took place ashore. Life on board was governed by its own routine, from the moment the men were aroused from their sleep at six in the morning until their hammocks were reslung and Lights Out sounded at ten in the evening. The ship's officers were sticklers for order and cleanliness. Slovenliness was not tolerated for a moment: everything had to be scrubbed and scoured, polished and painted.

Very occasionally the Welfare Service would break the monotony by providing more urbane amusements. On one occasion *Reichkommissar* Josef Terboven (Hitler's ruthless Reich Commissioner in Norway) arranged for the 2,000-ton *Kraft durch Freude* (Strength through Joy) vessel *Emanuel Rambur* to visit the ships holed up in the Lang fjord, there to put on theatrical performances twice a day for the ships' companies.

When we got there, each member of the party was offered a glass of red wine, biscuits and a packet of cigarettes stamped 'A gift from Terboven'. The first part of the show consisted of songs and music performed by five Red Cross nurses and fifteen Norwegian girls who were said to be stewardesses. In the second half three female nightclub entertainers, all of them getting on in years, did their stuff, to the accompaniment of a sextet which had once played at one of Berlin's less fashionable cafés. As soon as it was over we were taken straight back to the *Scharnhorst*. There were many outspoken complaints about the fact that the officers either spent the night on board the *Emanuel Rambur* or took some of the girls back with them to their own cabins on board the *Scharnhorst*.

That apart, the almost two thousand ratings on board the battlecruiser had to provide their own entertainment. New theatrical troupes and bands were formed. The ship's three cinemas showed all the latest German films, including propaganda films and newsreels. The library was well stocked with novels and popular fiction, but contained few political books.

According to the British *Interrogation Report*, most of the men's time off was spent playing cards. Playing for money was widespread and large sums were won and lost. Gambling was officially frowned upon, but the officers turned a blind eye to it. Helmut Feifer was one of the ship's best cardplayers. 'He was very clever. He used to play poker at one table and chess at another, going from one to the other. He very rarely lost,' Helmut Backhaus remembers.

For the sports-minded, the Lang fjord area was just the thing. *Organisation Todt* had built two piers near Sopnes called Hansa and Blücher. Every day, at about two o'clock, boats left the ship to take ashore men who were not on duty. Up to about half-past five in the winter there would be skiing, and in summer men would go mountain climbing, play football or pick berries and mushrooms. 'The skiing was fantastic, and after a while many of us got to be quite good at it,' says Backhaus, who seized every opportunity to get out into the wilds.

Kapitän-zur-See Hüffmaier's run of bad luck was not yet at an end, however. On 8 April 1943 the *Scharnhorst* was rocked by a violent explosion in the depths of the ship. 'The whole ship shuddered and shook. The magazine of C turret was flooded, and at first we were afraid it was sabotage. In the event, however, it turned out to be the result of spontaneous combustion in a compartment where they stored gas and chemicals,' Feifer remembers. 'The chaps who had to clear up afterwards had a terrible job. By the time they had got out all the buckled and twisted steel plates and timbers they'd found the mangled remains of seventeen bodies.'

Shortly afterwards one of the battlecruiser's Arado floatplanes hit an overhead powerline and crashed, killing the pilot. All eighteen men were buried with full military honours in the German cemetery at Elvebakken in Alta. Their families were told that their deaths were the result of enemy action.

The *Scharnhorst*'s boilers burned fuel oil, which was in very short supply and had to be strictly conserved. A whole month was to pass before the battlecruiser carried out its first tactical exercise, which took place in Stjern Sound towards the end of April. Three weeks later the entire Battle Group put to sea, with *Tirpitz* in the lead – but only for a day. A further month later the *Scharnhorst* and *Lützow* were

transferred to the Kå fjord, there to meet the three commanders in charge: the local chief of operations, *Admiral* Oskar Kummetz; the operations chief for northern Norway (*Admirals Nordmeer*, Narvik), *Konter-Admiral* Otto Klüber; and the Fleet Commander (*Gruppe Nord*, Kiel), *Generaladmiral* Otto Schniewind. It was a most impressive ceremony. Naval bands played martial music, Nazi flags strained and flapped in the wind and the gold braid of caps, cuffs and shoulder straps gleamed in the sunshine. It was to no avail: neither bellicose speeches nor the pomp of the occasion could disguise the fact that frustration and despondency were beginning to take hold, and matters were not improved by the gloomy news from home.

Hüffmaier summed matters up in the war diary for August:

> Six uneventful months lie behind us. . . True, refresher courses have been held . . . Arctic championships in various sports have been organized, as have courses in raffia work with the aim of making Christmas presents for the children, and there have been instructional talks on mushrooms and fungi that aroused considerable interest. . . . But none of the foregoing activities have been able to prevent the spread of a disquieting feeling among the men that they are far safer here than are their loved ones back home, exposed as they are to the bombing attacks of the British and Americans; this is especially true of the many who come from the Ruhr. . . . There is now a widespread urge to strike back with the ship on behalf of the [men's] next of kin. . . . To keep the blade sharp, action is necessary.

One of those who had found the past six months very frustrating was 21-year-old Heinrich Mulch from Giessen. As a ship's writer on the Admiral's staff, his security clearance allowed him to handle confidential documents. In consequence, he saw and understood more than the majority of his shipmates, but in his letters home he had to be circumspect: 'I arrived here early this winter. The air fairly crackled with frost, ship and fjord alike were wreathed in fog, and the rigging and aerials howled in the snowstorms. It was a cold, grey period – but then came the spring and we made a few short trips round about. We were, of course, hoping for a really long voyage, now that we were up here in the Arctic Ocean, but May came – and with May, you, my dear little girl.'

As already noted, the correspondence between young Mulch and the goldsmith's apprentice Gertrud Damaski in his home town of Giessen had begun by chance in the shape of an impersonal letter addressed to an unknown sailor. 'A girlfriend of mine asked me to write. I had no ulterior motive, there was nothing special behind it, no plans or desires of any kind, I was just doing what I felt was my duty, to convey a little warmth from home to someone at the front,' Gertrud says.

The first letter was one of many. In July 1943 Heinrich was granted leave. He took the bus to Alteidet and set out on the long journey south through Norway and Denmark. Gertrud recalled, 'Suddenly my eye was caught by a sailor standing just across the street. The goldsmith suggested that I call it a day. I didn't know quite what to do, but he was a handsome-looking lad. I felt myself trembling. The atmosphere between us was electric. I took him home to meet my family. After that, we spent as much time together as we could.'

It was a wonderful August for them both. They spent the long, balmy summer evenings walking hand in hand. Slowly, as they conversed, meaningfully and at length, love began to dawn. Whenever they felt themselves unobserved, they would steal a kiss and a cuddle:

Something happened between us in the course of those four weeks. We had a sense of intimacy and tenderness. We could talk about everything. I still vividly remember the day we went to see him off at the station. He was going back to Alta. The train was late. His mother and sister were there too. He drew me to one side and said, 'You're strong. You mustn't cry.' That was what they all said, 'Gertrud's strong'. And I *was* strong! I fought back my tears, but inside I felt completely empty.

On his return from leave Heinrich's letters took on a new note.

I didn't have any plans either. I had nothing special in mind. However, nothing ventured, nothing gained! I have never felt daunted by admirals and staff officers, so why did I feel so ill at ease in your home together with your father and stepmother? . . . Do you know how wonderful that evening was when we exchanged our first kiss, it was so truly magical as to defy description. . . . You made me so happy – and then we had to part, and it was so terribly sad. . . . I think of you with tremulous yearning. You are my eternal dream.

But Dönitz had not defied Hitler and despatched the Battle Group northwards in order that the ships' companies should while away the hours raffia weaving, picking mushrooms and penning romantic letters to their girlfriends back home. The ships had been sent north to fight. The Grand Admiral's salvation lay in the fact that the convoys were still not running. He was determined that as soon as sailings resumed the convoys would meet a battle group that with 'courage and ardour' would put the *Führer*'s abusive words to shame.

This brave pronouncement notwithstanding, the admirals who in February and March 1943 had been eager to 'fight and, if necessary, die' had already begun to doubt whether 'a crushing blow against the convoys' was at all feasible. Success would depend on the fulfilment of certain criteria – first and foremost that the *Luftwaffe* was capable of carrying out the required air reconnaissance. But *Luftflotte 5*, which was responsible for the northern territories, had been greatly enfeebled. Many squadrons had been transferred to the Eastern front and the Mediterranean, where the German forces were in full retreat. Moreover, *Reichsmarschall* Hermann Göring was a dangerous rival: he would not take kindly to playing second fiddle as back-up for the *Kriegsmarine*. On the contrary, Göring wanted his airmen to have the leading role. It was they who would provide the destruction of the convoys – the Battle Group would have to be content with the escorts.

As early as April the man whose duty it would be to lead the Group into battle, *Admiral* Kummetz, confided his doubts to Dönitz. He no longer believed that the stage was set for a successful operation. '*Luftflotte 5* has still not grasped what these joint operations we are planning entail,' he said. 'As things stand at present, I don't think the *Luftwaffe* is in a position to provide the prerequisites of success. They will neither be able to carry out the reconnaissance that is needed nor keep the heavy units at bay.'

These were pessimistic and defeatist words to be uttered by a man who held the lives of the Battle Group's ten thousand young sailors in his hands. By what right could Kummetz, Klüber and Schniewind demand the ultimate sacrifice of their men when they themselves no longer believed in victory?

On 6 July, in glorious summer sunshine, the Battle Group carried out its first and only war game, off the island of Sørøya. The *Tirpitz*, *Scharnhorst* and three destroyers were the 'Blues', representing the German Battle Group. The *Lützow* and five destroyers, the 'Yellows', constituted the enemy, a British battleship of the King George V class and its escorts – which was precisely the force the *Scharnhorst* was destined to meet off the North Cape six months later. The Blue force put up a good show and came out well. But the Battle of the North Cape was no war game; nor was there a 'Blue' section. Then, the *Scharnhorst* was alone.

While the guns roared and thundered and the war game proceeded according to plan, other developments were taking place ashore. *Kapitän-zur-See* Hüffmaier had long been concerned by the need to strengthen counter-intelligence measures. He warned against the damage spies and saboteurs could do. In point of fact at that time the Battle Group had little to fear – but that was soon to change.

CHAPTER SEVEN

London Comes to Life

THE KÅ FJORD, AUGUST 1943

A few weeks after the Battle Group's war game a young man wheeled a ramshackle ladies' bicycle ashore from the local steamer at Alteidet. The day was bright and sunny and in the sheltered valleys round about the potato fields were in full flower. Taking his time, the man mounted his bicycle and pedalled off up the gentle incline of the unmetalled road that *Organisation Todt* and the Highways Department had built across the mountains all the way to Alta. Some 100 kilometres in length and heavily guarded, for the cyclist its principal attraction was the panoramic views it afforded of the German anchorages, complete with their anti-torpedo nets, anti-aircraft batteries and other defensive installations.

The cyclist was Torbjørn Johansen. Courageous, and with a good head on his shoulders, he was the youngest son of the manager of the Tromsø Electricity Board; although only twenty-three years of age, he was already a seasoned member of the Resistance movement in northern Norway. His ride was destined to result in one of the most noteworthy intelligence reports to pass between Norway and London throughout the entire war.

Johansen had received his assignment from the telegraphist at the meteorological station in Tromsø, Egil Lindberg, who operated a clandestine wireless transmitter, Upsilon II, from the loft of the local hospital. Lindberg, in turn, was acting on behalf of the British Secret Service, which had begun to take a keen interest in the enormous German naval base in western Finnmark.

'Have a look at this, Torbjørn,' Lindberg had said. 'It's a signal I've had from London – it's about the *Tirpitz* in the Kå fjord. Not only do they want an accurate sketch map showing the position of the anti-torpedo nets, but also

exact measurements of the specific gravity of the water surrounding the ship. It's asking a bit much. Still, it'll give you something to think about!'

Good with his hands and of a technical bent, Torbjørn Johansen was a student at the University College in Trondheim; at the time he was enjoying the summer vacation in Tromsø. His first task was to construct a sampler, a vial which he secreted in the hollow butt of a fishing-rod, and his second to borrow a bicycle. As he pedalled along the shore of the Lang fjord that August day, he took in the sight of the pocket battleship *Lützow* at anchor north of Sopnes, together with a number of destroyers and the supply ship *Dittmarschen*. He found temporary employment at a fox farm located deep within the Kå fjord, not far from where the *Tirpitz* and *Scharnhorst* were moored some 200 metres from each other, ringed about by ten to fifteen tugs, tankers and other auxiliary vessels.

Some days later, at about the same time as *Kapitän-zur-See* Friedrich Hüffmaier was confiding his pessimistic reflections to the war diary, Torbjørn Johansen rowed slowly past the battleships, trailing on the end of his fishing-line not a lure but his homemade water sampler. Only when he replaced it with a real lure did his luck change. 'There was a sudden tug and Torbjørn reeled in a good-sized coalfish. . . . The sound of clapping came across the water and he looked up to see a group of German sailors lining the rail and applauding. He waved to them and proudly displayed his catch. . . . They were greatly impressed.'

A week later Johansen cycled back the same way he had come carrying the water sample he had surreptitiously taken and, tucked away among the pages of the Nazi propaganda newspaper *Fritt Folk*, detailed sketch maps of the two bases. These maps, like the sample and report that accompanied them, were just what the British were after; an extract of the report was sent from the Upsilon station to London in the shape of two long transmissions on 16 and 21 August. The report ran: 'The battle cruiser *Scharnhorst*, which the informant definitely recognised from the plan of the fleet, is anchored in the Kaafjord in position 69°57'6'N : 23°08'E.' It continued:

In May, there was a heavy explosion on board and everyone living in the district heard it. . . . Twenty ratings were killed in the explosion. In order to make coffins for them, the Germans pulled down the snow screens belonging to the Roads and Highways Department. . . . Also lying in the Kaafjord is a workshop ship of about 6,000 tons. She looks like a normal merchant ship and was ordered alongside the *Scharnhorst* after the explosion. . . . On the 4th July 1943 the whole fleet of 15 ships was out and the Germans stated later that they had been to Bear Island. . . . The *Scharnhorst* does not have a permanent anchorage. Sometimes she anchors in the Lang fjord, at others in the Kå fjord, and also in the Skille fjord. . . . The anchorage [in the Lang fjord] . . . was in use from March to 15 June. . . . [It is blocked] . . . by a double torpedo-defence net with an opening 25 metres wide. The distance from the shore to the opening is about 50 metres.

With a few exceptions, Torbjørn Johansen's information was astonishingly correct. As noted above, the explosion actually occurred in April, killing seventeen men. The ship that was brought in to repair the damage was the *Neumark*. The sortie referred to was the Battle Group's war game. The sketch maps Johansen had made were even better than they appeared at first sight, as they showed with a remarkable degree of accuracy not only the two fjords but also the German anchorages and nets. 'It was one of the most important signals any Norwegian wireless station ever sent,' says the official history of Norwegian Intelligence in the Second World War. Johansen's report, together with his sketches of the anchorages and the water sample he had taken, were despatched by courier to Sweden.

Lindberg and Johansen's controller in England was the Secret Service's Scandinavian section, which in 1943 was headed by a 46-year-old chemist, Lieutenant-Commander Eric Welsh. Inclined to stoutness but bursting with energy, since 1919 Welsh had lived in Bergen, where he was technical manager of a company specializing in marine paints. Married to a Norwegian, Johanne Brun Svendsen, he spoke the language fluently, albeit with a Bergen accent; the couple had three children. Welsh returned to England when the Germans invaded Norway and in time became a competent, though controversial, department head in the Secret Intelligence Service (SIS), with Norway as his special field of responsibility.

From the more than two hundred agents who were sent back to Norway during the war, Welsh's office received a constant flow of reports. But Welsh was not these agents' true employer. Their assignments came from a totally different and equally covert source, the Operational Intelligence Centre (OIC), which was housed in a bombproof cellar beneath the Admiralty in London.

The wireless reports from Tromsø detailing the results of Torbjørn Johansen's bicycle reconnaissance found their way to the OIC section dealing with German surface vessels, which was run by the legendary Lieutenant-Commander Norman Denning. Denning and his staff played an important part in keeping tabs on the whereabouts of the German High Seas Fleet and trying to guess the German admirals' plans. To assist him in this work Denning received a wealth

of information from a wide range of sources. From the Government Code and Cipher School at Bletchley Park came a steady stream of decrypted German wireless intercepts, and Welsh's department provided him with the eye-witness reports of Norwegian agents on the spot. The Royal Air Force contributed aerial photographs and the Security Service the results of their interrogations of German prisoners.

Things had been quiet in Arctic waters since the Russian convoys had ceased to run in March. Despite this, the German naval force still maintained a high state of readiness and appeared to be exercising more frequently than it had in the past. Stalin had already voiced vociferous complaints about the hold-up in supplies, and everything pointed to the resumption of sailings with the advent of darker nights in the autumn. This generated a need for more agents in the vicinity of the German bases; a bicycle trip every now and then would no longer suffice.

Some preparations had already been made. In the summer of 1942 Finn Lied, a courier who was later to be appointed Norway's Minister of Industry, crossed over from Sweden to Norway carrying a wireless transmitter designated Lyra. The transmitter was deposited in a safe hiding-place, where it remained until another agent, 21-year-old officer cadet Nils Hornæs, was detailed to arrange for its positioning close to the German fleet, which at that time was in Narvik. Before Hornæs could find someone to carry out the order, however, the ships were moved further north.

It was not until the spring of 1943, after the transmitter had several times been moved from one hiding-place to another, that an opportunity presented itself. With the aid of various go-betweens, Hornæs got in touch with 32-year-old Rolf Storvik, who ran a village shop that also doubled as a post, telegraph and shipping office. It was located in the small community of Porsa on the shores of Varg Sound, midway between Alta and Hammerfest. Storvik, a staunch patriot, had fought in the battles that raged around Narvik in 1940. His forebears had moved to the north when rich deposits of copper were found in the Porsa mountains shortly after the turn of the century. But Porsa was no Klondyke and after a few hectic years mining operations petered out. The man who owned the mining rights died and the executors neither could nor would carry on working the mine. In consequence from 1932 onwards the galleries stood deserted and the aerial cableway that ran through the scenic Porsa valley gradually became derelict and rusted away.

Now, some ten years or so later, Porsa was near-moribund, although the Storvik family continued to cling on, together with about ten others. They pinned their hopes on the new power station that had opened nearby in 1940.

Capable of generating 450kW, it was designed to supply the nearest town, Hammerfest, with electricity.

Early in June 1943 Nils Hornæs, together with his liaison, Emil Samuelsberg, disembarked at Porsa from one of the Finnmark County Shipping Company's coal-burning steamers. Hidden in their luggage they carried the Lyra transmitter, a Colt pistol, binoculars, four models of German warships, a map of Alta and 800 kroner (£40 in 1940s) in cash. It would be interesting to know what went through the urbane Hornæs's mind when the ship rounded the promontory and the huddle of houses that was Porsa came into view. He must have wondered how the military chiefs back in the teeming metropolis of London could be kept updated on happenings at northern Europe's biggest naval base from such a tiny settlement. The Porsa fjord was not a fjord in the true sense of the word but merely a bay in which the water remained deep right up to the shore. From the fringe of the bay the land rose steeply to a morainic ridge which constituted the start of the Porsa valley proper. Looming large among the scattered houses was a white-painted villa with mullion windows and a glassed-in verandah where the mine manager had once been wont to sit and admire the view across the sound.

Storvik had already prepared the ground. He had confided his plans to one of the engineers at the power station, 32-year-old Trygve Duklæt, a former merchant seaman. 'We discussed where to install the transmitter and concluded that, all things considered, the best place would be Rolf Storvik's storeroom,' Duklæt explained in a report he compiled in 1945. As Duklæt had a nodding acquaintance with Morse code from his seafaring days, it was decided that he should be the wireless operator.

Whenever opportunity offered, Hornæs and I practised Morse. Because of the inquisitiveness of the local population and the fact that everyone knew everyone else's business, we thought it safest that Hornæs should leave after about five weeks. . . . A couple of days before he was due to depart, thanks to the aerial we had put up – it was hidden in the gutter – I got through without difficulty to the Home Station in London. I informed them that we were operational and that, circumstances permitting, we would report on shipping movements in Varg Sound and at the naval base in Alta.

In London, Welsh recorded that the first contact with Lyra had been established on 2 July 1943, which was only three days before the dreaded Battle Group carried out the summer's war game in the open sea. With an unhindered view of

Varg Sound, and contacts in Alta and Hammerfest, the agents could now keep the base's northern exits under constant surveillance.

Shortly afterwards the transmitter was moved from Storvik's storeroom to Duklæt's flat in the former manager's villa. It was a complicated operation and one not without risk. In the flat next door lived another engineer from the power station, Rolf Arnt Nygaard. Not only was Nygaard a member of Vidkun Quisling's *Nasjonal Samling* (National Union) party and chairman of Kvalsund County Council, he was also one of Finnmark's most ardent Nazis and a secret agent of the *Abwehr*, the military intelligence service of the High Command of the German Armed Forces (OKW).

CHAPTER EIGHT

Off Bear Island

THE BARENTS SEA, SEPTEMBER–DECEMBER 1943

There can be few more desolate and empty regions in the world than the waters surrounding Bear Island. A forbidding grey hump of rock set in an oceanic no-man's-land, the island thrusts its way up out of nowhere 240 nautical miles north of the North Cape. More often than not it is shrouded in fog. Battered by a constant barrage of heavy breakers, the steeply shelving beaches make landing almost impossible. In the east the island's highest mountain, aptly named Misery Mountain, rises sheer to a height of 500 metres. In winter the polar ice encroaches ever nearer, making, if possible, this rocky outpost still more gloomy, bleak and inaccessible.

Bear Island stands on a broad underwater plateau. The sea round about is shallow and the bottom foul, but to the south the seabed plunges deeply to a depth of 500 metres. This chasm is the Bear Island Trench, which divides the Barents Sea into two.

Throughout the war Allied convoys braved this exposed expanse of ocean to carry vital supplies to Murmansk. Here, too, German U-boats maintained constant patrols. It was a stretch of sea greatly feared by those who had to sail it. The German Navy called it *Hölles Meer*, Hell's Ocean, the British, the Devil's Dance Floor. 'There was a special horror about working up there on the icy roof of the world which struck at a man's heart. It was an emotion compounded of the sick fear of those dark, desolate, waters, which froze a man as he fell into them; fear of the treacherous weathers [*sic*]; fear of the enemy sea and air raiders; and last but not least, a nagging distrust of the almost unknown Russians themselves.'

Winston Churchill was undeniably one of the twentieth century's most uncompromising anti-Communists. But he was also a pragmatist and master of *Realpolitik*. As early as the evening of Sunday 22 June 1941, after Hitler had unleashed his armies against the Soviet Union, in a wireless broadcast on the BBC he promised Stalin assistance on a massive scale, though he made clear from the outset that his generosity was not prompted by love of the Bolsheviks. The Nazi regime was, he said, 'indistinguishable from the worst features of Communism. . . . It excels all forms of human wickedness in the efficiency of its cruelty and ferocious aggression. . . . No one has been a more consistent opponent of Communism than I have for the last twenty-five years.'

After that opening salvo, however, he moderated his tone. 'But all this fades away before the spectacle which is now unfolding. The past, with its crimes, its follies, and its tragedies, flashes away. I see the Russian soldiers standing on the threshold of their native land, guarding the fields which their fathers have tilled from time immemorial. . . . I see also the dull, drilled, docile, brutish masses of the Hun soldiery plodding on like a swarm of crawling locusts.' Germany's invasion of Russia, he continued, was 'no more than a prelude' to an attempted invasion of Britain. 'The Russian danger is therefore our danger, and the danger of the United States, just as the cause of any Russian fighting for his hearth and home is the cause of free men and free peoples in every quarter of the globe.'

Churchill recognized that it was in Britain's own interest that the Soviet Union should be able to withstand the German onslaught. To this end, with Roosevelt's backing, he offered Stalin unlimited material aid on favourable financial terms. In the first instance it was a matter of motor vehicles, aircraft and other military matériel – a billion dollars' worth in all – all to be paid for in gold and silver. His private secretary Sir John Colville recorded that, chided for his *volte-face*, Churchill once remarked: 'If Hitler invaded Hell [I] would at least make a favourable reference to the Devil.'

The first regular convoy, which comprised ten merchantmen, reached Murmansk without loss in September 1941. Between then and Christmas a further seven convoys made the voyage there and back with the loss of only one ship, which was torpedoed off Bear Island. However, 1942 was far bloodier: before the year was out sixty ships had gone to the bottom. These losses notwithstanding, 1.35 million tons of supplies reached Russia through the Barents Sea.

Now, in the autumn of 1943, the convoys had been suspended since March and Stalin was growing increasingly impatient. Relations between the Soviet Union and Great Britain had never been overly warm, neither in the higher echelons of power nor among the population in general. The sailors who, locked up in the confines of Vaenga Bay, were condemned to wait for weeks on end to discharge their valuable cargoes, complained bitterly of the wretched conditions under which they were forced to live and of the inefficiency, suspicion and petty-mindedness displayed by local Party officials. The Royal Navy contingent of 170 officers and men waged a seemingly hopeless battle against Bolshevik bureaucracy. The British sailors evinced little understanding of the fact that until quite recently Russia had been a backward feudal society, a country which had first been rent by a bloody revolution and then had undergone a process of enforced industrialization driven through by a merciless reign of terror. Hitler's brutal assault had dramatically increased the nation's sufferings; millions of Russians had already been killed in battle. Since 1941 Murmansk had been under siege and, bombed as it was almost daily, was a heap of ruins. Viewed in this light, to many Russians the British complaints were founded on ignorance and arrogance. An aggravating factor was that it was precisely in Murmansk and Archangel that, only some twenty years earlier, the British had landed troops to fight in the civil war on behalf of the Whites. It was a historical fact that few Russians had forgotten.

From the Allied point of view the Russians' attitude was hard to accept. By that time the fortunes of war had changed and Nazi Germany was in retreat on all fronts. The Allied victory in North Africa in the winter of 1943 had been followed by landings in Italy which had directly affected the fighting in the north. *Luftflotte 5* had been compelled to release some of its best and most experienced squadrons from service in Finnmark to bolster German forces in southern Europe. On the Eastern front the Red Army had won decisive victories at Kursk, Orel and Kharkov. The *Wehrmacht* was in retreat from Moscow in the north to the Black Sea in the south; and over Germany bombs continued to rain down by night and day, leaving city after city a heap of smouldering ruins. Operation Overlord, the invasion of Occupied Europe, was scheduled for 1944; with it, Stalin would have the Second Front he had pressed for for so long.

In September 1943 Churchill decided that the time had come to exert pressure on the Russian dictator – before convoy sailings were resumed. He wanted to put an end to the everlasting succession of petty annoyances that were making life so unbearable for the merchant seamen and naval ratings cooped up in Murmansk. The list was a long one: restrictions on their freedom of movement, the Russians' insistence on searching their personal belongings, the volumes of paperwork attendant upon the issuance of passports and visas and the demand that letters be sent to Moscow for censorship. In themselves, these may seem minor

inconveniences, but for the men whose job it was to keep the convoys sailing the problems to which such pinpricks gave rise were a reality of daily life. To top it all, while waiting in the White Sea port of Ekonomiya for a return convoy to assemble, the bo'sun and cook of the merchant vessel *Dover Hill* had got into a fight. After indulging rather too generously in highly potent vodka, the only product that appeared to be in plentiful supply, a couple of Russians had broached a sensitive question, that of the long-awaited landing in Europe. They intimated that by holding back the British were letting their allies down. What began as a simple exchange of views ended in a free-for-all. One of the Russians happened to be a member of the Communist Party and the authorities were outraged. The two British sailors were arrested and given sentences that were out of all proportion to the offence – four and seven years' imprisonment. News of the scandal came to the ears of Downing Street. Churchill was furious and refused to countenance further convoys until the two men had been released and the Russians assumed a more humane attitude all round.

The upshot was a diplomatic controversy that was not resolved until Foreign Minister Anthony Eden met Molotov in Moscow and managed to smooth things over. On 1 October 1943 Churchill announced that the suspension would be lifted and that the next convoy, consisting of thirty-five ships, would leave Scotland on 15 November. From then on, he said, supplies would continue to be despatched at monthly intervals until February 1944. Taken all round, this amounted to 140 shiploads, totalling 1 million tons of tanks, fighter aircraft, motor transport, heavy artillery, ammunition, clothing, medical supplies, rubber, tin, copper and other raw materials.

Churchill's promise would eventually give *Grossadmiral* Dönitz his long-awaited chance to show what the Northern Battle Group was capable of. But, undermined by a long run of reverses, the morale of the men confined in the Lang and Kå fjords was by then at a low ebb.

Early in September *Admiral* Oskar Kummetz had taken the *Tirpitz*, *Scharnhorst* and a destroyer escort to Svalbard (Spitsbergen) and returned in triumph. A bombardment by the battleships' heavy guns that lasted for several hours had left Longyearbyen and Barentsburg in ruins. Six Norwegians were killed, thirty-eight taken prisoner. The rest of the garrison, some 150 men, sought refuge in the mountains. The German propaganda machine hailed the attack as a resounding victory, but the truth was far different. From a military point of view there was little point in wasting ammunition on slagheaps, tumbledown shacks and warehouses. The real purpose of the raid was to stiffen morale on board the battleships and give Hitler something to boost his ego.

To judge by the relevant entry in the ships' war diaries, the first object was successfully achieved. 'The enterprise was greeted with great satisfaction by the men. A sigh of relief ran through the ship. . . . The men felt that they had been charged with a task which again had a point to it . . . particularly in view of what was happening to the elderly and to women and children in Germany. . . . These feelings must be exploited . . . before the onset of the polar night makes action impossible,' wrote Hüffmaier on board the *Scharnhorst*.

The Commander of the 4th Destroyer Flotilla, *Kapitän-zur-See* Rolf Johannesson, was equally optimistic: 'The men have undergone their baptism of fire. This successful sortie has welded them together in a common act of war. . . . Their self-confidence strengthened, they are now ready for new tasks.'

Neither officer mentioned an act of war that engendered more gloom than joy on board the ships that had taken part in the raid. When a landing party was sent ashore on Spitsbergen, the nerve of a sailor on one of the destroyers had broken and he had hidden instead of joining the shore party. Such conduct could not be condoned. After a summary court martial the wretched man was sentenced to death and executed by firing-squad on the quarterdeck of the *Scharnhorst* in the presence of the entire ship's company.

Behind all the bravado were other and more serious realities. Both the *Tirpitz* and the pocket battleship *Lützow* were living on borrowed time. Both should long ago have been docked for a refit and repairs in Germany. It had already been decided that the *Lützow* should sail for home on 23 September. But what would happen to the Battle Group if the *Tirpitz* were to follow in her wake? The *Scharnhorst* would be left alone to strike the 'crushing blow' against the convoys that Dönitz had promised Hitler. It was a prospect few thought had any hope of success.

The naval chiefs were still pondering the pros and cons of the situation when the British made up their minds for them. Early in the morning of 22 September 1943 lookouts on the *Tirpitz* spotted what appeared to be two small submarines close alongside the ship. Those gunners who were able to depress their guns sufficiently opened fire, and desperate attempts were made to move the steel giant out of danger. It was in vain. At 10.12 powerful charges exploded beneath the ship's keel. 'Two explosions to port at 1/10-second intervals. The ship shuddered violently in a vertical direction and twisted to and fro between her anchors,' was the laconic entry in the ship's war diary.

The explosions were actually the result of one of the war's boldest and most successful acts of sabotage, an attack by two midget submarines, the *X6* and *X7*. Six such underwater craft had been towed from Scotland to a position offshore

from where the *Tirpitz* lay at anchor, two being lost on the way. After a heroic struggle two of the remaining four managed to penetrate the anti-submarine nets and place charges consisting of 8 tons of amatol beneath the battleship's hull – probably with help from the sketch maps and report Torbjørn Johansen had sent through to London after his bicycle trip in August. The *Tirpitz* remained afloat but the explosions caused serious damage to her hull, engines and guns. The damage was so extensive, in fact, that it ruled out all hope of a return to Germany to repair it; instead, a requisition was put in for the materials and labour required to repair the damage on the spot. The *Tirpitz* was likely to be out of action for at least six months.

Heinrich Mulch made no mention of this incident in his letter to Gertrud following the explosion – apart from saying that all cameras on board were being impounded. He also said that a third of the men were being sent home on leave. To his disappointment he was not one of the lucky ones, but he wrote that he expected a new opportunity to arise fairly soon. 'It was the best holiday I have ever had . . . and for that you deserve much of the credit. So you have no need to worry. As soon as I am able, I'll be back. . . . Should home leave prove absolutely impossible, we shall just have to wait. You – and I, too.'

On a later occasion he wrote:

It is late in the evening and I have locked all the drawers in my desk so as not to see any more of the paper war. Outside it is pitch-dark, I can't see very far. On both sides, black and threatening, tower the mountains – and above them stretches an overclouded, slate-grey sky. Darkness falls as early as five in the afternoon, blotting out the landscape round about. In the dark of the evening the sea loses its glitter. In fact it is hardly possible to make out the shapes of the big rocks on the shore. Sea and sky merge in varying shades of grey. The stars don't shine the way they do at home. But if there's a break in the overcast, one can see, high in the heavens, like a slowly waving veil, the Northern Lights. The trees have long since lost their leaves in the autumn storms that lashed the fjord. All the green of summer has vanished from a landscape dominated by these sombre mountains. . . . Fate has decreed that we shall not see each other again this year. But life goes on, and December is always followed by May. Then we shall once again be able to think about a holiday. . . . In the meantime you must remember that all along you have been a wonderful source of pleasure to me, giving me above all lots of love and comradeship. You have given me faith in a wonderful future together . . .

For once Friedrich Hüffmaier was in luck. The evening before the attack he had taken the *Scharnhorst* out into the Alta fjord in preparation for a gunnery exercise the following day. After the attack on the *Tirpitz* he hurriedly returned to the safety of the Lang fjord, where new and rigorous security measures were immediately instituted. Three weeks later he bade the *Scharnhorst* farewell. The men had long suspected their captain of having induced Dönitz to send the battlecruiser north for the simple reason that his greatest ambition was to win a Knight's Cross. True or not, in the event Hüffmaier's hopes were dashed, as he was promoted to Rear Admiral and posted to a staff job in Berlin. On 14 October he welcomed his successor, *Kapitän-zur-See* Julius Hintze. Hintze, who was forty-two years of age, was born and had grown up in Bad Bevensen on Lüneberg Heath, south of Hamburg. The son of a miller, he lived and breathed for the life of a naval officer.

'He was a warm, sprightly man, considerate and good-humoured,' recalls his niece and goddaughter, *Frau* Karin Woltersdorf. 'Ever since he was a child he had dreamed of a life at sea. The walls of his bedroom were plastered with pictures of ships. He even hung models of the Imperial Navy's frigates on the Christmas tree!'

In the autumn of 1918 Hintze entered the Imperial Cadet Training College but the First World War came to an end before he could complete the course. Germany had lost and was forced to sign a humiliating peace treaty. The future held no promise for a career officer, so seventeen-year-old Hintze reluctantly turned to banking.

'But life ashore was nothing for him. At the first opportunity, in 1920, he applied to rejoin Germany's new navy, which was then in its infancy. He was determined to realize his childhood dream of becoming a sailor.' Up until the time in the mid-1930s when Hitler tore up the Treaty of Versailles, the Navy was subject to severe restrictions. Its ships were few and outdated, and career prospects were anything but bright. But Hintze eagerly seized every chance that offered – from training courses at the Marineschule Flensburg-Mürwik to service at sea in the 1920s on board minesweepers, torpedo boats and the elderly light cruisers *Arcona* and *Amazone*, both of which had been built before the turn of the century and which the victors had magnanimously allowed Germany to retain. His first chance to sail with one of the nation's new naval vessels came in 1932, when he was appointed *Kapitänleutnant* and torpedo officer on board the 6,000-ton cruiser *Köln*, which had been launched three years earlier. His subsequent postings were all land-based until 1938, when he found himself on board the cruiser *Emden* as captain and navigation officer.

Some months later, after attending a staff officers' course in April 1939, he was posted as navigation officer to the brand-new heavy cruiser *Admiral Hipper* (18,000 dwt), which was armed with eight 8-inch guns and had a top speed of close on 33 knots.

'My godfather was a real family man,' *Frau* Woltersdorf says. 'He often visited my mother, his sister, and I still remember how proud and happy we were at [the success of] his career.'

With the rank of *Fregattenkapitän*, from 1940 onwards Hintze sailed the seas from Spitsbergen in the north to Africa in the south as navigation officer, serving under two captains, first *Kapitän-zur-See* Hermann Heye and later *Kapitän-zur-See* Wilhelm Meisel. He experienced violent gales in the Norwegian Sea and storms and icing in the Denmark Strait. His baptism of fire occurred off the Norwegian coast during the German attack on Trondheim on 9 April 1940, when the *Hipper* sank the British destroyer *Glowworm* which, in the course of a brief and bloody battle, had rammed the cruiser. In December 1940 Hintze again found himself in the thick of things when his ship engaged the British cruiser *Berwick* on the *Hipper*'s first Atlantic sortie. The German cruiser was damaged and an Allied ship sunk. The next raid, which took place in February 1941, was more successful. Not far off Madeira the *Hipper* chanced upon an unprotected convoy; shortly afterwards seven merchantmen had been sent to the bottom and a further three damaged. This episode was followed by several months in dock in Germany, before Hintze returned to the Arctic. The *Hipper* was part of the force which in July 1942 sallied forth from the Alta fjord to attack convoy PQ17, an attack which came to naught because the flotilla was recalled. When, in the late summer of 1942, Hintze was promoted to the rank of *Kapitän-zur-See* and put in charge of the Experimental Torpedo Station at Eckernförde, not far from Kiel, he could look back on three dramatic years packed with exciting incidents. They had endowed him with a wealth of experience in the handling of big ships in wartime, which meant that his sojourn at Eckernförde was merely an interim posting. In the autumn of 1943 Hintze learned that he had been chosen to captain the battlecruiser *Scharnhorst*; it was an appointment that undoubtedly had the blessing of his onetime superiors on the *Hipper*, Heye and Meisel, both of whom had in the meantime been promoted to the rank of admiral and were in important staff jobs. Heye was Chief of Staff of *Gruppe Nord* in Kiel, while Meisel was Chief of Staff at Naval Headquarters in Berlin.

With this appointment Hintze's lifetime ambition had been fulfilled. Looking back, Karin Woltersdorf says:

For him it was absolutely wonderful to be charged with responsibility for one of the Navy's biggest and best ships. But at the same time it was a task that weighed heavily upon him, no doubt because he knew of Germany's great inferiority at sea and the difficulties inherent in the job he had taken on. He visited us before leaving for the north. It was a chilly day in October 1943. Instead of the usual cheeriness and warmth, this time the parting was marked by deep sadness. My godfather knew what lay ahead, and he wasn't at all happy about it.

Only three weeks after Hintze's arrival at the naval base in Alta, a new and surprising change of command took place. *Admiral* Oskar Kummetz had promised 'to fight . . . and, if necessary, die' when he was permitted to retain his post as Squadron Commander. His tour of duty in Norway had been anything but propitious, however. As commander of the force earmarked for the occupation of Oslo on the night of 8/9 April 1940, he had had the *Blücher* sink beneath him and barely escaped with his life after dragging himself ashore on to a rocky islet in the Oslo fjord. New Year's Eve 1942 was another date he would have preferred to forget. Now, after eight far from successful months spent kicking his heels in the Arctic, he had applied for and been granted prolonged sick leave. In his absence one of the *Kriegsmarine*'s most experienced destroyer captains, *Konter-Admiral* Erich Bey, was appointed to replace him.

When the rumour that Kummetz was going on extended leave began to circulate, it gave rise to a certain amount of discontent among the Battle Group's officers, foremost among them the forceful 43-year-old Commander of the 4th Destroyer Flotilla, *Kapitän-zur-See* Rolf Johannesson, who in 1958 was to be promoted to the rank of *Konter-Admiral* and appointed Commander in Chief of West Germany's *Bundesmarine*. Like Kummetz, Johannesson was a veteran naval officer who could look back upon a long and varied service life that had begun in 1918. For his achievements as captain of the former Greek destroyer *Hermes* in the Mediterranean, he had been awarded the prestigious Knight's Cross in 1942. Many years later Johannesson was to write: 'In September 1943 there were rumours in Alta that the Commander of the Battle Group did not intend to spend the winter up there in eternal darkness but to take leave of indefinite duration. I found it impossible to believe that he would abandon his squadron and leave his flag hanging there like a meaningless symbol. For that reason I invited him to supper on board my own ship and endeavoured with the aid of my Flag Captain to persuade him to stay – in vain.'

Writing in the war diary, Johannesson expressed his disappointment in the following words: 'The general impression of this planned "replacement commander" is very reminiscent of 21 October 1939.' This was a reference to the day *Grossadmiral* Raeder had dismissed *Admiral* Hermann Boehm and other high-ranking officers including Kummetz. When Kummetz urged Johannesson to delete this remark, he refused: 'In my eyes it was simply stating a fact that there was no reason to hide. On the contrary, it was essential to inform the Fleet Commander and Naval High Command of feelings at the Front.'

The response was not long in coming. When a copy of the diary reached the Commander of *Gruppe Nord* in Kiel, *Generaladmiral* Otto Schniewind, it occasioned a chilling reprimand: 'I consider this remark . . . a most unseemly criticism of decisions taken at a higher level. I deem the statement quite improper and something the Flotilla Commander cannot overlook.'

After this the murmur of discontent died away, and on 9 November 1943 Kummetz left Alta. His farewell address ran as follows:

With effect from today I have handed over responsibility for the Battle Group to *Konter-Admiral* Bey while I am on leave and at the disposal of the C-in-C of the Fleet. Looking back, I can but regret that the high hopes we had for the Battle Group when I again came north in March 1943 have not been completely fulfilled. It may well be, however, that the very presence of the Battle Group has in itself precluded an attack on the convoys, as our adversary has not been able or willing to release the escort forces that the existence of the Battle Group has necessitated.

He concluded:

I should also like to express the hope that willingness to deploy surface vessels against the enemy will also result in those ships presently serving as training ships and/or that have been decommissioned in Germany, being sent to join the Battle Group in the north. That would greatly enhance the [Group's] striking power when I return. It will also be necessary to ensure that repairs to my flagship *Tirpitz* are completed by 15.3.44. Without this ship the Battle Group will carry no real weight.

No one dared to say so out loud, but everyone knew what Kummetz meant. He was taking leave because he did not believe that the Battle Group would see action until the *Tirpitz* had been repaired, which would not be until the winter of 1944. Bey and Hintze were *de facto* caretakers, condemned to mind the shop during the dark days of winter, pending Kummetz's return.

The only German units in the autumn of 1943 to continue offensive operations in the Barents Sea were the U-boats. Under the overall command of Dönitz, throughout the whole of 1943 a gradual extension of the network of bases in northern Norway had taken place. As early as 18 January a new post as Commander of all U-boat operations in the Arctic had been established. The new *Führer der Unterseeboote Norwegen* (abbreviated to *FdU Norwegen*) set up his headquarters on board Hitler's former yacht, the *Grille*, which was moored in Narvik harbour, along with a commandeered Norwegian tourist ship, the *Stella Polaris*, and a number of tankers and auxiliary vessels. A highly experienced and versatile torpedo officer, 44-year-old *Kapitän-zur-See* Rudolf Peters, was given command of the new U-boat fleet. Peters had been both second-in-command of the battlecruiser *Gneisenau* and Commander of the 21st U-boat Fleet in Memel in the Baltic, where prospective U-boat captains were given intensive gunnery instruction. However, Peters's undisputed qualifications notwithstanding, the appointment did not meet with universal approval. 'Peters was accustomed to big decks. He wasn't one of us, he didn't belong in the U-boat arm, he didn't have the requisite experience. Nor did he have a grasp of submarine warfare. He didn't understand what it entailed,' says one of the few U-boat captains to survive the war in the Arctic, Hans-Günther Lange, holder of the Knight's Cross of the Iron Cross with Oak Leaves for his achievements as Captain of *U-711* in the Barents Sea.

> There was one thing in particular that he did wrong: he wanted to control the U-boats down to the minutest detail. He would come in over the radio and want to know our position. We were constantly having to surface and say where we were. We ourselves would have preferred to lie quietly submerged and listen for the enemy, but Peters wanted to keep tabs on the fleet from hour to hour. It was a totally misguided tactic. We complained about it, but he wouldn't budge. He just didn't have the necessary knowledge.

Although Peters was never accepted by the U-boat captains, he did at least take the offensive. In the first two years of war the German wolf packs had operated from Kirkenes, where a commandeered whale factory ship, the *Südmeer*, did service as mother ship. At Peters's behest another requisitioned ship, the Fred Olsen Line's 5,000-ton steamer *Black Watch*, was fitted out to take over the *Südmeer's* role. Shortly after New Year 1943 the *Black Watch* was moved to

Hammerfest and moored between two new landing-stages deep within Fuglenes Bay – only 200 metres or so, in fact, from the house into which this author's parents moved when they married in 1938. The *Black Watch* provided all the comforts the U-boat crews could ask for in the shape of washing and laundering facilities, good food and, not least, rest after gruelling patrols, some of which might last for forty days or more.

'It was a luxury ship. It was fantastic on our return from an arduous patrol to be able to relax on board with a sauna, clean clothes, film shows and tip-top food,' remembers Peter Junker, a wireless operator on board *U-716*.

Moored on the town side was a cargo vessel, the *Admiral Carl Hering*, laden with torpedoes and ammunition. Captain-cum-chief engineer Friedrich Walther Müller was placed in command of this new forward base, which was known as *U-boot-Stützpunkt Hammerfest*. According to Lange,

> Müller was an elderly man who wasn't too happy in the company of the young lads we had on board. The [U-boat] service was a demanding and dangerous undertaking. At sea no one could afford to relax for a moment – spirits were strictly taboo. For that reason the men used to save up their ration, which meant that quite a few litres had accumulated by the end of a forty-day patrol. We couldn't leave any undrunk, of course. No one was going to have our ration if we didn't get back, it had all to be disposed of. Things could get pretty lively at times and Müller wasn't at all pleased.

The *Black Watch* had barely settled at her moorings behind the anti-submarine nets in January 1943 when the first U-boat returned from patrol. This was *U-255* under her famed skipper Reinhard Reche. Reche was only twenty-six years of age when, in the spring of 1942, he was posted to the Arctic, but he very soon demonstrated an exceptional talent for unrestricted U-boat warfare and was one of the brains behind the destruction of the ill-fated convoy PQ17. In the course of one week in July he sank no fewer than four merchantmen from the convoy off Novaja Semlja. But he could also be chivalrous. When the Liberty ship *John Witherspoon* was sent to the bottom, he drew alongside the lifeboats and distributed water, cognac and cigarettes among their occupants. With the *Black Watch* as his base, in February and March 1943 he continued to attack whatever Allied ships came his way, and in rapid succession sank the Soviet icebreaker *Malygin*, the steamer *Ufa* and three American merchantmen, the *Greylock*, *Executive* and *Richard Bland*. The last-mentioned vessel was a brand-new Liberty ship which Reche shadowed all the way to Iceland, where he succeeded in torpedoing her for a second time. On 17 March he was thanked by the *Führer* for having sunk more than ten enemy ships in the course of a bare six months. He was awarded the Knight's Cross of the Iron Cross and subsequently joined Rudolf Peters's U-boat staff in Narvik.

Reche belonged to a breed that was already dying out, the Third Reich's first contingent of all-conquering U-boat captains. They constituted the undisputed elite of the German Navy. For one thing they had experienced the 'Happy Time', when the seas were everywhere full of unprotected ships. In those days the Allies had been short of escort vessels and had still not learned how to counter the wolf packs. In the Barents Sea the U-boat commanders were long able to operate virtually at will among the convoys. They were men like thirty-year-old Siegfried Strelow, who, in *U-435*, sank thirteen ships totalling more than 57,000 tons to win the Knight's Cross as early as the autumn of 1942; Günther Seibicke, who was of the same age and in *U-436* torpedoed eight Allied ships; 27-year-old Max-Martin Teichert of *U-456*, who sank seven ships and disastrously damaged the cruiser *Edinburgh*, which was carrying 5 tons of gold; and the urbane Heinrich Timm, who had a predilection for playing classical gramophone music over *U-251*'s loudspeaker system.

All were young and all had earned the right to wear the Knight's Cross on a silk band around their necks. But their time was running out. Thanks to a massive campaign mounted by aircraft and destroyers in hunter-killer groups, together with the introduction of 10-centimetre (actually 9.7-cm) radar, huff-duff (HF/DF) and up-to-date Ultra decrypts, the Allies were fast gaining the upper hand. Of the 180 U-boats that accompanied *U-255* to her base in Hammerfest, many would in the course of the next two years find a watery grave at the bottom of the Barents Sea.

'The change came in 1943. We found ourselves on the defensive. The escorting destroyers increased in number and grew better at their job. As soon as you fired your first torpedo, you had to expect a well-coordinated counter-attack. Our losses were colossal,' says Lange.

In the Barents Sea the suspension of the convoys in 1943 was followed by a period of comparative inactivity. There was less to do for the U-boats, which instead were charged with other tasks. Weather buoys were placed in position, meteorological expeditions were landed on Spitsbergen, Bear Island and Hopen, and mines were laid in the Kara Sea, far to the east.

The Atlantic Ocean was still the U-boats' most important hunting ground, but here matters were nearing a climax. A succession of major convoy battles in May 1943 decided in practice the outcome of the U-boat war in the Atlantic in

the Allies' favour. In the course of a few short weeks twenty-five German U-boats were sunk, including one in which one of *Grossadmiral* Karl Dönitz's two sons was serving. After this the Grand Admiral decided that he needed time for reflection and accordingly withdrew his wolf packs from the convoy routes linking Canada and Britain.

In Narvik *Kapitän-zur-See* Peters repeatedly begged for reinforcements to be sent to the Arctic, where he expected the Russian convoys soon to resume sailings, but Dönitz preferred to bide his time. When, on 14 September 1943, Peters ordered his U-boats to man a new patrol line south of Bear Island, he had only two available to do so – nowhere near enough to cover that desolate expanse of ocean. This prompted him to give the few U-boats under his command a name with rather ambiguous connotations, *Gruppe Eisenbart* (Iron Beard), Eisenbart being the name of a legendary doctor of doubtful repute. It was a name that would for ever afterwards be associated with Bear Island and the forthcoming Battle of the North Cape.

CHAPTER NINE

Operation Venus

SENJA, SEPTEMBER 1943

The time was half-past one in the afternoon of Sunday 5 September 1943 when the Norwegian submarine *Ula* dived and began to pick her way slowly across the Sven Shallows. A light wind from the north had dispersed the clouds, leaving the distinctive outline of the Senja mountains etched against the deep-blue autumn sky. It was nerve-racking work for the submarine's captain, Reidar Michael Sars, as, his voice low and controlled, he gently guided the submarine deeper and deeper into the fjord. The bottom was notoriously treacherous, bestrewn as it was with a host of poorly charted submerged rocks. In some places clearance between the seabed and the submarine's keel was no more than a few metres.

Understandably Sars took his time, and it was not until ten hours later, at 23.10, that he blew his tanks and took the *Ula* to the surface. His navigation had been spot-on: he had reached the head of the narrow Me fjord unobserved. With the bow of the submarine almost on the beach, landing proceeded apace. 'Crates and containers were handed up from the hold by a chain of seamen and the rubber dinghy was hauled ashore on the end of a rope. . . . A few quiet words of command now and then and an occasional splash were the only sounds. The silence served only to intensify the tenseness of the atmosphere.'

Two hours later the *Ula* turned about and, showing not a glimmer of light, stole back out of the dark fjord on the surface. She left behind three Norwegian agents: lone cyclist Torbjørn Johansen's elder brother Einar, an engineering student from Tromsø; Torstein Pettersen Råby from the Lofoten Islands, the son of a schoolteacher; and Per Ingebrigtsen from the island of Kvaløya, the son of a prominent Labour politician.

Operation Venus, the biggest operation to be mounted in northern Europe by Eric Welsh and the Scandinavian Section of the British Secret Service during the whole war, was off to a promising start. With them the three Norwegians had no fewer than ten wireless transmitters, complete with petrol-driven generators and accumulators – 3 tons of equipment in all, including 900 litres of petrol and 50,000 kroner (some £2,500) in cash.

The Lyra transmitter had been in operation in Porsa since July 1943. It was intended that the new transmitters should cover the other exits from the German anchorages in the Lang and Kå fjords, and also in Hammerfest. In future, no warship would be able to leave these German bases unseen and without its departure being reported to London.

It was an ambitious undertaking and one fraught with danger for those whose task it was to carry it out. Only fourteen days later, when Råby crossed the mountains to the nearest ferry terminal, things very nearly went awry. In a report he wrote on his return to London in July 1944 he recounted a close shave he had had on a milk boat sailing to Tromsø:

After a few hours a man came on board whom I knew from before, but whom I certainly did not want to meet. Fortunately he did not recognise me in the clothes I was wearing, and I took refuge in the saloon. As soon as I opened the door, the first person I saw was a girl I knew very well, and whom I had even less wish to meet. There was nothing else to do, but for me to get ashore as soon as possible which I did at Tisnes.

When, some time later, Einar Johansen and Per Ingebrigtsen hired a cutter to transport some of their equipment from the Me fjord to the group's central store on the island of Kvaløya, they too ran into danger. No sooner had they set off than a German destroyer entered the fjord, forcing them to jettison the entire deck cargo. The destroyer was searching for a Russian prisoner of war who had escaped from a camp beyond the mountains, and accordingly didn't take the trouble to inspect the fishing boat; instead it simply turned round and sailed back the way it had come. By then, however, several wireless transmitters and a case containing the agents' forged passports and papers had been irretrievably lost.

Torstein Pettersen Råby, aged twenty-three, had been allotted the difficult task of penetrating to the heart of the German naval base in western Finnmark. His transmitter was codenamed Ida, having, typically for him, been named after one of his numerous old flames. All things considered, few of the two hundred agents in Norway have left behind a more colourful reputation than Ida's wireless operator, who made a name for himself as an exceptionally resourceful and fearless agent, an incorrigible raconteur, a convivial companion and a ladies' man of the first water. Something of a tearaway in his youth, Pettersen Råby attended wireless school in Oslo (which was where he met the legendary Ida) and when Germany invaded Norway in April 1940 he was working as a wireless operator in Vadsø. Resistance and initiative were in his blood: by the time he made his way to England via Sweden in 1942, he had already operated one clandestine transmitter – working from northern Norway to Murmansk. Now, at the end of September 1943, he was issued with a new set of forged papers in Tromsø and sent north to Hammerfest on board a fishing boat, the *Skandfer*, which was doing duty as a replacement for the larger coastal-express steamers.

> I had been instructed to contact Paul Johnsen [mate of the local ferry, the *Brynilen*], but he demanded a password, and no one had thought to give me one. So there I was, stuck. Luckily I knew the man in charge of the local telegraph office, Alf Pedersen. He was likewise engaged in undercover work and accompanied me to Johnsen to vouch for me.

Johnsen sailed with the *Brynilen* twice a week from Hammerfest to Sopnes in the Lang fjord and was thus in a position to get a good look at both the *Tirpitz* and the *Scharnhorst* on his way there and back. He was a true patriot and one of those who regularly reported to Lyra when the *Brynilen* put into Porsa. In Johnsen's home the newcomer was introduced to the man behind the Lyra transmitter, Rolf Storvik, whom Welsh in London had instructed to prepare the ground for Ida. This introduced a new and very grave risk. As Råby wrote in his report:

> Why must there be so many organisations outside Norway which are engaged in collecting the same information? . . . Everybody knows how delicate the situation in Finnmark is. There are not many people to be used as contacts, and every agent is forced to use much the same courier and transport routes. Skipper Jacobsen and Mate Johnsen were used by Lyra and myself and also by the organisation to which Mjøen belonged. [Mjøen ran an escape route from Alta to Karesuando in Sweden.] . . . How on earth can one know whether one is in danger or not, while one is in Norway? It can happen that a man may be arrested one day, whose name one does not even know, and a couple of days later you yourself may be arrested because the man in question knew all about your business.

These were prophetic words, penned in the clear light of hindsight. But Torstein Pettersen Råby was not one to be put off by the risk he was taking. He and Johnsen set about looking up Storvik's contacts. But no one was willing to have anything to do with a man who had a brand-new Mark V wireless transmitter in his suitcase and a loaded pistol and thousands of kroner in his rucksack.

Torstein's luck changed when he reached Burfjord. There he was informed that a friend from Vadsø, 27-year-old Karl Rasmussen, had moved to Alta. 'He was living with his parents-in-law in a house in the Tverrelv valley. I approached him and he proved very amenable. We sat chatting for half an hour or so – it was a Sunday afternoon – and in the end he asked me to go outside with him for a moment. Once out of the house he turned to me and asked in a surprised voice, "But aren't you supposed to be in England?"'

This was in October 1943. Karl Rasmussen had been married for a bare two months and was sharing a room with his pregnant wife, twenty-year-old Sigrid Opgård Rasmussen, on her parents' smallholding. He was used to cramped quarters. His father was headmaster of Vadsø elementary school and Karl was the fourth of nine children. He was cast in the same mould as Råby, being both outgoing and of an optimistic disposition. As noted earlier, he was a popular gymnast, gym teacher and amateur actor. He studied at the Infantry Officers' Training School in Harstad and had done his military service as a second lieutenant with the Varanger Battalion. Since the summer of 1939 he had been office manager and bookkeeper under the Highways Inspector, Trygve Gimnes, in Vadsø. It was then that he had first made the acquaintance of Torstein Pettersen Råby who, on completion of his technical training, had travelled up from Oslo to work at the Finnmark Broadcasting Station. The station was bombed on 2 June 1940, after which Råby simply disappeared. When, two years later, Gimnes moved to Alta, where the Highways Department, together with the German *Organisation Todt*, was planning a series of major building and construction projects, Karl Rasmussen went along as cashier with responsibility for the whole region.

He could easily have said no when, standing in the yard outside the house, the agent from London told him about the difficulties he was having. By now Karl was a family man and beginning to settle down; furthermore, his comely wife Sigrid was awaiting their first child and needed his support. But Karl Rasmussen never invoked any of these arguments. It seemed as though he had been waiting for just such an assignment. Without hesitation he said yes and became Råby's partner.

As it happened, one of the chaps in the cashier's office had just left and he said that as I could type, I could take his place. That's how I came to work there as an assistant – I kept the job for ten months. Karl – or Kalle, as we called him – made an ideal accomplice. He was intelligent, quick-thinking and full of drive. He had always been a keen amateur actor and it was later to stand him in good stead. I'd say he was pretty much a born agent.

Together with his transmitter Torstein Pettersen Råby was installed in one of the Highways Department's huts in the middle of the little township, some 200 metres from the nearest German camp. The two Norwegians immediately set about their dangerous task together. Nothing was said to Sigrid or her parents, and to disguise what they were doing they started to talk in loud voices and act like a couple of real boozers. It came easily to Torstein: he was well known as being a bit of a rowdy and fond of a drink, but for Karl the role was more difficult to play. He could see how Sigrid was suffering because of his behaviour, but didn't dare enlighten her as to the reason for it – he didn't want to add to her burden.

After much difficulty, in November 1943 Torstein and Karl managed to get through to London. 'You will be interested to know that we have established contact with our IDA station. This station was first heard on the air 11.11.43 and reported that he is operating from Elvebakken in Altafjord,' wrote Eric Welsh in a confidential communication to the Intelligence Office run by the Norwegian government-in-exile in London. The man who was really behind the operation, Norman Denning in the Admiralty's Operational Intelligence Centre (OIC), had achieved his purpose.

Two transmitters, Lyra and Ida, were now in place close to the German naval bases. The agents who operated them were running an enormous risk. They not only worked together, they also used the same network, but in the opinion of their British handlers it was a risk that had to be taken. Only four days were left until 15 November, which was when the first convoy to resume sailings from Scotland was scheduled to depart for Murmansk. It was essential to know whether the German Battle Group was planning to put to sea. It was also necessary to run risks for other, totally different, reasons – but neither Torstein, Karl nor any of the others involved had any inkling of this.

CHAPTER TEN

An Unexpected Catch

OSLO, SUMMER 1999

In the spring and summer of 1999 I did the rounds of some of the principal Norwegian fishing companies with experience of the forbidding seas north of the North Cape, interviewing trawler owners in Hammerfest, the Lofotens, Ålesund and elsewhere. I made careful notes, which I subsequently perused with a growing sense of despair:

> 29 April: Edvard Gabrielsen, captain of the *Kjøllefjord*. Consults his chart at home and comes up with N 72.16.14 E 28.41.48, alternatively N 72.15.5 E 28.38. Hasn't been there himself. Thinks the position has been passed on from mouth to mouth.
>
> Kåre Ervik, captain of the *Safir II*. Gives the following positions: N 72.12.33 E 28.41.37 or N 72.12.15 E 28.42.5. Hasn't seen the wreck himself.
>
> Jan Pedersen of the *Kjølnes* comes up with 72.13/28.41 right off the cuff, but goes on to say that there are two positions where the *Scharnhorst* is thought to lie. Can't recall ever having been there himself. Thinks the ship's position has been passed on by word of mouth.
>
> 6 May: Captain Yngve Karlsen of *Berlevågfisk I* has the wreck of the *Scharnhorst* plotted as N 72.16 E 28.40. He hasn't seen the chart himself but he has an English chart on which are marked two wrecks close together at N 72.13 E 28.42.
>
> 11 May: Lars G. Jensen of the *Makkaur* says there is a position within a circle some 20 to 30 km in diameter which it is advised to steer clear of and which is where the *Scharnhorst* lies, viz. N 72.16.2 E 28.42.1.

4 June: On board the *Ifjord* everything is computerized. The wreck marked as the *Scharnhorst* is at N 72.18.0167 E 28.44.9085. . . . Captain Geir Svendsen has no idea of who has pinpointed the wreck. Not surprisingly, he believes that the GPS position is a better bet when it comes to locating the wreck than the old Decca figures, which become increasingly inaccurate the further north of lat. 72 one goes.

Despite minor variations, a general pattern emerged quite clearly: the great majority of Norwegian trawler captains believed the wreck of the *Scharnhorst* lay in a position identical, or almost identical, with the officially accepted location given by Admiral Fraser. Someone must once have noted the position he reported and it had afterwards been handed down from ship to ship – and as the years passed its 'accuracy' had increased to the point where it was now being read off from the satellite-assisted navigation systems to four decimal places! There was just one problem: we had combed the vicinity of the position given by Fraser with the side-scan sonar and discovered that where the *Scharnhorst* was supposed to lie there was nothing, absolutely nothing. The charts were wrong.

Reports obtained from England proved equally disheartening. One of Hull's leading trawler skippers, Kenneth Knox, who had sailed for Hamlyn Bros for more than twenty-five years and had since worked for Kingfisher Charts, said without hesitation that the position we were after was N 72.16.33 E 28.41.00. He also showed us a chart on which the wreck of the *Scharnhorst* was marked with a swastika in the same position and a rough sketch of the wreck which he himself had copied from an echogram. 'If you don't manage to find the wreck with this to help you,' he said confidently, 'then you don't deserve to find it at all.'

However, I happened to know the bullion-hunter Keith Jessop personally. When, in the late 1970s, he set out to search for the wreck of the British cruiser *Edinburgh*, which was carrying bullion worth more than £40 million, he too had been to see Kenneth Knox.

On that occasion Knox had done exactly the same as when we approached him, pulling out his charts and notes and pointing to where he was convinced the wreck lay. 'Use your Decca,' he said to Jessop, 'and you'll find her 300 metres or a little more from this point. . . . I know, because I once spent more than eighteen hours caught up on the wreck.' It was quite impressive. Knox had apparently become entangled with the wreck of the *Edinburgh* on the Skolpen Bank and had seen and marked the location of the *Scharnhorst* on the North Cape Bank.

In the event, however, it took Keith Jessop twenty-seven days to find the wreck of the *Edinburgh* – and when he did it was almost 30 nautical miles from the position Knox had given him. Jessop was backed by wealthy shipowners who stood to make millions if all went well, and for that reason he could afford to spend close on a month at sea. I had no millionaires behind me, only a television company; that meant that I had to locate the wreck in the course of twenty-seven hours, not twenty-seven days. I couldn't afford to take chances: I had to do my homework thoroughly before I could think of setting off on another search.

I had spent the spring and summer collecting charts and positions from more than a hundred fishing vessels – Norwegian, British and German. Almost without exception the position marked on their charts was that reported – erroneously – by Admiral Fraser. There were, though, a few pieces of evidence deserving of closer study.

On 22 November 1993 the factory ship *Nordstar* had been fishing for cod off the North Cape Bank. 'When we winched in the trawl, we found that we had netted an almost 6-metre-long torpedo. The warhead was still intact, all that was missing was the rear section, where the motor had been,' the captain, Reidar Nygård, told me.

Unwilling to risk his ship and crew, he made for the coast at the best speed he could muster. Alerted by wireless, a Sea King helicopter took off from the airfield at Banak carrying three divers from the Mine Disposal Unit at Harstad. In the Troll fjord, not far from the Cape, the crew of the *Nordstar* were evacuated to the fisheries protection vessel *Stålbas*, while the divers swung the torpedo overboard on to six empty oil barrels. Once they had manoeuvred this makeshift raft into shallow water, they sank the barrels by the simple expedient of riddling them with bullets fired from an AG-3 automatic rifle, whereupon the torpedo was blown up with 5 kilograms of dynamite. 'The spout of water from the explosion rose sky-high,' said Nygård. 'I heard afterwards that the warhead contained 67 kilos of TNT.'

The divers identified the torpedo as a 21-inch British Mark 8, mod. 2, a type used in the Second World War by both submarines and surface vessels. In the course of the battle fought off the North Cape the twelve British ships engaged in it, together with the Norwegian destroyer *Stord*, had fired a total of fifty-five such torpedoes at the *Scharnhorst*; how many had found their mark was not known, but it was something between ten and fifteen. The remaining forty to forty-five torpedoes had run on until their fuel was exhausted and then simply plunged to the bottom. Could the torpedo recovered by the *Nordstar* have been one of them?

On board the *Nordstar* the crew had mounted the rear section of the torpedo in the mess as a reminder of a dangerous encounter they had no wish to repeat. The ship's position when they had hauled in the torpedo was engraved on a small metal plate: lat. 72°32' N, long. 28°20' E. That was more than 20 nautical miles west of the official position given by Admiral Fraser. A Mark 8 torpedo had a range of about 8,500 metres, which meant that if the *Nordstar*'s position was correct, it would be a simple matter to construct a 'search box' around the spot measuring 8 × 8 kilometres, in which case it would take only a couple of days to go over the area completely.

The problem lay in determining precisely when and where the torpedo had found its way into the trawl. According to the *Nordstar*'s log the trawl had been out for three hours and fifty minutes and the ship had been doing 4 knots. That meant that the trawl had been towed behind the ship for some 16 nautical miles, so there were still far too many unknown factors in the equation. Moreover, the logbook said nothing about the direction in which the trawl had been towed. I inscribed a circle on the chart with a diameter of 16 nautical miles around the *Nordstar*'s last position. The area we would need to search was truly vast, and far too large for us to attempt with the limited means at my disposal.

I sat down to ponder the matter. Was the torpedo really one of those that had been fired during the battle? I wondered. And if it was, had it been fired by the *Stord* at a range of 1,800 metres at 18.55 or by the *Jamaica* from 3,750 metres at 19.37? How far had the *Scharnhorst* sailed in the meantime? And which was more probable, that the torpedo had been picked up by the trawl early in the towing process or late? If early, would it have withstood being dragged across the seabed for nearly four hours without exploding?

It was at that point that I came across a piece of information I had received earlier that spring. I had got in touch with my old friend Arne Jensen, who had once skippered the *Gargia* and who, in April 1977, had first shown me the location of the wreck of the *Scharnhorst* on his chart. At that time Arne had been Norway's youngest trawler captain. Now he had swallowed the anchor and was working in the Harbourmaster's office in my home town of Hammerfest. The chart he had shown me had been lost but Arne, as enterprising and helpful as ever, gathered three of his pals from the Findus fleet on board the trawler *Doggi* and asked for their help in reconstructing the position of the wreck from such old charts as they might have in their possession.

The first note I had jotted down after the unsuccessful expedition on board the *Risøy* described what transpired.

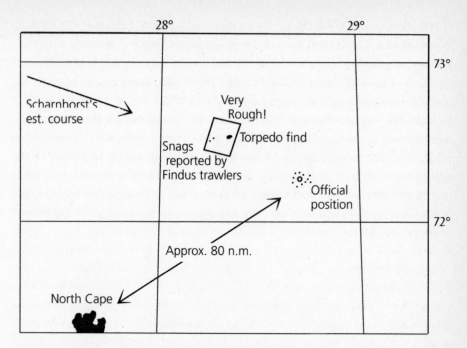

Marked on the charts of nearly every fishing vessel in northern Norway as the spot where the *Scharnhorst* lay was the 'official' position given by Admiral Bruce Fraser, 72° 16'N 28° 41'E. The chart used by the Findus fleet placed the wreck some 25 to 30 nautical miles further west, close to the spot where, in 1993, the factory ship *Nordstar* picked up an unexploded Second World War torpedo.

28 April. Arne Jensen got together three Findus skippers on board the *Doggi* and asked them to point out the *Scharnhorst*'s position. Arne Jensen had himself sailed over the estimated position with his echo sounder in operation and had observed a 25- to 30-metre-high steel wreck. He thought from the markings on the chart that it must have been at N 72.42 E 30.01. However, the other two captains, Albert Iversen and Jegvar Nilsen, disagreed; they thought the correct position was N 72.29.5 E 28.15. After discussing the matter at length, all three agreed that the latter position was probably the right one.

Another old friend of mine, Jan Pedersen, also a trawler captain, had been master seiner on the stern trawler *Thue Jr* in the late 1960s when I took a temporary summer job on board. He was a seasoned trawlerman, and marked on his charts was a formidable obstacle in what was almost the same position, N 72.31.55 E 28.15.52.

The *Nordstar* had hauled in the torpedo only 5 nautical miles east of these two positions. Could it all be no more than a coincidence?

I returned to the copies of the charts I had acquired from England. About 35 nautical miles north-west of the swastika there was a large area marked in red and accompanied by the following warning: 'Very bad'.

Both the torpedo find and the two positions given me by the Hammerfest trawlermen lay within the same area. My pulse quickened! There *was* an obstacle in the western sector of the search area that might be linked to the *Scharnhorst* – though at that point only tenuously. There were ten or so other wrecks from the two world wars in the vicinity, so I couldn't allow my enthusiasm to run away with me. But I did go so far as to put a large question-mark on the chart.

CHAPTER ELEVEN

Alarums and Excursions

THE BARENTS SEA, NOVEMBER–DECEMBER 1943

So far it had been a dull patrol for *U-307*, a 760-ton type VIIC submarine launched at the Flender-Werke yard in Lübeck a year earlier. The U-boat's patrol area extended from Bear Island to a line 60 nautical miles south, but nothing had been seen other than a grey expanse of gale-lashed ocean. Day after day since the end of October the lookouts had vainly scanned the horizon for enemy ships, while the U-boat zig-zagged to and fro, nine hours one way, nine hours the other. The skipper was 33-year-old *Oberleutnant-zur-See* Friedrich-Georg Herrle from Rheinland-Pfalz. *U-307* was his first command. He had been on board since taking over in November 1942; after undergoing five months' training in the Baltic, in July 1943 he had joined the 13th Flotilla and was sent to Hammerfest. 'Herrle and I became close friends. He was a fine man and a great leg-puller,' says Hans-Günther Lange:

I remember that we once took along a doctor as a supernumerary. We rendezvoused in the open sea, shot a line across from conning-tower to conning-tower and started to haul the doctor over to us. He was in need of a bit of excitement, so Herrle gave it to him. When he was halfway, Herrle suddenly shouted, 'Dive!'. I bundled the doctor down the hatch and we dived. To give us a bit of a fright, Herrle had made up a bundle of hand grenades, which he lobbed overboard. Unfortunately, he had miscalculated their explosive power. There was an almighty bang. When I took the boat back up, it was to find that the gun on the foredeck had vanished.

It may sound strange today, but the fact is that every U-boat had fifty young lads on board. Death was ever present. You had to try to laugh to stick it. There weren't many Nazis in the Navy; on my boat there was, in fact, only one. I well remember that the Party sent a brown-uniformed political officer to Narvik, one of the type we used to call 'Golden Pheasants'. His job was to teach us to think along the right lines. But we got him drunk and dumped him in a vat full of paint. When he came round, he'd become one of us. His uniform had turned blue.

But now it was autumn and there was no time for larking about. Herrle still had a week to go to complete his forty-day patrol. Both the U-boat and its crew reeked of diesel oil, salt and stale sweat. Everyone was looking forward to a break on board the *Black Watch* in Hammerfest, where there would be hot baths, clean bed linen and fresh food.

Early in the morning of Thursday 1 December, *U-307* was 45 nautical miles south-west of Bear Island when, without warning, the klaxon sounded. In the murky darkness the lookout had spotted a dim silhouette, which was soon to multiply into more vaguely discernible shapes. Their outlines in the binoculars of the men in the conning-tower rapidly enlarged to the point where they could see that it was a squadron of warships sailing westwards at high speed. To be caught by an escort of that magnitude was the worst nightmare of every U-boat commander. Herrle didn't hesitate. He crash-dived while the crew prayed that they had not been spotted. Their prayers went unheeded. From the bridge of the British destroyer *Inconstant* the outline of the U-boat had been seen sharply etched against the horizon only a few hundred metres distant. The order rang out for full speed ahead, a searchlight pierced the darkness and the destroyer opened fire. A few minutes later the *Inconstant* raced over the spot where *U-307* had dived and dropped ten depth-charges.

We hadn't even reached the prescribed depth when the first charges went off . . . dong-a-dong-dong, dong-a-dong-dong, dong-a-dong-dong. . . . The detonations were unbelievably sharp – piercing, metallic clangs and crashes that made a clap of thunder sound like the cheerful click of falling pins in a bowling alley. The steel hull acted as an amplifier, exposing our nerves to the hammer blows of the enemy. Explosions take agonizingly long to travel through the water and they intensified our feeling of being cut off from the world outside. . . . There wasn't a sound on board the boat. All the machinery had been shut down so that the enemy couldn't hear us. Everyone stood immobile at their posts. From the sonar room came the wireless operator's low voice as he reported to the Command Centre. 'Propeller noises at 190 degrees . . . heading constant . . . getting louder.' As the men waited, tension rose. The next lot of depth-charges outdid all that had gone before. They fell right up close to the boat. They couldn't have come any nearer. We exchanged glances. The men looked questioningly at the faces of the officers. Now was the time for ice-cold composure. The crew crowded together in the forward passageway. The only sound to be heard in the cramped confines of our steel cylinder was that of heavy breathing. . . . Where would the next lot land? . . . Then the noise of propellers began to fade. The depth-charges started to explode further away. The enemy had failed to locate us in our new position! . . . Slowly we relaxed. We all began to smile . . . we were reborn! Laughter relieved the tension after the unbearable strain to which our nerves had been subjected.

Led by the *Inconstant* and the Canadian destroyer *Iroquois*, the hunt lasted for several hours. Not until half-past eleven in the morning, when the pursuers had finally given up, did Herrle dare to take *U-307* back to the surface and wireless U-boat Command HQ in Narvik, 'PROBABLE WESTBOUND CONVOY. DEPTH-CHARGED FOUR HOURS BY THREE ESCORTS.'

Herrle carefully nursed the badly damaged *U-307* back to Hammerfest at slow speed and thence to his home base in Trondheim for repairs. He was unaware that he had been close to an historic and extremely valuable prize, the British cruiser *Kent*. This ship was part of the escort of the westbound convoy RA54A, which had left Murmansk on 26 November. In the cruiser's hold were 4 tons of gold bars and 50 tons of silver, part-payment for the weapons of war and other supplies sent to Stalin.

At 14.25 on 1 December the alarm sounded on board the *Scharnhorst* as she lay at anchor in the Lang fjord. The ship's company was put at three hours' readiness in expectation of further signals from the Barents Sea. The ship got up steam and the men hurried to their stations – though more out of a sense of duty and from force of habit than in the belief that they would soon find themselves at grips with the enemy.

There had been many false alarms that autumn. The officers' nerves had been badly on edge since the attack on the *Tirpitz*. In October suspicious noises had been heard close to the anti-torpedo nets. Depth-charges had been dropped and patrols sent out 'to apprehend Norwegians endeavouring to contact any surfacing midget submarines'. One night in November a mysterious light was observed on

the shore nearby. The *Scharnhorst*'s powerful searchlights were turned on it and an unsuspecting soldier with a flashlight got the shock of his life!

Kapitän-zur-See Fritz Julius Hintze proved himself both dynamic and efficient. Despite an acute shortage of fuel, he had been given permission to carry out a series of gruelling exercises, with the emphasis on radar-controlled gunnery. From the end of October onwards one salvo after another shattered the peace of Stjern Sound, right up until 10 November, when a violent storm swept in from the west. 'The fjord acted like a nozzle. The strength of the katabatic wind was so strong as to defy all measurement, and especially so at the mouth of the Lang fjord. In stark contrast to conditions there, the storm was barely noticeable in the inner reaches of the fjord, which once again proves what a favourable anchorage this is,' Hintze succinctly noted in the war diary.

The men had held their breath the day their captain took the battlecruiser into the Store Lerres fjord to test its worth as an anchorage. At low tide the *Scharnhorst* had listed to port. A hurried sounding revealed that she was aground in unmarked shallows. Unrattled, Hintze waited till high tide, then gently eased the ship off – without a scratch.

Unlike Hüffmaier, Hintze was a sailor to his finger-tips, the men said; they regarded him with increasing respect. He appeared to be genuinely concerned about the welfare of his men and often attended film shows together with the ratings. He was very much a 'B' type, rarely rising before ten in the morning, when he would start the day with an hour's brisk pacing to and fro on the quarterdeck. But one thing was sacred: the Captain's siesta. Hintze's cabin lay directly beneath the forward 10.5-cm anti-aircraft gun. Between one and three in the afternoon absolute quiet reigned: no one dared to walk about on deck or touch the gun. It was a peculiar state of affairs, but the prohibition was respected and merely served to heighten Hintze's popularity.

On 18 November Hintze gave permission to fire A turret's three 11-inch guns in the narrow confines of the Lang fjord. Ten salvoes were fired blind high above Alteidet at the tiny island of Sukkeret ('Sugar Lump'), 21 kilometres distant. The precision of the range-finding was astonishing. The islet was a bare 100 metres across, but one salvo scored a direct hit and five others fell close by. Hintze was determined to prove that the *Scharnhorst* could act as a floating gun emplacement and defend the surrounding area against enemy attack. 'At least the enemy will now learn through his agents that the big ships have the entry fjords indirectly covered, and that will have a deterrent effect,' he wrote.

Four days later, on the evening of Monday 22 November, the first major alarm was sounded. That same day, after some ninety hours' arduous toil, the cryptologists of the *Kriegsmarine's B-Dienst* (Monitoring and Direction-Finding Service) had succeeded in deciphering a signal sent on 18 November by the Admiralty in London to an unknown recipient in the Barents Sea: 'CHANGE COURSE OF STRAGGLERS AS FOLLOWS: FROM POS. (E) TO (O) 74 19 N 28 20 EAST'.

To the intelligence staff in Berlin the meaning of the signal was clear: 'stragglers' meant ships which for one reason or another were unable to keep up with the rest of the convoy. This meant that the convoys for which Dönitz had been waiting since March had resumed their sailings.

At 19.00 the teleprinters in *Konter-Admiral* Erich Bey's Staff Office on board the still-disabled *Tirpitz* in the Kå fjord rattled out: 'THREE HOURS' READINESS FOR BATTLE GROUP. PREPARE TO PUT TO SEA.' Two hours later the following signal reached the *Scharnhorst*: 'POSSIBLE PQ CONVOY OFF BEAR ISLAND. THREE HOURS' READINESS. TOP UP ALL FUEL TANKS. IF WE SORTIE, BDK [BEY] WILL JOIN *SCHARNHORST* IN *Z 30*.'

The Germans had interpreted the British signal correctly. It was an instruction from the Admiralty to the eighteen ships of convoy JW54A, which had left Scotland on 15 November, the first convoy to do so for nine months. But the area around Bear Island was shrouded in fog and the cloud base was so low that the aircraft despatched to search for the convoy found nothing.

That same night the *Scharnhorst* had taken on board 4,800 cubic metres of fuel oil from the tanker *Jeverland*. In the event the order to sail never came, and two days later the men were stood down. His tanks full, Hintze grasped the opportunity this offered. The *Scharnhorst*'s engines had not been properly tested for over a year, so on 25 November he took the battlecruiser into Varg Sound and ordered full speed ahead.

The man in charge of the *Scharnhorst*'s complex and highly sophisticated engine-room was another of the battlecruiser's key officers, *Korvettenkapitän (Ing.)* Otto König from Paunsdorf, near Leipzig. König was a popular and gifted officer who, in a poll taken among his classmates at Cadet Training College in 1928, had been voted the one most likely to attain the rank of admiral. After many years' service on land and at sea, including a stint as engineer officer of the torpedo-boat *Möve*, in October 1943 König had transferred to the *Scharnhorst* in the same position. This appointment meant that, young though he was (he was only thirty-four), König had already risen to hold one of the *Kriegsmarine*'s most coveted and responsible posts in the Engineering Branch. With her twelve high-pressure boilers, three state-of-the-art turbines and kilometres of pipes and hoses for steam and oil,

the battlecruiser's machinery represented the acme of contemporary technology. The engine-room was really the ship's most vital asset: speed was of the essence if the *Scharnhorst* were to have a chance of mounting a surprise attack on the enemy; it might also prove her salvation if things went radically wrong. It was therefore crucial to the battlecruiser's survival that her engines should not fail – as they had on several occasions in the past. Operational reliability was a must, necessitating constant maintenance. This imposed a heavy burden on König. To make matters worse, at about the same time as he took up his appointment as Chief Engineering Officer, some one hundred or so midshipmen, a number of them from the engine-room, had been posted away. It was soon found that their replacements lacked experience. On one exercise König discovered to his horror that execution of several damage-control orders had been delayed for forty minutes owing to a breakdown in communications and because the men involved didn't know enough about the relevant machinery. In a battle, forty minutes might well decide the outcome. König commented in the war diary: 'Giving the new personnel special training is paying off, but the results are slow in coming. That is because hardly any of them have previous knowledge of high-pressure steam engines.'

Now, at nine in the morning, in fine weather, the chief of the engine-room staff slowly increased the pressure in the boilers. As she raced through the sound, the *Scharnhorst* gathered speed – from 25 knots to 27 knots until, round about noon, she reached top speed. From a technical point of view everything went without a hitch, but the result was none the less disappointing. In 1940 the ship had attained a maximum speed of 31.14 knots; now she could manage only 29.6 knots. 'The overall result of the speed trial is highly satisfactory,' König wrote. 'The engines ran smoothly at full power, also during the two hours they delivered revolutions for 29 knots or more. . . . The loss of speed . . . is ascribable to the ship's being heavily laden. Compared with the speed trials of 1940 and 1942 she now lies more than half a metre deeper in the water.'

Although the technical aspects of the trial had gone off without mishap, *Konter-Admiral* Bey was dissatisfied with the only one of his big ships still operational. 'A decrease in speed of 3 knots, as in the case of the *Scharnhorst*, is unacceptable. It must be possible to demand that the engines of a warship have sufficient reserves to prevent her top speed falling by 10 per cent when fully laden.'

Isolated as they were in a forward base like Alta, beyond giving of their best when called upon there was little the engine-room staff could do to put matters right. In the meantime confusing information continued to come in from U-boats and aircraft in the Barents Sea. On 29 November, for example, *U-636* set alarm bells ringing when she reported having sighted 'a wheeled aircraft' off Bear Island. In this area an enemy plane equipped with landing wheels could only have come from an aircraft-carrier. The Battle Group was besieged by anxious telephone calls. Could an invasion force be on its way? The answer was no. Closer investigation revealed that the aircraft seen by *U-636* was the *Luftwaffe*'s 'weather plane' on its daily flight from Banak to Spitsbergen and back. 'Reports of carrier-based aircraft tend to generate intensive counter-measures, so be precise,' *Kapitän-zur-See* Rudolf Peters, U-boat C-in-C in Narvik, admonished the hapless captain.

On 1 December enemy forces had compelled *U-307* to dive. The following day *U-636* observed a cluster of red lights on the horizon, again giving cause for alarm. But once more neither aircraft nor U-boats could find the convoy. Both convoy no. 2, JW54B, comprising fourteen ships, and the return convoy RA54B, escorted by, among other warships, the bullion-laden cruiser *Kent*, reached port without loss.

For *Kapitän-zur-See* Peters, who was responsible for manning the cordon south of Bear Island, the weeks that followed brought nothing but frustration and uncertainty. *Gruppe Eisenbart* had been badly depleted. To start with, *U-307* had had to go into dock in Trondheim owing to bomb damage, then *U-713* ran aground north of Bear Island while putting ashore men to man the meteorological station there. That left Peters with only four U-boats at his disposal. His requests for reinforcements went unheeded, 'despite the fact that in all probability the convoys have resumed sailings', as he wrote.

It wasn't only the U-boats that had become fewer: the lustrous winners of the Knight's Cross had gradually been either withdrawn from the Barents Sea area or killed. The more fortunate among them had been posted to staff jobs ashore. Others, among them Max-Martin Teichert, Günther Seibicke and Siegfried Strelow, had been lost, together with their U-boats, in the bloody spring of 1943. Their replacements, who had been rushed through U-boat training courses in the Baltic, were not of the same high calibre.

Only two members of the *Eisenbart* Group were thoroughly at home in the Arctic. One was 33-year-old *Kapitänleutnant* Karl-Heinz Herbschleb, skipper of *U-354*, on the conning-tower of which was painted the 11th Flotilla's celebrated red emblem, a U-boat in the powerful embrace of a polar bear. Herbschleb had assumed command of the U-boat, a type VIIC, in April 1942 and was stationed for a time at Brest before being transferred to Bergen and then despatched northwards shortly before Christmas. It was his disastrous report from the scene of the battle off Bear Island on New Year's Eve 1942

('All I can see is red') that had led Hitler to believe that an Allied convoy was in process of annihilation. 'He was a big, burly fellow, Herbschleb, always talking in a loud voice. He was famous for that. He talked loudly and at great length,' says Lange.

Unlike most of his fellow captains, Herbschleb had seen action. He had sunk the new 7,000-ton Liberty ship *William Clark* and damaged two Soviet steamers, the *Petrovsky* and *Vanzetti*. Both he and *Kapitänleutnant* Rudolf Büchler on board Herbschleb's companion U-boat, *U-387*, had been patrolling south of Bear Island since 22 October. But Büchler didn't have Herbschleb's experience. He was only twenty-eight years of age and had never fired a torpedo in action and seen a merchant ship burst into flames. This was his first prolonged patrol in the Barents Sea and he was looking forward to being relieved. After forty-five days at sea the U-boats put into Hammerfest on the morning of 6 December. But *Kapitän-zur-See* Peters hardly gave their crews time to shower and change their clothes. The very next day *U-354* and *U-387* had to cast off from the *Black Watch* and set a return course for Bear Island, where *U-636* and *U-277* were holding the line alone.

The skipper of *U-636*, 31-year-old *Kapitänleutnant* Hans Hildebrandt from Bremen, was the other veteran in *Gruppe Eisenbart*. He had been operating in the Barents Sea since the spring of 1943 and had sunk two Soviet ships, the 7,200-ton steamer *Tbilisi* and an armed trawler, *SKR-54*. He was returning from a minelaying assignment that had taken him into the Kara Sea, far to the east, when a countermanding order reached him. There was no question of shore leave and a rest: *U-636* was ordered to join *Gruppe Eisenbart* without delay. It was Hildebrandt who had put the wind up the naval chiefs in Kiel and Berlin when he had incorrectly identified a Ju 88 of the *Luftwaffe*'s Meteorological Flight as an enemy aircraft. As was standard practice, his mistake was marked against him on his service record. The U-boats and the men who manned them were driven hard. They were shown no mercy – and neither were the men who served on board the merchant ships that were their quarry. Like Büchler, *U-277*'s 27-year-old captain, Robert Lübsen, had never made a kill. He had arrived in the Arctic in August and, though now on his fourth patrol, had still not seen an enemy ship. On this occasion he had been detailed to patrol the edge of the polar ice a few miles north of Bear Island:

> When, in the morning, we climbed out of the conning-tower hatch, it was to see stretching out before us the ragged edge of the pack. Hummocks of ice towered up in a blaze of blue and green. Flocks of seabirds lined the water's edge.

Seals disported themselves in the water. Small chunks of ice constantly broke loose and drifted past us. There was a chill in the air and the sky was a uniform grey.

For *Kapitän-zur-See* Peters in Narvik the situation was desperate. All the evidence suggested that convoys were sailing to Murmansk and back without being intercepted by his U-boats. 'I have to acknowledge that surveillance of the Bear Island Gap is not practicable with the means at my disposal,' he noted resignedly in his 7 December entry in the war diary.

Signs that the convoys had resumed sailings gave rise to heated discussion among the admirals in the Kå fjord and at Narvik and Kiel. The Battle Group had been formed, contrary to Hitler's wishes, to strike 'a crushing blow' against the convoys. But the Group's flagship, the *Tirpitz*, was out of action behind her anti-submarine nets, and the pocket battleship *Lützow* had returned to Germany. In mid-November the Battle Group was further depleted when the 6th Destroyer Flotilla was despatched to southern Norway to ward off a feared invasion. Only the *Scharnhorst* and five destroyers were left.

'The 17th of November 1943 is a day that deserves to be remembered. That was the day we relinquished all initiative in the war and went on to the defensive as far as surface vessels are concerned,' the C-in-C of the 4th Destroyer Flotilla, *Kapitän-zur-See* Rolf Johannesson, wrote in the war diary. His five destroyers were all of the new Narvik class, and three of them were equipped with twin 15-cm guns forward. They were larger and more heavily armed than their British counterparts, but the weight of the foredeck turrets detracted from their seakeeping properties. In bad weather they shipped enormous quantities of water – not that that mattered much, as the Flotilla Commander no longer viewed his destroyers as an offensive weapon against Allied convoys. 'Whereas we have hitherto had an operative purpose . . . our task now is to safeguard the *Scharnhorst*,' he wrote bitterly.

The original order for the operation codenamed *Ostfront* was still in force, but no one believed any longer that it would ever be implemented. Aircraft reconnaissance was poor, the available U-boats few and cooperation with the *Luftwaffe* still left much to be desired. On their own the *Scharnhorst* and her escort of five destroyers would have little chance of success in an attack on a strongly protected convoy.

Most of those in a position to do so warned the new Squadron Commander against adventurous sorties. Kümmetz exhorted Bey to wait until the *Tirpitz* had been repaired, so that the two ships could operate in concert. Alone, he said, the

Scharnhorst would be extremely vulnerable in the face of British destroyers equipped with superior radar, which enabled them to launch torpedo attacks in the dark. Bey was equally pessimistic about the way things were, but he wasn't prepared to throw in his hand there and then. He envisaged a possible attack by destroyers under covering fire from the *Scharnhorst*. On 22 November, when the ships had been brought to a state of readiness for the first time and had remained for a while awaiting orders to put to sea, he had expressed his views in the following words: 'I am aware that an attack on a convoy in winter, with the Battle Group in its present state, could only be carried out with difficulty. . . . All would depend on luck . . . or on the other side's making momentous errors. However, despite our inferiority, the war at sea has afforded our naval forces some excellent opportunities. That justifies our hoping that luck will once again be on our side.'

The man who committed *Konter-Admiral* Bey's ill-founded hopes to paper was in all probability his writer, Heinrich Mulch. At that time Mulch, head-over-heels in love as he was, had other things on his mind than bickerings between the admirals. Gertrud had written to him of her fear of the bombs raining down on the Ruhr, and Heinrich did his best to comfort her. 'Nerves are very much in evidence at such times,' he wrote, and went on:

> In the light of the first shock a lot tends to be said that is not in accordance with the facts. Some people listen to the English wireless and because of that unconsciously become our enemies. I am in a position to check what is said against the true facts. Some of it is false, some greatly exaggerated and employed as part of the propaganda war and war of nerves. . . . So far it has *not* rained phosphorous, my dear . . . so don't be afraid, things are never as bad as they seem . . .

He had an additional and still more pressing problem to contend with. At home in Germany his family had finally realized that his correspondence with Gertrud had blossomed into a full-blown love affair. That was more than his father could countenance. Admittedly, Gertrud was vivacious and good-looking, but she was, after all, only a waiter's daughter. Heinrich's family had striven hard to pay for his education: they insisted that he find himself a girlfriend of his own class, someone with money and of an appropriate social background. Gertrud found this both hurtful and humiliating, but Heinrich wrote:

> My dear girl, the battle surrounding our love has begun. Now they are all hard at it. It's a matter of not being afraid, of not answering back and not giving in.

. . . You know, of course, that it was a sacrifice for my parents to allow me to attend school for an extra two years . . . and that it has undoubtedly surprised everyone that we found one another so soon and fell in love with each other. . . . I have written to my father and informed him of how I feel, politely and firmly. What I want to say to you is this: what has been said does not trouble me, as we must take into account that my parents are worried about my future, and therefore also about yours. What occupations one's parents have means nothing. The only thing that is important to me is that I wish to share my life with a woman who is loving, faithful and a good friend, who will stand by me in good times and bad, who has confidence in me and who gives me faith in the future. . . . Beauty is only skin-deep; I don't attach much importance to it. What I wish for are healthy children, peace of mind, a warm heart and an ordered life. . . . That is why you must not be sad and depressed, my dear little girl. I love you more than ever. . . . I foresaw this conflict and will pursue it to the end. It does nothing to change our love. I know that you love me very dearly and trust me, so it is up to me to trust you and make you, only *you*, happy – despite all the concern about your background, despite those venomous tongues and despite all the grumbling and admonitions.

For *Konter-Admiral* Bey there was no question of a sortie in November. The weeks dragged by, and Christmas was coming up; but neither the *Luftwaffe* nor his U-boats reported any new sightings. After waiting impatiently for two weeks, on 14 December Hintze again ordered the *Scharnhorst* to weigh anchor. He spent the night in the Skille fjord, then took the battlecruiser round Loppa Point and into the Bur fjord. Hintze had learned the lesson of the raid on the *Tirpitz*: he wanted a choice of anchorages should the British attempt to repeat their success. 'The enemy is sure to know through his agents of the Battle Group's frequent exercises in the Alta fjord, and in favourable circumstances can launch a Commando raid . . . if their target . . . remains at anchor, stationary and unprotected,' he wrote in the ship's war diary.

  Hintze's suspicions were well grounded. From November onwards both Lyra and Ida had regularly transmitted reports from the Kå and Lang fjords, but none of the agents was finding things easy. In Porsa, Trygve Duklæt was forced to rub shoulders day after day with a local informer and ardent Nazi. They both worked at the power station and lived in the same house; and it was there that the aerial had been boldly concealed in the gutter. 'This aerial system later proved useless, and I was unable to communicate with London again until I hit upon the idea of replacing one of the telephone wires . . . by an aerial strung

between the first telegraph pole and the wall of the house in which I lived. This proved to work well, and after that I was in contact with the Home Station every day,' Duklæt said in his postwar report.

In reality he and Rolf Storvik had displayed considerable ingenuity in hiding Lyra. In full view of curious onlookers round about, they had excavated a small cellar beneath the back porch of the former mine manager's villa. On top of it they placed a wardrobe containing an ingenious mechanical device. By turning what was to all intents and purposes just a wooden peg, the bottom of the wardrobe could be moved aside. From the opening thus revealed, steps led down to the chamber in which the transmitter stood. 'A stove was installed in the "studio" to keep everything dry. We used the equipment right up to 6 June 1944,' Duklæt wrote.

The first recorded report was dated 5 November 1943 and read as follows: 'The hospital ship *Posen*, carrying torpedoes for the submarine depot ship at Hammerfest, arrived there yesterday, the 4th November.'

On 10 November Storvik and Duklæt followed this up by saying: 'It is reported that the *Stavangerfjord* [a commandeered Norwegian transatlantic liner] has been fitted out as a repair ship and sent north with a German crew on board to carry out repairs on the *Tirpitz*.' Although mere snippets, these were valuable pieces of information. They improved British understanding of the local situation and would come in useful when the time came to plan an attack.

Other reports contained a note of desperation. That of 29 November, for example, ran: 'We are not getting anything done on account of the lack of means of assistance. It is money and tobacco we lack most. The address given does not answer. We had in the beginning 800 kroner. Our private means are very limited. We cannot get help without paying.'

In Alta Torstein Pettersen Råby had been taken on by the Highways Department, ostensibly as assistant to Karl Rasmussen. In his capacity as cashier, every week Karl drove the long distance to Langfjordbotn to pay the wages of the men working there. It was a heaven-sent opportunity to gather information – and also to recruit new helpers. Among them were Sigrid Rasmussen's brother Halvor Opgård, a carpenter, who built a hiding-place for Ida under a desk in the Highways Department office; Harry Pettersen, a driver, whose childhood home stood close to where the *Tirpitz* lay in the Kå fjord and who drove a 1937 Ford; accordionist Elias Østvik from Hammerfest, who also worked at the Highways Department and helped with transmissions; and shopkeeper Jens Digre, and former police officer Jonas Kummeneje, both of whom lived on the shores of the Lang fjord.

'Karl knew a lot of people, and he was the type no one would suspect. If he asked someone to do him a favour, they never said no. That was him in a nutshell.' The German *Feldgendarmerie* (Military Police) were very vigilant and the agents often found themselves in tricky situations. 'We were often stopped at checkpoints. Our pistols were hidden in the car. We had been instructed to shoot our way out if things went wrong, but always to save the last bullet for ourselves. Those were our orders,' says Harry Pettersen, whom Karl recruited at Christmas 1943. Writing later, Råby said:

He [Pettersen] went home to Kaafjord, and the very next day started by going on board *Monte Rosa* on the pretext of selling fish. He soon became a good drinking comrade of the workers on board, and so long as *Monte Rosa* lay in Kaafjord, there was no difficulty in finding out what was going on. Once he came grinning into our office to say that he had been on board the *Tirpitz*. He had found out the following dodge. If you forgot your pass and went past the *Tirpitz*, the sentry took you on board to an officer. The Germans would then check up with the Sheriff to see whether your explanation was correct; if it was correct, you were released with a stern warning. This was exactly what Harry had done, but unfortunately he did not see very much.

Back home on her parents' farm, Sigrid Opgård Rasmussen had only a month to go before her baby was due, but by that time the happiness of the early months was a thing of the past. As she learned more and more of what was going on, she became increasingly fearful:

Kalle often used to bring the transmitter home with him. He used to hide it behind a chest-of-drawers with a mirror that stood in a corner of our bedroom. He would often dump the rucksack it was in on the floor of the bedroom when he got home at night. I asked him on several occasions whether he really intended to leave it there. He answered that it was his responsibility. . . . Kalle used to have bad dreams. He would wake in the night and call for me. Once he took the revolver he always kept under his pillow and said, 'With this I intend to take my life before the Germans do'. Things grew tense between us. I wasn't allowed to ask about anything, but it wasn't easy not to. Kalle was on edge, too – everyone could see that. He'd changed. My mother said to me one day when he was sitting in the living-room with the newspaper before him, 'He's not reading it, you know, he's just

staring at it'. . . . Torstein was equally worried. He often used to visit us. One Sunday morning, it was very early, he burst into our bedroom. He had to reassure himself that Kalle was there.

Only three of the reports transmitted by Ida in the autumn of 1943 have survived. One, dated 13 November 1943, read: 'The *Scharnhorst* is reported to be in Langfjordbotn. The fjord freezes as far out as Eidsnes, but at present it is open.' They were simple pieces of information, but they were proof, if proof were needed, that the agents were keeping the German fleet under close observation.

A whole month was to pass before the U-boats again found a convoy. The third convoy of the season, JW55A, numbering nineteen ships, was passing Bear Island on 18 December when Hans Hildebrandt reported 'SINGLE VESSEL WITH BUOY, AM FOLLOWING'. It was yet another confusing signal from *U-636* and, not surprisingly, was viewed with some scepticism. 'This report is at the moment quite incomprehensible,' Schniewind commented acidly in the war diary. It was not until some two hours later, when Hildebrandt reported having seen two destroyers and the *B-Dienst* intercepted new instructions to the convoy, that the alarm was raised. *Gruppe Eisenbart*'s two operational U-boats were sent east in search of the convoy. *Kapitän-zur-See* Peters was allocated four new U-boats and the *Luftwaffe* took to the air. On the night of 18/19 December *Kapitänleutnant* Herbschleb on board *U-354* reported that he had seen star-shell on the horizon and heard a succession of bangs. Everything indicated that a new convoy had got through without the *Kriegsmarine* having been able to intercept it.

For one man, however, these sparse observations were enough. That man was *Grossadmiral* Karl Dönitz. The moment he had been waiting for since March had finally come. He had staked his reputation on an attack; now it was time to act. That same day he flew to Hitler's 'Wolf's Lair' in Rastenburg in East Prussia with dramatic news. 'The *Scharnhorst* and destroyers of the Battle Group will attack the next convoy from England to Russia,' he said, 'if success would seem to be assured. If the convoys begin to sail regularly, it will pay to reinforce the U-boat fleet in the north. I have already ordered more U-boats to the Arctic.'

Realpolitiker that he was, Dönitz had made a slight reservation, but his underlying intention was clear: the honour of the Battle Group was to be redeemed by a bold stroke.

Meanwhile the *Scharnhorst* had returned from the Bur fjord and was on standby, ready to put to sea, in her old anchorage at the head of the Lang fjord.

But by then the merchantmen of JW55A were already entering the Kola Inlet. Again an attack had to be called off. It was most frustrating. In Narvik yet another of Hitler's admirals, the cautious Otto Klüber, had gone home on compassionate leave, *Kapitän-zur-See* Rudolf Peters having been appointed his temporary replacement. Writing in the war diary, Peters made no attempt to disguise his disappointment: 'For several months we have been in doubt about the enemy's movements in the polar region. So far we do not know whether convoys are sailing or not. The means at my disposal do not make up for the lack of aerial reconnaissance.'

The date was 20 December 1943. Peters was still unaware that a new convoy had left Scotland, the fourth in five weeks. It was soon to be brought home to him with unwonted clarity exactly what the situation was.

CHAPTER TWELVE

Further Setbacks

OSLO, AUGUST–OCTOBER 1999

Summer was drawing to a close. Until the last I had nourished a faint hope that it would be possible to mount a new expedition before autumnal storms made my quest impossible. Even in September the Barents Sea can be kindly disposed towards those who sail it, greeting them with cool, south-easterly winds, a calm sea and magnificent sunsets. It is in October that the risks increase: the temperature falls and, slowly but inexorably the polar ice edges its way southwards. When cold air from the north meets warm air from the south, the resulting turbulence drives deep depressions in towards the coast. At such times it is unwise to risk costly underwater scientific equipment.

In mid-September Stein Inge Riise and I searched an area off Senja for the wreckage of the *Utvik Senior*, a fishing boat which in February 1978 had disappeared in mysterious circumstances with the loss of all nine on board. The sea here is about 40 metres deep above the narrow ledge of the Continental Shelf, which, a few nautical miles further out, plunges steeply to 1,000 metres. This is the area fishermen call Stordjupta (Great Deep) and through which vast shoals of cod pass each year on their way to their spawning grounds in the Lofoten Islands. From the south the Gulf Stream sweeps across the plateau in an irresistible flood. Where wind and current collide, storms of terrifying violence often rage.

We, however, enjoyed two halcyon days on board the *Risøy* as we quartered an area 4 nautical miles from precipitous Mount Oksen. There wasn't a breath of wind, the ship rocking gently to and fro in the barely perceptible waves that came rolling in from the trackless ocean further out. At night a full moon

transformed the ripples into a shimmering silver filigree. Although there was a 4-knot surface current, Stein Inge dived to a depth of 40 metres. The winches had no difficulty in hauling aboard the pieces of wreckage we found.

In between times we discussed the *Scharnhorst*. I had plotted on a chart all the reported positions I had been able to obtain between 72 and 73 degrees North and 28 and 29 degrees East. Although they were in the hundreds, they showed a definite pattern. In five different areas the concentration was extremely high – the dots were so tightly packed, in fact, that they almost overlapped.

'They're wrecks, that's obvious,' Stein Inge said.

'But which of them is the *Scharnhorst*?' I asked.

'We shan't know that until we send the "fish" down to have a look,' he replied.

There was only one problem: it was 60 to 70 nautical miles between the two extremities. I couldn't help feeling rather foolish. I'd spent untold hours gathering this information, and at home I was knee-deep in charts. My aim had been to narrow down the area of search, but what I had actually done was greatly to extend it. We had started with a box of 4 by 7 kilometres and now we found ourselves with one of 120 by 120 kilometres, an area some 15,000 square kilometres in extent. It was becoming increasingly apparent that I had embarked upon a project in which the obstacles were insuperable. I felt like a rambler who, after having laboriously made his way up a mountainside, reaches what he thinks is the summit only to see before him, stretching away into the distance, ridge after ridge, battlement piled on battlement. When despondency overwhelmed me, I was tempted to give up and write the whole enterprise off as an over-ambitious dream. I began to think that I had bitten off more than I could chew. On the other hand I had devoted more than thirty years of my life to journalism and was accustomed to taking chances. Looking back, with a bit of good will I could say that I had won just as many times as I had lost. It was a poor consolation, though.

Stein Inge and I calculated that we could cover the key areas with the side-scan sonar in seven days. We pondered the wisdom of taking a chance and sailing straight from where we were to the North Cape Bank.

I was sorely tempted, but finally decided against it. The *Risøy* had spent the summer investigating the wartime wrecks that littered the seabed in Narvik harbour, and both the ship and her crew were in need of a rest. I myself had somehow managed to fall off my bicycle and crack several ribs. I could neither laugh nor cry, and getting in and out of my bunk was agony. What a rough sea would do to a lumbering 100-kilo man like myself who had difficulty in keeping his balance didn't bear thinking about. The crew teased me unmercifully. 'Stay clear of the hard stuff next time,' they laughed. 'Don't drink and ride.' It was most embarrassing, not least because the accident had happened on a flat stretch of road and I had been stone cold sober.

Weather reports from the Barents Sea varied. We might, of course, be lucky and hit on the wreck the very first day. But you can't depend on luck 100 nautical miles off the North Cape when you're on an open deck. You need thorough preparation and planning. Reluctantly we decided to abandon the expedition. It was yet another setback and I was saddened by the thought. The season for underwater work was almost over. In the event the project had to be put off for a year. I returned to Evenes and took a plane home to Oslo. As we neared the capital we ran into turbulence; with every bump I felt as if a dagger was being driven into my spine. When I got home I lugged my bicycle down into the cellar and poured myself a stiff drink. I was foolish enough to think that it would help.

III

CHAPTER THIRTEEN

Studied Indifference

THE NORWEGIAN SEA, 20–23 DECEMBER 1943

The fast convoy JW55B sailed from Loch Ewe in Scotland at half-past two on the afternoon of Monday 20 December 1943. It comprised nineteen steamers sailing in six lines, and maintained a cruising speed of 10 knots. The Commodore was Rear-Admiral Maitland W.S. Boucher, who had been recalled from retirement for active service. He hoisted his flag on board a new Canadian-built Liberty ship, the 11,500-ton *Fort Kullyspell*. The escort consisted of two destroyers, three minesweepers and four corvettes.

The heavily laden merchantmen carried in their holds some 200,000 tons of ammunition, tanks, aircraft fuel and other essential supplies for Russia. They made a tempting prize. This valuable cargo notwithstanding, the convoy was ordered to follow an unusual course north, a course that would take it only 400 nautical miles from the Norwegian coast. This put it outside the range of German bombers but within the range of reconnaissance aircraft. The intention was that the convoy should be spotted. The ships, and the men who manned them, a thousand in all, were the stake in a deadly game of poker. The British Admiralty, spurred on by Churchill, had set out to entice the Battle Group holed up in the Lang and Kå fjords to sally forth and attack.

Shortly before eleven in the morning of Wednesday 22 December, when the convoy was just about level with Trondheim, lookouts on board the minesweeper *Gleaner* saw, some distance astern, an aircraft making for the Norwegian mainland. It was a twin-engine Ju 88 weather plane from the airfield at Værnes on a routine patrol – and despite the low cloud base the pilot could not have failed to observe the convoy.

At 12.46 teleprinters at the headquarters of the Fleet Commander in Kiel, *Generaladmiral* Otto Schniewind, clattered into life. '*FLIEGERFÜHRER NORD (W)* REPORTS: AT 10.45 IN SQUARE AE6983 [100 nautical miles north-east of the Faeroes] 40 TROOPSHIPS AND ESCORT VESSELS, PROBABLY WITH AIRCRAFT-CARRIER. COURSE 45 DEGREES. SPEED 10 KNOTS.'

The British ploy had worked: the convoy had been seen. But the disappointments of the last months had taught Schniewind prudence. He wrote in the war diary:

The report is surprising. Neither the position nor the composition of the convoy is easy to interpret. At the moment I incline to the view that there are many sources of error attaching to [a report from] a weather plane. To say the least, identification of [ships as] troopships would seem to be impossible. . . . Further reports should be awaited. An attempted landing appears highly improbable. It is more likely to be a PQ convoy on a course previously unfamiliar to us.

The Germans' uncertainty notwithstanding, the teleprinter lines between the C-in-C in Kiel and *Kapitän-zur-See* Peters in Narvik began to hum. Hitler had long feared an invasion of northern Norway. The three U-boats that were on their way northwards were re-routed to the Vest fjord, and pilots were summoned from Tromsø to assist the Battle Group in case it should find itself engaged with the enemy among the maze of islands that make up the Lofotens.

In the Lang fjord the men of the *Scharnhorst* and her attendant vessels were preparing for a quiet Christmas. The weather was fine and the temperature around freezing-point. The shortest day of the year had come and gone. A canopy of stars glittered above the snow-clad mountains, and every so often a magnetic storm in the atmosphere would send the leaping flames and probing yellow, green and violet fingers of the Aurora Borealis darting and flickering above the anchorage.

At about half-past eleven in the morning of 22 December the minesweeper *R 121* anchored alongside the battlecruiser. *Konter-Admiral* Erich Bey had arrived, bringing extra rations for Christmas. 'The men were looking forward to a peaceful, cheerful Christmas at their moorings and were hoping that the period of relaxed discipline would last until over the holiday. . . . A large quantity of Christmas comforts had come in. . . . The Captain's rounds were informal. Greater importance was attached to the comfort and well-being of the men than to efficiency and spit-and-polish.'

Only eighty of the ship's officers and men had been granted fourteen days' Christmas leave; jubilant at the prospect, they had already left Alta. One of them was the ship's jovial Bavarian hairdresser, 41-year-old Karl Ernst Weiss, who had been in the Navy since the early 1920s. He was a great admirer of Hitler and, thanks to his political connections, in 1939 had succeeded in getting himself put in charge of the hairdressing salon on board the *Scharnhorst*, with three civilians to help him. He was also the representative of the NSDAP (Nazi Party) on board the battlecruiser. One of his surviving grandchildren, Oliver Weiss, says:

On every trip he brought with him a cartload of shaving-gear, aftershave lotions, shampoos, toothpaste and brushes. He had it made. With almost 2,000 men needing a haircut every other week, he was in clover. Grandfather was very proud both of his work and of the ship itself. I remember his saying that it was almost impossible to shave the Captain: his cheeks were so weathered, it was like scraping the skin of a pig! He was overjoyed at being one of those lucky enough to be given leave.

For the men left on board, being away from home was an added burden, not least because the postal service to and from Alta had left much to be desired all through the autumn. Weeks might pass before a letter reached its destination. On 16 December Heinrich Mulch on board the *Tirpitz* complained that he was both tired and nervous – letters from home seemed to be his only solace. 'I always await your letters with longing,' he wrote to Gertrud. 'You have become my whole life, you are, as it were, the quintessence of all that is beautiful and loving. Nothing can any longer come between us. Fate will be kind to us.'

Heinrich's service as the Admiral's writer was coming to an end. He had applied to be allowed to continue his education in Frankfurt, and there was every chance that he would be released before the end of the year. His tone grew more hopeful with every letter he wrote, though he had his ups and downs. On 19 December, for example, he wrote: '*Was sich Soldaten wünschen?* [a Forces request programme] That's the title of that wonderful programme on the wireless on Sunday afternoons, and what we wish for most of all is a sackful of letters! Today it is three weeks since one came. Our wish has not once been fulfilled. How I have longed for a little letter from you! . . . Alas, there was nothing today.' However, the rest of the letter was more optimistic:

Before this letter reaches you four months will have passed since we last saw each other, my dear. If we add another four, it will be the last time I leave here.

I may also be demobbed earlier. Just let's hope that the war doesn't spoil things for us! I have still not received an offer of further schooling, but a decision will be taken in the course of the next eleven days – fairly soon, in other words. I am counting on my fingers: Shall I or shall I not raise your hopes? . . . Let Fate decide. Whatever happens, one day I shall again be by your side . . .

Two days later he was more cheerful still: 'After almost four weeks the great day came at last. I received another batch of letters – also from you! . . . Something else of importance has happened: the new writer arrived today! With God's help . . . we shall be able to attend school together . . . a simple pleasure will have far-reaching consequences . . .'

But hopes of a quiet Christmas were about to be rudely shattered. The men had hardly had time to open their letters before they were again put at three hours' readiness, at about two in the afternoon of 22 December. On board the *Scharnhorst* Bey, Hintze and the ship's senior officers met to discuss developments. The C-in-C of the 4th Destroyer Flotilla, *Kapitän-zur-See* Rolf Johannesson, and his Flag Officer, *Korvettenkapitän* Theodor von Mutius, on board *Z 29*, also conferred: 'There was no Christmas for Mutius and myself. We spent it plotting the convoy in my cabin.'

Writing in the war diary, Johannesson recorded: 'Is it an aircraft on a meteorological flight that has discovered the convoy by chance? Whatever, it was a stroke of luck. We shall know tomorrow whether the report is correct.'

As soon as the Ju 88 landed at Værnes, the pilot was debriefed. At 15.56 *Generaladmiral* Schniewind's misgivings were borne out. The pilot admitted that he had not been able to identify the ships with certainty, as visibility had been too poor. He changed his story and said that they weren't troopships after all, but two- to three-thousand-ton merchantmen. 'In the light of past experience, and judging by the size of the ships, the observation may be completely wrong,' Schniewind wrote. 'It may be nothing more than a fleet of fishing boats.'

Despite the doubt surrounding the sighting, the state of readiness was maintained. The new U-boats were re-routed from the Lofotens to Bear Island and the *Luftwaffe* was urged to send out more aircraft on reconnaissance. Only one U-boat failed to reach its destination. Hans-Günther Lange's *U-711* should have been the ninth member of *Gruppe Eisenbart*, but in the narrow confines of Tjeld Sound the U-boat was run down by a German patrol vessel that was travelling faster than it should have been. The U-boat sustained severe damage to her hull and had to enter the floating dock in Trondheim for repairs. The captain of the patrol boat panicked after the collision and ordered his men to jump overboard. 'He made a tragic mistake that cost many young men their lives. It was dark, so we only managed to pick up a few of them. The tragedy affected him so strongly that shortly afterwards he shot himself. For us the collision was a sad affair. True, we were given unexpected Christmas leave, but it was off Bear Island we should have been,' says Lange.

On the morning of 23 December the convoy was observed for a second time some 400 nautical miles west of the Lofotens. From airfields in the north Junkers Ju 88 bombers, four-engine Focke-Wulf 200 Condors and ungainly Blohm & Voss 138 flying-boats took it in turn to shadow the Allied ships throughout the day. As the clouds began to clear, the wind freshened to a moderate south-westerly gale accompanied by rain showers. The rain notwithstanding, visibility remained good, allowing the German aircrews to determine that it was not a fishing fleet after all but a convoy of some twenty merchant vessels escorted by about a dozen corvettes and destroyers.

The only worrying factor was the convoy's apparent indifference to the presence of the German reconnaissance planes. 'The convoy is steaming northwards 400 nautical miles from the Norwegian coast, barely outside the operational radius of the *Luftwaffe*'s bombers. It clearly sees no reason to remain out of range of our aerial reconnaissance. Probably it feels equal to the Battle Group, or it is not expecting to be attacked' was the considered opinion of *Kapitän-zur-See* Johannesson on board *Z 29* in the Lang fjord.

In Kiel, *Generaladmiral* Otto Schniewind was even more precise in his findings:

By noon on 26.12 the convoy may be abreast of Bear Island. . . . The only surprising thing is that it is sailing so near to the coast, 380 nautical miles distant. The reason may be the weakness of our forces, but there may be another explanation. The possibility cannot be ruled out that the convoy is being used as bait . . . and that there are strong forces in the vicinity ready to annihilate the German Battle Group if it ventures to attack.

Gathered round the plotting-tables in the Kå fjord and in Narvik and Kiel, the German admirals could follow the path of the convoy as it sailed northwards at a steady 10 knots. It was heading for the *Eisenbart* Group's cordon – and the point where it would be within range of a lightning attack by the *Scharnhorst* and the five destroyers of the 4th Flotilla.

Almost a year had passed since Kummetz had been humiliated in the same area, prompting Hitler to demand the decommissioning of the entire High Seas Fleet. This was the first real chance to redeem the honour of the Fleet by dealing the convoys to Russia 'a crushing blow'.

The prize was a valuable one, and temptingly close. It was, in fact, almost too good to be true, and the naval chiefs vacillated between optimism and nagging doubt. As Rolf Johannesson wrote in the war diary: 'It is amazing how calmly and on what a straight course this convoy is heading for Bear Island at the speed of a motorboat. It is as though neither the *Luftwaffe* nor the Battle Group exists.'

But on this point Johannesson was wrong: the British were very well aware of the existence of the German Battle Group.

CHAPTER FOURTEEN

The Mystery of the Logbook

OSLO, AUTUMN 1999

By this time I had managed to assemble copies of most of the available documents relating to the Battle of the North Cape in public archives: the Public Record Office in London, the Militärarchiv in Freiburg, Germany, the National Archives in Washington and the Naval Museum in Horten, Norway.

Admiral Bruce Fraser compiled two detailed reports. The first was dated 31 December 1943 and was written on board the flagship *Duke of York* on her return voyage from Murmansk to Scapa Flow; there was nothing in it to indicate where the *Scharnhorst* had gone down. The other report was dated 28 January 1944 and contained the following passage: '*Jamaica*, *Matchless* and *Virago* were the last ships to sight her at about 1938; at 1948 when *Belfast* closed to deliver a second torpedo attack she had definitely sunk in approximate position 72°16'N. 28°41'E.'

By then, four weeks had elapsed since the battle and Fraser had had a chance to rest. Back at the Fleet's home base of Scapa Flow, the Admiral found plenty of time to study the relevant charts and reports, and to confer with his captains. Vigilant and conscientious to a degree, he kept his navigators very much on their toes. As he himself recorded in his report after the battle, 'Plotting arrangements in the Fleet Flagship worked well, and were of great assistance both to me and to the ship. I myself alternated between the plot and the Admiral's bridge, the Chief-of-Staff remaining in the plot. I feel very strongly that the officers in the plot must always be in the closest contact with the Admiral who should obviously be on the bridge.'

Fraser's Chief-of-Staff was Captain William ('Bill') Slayter, who had joined the *Duke of York* shortly before the battle. Tall and bald-headed, he had 'a rather

red face and a very long nose'. He was a strict disciplinarian, 'always dishing out the maximum for whatever offence'. In action, however, 'he was cool and a great builder of confidence. . . . He always wore his anti-flash gear and tin helmet at action stations and expected others to do the same.'

Slayter also supervised plotting of the *Duke of York*'s and the remainder of the fleet's movements as the battle unfolded from minute to minute. Under his command he had a staff of navigators, both officers and ratings, whose task was to ensure that Fraser knew exactly where he was at any given time.

This wealth of expertise notwithstanding, somehow a grave error was made: the *Scharnhorst* had not met her doom where Fraser was told she had. Navigators on board British ships – and especially a team working under an admiral's critical gaze – were renowned for their thoroughness and the accuracy of their observations. That being so, what went wrong?

The *Duke of York*'s handwritten log did nothing to solve the mystery; if anything, it added to it. The entries were brief and to the point:

1929 Checked fire range 4000x. Cruisers and destroyers went in to finish off the enemy with torpedoes.
1945 German battlecruiser *Scharnhorst* sank in position 72.29 N 28.04 E.

It was very strange. The position recorded in the ship's log for the *Scharnhorst*'s sinking was quite different from that Fraser gave in his official report. It wasn't a minor difference either: the position recorded in the logbook was no fewer than 37 nautical miles further to the west.

I assumed that the entries in the logbook had been made during or immediately after the battle. What had occurred between 26 December 1943 and 28 January 1944 to cause Fraser to amend the position? It was clear that those involved had discussed the matter between themselves. It appeared from the various logbook entries that there had been a difference of opinion between the *Duke of York*'s navigators and those on board the *Belfast*, Vice-Admiral Robert Burnett's flagship – and that the latter had emerged triumphant. The official position had actually been copied straight from Burnett's report of 1 January 1944: 'At 20.02 thick oil was observed on the water in position approximately 72°16'N. 28°41'E., and the strong reek of burnt oil was very noticeable.' It was correct that the *Belfast* had been closer to the spot where the *Scharnhorst* had plunged to the bottom than had the *Duke of York*, which had withdrawn from the scene before the battlecruiser sank. But was that enough to justify the belief that Fraser had relied more on the accuracy of the cruiser's navigating skills than on those of his own officers? That in his official report he had chosen to overlook the work done by Slayter and his staff in favour of that performed by the navigation staff on board the *Belfast*?

How had the two divergent positions been arrived at? On 26 December 1943, St Stephen's Day (often erroneously referred to in the literature as Boxing Day, which it was not, as it fell on a Sunday), a strong gale had been blowing from the south and south-west, accompanied by snow showers. It was pitch-dark, the sky was probably overclouded and the wave height was 8 to 10 metres. In those days only traditional navigational aids were available: chronometers, slide rules and sextants. It was winter and the sun never rose above the horizon. Had someone caught a glimpse of the moon or stars? If they had, would they have been able to take the altitude with any real degree of accuracy with the sea as rough as it was?

Closer study of the logbooks revealed that for most or all of the time the ships' navigators had relied on dead reckoning, meaning that they had estimated their position on the basis of their own ship's course and speed, with adjustments for the probable effects of wind and current.

Only one of the navigation officers who took part in the battle was still alive when I began my investigations, 78-year-old Rex Chard, who in 1943 had been a young lieutenant-commander on the destroyer *Scorpion*. What he had to say when we finally tracked him down in Bristol was hardly encouraging:

To be perfectly honest we had better and more important things to do than plot our position at any given moment. Although I was the navigational officer on board HMS *Scorpion* I had a different battle station, in charge of the star-shell guns and close-quarters armaments.

The only real navigational position we would generally have taken notice of would have been our position relative to the flagship. All changes to our course were made to keep us in position with other ships, or out of the way of the *Scharnhorst*.

I would suggest that, considering the weather conditions at the time, the calculated position for the sinking of the *Scharnhorst* could be at least 10 nautical miles out. The navigation was all done by dead reckoning from the position given by the flagship. We didn't have fancy navigational aids like today. Half the time we didn't know where we were – only that we should be where the Admiral on the flagship *wanted* us to be.

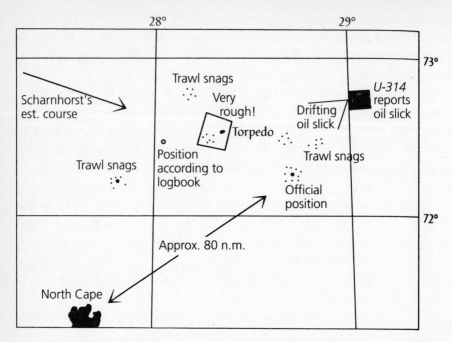

An analysis of obstacles on the seabed with which the fishing gear of more than one hundred vessels had become entangled revealed marked concentrations at several places in the search area. Strangely, the position recorded in the logbook of Admiral Fraser's flagship *Duke of York* for the sinking of the *Scharnhorst* differed markedly from that given in his official report.

In reality, then, it was only on board the *Duke of York* that any navigation work was done during the battle; the other ships in the squadron simply took care to maintain station in relation to the flagship.

At 45,000 tons the *Duke of York* was very stable. Moreover, Slayter's staff had no other duties during the battle than to navigate: that was their one and only job. They needed to know their own and the enemy's position and be ready at any moment to provide Fraser with accurate figures.

The *Duke of York* had also navigated by dead reckoning – except at one crucial moment in time: 12 noon on 26 December 1943, a bare eight hours before the German battlecruiser keeled over and sank. Then, according to the ship's log, the navigator had succeeded in obtaining an accurate fix, viz. N 72.07 E 20.48. What had happened? Had an opening suddenly appeared in the overcast? Had they been in radar contact with land? Or had they taken a sounding?

There was no one who could provide a definite answer. But in any navy an 'observed position' was traditionally looked upon as an accurate position, based as it normally was on at least two sources. If this position, which was determined a little less than eight hours before the *Scharnhorst* went down, really was correct, could we use it to test the truth of Fraser's report? Use it, in other words, to work out the position of the wreck?

There was one important reason why the position entered in the logbook began to preoccupy me more and more. It was only 10 to 12 nautical miles from where the torpedo had been recovered by the *Nordstar*, and was even closer to the position Arne Jensen and the Findus fleet's trawler captains had given. If the navigators on board the *Duke of York* really knew what they were about, we might be getting warm. I felt a surge of hope, but it was still far too early to draw any firm conclusions.

I had only a nodding acquaintance with navigation and realized that I needed expert assistance. But who could provide it? Fortunately, I had recently got to know one of the Norwegian naval staff's most industrious and enthusiastic officers, Commander Marcus Einarsson Osen, a keen student of naval history. If anyone could help me, he could.

CHAPTER FIFTEEN

Admiral Fraser's Plan

THE BARENTS SEA, 23–24 DECEMBER 1943

There was a very good reason why convoy JW55B was steaming northwards 380 nautical miles off the Norwegian coast in what was to all intents and purposes complete disregard of the enemy. The convoy was not alone. It was a key factor in a plan that had been taking shape in the mind of 55-year-old Admiral Bruce Fraser ever since he took over as C-in-C of the British Home Fleet in the spring of 1943. It was a simple plan, designed to lure the German Battle Group out into the open sea, there to be surrounded and annihilated by superior British forces. Like the two convoys that had preceded it, convoy JW55B was bait. All three convoys had taken the same course, but the first two had not been sighted in time by the Germans. However, 'with the safe arrival of JW55A I felt very strongly that the *Scharnhorst* would come out and endeavour to attack JW55B,' Fraser wrote in his 'Despatch' after the battle.

Fraser had joined the Royal Navy in 1902 as an officer cadet at the tender age of fourteen. By now, after forty years' experience of life at sea, many of them spent on board the Navy's big surface vessels, he possessed an intuitive grasp of the complexities of naval warfare. He had served as a gunnery officer on board a succession of cruisers and battleships, among them the light cruiser *Minerva* in the Red Sea during the First World War and the battleships *Queen Elizabeth* and *Warspite* in the Mediterranean after the war. As gunnery officer on board the *Resolution*, he had even led a party of thirty sailors into the oil town of Baku in Azerbaijan in 1920 to fight against the Bolsheviks. When the local population changed sides and lent their support to the revolution, Fraser and his men were thrown into prison, where they languished for six long months. He personally

thus had no reason to love Stalin and his henchmen, although, ironically, his primary task now was to help sustain the very regime he had once fought against. In the 1930s Fraser had captained the cruiser *Effingham* and the aircraft-carrier *Glorious*. Then followed a number of attractive appointments on the Naval Staff, including the important posts of Director of Naval Ordnance and Controller of the Navy. All this was proof, if proof were needed, that Admiral Fraser was a first-rate sailor. But there was more: he could also handle the powers-that-be in government offices in London.

Phlegmatic, self-assured and affable, Fraser was the epitome of a British naval officer. He had been trained as a defender of the Empire, but if this had given him a feeling of superiority he revealed no trace of it. According to his adjutant, his attitude to life was simple: he and his fellow sailors, from the oldest officer to the youngest rating, had the good fortune to be serving in the finest navy in the world. No matter what their rank, Fraser treated one and all as equals, and in consequence was greatly respected by all who came into contact with him.

An inveterate pipe-smoker, he was short of stature and inclined to stoutness. 'He never raised his voice,' remembered Sir Henry Leach, who served as a junior officer under Fraser on board the *Duke of York*, 'but the quiet, cold statement "That's bad" was reproof enough for most.' He could be quite ruthless, though, if the situation called for it. Officers who fell into disfavour risked having to pack their bags and depart within half an hour; ratings were dismissed on the spot.

Unmarried, at sea Fraser spent much of his time alone in his cabin, 'just thinking' and sucking on a large pipe. But his thoughts were not idle ones. 'He was constantly turning over in his mind problems of strategy and tactics, examining alternatives, rehearsing his response to every conceivable manoeuvre his likely opponents might make.' According to Vernon Merry, his Flag Lieutenant, 'he would fight hypothetical fleet actions, rehearsing dispositions, ranges, "A" arcs, factors of light, wind and weather and enemy capabilities and courses of action'. Long before it took place his battle against the *Scharnhorst* had many a time been fought out in his mind.

When, looking back, Fraser wrote that in the light of his long service and wide experience, he 'felt' that the *Scharnhorst* would launch an attack, he may well have been correct. It is more probable, however, that his wording was deliberately chosen to disguise the fact that throughout the autumn he had received from Norman Denning at the Operational Intelligence Centre a stream of intelligence reports relating to the German Battle Group. The strange thing is that these reports seemingly did not originate with the Norwegian agents in

Porsa and Alta, who, at risk of their lives, were keeping watch on the German naval bases there; in fact, they emanated from a completely different source: decrypted wireless signals exchanged between the German admirals in Kiel, Narvik and the Kå fjord. 'When, from the middle of December 1943, Ultra told him [Fraser] of *Scharnhorst*'s intensive exercises he became convinced that the German leadership would send out the Battle Group, not only to deny supplies to the Russians, but also to provide the German population with something to take their minds off defeat and aerial bombardment.'

As C-in-C of the Home Fleet, Admiral Fraser had at his disposal all the means he required. His flagship, the *Duke of York*, was a 45,000-ton steel giant of the King George V class. Commissioned in September 1941, she was armed with ten heavy 14-inch guns with a range of 33 kilometres. Each shell weighed 725 kilograms and could penetrate armour plating 40 centimetres thick. The battleship's secondary armament was no less formidable, comprising as it did more than one hundred guns of varying calibre. With twelve radar transmitters the *Duke of York* was far superior to her German opponents in her ability to fight at night. She had a top speed of more than 29 knots, which was very high, although the tremendous weight of her forebody meant that she battered rather than clove her way through heavy seas. Because of an error in design, she and her four sister ships tended to plough their way through the water, and it didn't need much of a sea for the *Duke of York* to ship tons of water over her foredeck.

Fraser had with him his own escort, which consisted of the 8,000-ton light cruiser *Jamaica* and four S-class destroyers, the *Saumarez*, *Savage*, *Scorpion* and *Stord*, the latter a Norwegian ship under the command of Lieutenant-Commander Skule Storheill.

The squadron had not operated as such for very long. In mid-December Fraser had taken the battleship and her consorts through the Barents Sea to Murmansk, where they carried out night exercises for the very first time. In Murmansk, which was still under siege, Fraser was the guest of the C-in-C of the Soviet Northern Fleet, Admiral Arseni Golovko, who was at a loss to understand the reason for the visit.

After two days of exchanging courtesy calls, accompanied by lengthy toasts and musical entertainments, on 18 December Fraser's ships abruptly weighed anchor and sailed away as unexpectedly as they had come, leaving Golovko more baffled than ever. He wrote in his postwar memoirs: '[A]fter receiving a wireless message of some sort from sea, the *Duke of York* and escorting ships weighed anchor and left the Kola Inlet in such haste that Fraser sent his apologies to the Mission, explaining that he was returning to England.

A strange hurry. Where are the British racing off to now? To meet the convoy and support it?'

Fraser's sudden departure had a simple explanation. Neither Golovko nor any of the other Russians knew that the British were reading the German naval codes; only Fraser himself and a handful of his most senior officers were privy to the secret. That was why he could not inform the Soviet admiral of the wireless messages he had received from the Operational Intelligence Centre and of what he knew about developments in the Alta fjord.

Three days later, on the morning of Tuesday 21 December, the *Duke of York* and her escorts swept into the narrow Eyja fjord on the north coast of Iceland and dropped anchor off the tiny fishing village of Akureyri. Fraser was pressed for time. He needed extra fuel oil – he had no intention of being caught out if the *Scharnhorst* showed signs of making a move. He put his faith in the *Duke of York*'s radar, the best in the Navy, but no matter how efficient it may have been, the men on the destroyers that followed in the battleship's wake were 'amazed and somewhat frightened by the speed at which we entered these hazardous waters'.

One by one the ships of what by then was designated Force 2 topped up their fuel tanks from an oiler anchored in the roads, while Fraser waited for the order to put to sea. Refuelling went on until well into the morning of 23 December. It was bitterly cold and the Eyja fjord was beginning to freeze over. Fraser went ashore to do some Christmas shopping, but soon returned to the flagship. 'When we got back on board all the Icelanders ashore were skating, by light – we were in darkness, of course. I asked the band to come up on deck and play Christmas carols; and really, it almost brought tears to your eyes.'

By this time convoy JW55B had been sighted by the *Luftwaffe* and was being continuously shadowed as it sailed northwards. Fraser knew that he still had time, as Denning kept him well supplied with deciphered German wireless signals. A Soviet Spitfire equipped for photographic reconnaissance had been over western Finnmark on the morning of 23 December. The sky was clear and the pilot had seen both the *Tirpitz* in the Kå fjord and the *Scharnhorst* and two destroyers in the Lang fjord, surrounded by auxiliary vessels.

At 19.00 Fraser summoned the Commanding Officers of Force 2 to a meeting in his cabin on board the flagship for a final conference. He wished to assure himself that they all understood his plan and to this end he impressed upon them that 'every officer and man [had to] be doubly sure that he knew his night action duty'. He added, however, that 'such a reminder would hardly seem necessary, except that within the Home Fleet there are frequent changes of officers and men, and, with constant escort requirements, adequate training is not easy to achieve'. Fortunately, as the Battle Summary points out, by then Force 2 had been in company for nearly a fortnight and they knew each other and had practised night encounter tactics together.

Even with full fuel tanks, the destroyers' range was limited. To conserve fuel it was planned to steam towards the area south of Bear Island, where it was expected that battle would be joined, at a speed of 15 knots and to remain 200 nautical miles astern of the convoy. If the Battle Group did come out, the *Duke of York* and her escorts would make for the North Cape at full speed and cut off the Germans' retreat.

Apart from a grey twilight in the middle of the day, the whole area was enveloped in impenetrable Arctic blackness. The weather forecast was poor. A gale was on its way from the south-west, accompanied by rain and snow showers, which meant that in all probability the battle, if it occurred, would be fought in pitch darkness with zero visibility. Fraser was not only highly intelligent, he also possessed an above-average knowledge of technology, which encouraged him to rely on the *Duke of York*'s twelve radar transmitters – at that time the most advanced anywhere in the world. The main radar, type 273QR, was installed in a plastic radome on top of the battleship's superstructure and was capable of detecting an enemy vessel at a range of over 40 kilometres. The corresponding German radar on board the *Scharnhorst* was much more primitive and had a range of only 13.2 kilometres – and that was under the most favourable circumstances. This Fraser knew, and it gave him an advantage that he had every intention of exploiting to the full. If he succeeded in cutting off the battlecruiser's retreat, he intended to hold his fire for as long as possible, and then, when he judged the time was ripe, to fire star-shell at a distance of 11 kilometres. By then his presence would probably have been discovered by the German radar anyway, but it would be too late: the *Duke of York*'s heavy guns would pound the *Scharnhorst* unmercifully, to the point where all her guns were silenced, whereupon the destroyers would race in to deliver the *coup de grâce* with torpedoes.

At about eleven on the evening of 23 December Force 2 weighed anchor and set off from the Eyja fjord, the destroyers in the van. Iceland's mountains were invisible in the darkness and it was still bitterly cold. Somewhere beyond the horizon, between Jan Mayen and the Norwegian coast, the nineteen ships of convoy JW55B were ploughing northwards in the grip of a rising gale.

Still further to the east, off the Kola peninsula, the twenty-two ships of the returning convoy, RA55A, their precious cargoes discharged, were forming up for the long voyage back to Loch Ewe on the north-east coast of Scotland. Their close

escort was a strong one, consisting as it did of ten destroyers, three corvettes and a minesweeper under the overall command of a veteran captain, 'Scotty' Campbell, on board the *Milne*. In the south, between the coast of Finnmark and the convoy, waited the distant escort – three cruisers, the *Belfast*, *Sheffield* and *Norfolk* – under the command of 55-year-old Vice-Admiral Robert Burnett.

'Nutty' Burnett was an old hand on the convoy route to Murmansk. In September 1942, as captain of the cruiser *Scylla*, he had spent fifteen days fighting a ruthless running battle against German aircraft and U-boats, and had seen thirteen of the thirty-nine ships that made up convoy PQ18 burst into flames and sink. He later transferred his flag to the *Sheffield*, and on New Year's Eve 1942 took part in the battle to protect Convoy JW51A. It was shells fired by Burnett's cruiser force that had damaged the *Admiral Hipper* and reduced the destroyer *Friedrich Eckholdt* to a blazing hulk. In reality it was Burnett, together with Captain Sherbrooke, who had put Kummetz to shame and aroused Hitler's ire.

Now he was back in the same dangerous waters. Although no intellectual, Burnett was an aggressive admiral, powerfully built and fighting fit. He had not done very well in theoretical subjects at Naval College, but he played rugby, football and water polo like a professional. In his typically English manner, he was self-deprecating to a degree and used jocularly to refer to himself as 'a stupid fellow who had been lucky'. He was wont to declare that his promotions – to captain and later to rear-admiral – were 'neither expected nor merited'.

'He used to say, slapping himself on the stern, "This is where all my brains are,"' recalled his friend Frederick Parham. 'But he was a tremendous personality and . . . a *fighting* admiral, with a sort of fighting instinct. Of course, he was *immensely* popular. I remember going to concerts . . . and as we came in the whole place would burst into cheering!' Parham was destined to rise to the rank of admiral, but at the time of the Battle of the North Cape he was captain of Burnett's flagship, the *Belfast*.

While the empty ships of convoy RA55A were pounding their way westwards along the edge of the polar ice and in the teeth of a rising wind, Vice-Admiral Burnett set a course for the North Cape. Force 2 was to be the anvil, the three cruisers of Force 1 the hammer. Between them they intended to crush the *Scharnhorst* and the remainder of the German Battle Group.

The success of the operation hinged on one vital question, and that was still unanswered: would the German squadron take the bait?

CHAPTER SIXTEEN

The Dream of Oil

OSLO, AUTUMN 1999

I spent the next week gathering together the threads of my investigation. I was determined to leave no avenue unexplored, and for this reason had contacted the Norwegian Petroleum Directorate, which contained in its archives and databases all the information that had been garnered in regard to the Barents Sea in the last thirty years.

The first seismic exploration vessels were despatched to the region by various oil companies in the 1960s. Since then, millions of kilometres of ocean floor had been seismically charted with a view to pinpointing probable deposits of oil and gas.

The Barents Sea was still looked upon as a promising source of oil, although there was nothing to show for twenty years' hard work other than sixty or so mostly dry holes. Things had been different in the 1970s, when the dream of vast underwater deposits had conjured up visions of a new Klondyke. All the signs were propitious: the sedimentary layers were extensive and seismic studies had revealed the presence of formations that might well conceal gigantic reservoirs on a par with the largest in the North Sea. I well remember once driving with a county official. He stopped the car and pointed to a desolate stretch of mountainous countryside: 'That's where the town will grow up,' he said. 'Three or four thousand new homes. They'll house roustabouts and engineers, drilling managers and geologists. As soon as we get the oil ashore. You'll see!' I was a cub reporter at the time and I felt my pulse quicken at the thought. Oil would be Finnmark's salvation and confer on the people an affluence the like of which had not been seen since the peak years of the capelin

fishery, when jubilant fishermen took taxis all the way from Hammerfest to Tromsø for the sole purpose of dining out at a restaurant.

That had been nearly thirty years ago, and things hadn't turned out the way people had hoped. Drilling started in 1980. A few years later a deposit of gas, the Snow White Field, had been discovered, but every hole drilled since then, and there were many, had proved dry. The most promising formations revealed clear traces of hydrocarbons, but there was no oil – and no one knew where it had gone. Only now, when the geologists had reassessed their data and suggested new areas of exploration, had hope been rekindled.

It was this that interested me. From 1989 onwards a number of holes had been drilled in the area where the *Scharnhorst* had gone down, one of them only 7 or 8 nautical miles north-east of the officially recognized position given by Fraser. Before the platforms were anchored in place and drilling commenced, a great many seismic shootings had been carried out to yield seabed profiles, detailed three-dimensional studies and site surveys 4 × 4 kilometres in extent around each hole. Before and during such operations a supply ship and other specialist vessels would have been standing by in the vicinity. I reasoned that, if I were lucky, one of them might have observed a large wreck nearby.

I wrote to the Norwegian Petroleum Directorate:

When I saw these wells marked on a chart, it struck me that the oil companies concerned, or you yourselves, must have accumulated large quantities of seismic data about this region and, I should imagine, also obtained profiles of the sea floor and other information. I therefore wonder if, at the same time – as a byproduct – information was also recorded of any large wrecks there may have been in the area. As the wreck of the *Scharnhorst* is of thick armoured steel and some 230 metres in length, it would show up very distinctly on an echo or sonar diagram.

I wasted a lot of time pursuing this lead without becoming much wiser. Seismic data are stored in vast databases and cannot be retrieved simply by pressing a button. The experts I consulted doubted whether ordinary seabed profiles would reveal the presence of wrecks – and in any case, to search all available data at random would be far too costly and complicated a process to be practicable. The Petroleum Directorate's office in Harstad was good enough to check its site surveys, which had been carried out to chart any obstacles there might be on the seabed in areas where drilling was scheduled to take place.

Their answer came promptly, and it was anything but promising: no wrecks had been located around any of the drillholes.

I also wrote to the Norwegian Mapping Authority and asked whether they could help me. After I had twice given them a gentle nudge, they replied that there was no record of any obstacle within a radius of 9,000 metres of the positions I had enquired about.

The truth was slowly beginning to dawn. We were one of the world's wealthiest countries, we possessed enormous resources in the sea and seabed – fish, minerals, oil and gas – and we were a nation with long seafaring traditions. All this notwithstanding, I had to face the fact that we knew very little about what lay beneath the surface of the sea. There were no reliable charts of the seabed in the north, nor did a relevant database exist. Even many of the charts regularly in use in coastal navigation were based on surveys that had been performed anything from fifty to one hundred years earlier. Much of the ocean that we called ours was in reality a *mare incognito*.

By this time I had become pretty well immune to bad news. Somewhere or other lay the wreck of the *Scharnhorst*, and I intended to find it. It was no longer a dream: it had become an obsession.

CHAPTER SEVENTEEN

The Report from U-601

THE BARENTS SEA, SATURDAY 25 DECEMBER 1943

Somewhere above the solidly packed waste of ice between Spitsbergen and Greenland warm air from the south and cold air from the north had collided, forcing mild currents of air upwards, where they formed gigantic, unstable banks of cloud. The temperature began to fluctuate and barometers to fall. The German military meteorologists huddled in their lonely cabins on Hopen, Bear Island and the eastern shore of Greenland had noted the signs and knew what to expect. A front was developing – and over Christmas it would sweep across the North Cape with ferocious force.

Early on Christmas Day morning 1943 *Oberleutnant-zur-See* Otto Hansen noticed the first signs of a change in the weather. The south-westerly wind that was blowing grew stronger, the waves about him crested and broke and the barometric pressure sank to almost 980 millibars.

'The weather is worsening from hour to hour,' he noted in the war diary. At twenty-five, Hansen was one of the youngest U-boat skippers in the *Eisenbart* Group. Only four weeks earlier he had taken command of one of the veteran Arctic U-boats, *U-601*. The year before, *U-601* had wreaked havoc among merchant ships as far east as the mouths of the Ob and Yenisey, two large rivers that debouch into the Kara Sea. Three Soviet steamers had been left as burning hulks. At that time the captain had been Peter-Ottmar Grau, who could look back on seven wartime patrols. Now Otto Hansen was in command. He was on his first winter patrol and feared the worst. His problems had begun early on, when he set out on the long voyage north. He was carrying letters addressed to the U-boat Commander in Narvik, Rudolf Peters, and six new Naxos- and Borkum-type radar

detectors. The technological war was gaining increasing momentum: the Naxos and Borkum sets had been developed as a counter to the ever more sophisticated British air- and shipborne radars. They were highly sensitive instruments. If they detected enemy radar pulses the alarm would be sounded and the U-boat would have time to dive before an attacker reached the scene.

The trouble was that not one of the U-boats operating in northern waters was equipped with a Naxos or Borkum radar detector. Otto Hansen had the first six with him. They ought by rights to have been handed over in Narvik, together with the Christmas mail, but with the discovery of the British convoy *U-601* had hurriedly been directed to make straight for Bear Island. In the open sea off the coast of Finnmark Hansen had lain to alongside *U-277* and the mail and three of the new radar sets had been passed over before the U-boats went their separate ways. *U-277* had already spent forty days patrolling the area between the edge of the polar ice and Bear Island. She was running short of diesel oil and her crew were showing signs of fatigue. There was no question of a rest, however. As soon as she had refuelled while moored alongside the *Black Watch*, she was ordered to return to Bear Island and there hand over two of the three radar sets she had on board to other U-boats of the *Eisenbart* flotilla. It was all very complicated, and matters were not helped by the fact that no one on board the *Black Watch* was familiar with the new technology involved. They knew neither how to install the sets nor how to operate them. But that wasn't Otto Hansen's problem. He had done his bit by handing them over, and now set out to celebrate Christmas Eve submerged off Bear Island.

On each plate is a packet of biscuits, a bar of chocolate, a box of pralines, a piece of marzipan, apples and bon-bons. The First Officer counts everything out and the wireless operator puts the goodies on the plates. . . . A long, white-draped table has been laid in the crew's quarters in the bow. The whole crew assembles there. Our sailors' Christmas tree, made of scraps of green-painted metal and rope ends, looms large at the head of the table. There are no candles on it – naked lights are forbidden because of the danger of an explosion. All lights have been switched off. Just one, in a Christmassy lampshade at the end of the table, is left on. . . . Our Captain says a few well-intentioned words about the meaning of the Christmas festival and why we are having to celebrate it up here in the far north, far away from home. A carol is sung. Then we are given permission to open our letters, which have been placed beneath the plates. The mail has not arrived, but earlier in the autumn girls in a town in the Saar wrote letters to all U-boat sailors in the north, so everyone gets something from home after all. . . . The best letters are read out aloud. There's a lot of laughter. This Christmas Eve the girls in the Saar would have needed to cover their ears!

It was all very simple and unsentimental. A Saviour had been born to bring peace to the world. Otto Hansen had brought with him something quite different: slim, sleek, steel 'fish' packed with high explosive. Round about ten o'clock the celebration came to a close. Hansen took the U-boat up to the surface and set a course south. Eight hours later he took up his position on the new cordon, 135 nautical miles south-west of Bear Island. When *U-277* returned, *Gruppe Eisenbart* would consist of eight U-boats.

Rudolf Peters and his staff in Narvik were very much on edge. A stream of new orders was signalled to the U-boats in an endeavour to concentrate them in the path of the convoy. If the convoy's speed had been correctly estimated, the merchantmen should soon heave into sight in the lenses of the U-boat captains' binoculars.

It was still midwinter and darkness reigned. Around *U-601* dawn didn't break in the accepted sense of the word, the blackness of the night merely giving way to lighter shades of grey. 'The northern horizon is hidden in bluish-grey shadows, but far off in the south a pale pencil of light is discernible against the sky, a faint gleam on the horizon. Shortly afterwards a red glow appears. We can just make out the presence of the sun. It is casting its beams over faraway lands, and the people who live there have no idea of how fortunate they are.'

At 08.52 Otto Hansen again gave the order to dive. He stabilized the U-boat at a depth of 60 metres and decreased the engine revolutions. A few minutes later the wireless operator leaned out of the sonar compartment and whispered excitedly, 'Vessel bearing 230 degrees. The noise is getting stronger.' The sound grew in intensity, until all on board could hear the churning of propellers and the whining and hammering of valves and pumps at work. The noise was overwhelming. Not only were there ships on both sides of the U-boat, there were others ahead and astern: laden tankers, wallowing merchantmen, sleek corvettes. Suspended in a thin-hulled, unprotected steel cylinder, the crew of the U-boat waited breathlessly. Above them was the convoy, below, 2,000 metres of icy water. They could do nothing but wait and hope. Twenty nerve-racking minutes passed before the noise grew weaker and eventually faded away to the east.

Otto Hansen waited for almost an hour before venturing to surface. At precisely 09.52 on Christmas Day 1943 the following coded signal went out from the

U-boat's aerial: 'RUN OVER BY CONVOY IN SQUARE AB6720. ENEMY STEERING 60 DEGREES. HANSEN.' It was one of the most significant and fateful signals ever transmitted in the history of naval warfare in the Arctic.

In Narvik, a deciphered copy of the signal was placed on *Kapitän-zur-See* Peters's desk half an hour later, at 10.20. Peters had every reason to feel proud. This time he had directed his U-boats to the correct position. But for once the normally outspoken U-boat commander was mindful of what he wrote, contenting himself with: 'The position of the convoy was established as planned in the morning of 25.12.'

In Kiel, the Fleet Commander, *Generaladmiral* Otto Schniewind, was equally succinct when he received the decrypt at 11.02. 'The convoy has been located by the U-boats. Its position accords well with our plot. . . . Its speed appears to be something in excess of 9 knots.'

On board his flagship, *Z 29*, in the Lang fjord, *Kapitän-zur-See* Rolf Johannesson noted: 'The convoy is sailing at a distance from the coast that is little more than 200 nautical miles. It does not seem to have any great respect for our air force.'

These sober comments disguised the tension that had built up in the German headquarters over the last three days. On their charts and plotting-tables staff officers had followed the convoy's bold progress north since its discovery on Wednesday 22 December. Now it was Saturday, and soon the convoy would cross the Bear Island Trench, less than fifteen hours' sailing from the Lang fjord. The time for a decision was growing ever closer – a decision for which the admirals had been impatiently waiting for nearly ten months. Should the Battle Group be sent out or not? The order to put to sea had already been drafted; what was lacking was the decision to issue it.

Up to that point handling of the situation had been exemplary. True, *Luftflotte 5*, depleted as it was, had complained that shadowing the convoy was imposing 'unnecessary strain on men and matériel', as it seemed that the *Kriegsmarine* 'did not intend to do battle'. But despite the *Luftwaffe's* disgruntlement, reconnaissance aircraft had regularly taken off from Banak, Bardufoss and Tromsø. From about noon on 23 December sightings had regularly been reported. Towards midnight on Christmas Eve the German analysts came to unanimous agreement: 'Course, speed and composition make it possible to say with certainty that this is a PQ convoy bound for Murmansk or the White Sea.'

Generaladmiral Schniewind noted in the war diary: 'I share this view. Such questions as still remain open may be expected to be answered when the convoy passes the U-boat cordon tomorrow morning.'

During the night of 23/24 December there had been a flurry of teleprinter messages between the U-boat Commander in Narvik, Rudolf Peters, and *Konter-Admiral* Erich Bey in the Kå fjord.

It must have been a strange time for Bey. Outside the windows of his cabin on board the crippled *Tirpitz* snow had begun to fall. The weather was mild and there was no wind. But the flag that hung limply over the stern was not his; it was still that of his predecessor, *Admiral* Kummetz. Instead, 45-year-old Bey had hoisted his flag on board the destroyer *Z 34* as if to demonstrate that he still belonged to the small ships, not the big ones. The fact was that he had not set foot on the deck of a battleship since he was a cadet during the First World War. According to his contemporaries, Bey was 'a person of massive build, a brilliant seaman and a born destroyer commander. Behind his forbidding exterior there beat a warm heart'. As Captain of a wide array of destroyers and, later, Commander of the entire destroyer force, Bey had won all-round respect. 'Like Kummetz, he had cut his seafaring teeth on board destroyers and gained considerable tactical experience in both war and peace. He was extremely efficient and knew a great deal about war at sea. He had done well in all the positions he had held,' wrote Dönitz. In the ferocious battle for Narvik in April 1940 Bey had assumed command when Bonte, the destroyer commander, was killed. But his first attempt to break the British blockade of the Vest fjord had been half-hearted and ended in disaster. All his ten destroyers were sunk, some scuttled by their own men when they ran out of fuel and ammunition. Bey's ship was among them. He had been compelled to open the seacocks and send his own flagship, the destroyer *Wolfgang Zenker*, to the bottom. He and his men then took part in the ensuing land battles until Norway fell to the Germans in June. His defeat at Narvik could have been a serious setback to his career, but it seems to have passed unremarked. As Rear-Admiral, in February 1942 he had led the escort that had accompanied the *Scharnhorst*, *Gneisenau* and *Prinz Eugen* on their triumphant dash through the Channel. Now he was back in northern Norway as Commander of Nazi Germany's last heavy battle group. But he had changed: in the six weeks that had passed since his arrival in November he had made no attempt to conceal the disappointment he felt over his new posting.

'When I reported to him on 8 November he was an embittered man. He felt that he had been unjustly dealt with. He had been appointed to stand in during the winter. This was at a time when the men at the top did not envisage that any battles would be fought. He spoke of his exile in extremely harsh terms. It saddened me to see that he was no longer the man he had been,'

wrote the Commander of the 4th Destroyer Flotilla, Rolf Johannesson, many years later. But he had little good to say of Bey's qualifications as Commander of the Battle Group:

> I had worked with him on gunnery exercises in peacetime and I knew that he didn't understand much about guns. . . . He neglected to foster team spirit in the Battle Group. He never went to visit the auxiliary units, he never had career or service talks with anyone, he never made plain what his intentions were, never staged war games, never took part in exercises or inspected the destroyers, never carried out any exercises involving all the units under his command and never made the personal acquaintance of the Admiral in Narvik. . . . It took eight hours to get from the Lang fjord, where the *Scharnhorst* and my destroyer lay, to the Kå fjord and back. I had been his Flag Captain in peacetime and carried out numerous operations in his company in war. I visited him only once. He made no attempt to hide his bitter disappointment.

Johannesson was harsh in his judgement. In short, he thought that Bey was unfitted to command a battlecruiser in action. He was mentally unprepared for battle, nor had he made the necessary preparations. Now, on Christmas Eve 1943, Bey was overtaken by events. He held 3,000 lives and Hitler's last battleship in his hands. What had not been done would have to remain undone; the sands had run out. Bey was cornered: if the order came, he would have to put to sea.

That he would do so with reluctance was manifested by the teleprinter signal received by *Kapitän-zur-See* Peters in Narvik at 02.30 on the night of 24 December:

> Reports on the convoy have so far left much to be desired. . . . A search for enemy covering forces is essential. . . . The best time for a tactical surprise [attack] would not be early dawn, measured astronomically, but at half-light in the middle of the day [i.e., between 11.06 and 11.51]. . . . At a probable northern meeting point there will be no light at all, which means that conditions will not be at all conducive to the employment of heavy guns.

Peters's response to this gloomy signal was not long in coming. In a signal sent to the Fleet Commander, *Generaladmiral* Schniewind, only four days earlier, he had once again expressed himself in angry and despairing terms about the *Luftwaffe's* lack of cooperation in the northern sphere of operations. 'It must be placed on record that the *Luftwaffe*'s reluctance and lack of strength in the north mean that there is no chance of a successful attack by the U-boats and the Battle Group. . . . It is essential that Fleet Command makes this unequivocally clear, so that the Navy is not blamed for the fact that supplies to Russia are passing through the Barents Sea without loss.'

The Admiral agreed but cannily decided that Peters's signal was too strongly worded to be passed on – especially as Dönitz and his staff already knew how things stood.

Now, on the morning of Christmas Eve, Peters's opinion of the *Luftwaffe* had mellowed. In his reply to Bey he said that, in his opinion, shadowing of the convoy had been adequate. It was, though, desirable that the expanse of ocean west of the convoy be searched within a radius of 300 nautical miles in case a heavy enemy force should be lurking astern of the convoy.

If the Battle Group's putting to sea does not become known to the enemy and tactical surprise is achieved, an engagement of two to three hours' duration may be counted on and nine to ten hours allowed for withdrawal. At best the opponent will be able to cover 300 nautical miles in this time, meaning that he will be unable to overtake the Battle Group. . . . In the light of experience gained on 31.12.42 it is possible to fight for at least two hours at a range of up to 17,700 metres. So far the weather outlook for 25/26.12 appears favourable.

Kapitän-zur-See Peters's reply was clearly intended to steel the will of the irresolute Squadron Commander. It must have served its purpose, as when, some hours later, the *Luftwaffe* confirmed that parts of the area in question would be thoroughly searched, Bey chose to back down. Replying at 18.45 on Christmas Eve, he remarked drily, 'It is requested that a promise be obtained that reconnaissance to a distance of 300 nautical miles west of a line extending from Lucie 1 [Point Lucie] and the battle zone really will be carried out,' which elicited from Peters the assurance that 'the Battle Group likewise considers that reporting on the convoy and its close escort is clear and satisfactory. . . . For the time being we shall have to wait to see to what extent locating of the supposed enemy covering force is feasible. An unambiguous and clear picture of *whether* and *when* intervention by this force may be expected is a presupposition for action by the Battle Group.'

Strangely, Fleet Commander Schniewind, who that same evening had been following the exchange of views between Bey and Peters, expressed himself as being largely in agreement with the former:

The Battle Group's opinion accords well with *Gruppe Nord*'s/the Fleet's views, viz., that the situation calls more for action by destroyers than by the entire Battle Group, unless an especially favourable situation in the battle zone materializes accompanied by good visibility, possibly in the shape of the Northern Lights, good weather and a clear picture of the enemy's dispositions. In the light of discussions with Naval High Command guidelines have therefore been drawn up for deploying the destroyers primarily in the winter. Because of their lack of strength, conditions do not really favour them, either.

The belief that a heavy covering force was lying in wait somewhere was well founded. Most of the earlier convoys had been protected by one or more battleships and cruisers, which normally remained 100 to 200 nautical miles further back. It was reasonable to suppose that a convoy that 'flaunted itself' the way JW55B was doing would be similarly protected. But how could anyone be sure, as long as the *Luftwaffe*'s reconnaissance aircraft were unable to find the rearguard?

At about 18.30 on Christmas Eve, while the admirals were still bickering among themselves, disquieting reports came in from two D/F stations, one in the German Bight, the other in Kirkenes. Both had obtained a cross-bearing on wireless signals from an unidentified British unit some 180 nautical miles west of the convoy.

In the war diary that same evening Schniewind wrote: 'The British unit on which bearings have been obtained at an extremely acute angle appears to be some 180 nautical miles astern of the convoy. This may be an approaching covering force.'

These reports notwithstanding, the Admiral chose to treat them as suspect. His next comment was little short of surrealist in its ambiguity: 'All in all we must take into account the presence of a second enemy force in the Barents Sea, unless it is assumed that the fix is so uncertain that it emanates from the convoy itself or a straggler. There is nothing new about this fix.'

On the one hand he was pretty certain that the convoy was a come-on and that heavy British units were lurking not too far distant, in which case he could not justifiably order an attack. On the other hand the whole situation was shrouded in uncertainty, which meant that an attack might be feasible after all.

In the Admiral's quarters on board the *Tirpitz* Heinrich Mulch had followed the discussions between Bey and Fleet Headquarters. If he was anxious, he gave no sign of it in the last loving Christmas letter he wrote to Gertrud:

My darling! When you open this letter it will be Christmas Eve. The fifth
wartime Christmas and my first Christmas with you, but so very far away. . . .
Your and my thoughts will each find their way – from the wonderful peace of
hearth and home to our world of ice. Soon we shall enter upon a new year in
our lives. The past year afforded us many delightful moments, moments that
warmed and gladdened our hearts. May our hopes be fulfilled in the year that
lies ahead! . . . This is my greeting to you on Christmas Eve 1943, my third
wartime Christmas in the north, in blizzards or beneath a tranquil Arctic sky,
in inky blackness or beneath a canopy of stars and weaving Northern Lights –
who knows, today, what the morrow will bring? Whatever it may be, I shall
be seated beneath a Christmas-tree on board a ship together with my friends,
thinking of you, my dear Gertrud. I close firm in the belief that we shall
enjoy a happy New Year and a happy future together. No matter what, we
two will remain together for ever. Warmest greetings. As always, with love to
you, your Hein.

At home in Giessen Gertrud was celebrating Christmas Eve quietly, happy at
the thought that her boyfriend would soon be coming home, perhaps for good.
But in Kiel *Generaladmiral* Schniewind was already formulating the order that
would send the Battle Group out to launch an attack.

At 23.37 on Christmas Eve the final draft was sent to Dönitz. It proposed that
the *Scharnhorst* and her five escorting destroyers should sortie the following day
with a view to attacking the convoy south of Bear Island on the morning of 26
December. Schniewind was aware that the battlecruiser would have its work cut
out and might be unable to break through the convoy's close escorts in the time
available for accurate bombardment with her heavy guns. It had been estimated
that there would be just over half an hour when it was light enough for accurate
gunnery, from 11.22 to 12.07. If she couldn't get through, the *Scharnhorst* was to
disengage and leave the closing phase of the battle to the destroyers. It wasn't a
very encouraging scenario. The *Scharnhorst* needed two destroyers for her own
protection, which left only three to attack the convoy, meaning that, 'taken all
round, the prospects of a successful outcome would be poor'.

When *Grossadmiral* Karl Dönitz received Schniewind's proposal, he was
celebrating Christmas together with the U-boat crews of *Gruppe West* in Paris. It
was almost ten months since he had entered into that tacit bet with Hitler that
he would strike 'a crushing blow' against the convoys. This was his first real
opportunity, but Dönitz was far from happy about it. A staff officer present at
the dinner, Edward Wegener, recalls that the Commander-in-Chief grew

increasingly grave and morose as reports continued to come in. 'In the Officers' Mess afterwards Dönitz took no part in the general conversation. He was far away, lost in his own thoughts.'

Shortly afterwards the Grand Admiral decided that the time had come to take his leave and returned to his headquarters – a collection of timber barrack huts known as 'Koralle' in a pine wood outside Berlin.

On board what had once been the *Führer*'s luxury yacht *Grille* in Narvik harbour, the Christmas celebrations were similarly subdued. *Kapitän-zur-See* Peters was worried. To the west a strong storm centre was rapidly building up. The day before three out of four radar-equipped flying-boats had had to abort, two owing to technical faults and one because of wind and icing. The optimism of Christmas Eve was beginning to fade. Peters was very much in doubt whether the necessary reconnaissance could be carried out. At five in the morning he ordered his Operations Officer, *Kapitän-zur-See* Paul Friedrich Düwel, to get in touch with his opposite number at Schniewind's headquarters, *Kapitän-zur-See* Hans Marks.

'The *Luftwaffe* pilots are doing all they can to locate the probable enemy formation. . . . But so far they have not been able to provide us with a completely clear picture . . . yesterday's bearings may relate to the approaching covering force,' Düwel said.

Marks's reply was both chilly and to the point: 'The Naval High Command knows that.'

Düwel tried again: 'The precondition [for putting to sea] . . . has been a clear picture of the enemy's dispositions, which in turn presupposes positive identification. We do not have that. . . . A move on the part of the Battle Group will therefore be attended with great risk.'

'That is also our opinion. It is up to the Commander to decide whether this undeniable risk is to be run. His decision is not yet forthcoming.'

By this time the convoy was pitching and tossing midway between Jan Mayen and the North Cape on a course which would take it about 50 nautical miles south of Bear Island. In all probability it was on the *Duke of York* that the German D/F stations had obtained cross-bearings on Christmas Eve. Admiral Fraser had had a disturbing Christmas. Regular wireless signals from the Admiralty had kept him informed that the convoy had been sighted and was being shadowed by long-range aircraft. He knew that the U-boats of the *Eisenbart* Group had been stationed across the projected course of the convoy, but he did not know what he wanted to know most of all, that is, whether the *Scharnhorst* had put to sea. They were nerve-racking hours for the Admiral.

He was responsible for the fact that the convoy would soon be sailing a mere 200 nautical miles from the German naval base in the Lang fjord. He had, in effect, staked the lives of 1,000 seamen and 200,000 tons of valuable supplies on the success of his bold plan. If the German Battle Group were to sortie without his knowledge, there would be a bloodbath. But the die was cast, and Fraser's anxiety mounted.

As the day wore on he took a drastic decision. He broke wireless silence and ordered the convoy to turn about and steam south-west for three hours. Half an hour later he ordered the in-bound convoy, RA55A, to steam north, at the same time requesting that four additional destroyers be sent to support JW55B. He then increased the speed of his own vessels, Force 2, to 19 knots. 'Although German surface forces had never before made a sortie to the westward,' he wrote, 'the convoy . . . was entirely unsupported and I was uneasy lest a surface attack should be made.'

The Commander of JW55B's close escort, Captain J.A. McCoy on board the destroyer *Onslow*, was a tough and seasoned officer. Through gaps in the overcast he occasionally caught a glimpse of the aircraft shadowing the convoy. Although the German pilots took care to remain out of range of his guns, every so often McCoy would order the gun crews to fire a few rounds at them, though it was simply wasting ammunition. In any case he had other things to think about. The weather, already bad, was getting worse and the convoy was proving to be one of the most unmanageable he had ever had in his charge. Ships continually lost station and fell behind. Signals were misconstrued and before long the merchantmen were scattered all over the ocean. Fortunately the resourceful McCoy knew exactly what to do. He decided, 'I must disobey this order, as to turn such a convoy through 360° and keep it coherent was a manifest impossibility. I therefore took steps to comply with the C-in-C's wishes in spirit if not in letter.'

What McCoy did was to reduce the speed of the convoy from 10 to 8 knots, which had about the same effect as if it had completely reversed course. It was Christmas Eve. The ships continued to plough their way north-east in a heavy following sea. At half-past seven on Christmas Day morning McCoy signalled the Commodore of the convoy by Aldis lamp: 'Situation today. Enemy will probably attack us today with U-boat and possibly surface craft. Four more Home Fleet destroyers should join us P.M. today. *Duke of York* is about 100 miles astern coming up at 19 knots or more. Three heavy cruisers somewhere ahead. Happy Christmas.'

Only an hour later McCoy and his convoy passed over the submerged *U-601*. The Battle of the North Cape had begun.

IV

CHAPTER EIGHTEEN

The Naval College Simulator

OSLO, WINTER 2000

I first met Commander Marcus Einarsson Osen of the Royal Norwegian Navy when he came to me with a story from the island of Senja which still upsets a lot of people. It all happened on 12 April 1943, three weeks after the German Battle Group had dropped anchor in western Finnmark. Around noon that day, a grey-hulled submarine stole into the area surrounding the Svensgrunnen Shallows, some 20 nautical miles west of Månesodden Point. Thirty or so fishing boats were busy with their lines and nets when the submarine came gliding in like a dark shadow. The gun on the foredeck was manned and there were men leaning on the conning-tower coaming. Some of the fishermen held up cod to let the crew of the submarine know that fresh fish was available for the asking. No one felt any fear – until there came a loud report and a shell whistled over their heads. By then it was too late. With calculated brutality the gun crew blew three of the fishing boats out of the water at short range, then boarded a fourth. It was later found drifting, abandoned, in the And fjord. Nine fishermen were killed in the attack, seven wounded and a further seven taken prisoner.

The submarine was the Soviet *K 21* under the command of Lieutenant-Commander Nicolay Lunin, who could boast of a resounding victory over four unarmed civilian fishing boats. The people of Senja were deeply shocked and embittered by the heinousness of the crime, and, not surprisingly, the occupying Germans exploited the propaganda value of the Soviet submarine's 'dastardly outrage' for all it was worth.

Osen came from a prominent family on the island of Sandsøy in the And fjord and had grown up with the story of the tragedy. One of his contacts,

Bjørn Bratbak, had made a detailed investigation into the incident, and in the process made an intriguing discovery. It transpired that a few hours after the Soviet submarine had left the fishing ground, the Norwegian vessel *Baren* had rescued a young lad from drowning. He proved to be the submarine's messboy, who had fallen overboard and had been callously left to die. Angry at what had happened, many people wanted to have the lad, nineteen-year-old Alexander Labutin, shot on the spot, but the local parson managed to restrain them. Instead, the Russian was sent to a prison camp near Tromsø.

When Osen came to see me in the autumn of 1999, he told me something known to very few. Bratbak had discovered that Labutin had survived the war and was living in a small town about 100 kilometres outside Moscow. Plans were afoot to invite him as the Navy's guest to a war veterans' reunion in Tromsø in June 2000. Osen wished to know whether I would be willing to help ensure that Labutin's return would receive the media coverage it deserved, and also whether it would be possible to make a documentary about it. Without hesitation I said yes, and was instrumental in arranging for the Russian to meet his rescuers again, for the first time in fifty-seven years. It was a memorable and very moving experience to witness the way Labutin embraced and thanked the surviving members of the *Baren*'s crew and asked for forgiveness for the despicable conduct of his captain.

I availed myself of the opportunity thus offered to acquaint Osen with the trouble I was having in finding the wreck of the *Scharnhorst*. He immediately expressed an interest. In the letter I wrote to him after our first meeting, I summed up my findings and opinion in the following words:

Through our own investigations we have determined that the *Scharnhorst* does *not* lie where it is officially reported to lie, a position that has hitherto been universally accepted as gospel. What significance this divergency may have in assessing the battle from a purely military point of view I do not know, as we are still not quite sure of where the wreck actually is. In our opinion it will be a most interesting challenge to locate and film the wreck in its new and so far unknown position in the light of an analysis of the large volume of data we have assembled. Accordingly, I would ask whether the Navy would consider taking part in the project, in the first instance by going through the material we have, then by participating in the actual search for the wreck in the Barents Sea.

The Inspector-General of the Navy, Rear-Admiral Kjell Birger Olsen, approved the project, and Osen took steps to secure the services of his predecessor,

Rear-Admiral (Rtd) Kjell Amund Prytz, to advise on naval matters. He did me another important favour, too: he introduced me to Jarl Johnsen, head of the Defence Forces Research Institute's Department of Submarine Warfare in Horten, an establishment that knows as much as, if not more than, any similar body in Europe about what goes on, and what is to be found, on and beneath the surface of the Barents Sea.

Then sixty-five years of age, Prytz was one of the Norwegian Navy's most knowledgeable and respected officers. A most likeable man, he had served as a frigate captain and Commander of the Coastal Defence Squadron, and later as Naval Commander Southern Norway and Inspector-General of the Navy, so he was well acquainted with staff work and the corridors of power. In his day he had assumed overall responsibility for the loss of the frigate Oslo and never wavered in the storm that followed. Many of his associates looked upon him as the Navy's mild and mellow Grand Old Man. He was to prove indispensable to me and the success of my quest.

I began by showing him all the material I had. He immediately focused on the position reported in the *Duke of York*'s logbook at noon on 24 December 1943 – 7¾ hours before the *Scharnhorst* sank. 'I trust the battleship's navigators,' he said. 'They knew what they were doing. If they logged a position as a fix, it meant that they had at least two reliable sources to go on. We don't know what those sources were, but I would be very surprised if the ship's position at midday was much out. We're talking about traditions in the Royal Navy. You don't write in a ship's log that sights have been taken and a position calculated unless you have accurate information to go on.'

Prytz had a surprising suggestion to make. To test our theories he proposed that the Naval College's brand-new computer-controlled navigation simulator be pressed into service. It would enable us, so to speak, to refight the last eight hours of the battle in a world of virtual reality – and then to see where we found ourselves. The idea caught my imagination immediately and I lost no time in making my way to Bergen, where the simulator was housed in a circular concrete building in the grounds of the college. Inside the building is a mock-up of a modern ship's bridge with a 360-degree field of vision and equipped with all standard navigation and control systems. When, for example, the approach to Bergen harbour or other areas of the Norwegian coast are projected on to data screens, complete with ambient noise and lighting, the effect is dramatic to say the least. The sense of being on the bridge of a ship at sea is astonishingly real. But it is all an optical illusion created by the powerful STN Atlas computers of the simulator. The simulator provides naval cadets with a unique opportunity for

realistic training, but for us it wasn't quite so simple. As the man in charge of the simulator, Commander Kjetil Utne, and the navigation instructor, Commander Petter Lunde, explained to me, 'What we need to simulate is HMS *Duke of York*, as it is the only ship to have taken sights at 12 noon. After that we shall have to plot the relative position of the *Scharnhorst* at the time it was sunk. But don't forget that the simulator is a "calculator" that is capable of presenting its findings in a virtual world. If its calculations are to be correct, the data on which they are based must be reliable.'

The basic data had to be reliable: that was the core of the matter. My heart sank when I realized just what that meant. The task facing us was staggering. To construct a realistic mathematical model of a ship's movements at sea, 800 specific items of information would be needed, ranging from the length and breadth of the vessel through the number of rudders and propeller blades to the turning radius and rudder area. When it came to it, we were only able to find a part of the information we required. The *Duke of York* had been scrapped long ago and battleships were a thing of the past. Like the dinosaurs, they had gone for ever. The databases that were available contained only models of clean-lined modern vessels.

I was quite at a loss, but Utne and Lunde brought their creative talents to bear. They selected a model of a container ship and fed into it all the data we had at our disposal. Thanks to a great deal of hard work, both on their part and that of other members of the staff, on 3 May 2000 it became possible to virtually re-enact the Battle of the North Cape, though there were gaps in the premises on which the 'battle' was based.

We knew that it would not be possible to calculate an optimal course for the *Duke of York* without an optimal model. However, by using the container ship we would be able to calculate the effects of wind and current on a large vessel, though not on the battleship itself.

In the course of two exciting days we engaged in a virtual foray deep into the heart of the Barents Sea. The result took us completely by surprise. Four computations were made, one purely mathematical and three involving different wind and current strengths. It is true that in a south-westerly gale the model of the container ship was driven some 20 nautical miles too far north, but that was not the most interesting result. More significant was the fact that all four calculations suggested that the official position was too far east. That meant we needed to concentrate our search on an area further west, somewhere around the position stated in the logbook and where the torpedo had been found, and which the Findus trawler captains had suggested.

Prytz's own conclusion was quite clear: 'The British Mk 8 torpedo that was found in the vicinity of the position entered in the *Duke of York*'s log as that where the *Scharnhorst* went down is, in my opinion, that where she actually sank. A torpedo has a range of about 5 nautical miles, that is, 8,500 metres.'

I felt like laughing. We had spent hours gathered around one of Norway's most sophisticated computers to confirm that my amateur assessment might be right after all. But I was careful to suppress the urge. After all, a computer that costs 3,500 kroner (about £325) an hour to operate is no laughing matter.

Adolf Hitler, with a party including *Generalfeldmarschall* Werner von Blomberg and *Grossadmiral* Erich Raeder, at the launching of the *Scharnhorst* on 3 October 1936. (*Naval Historical Foundation 306-NT-99098*)

Scharnhorst seen bow-on, early 1939. (*Naval Historical Foundation NH102537*)

Scharnhorst was commissioned on 7 January 1939 and placed under the command of *Kapitän-zur-See* Otto Ciliax. (*Naval Historical Foundation NH97536*)

Scharnhorst and *Gneisenau* in port, 1939. (*Naval Historical Foundation, NH97537*)

Scharnhorst after she received her new 'clipper' bow in July–August 1939. (*Naval Historical Foundation NH97504*)

Scharnhorst underway in autumn 1939. (*Naval Historical Foundation NH101558*)

The view from *Scharnhorst's* forward superstructure, looking towards the bow, in wintry seas, 1939–40. Note ice accumulated on her triple 283mm gun turrets. (*Naval Historical Foundation NH102529*)

Scharnhorst in the ice of Kiel harbour, during the particularly severe winter of 1939–40. (*Naval Historical Foundation NH101560*)

Scharnhorst's forward guns coated with ice, winter 1939–40. (*Naval Historical Foundation NH102526*)

Icy decks on *Scharnhorst*, 1939–40. (*Naval Historical Foundation NH101561*)

Gneisenau, *Scharnhorst* and *Admiral Hipper* at a Norwegian port in April 1940. (*Naval Historical Foundation* NH82407)

Scharnhorst firing on British aircraft carrier *Glorious*, 8 June 1940. (*Naval Historical Foundation* NH83981)

Glorious turns away from an escort on the afternoon before she was sunk. The Carley floats which can be seen on her stern were painted in camouflage, making them difficult to spot from the air and thus leading to the deaths of many who survived the sinking.

Admiral Ciliax addresses German crews in Brest before the 'Channel dash'. (*Imperial War Museum HU2228*)

Gneisenau (closer) and *Scharnhorst* (further away) en route from Brest to Wilhelmshaven, 12 February 1942. (*Naval Historical Foundation NH69744*)

A reconnaissance photograph showing Kiel harbour in early 1942. *Scharnhorst* was undergoing repairs there after the 'Channel Dash' of February 1942. (*Naval Historical Foundation NH97506*)

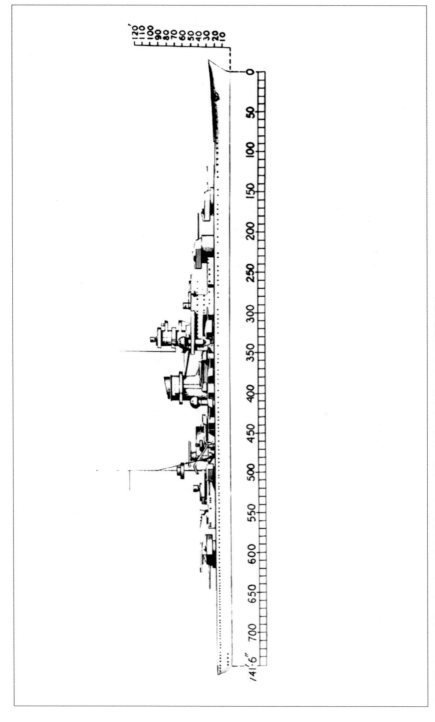

An Allied recognition drawing of the *Scharnhorst*. (*Naval Historical Foundation NH42204*)

Scene on *Gneisenau* with *Scharnhorst* in the distance. (*Naval Historical Foundation NH97538*)

Scharnhorst in the Alta fjord, Norway, 1943. (*Naval Historical Foundation NH71392*)

Matchless, *Musketeer* and *Mahratta* in an Atlantic gale. (*Imperial War Museum A20448*)

HMS *Jamaica* in 1942. (*Science & Society S1659*)

Survivors from *Scharnhorst* on board *Duke of York*. (*Imperial War Museum A21172*)

The victors, left to right: Captain The Honourable Guy Russell (*Duke of York*); Commander Lee Barber DSO (*Opportune*); Commander E.L. Fisher DSO (*Musketeer*); Commander Meyrick (*Savage*); Admiral Sir Bruce Fraser; Captain J. Hughes Hallett DSO (*Jamaica*); Lieutenant-Commander E.N. Walmsley DSC (*Saumarez*); Lieutenant-Commander Clouston (*Scorpion*) and Lieutenant Shaw (*Matchless*). (*Imperial War Museum A21164*)

The object picked out at a depth of 300 metres on the seabed by the multiple-beam echo sounder of the *H.U. Sverdrup II* at 72° 31'N 28° 15'E, a fractured 15- to 20-metre-high mound, 66 nautical miles north-east of the North Cape. The bulk of the hull is about 160 metres in length, the wrenched-off bow, which lies at an angle, some 60 to 70 metres. (*Author's Collection*)

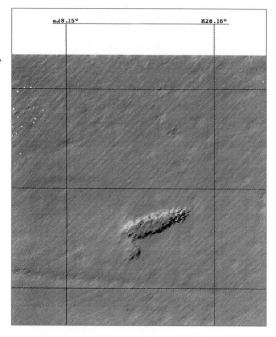

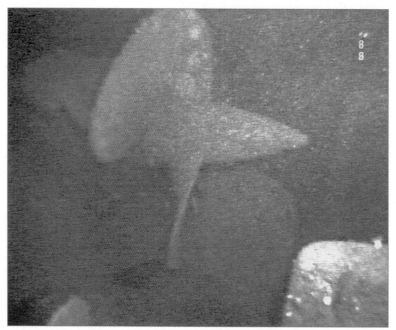

Above and overleaf: Underwater photographs of the *Scharnhorst* taken at a depth of 300 metres in 2000. Here the intact propeller is shown. (*Author's Collection*).

At least two torpedoes are stuck in the torpedo tubes. *Leutnant* Bosse made a desperate attempt to defend the *Scharnhorst* against attack from the destroyers. (*Author's Collection*).

The 10.5cm guns are still trained aft, indicating that they were never used against the destroyer. (*Author's Collection*)

CHAPTER NINETEEN

The Scharnhorst Puts to Sea

THE LANG FJORD, SATURDAY 25 DECEMBER 1943

It was noon on Christmas Day. Twelve hours had passed since *Generaladmiral* Schniewind had sent *Grossadmiral* Dönitz his draft order. Everything now hinged on Dönitz, but the Grand Admiral couldn't be reached: he was high above the blanket of clouds that covered the Continent. His comfortably appointed personal Ju 52 had taken off from Paris early that morning with the Grand Admiral and his staff on board.

An air of gravity hung over the discussions that took place in the cabin of the aircraft. German troops still stood firm from the Pyrenees in the south to the Fisker peninsula in the north. In the first years of the war Germany had been all-conquering. But Dönitz was a realist: the tide had turned, and in the east the Army had suffered one defeat after another. Unless the Soviet advance were halted, the Thousand-Year Reich would crumble and fall as quickly as it had arisen. As Commander-in-Chief of the *Kriegsmarine*, he was under obligation to use all the means at his disposal to avert a collapse. Consequently, as he saw it there could be no doubt about what he had to do. If he were not to lose face with Hitler, he would have to order the Battle Group to put to sea. He had procrastinated long enough; there was unlikely to be a better chance:

A convoy carrying war materials for Russia was sailing through an area that was well within range of the Battle Group. The convoy's cruiser escort would be no match for our battleship. The convoy's position, speed and course were known to us. The ice barrier off Bear Island would prevent the convoy from

making its escape. The superior speed of the German ships meant that it had no hope of evading an attack. Our air reconnaissance had not revealed the presence of an enemy force in the vicinity, though that did not mean, of course, that there *was* no such force at sea. But if there was, it would be a long way off and the *Scharnhorst* would have every chance of delivering a swift and successful attack. The twenty ships were carrying a very considerable quantity of war materials which would greatly increase the offensive capacity of the Soviet Union. Every available opportunity to prevent this had to be seized. In my own opinion, and that of the Fleet Commander and Naval Staff, this was an excellent opportunity for the *Scharnhorst*.

By the time the aircraft neared Berlin the decision had been taken. At 14.12 precisely the order was given, first by telephone, then by teleprinter: 'The Battle Group will go out in time to enable it to operate against the convoy.'

In Kiel, *Generaladmiral* Schniewind had been waiting for this dramatic decision for fifteen hours. He had already taken steps to have encrypted a suitable signal should things go the way he thought they would. Only some twenty minutes or so later, at 14.33, he was in a position to relay the order to *Kapitän-zur-See* Rudolf Peters in Narvik in the shape of a concise and fateful signal: '*OSTFRONT* 25/12.' Although the signal ratings on board the Commander's yacht in Narvik harbour used the standard Enigma cipher and not the more complex *M-Offizier* key, a whole hour was to elapse before the order reached the *Tirpitz*, whence, at 15.27, it was retransmitted to the *Scharnhorst* and her attendant destroyers in the Lang fjord, though this time with an important addition, so that it read: '*OSTFRONT* 1700/25/12.'

'This means that the Battle Group has been ordered to operate against the convoy. Here we go!' wrote *Kapitän-zur-See* Johannesson excitedly in the war diary when he received the signal a few minutes later.

Despite the senior officers' lingering doubts and prolonged discussions, the German planners had been busy since early that morning. Already at 07.00 the minesweeper *R 121* had left Tromsø with three pilots on board; it would be their task to take the Battle Group safely through the fjord and out into the open sea. As soon as the minesweeper reached the Kå fjord, it was ordered to continue to the Lang fjord, where the pilots were transferred to the *Scharnhorst* and to the destroyers *Z 33* and *Z 29*. At 12.30 two more minesweepers, *R 56* and *R 58*, were despatched from Hammerfest to the Lang fjord, where, four hours later, they lay to alongside the *Scharnhorst*.

The Captain of *R 58*, Werner Hauss, has left an eye-witness account of the scene:

It's like a millpond here at the head of the fjord after the violent squalls and raging seas further out. The destroyers are as carefully blacked out as the *Scharnhorst*. There is not a gleam of light to be seen, not a sound to be heard, only the faint soughing of the wind. Every now and then a few bluish-violet, ghostlike flashes of light can be glimpsed on the bridge of the battleship when a shaded Morse lamp flashes a signal to the destroyers. There is something spectral about the silence. High above the oppressive mountains, snow-covered and barren, the Northern Lights flicker against the star-spangled sky and contribute to the eerieness of the setting.

The two minesweeper captains, Hauss and Maclot, had been instructed to report to *Kapitän-zur-See* Fritz Julius Hintze and were taken over to the battlecruiser:

We are led through a confusing maze of passageways, watertight doors, companionways, cabins, workshops, telephones, cables, pipes, lower decks and messes. . . . There is feverish activity everywhere. . . . The ship is like an anthill that has been disturbed, with men scurrying about as though in a hundred-metres sprint, up and down ladders, back and forth through the passageways, as though ten seconds are all they have left.

After a long walk through stifling, narrow passages the two young officers finally reached the Captain's cabin.

The lieutenant knocks and opens the door. . . . We exchange a stolen glance. This is regal luxury compared with what the captain of a humble minesweeper is accustomed to. We salute, then step discreetly to the rear. A lot seems to be going on at the same time. . . . The Captain, his Second-in-Command, [*Fregattenkapitän*] Dominik and the Chief Engineer, König, are standing talking together beside the desk. The Adjutant stands next to him, a wireless signal in his hand. The Commander is clearly issuing instructions to the Chief Engineer. . . . We prick up our ears to catch his last words: 'We must speed things up. We must be ready to sail at 18.00!' . . . I suddenly become aware of the roomy, comfortable armchairs in the cabin, the paintings on the bulkheads, framed photographs on the desk – and a bowl of Christmas goodies. 'Of course,' I think, 'it's Christmas Day.' I would have forgotten had I not caught sight of all those apples and raisins, nuts and cakes, and the chocolates, pine branches and tinsel. The sight brings back memories and I lose myself in reverie.

Born in Gieboldehausen, 38-year-old *Fregattenkapitän* Ernst-Dietrich Dominik, second in order of seniority of the officers present, was a meticulous professional seaman. In 1924, as a cadet, he had undergone gunnery training and served on board the cruiser *Emden*; he was posted to the newly commissioned *Scharnhorst* in January 1939. Few knew the ship better than Dominik. He had been with her from the outset and had been in command of both the light and heavy armaments until, in the winter of 1943, he was made First Officer and became the Commander's right-hand-man. Dominik was a fighting sailor to the core. After four years' service at sea he had been appointed to a new position at Naval Headquarters in Berlin on 1 October 1943. But his replacement had not yet reached the Lang fjord, so Dominik was still on board.

His son, *Fregattenkapitän* Wulf Dominik, who made a career in the *Bundesmarine* after the war, says: 'A letter from my father reached my mother, who was living with her parents in Nordheim, near Hanover, at the time. In it he wrote: "I am thinking of my Fatherland. May God give us strength so that, with our proud ship, we may contribute to a victorious conclusion of this war." The letter was intuitively written as a last testament. I think the wording was typical of the spirit that imbued the entire ship's company.'

When Maclot and Hauss received their final orders from Dominik, he was in a hurry. There was a very good reason. The *Scharnhorst* had been at an hour's readiness since twelve that morning and had long had steam up; the same applied to the destroyers. But *Konter-Admiral* Bey was in the Kå fjord. Without the Squadron Commander the Battle Group could not leave the fjord. '*Admirals Nordmeer* ordered departure at 17.00. It is absolutely impossible. Bey has still not reached the flagship,' wrote the Commander of the destroyer flotilla, Rolf Johannesson, in the war diary.

Every minute was now vital. If an attack were to have the slightest chance of success, the Battle Group would need to be in position south of Bear Island next morning. But in the Kå fjord, almost imperceptibly, things had already begun to go wrong for the reluctant admiral. Bey had embarked on *Korvettenkapitän* Karl Lampe's *Z 30* with his staff of thirty-six from the *Tirpitz* at 14.00, but it was not until an hour later that the destroyer slipped her moorings from the supply ship *Nordmark*. Sudden showers and squalls made it difficult to open the boom that protected the entrance to the Kå fjord, and the tug sent to do the job was delayed. It was almost 16.00 when *Z 30* finally cleared the mouth of the Alta fjord and headed for Isnestoften – still at a leisurely 21 knots. Even when, at 18.15, Bey finally boarded the *Scharnhorst*, the battlecruiser stayed put.

'The destroyers have their engines running, but nothing is happening. I am very sorry that there is no exchange of views with the Squadron Commander,' wrote Johannesson with growing irritation. The fact was that on board the *Scharnhorst* a new, and acute, problem had arisen: the ship's radar warning system, which was crucial to any operation, was out of order. As a stopgap, *Korvettenkapitän* Gerfried Brutzer was ordered to hand over Z 38's radar detector to the battlecruiser, an operation that took three-quarters of an hour to complete.

Finally, at 19.01, the signal lamps on the *Scharnhorst*'s bridge flashed out 'weigh anchor'. Shortly afterwards a sloop slid alongside Johannesson's destroyer, Z 29. An officer came on board, bringing with him Bey's order for the attack, a two-page document that had clearly been dictated by a man badly pressed for time. Several typing errors had been corrected by hand. Not long afterwards another motorboat came put-putting into the fjord. On board was Petty Officer Wilhelm Gödde and a party of torpedo ratings who had been stationed as an extra guard at the anti-submarine net, depth-charges at the ready. Sub-Lieutenants Hauss and Maclot had each received personal instructions from Dominik and had long since left the flagship. Their job was to clear a channel for the squadron through Stjern Sound, and all they were waiting for was the order to set about their task.

From the bridge of the *Scharnhorst* the order is given by loudhailer to cast off. The crews of R 56 and R 58 spring to their stations and the two young captains are on their bridges in no time. Two shrill blasts of the boatswains' pipes and the moorings are quickly cast off, hauled in and coiled. The men know their business. Like phantoms, the two minesweepers draw slowly away, heave to and remain stationary, waiting.

In the dark, two small tugs had appeared from nowhere. 'The fjord is narrow at this point and the battleship is lying across it with her bow into the wind, so that the tugs have to turn her through an angle of 90 degrees before she can proceed under her own steam to the gap in the net at the mouth of the fjord.'

While the men of the starboard watch were bringing in the anchor and moorings, the rest of the *Scharnhorst*'s company assembled on the afterdeck.

The men on the lower decks, the officers in their cabins and messes, as one they hasten aft. . . . A tall, slim figure comes into view on the after armoured tower, *Fregattenkapitän* Dominik. He has served on board from the day the ship was commissioned. He is an experienced gunnery officer, and was in command

of the anti-aircraft guns and heavy batteries before being promoted to Second-in-Command. A stalwart, serious man who, during his long term of service on board, has proved that the welfare of the men is close to his heart.

The Chief Petty Officer handed the ship's company over to Dominik, who then mounted the dais. He gave a brief summary of the situation, concluding with the following words: 'A convoy is on its way with supplies for the Eastern front. Our task is to annihilate that convoy.'

Ten months had passed since the *Scharnhorst* and her escorts had entered the Lang fjord. For some weeks rumour had been rife, especially in the last few days. The ships had been held in a heightened state of readiness, and several times had got up steam. Only now, however, had matters come to a head.

The words are hardly out of his mouth before the men go wild. The sound of spontaneous cheering is borne across the fjord, and in their enthusiasm some ratings cast discipline aside and carry the ship's Second-in-Command triumphantly forward on their shoulders. They then hurry off to their action stations. Three minutes later, in record time, all are in their places. . . .

Stoker Feifer, who survived, recalls that moment:

With hindsight it may be hard to understand such a response. But we had been waiting for months. Anything was better than remaining where we were. We had complete confidence in the ship and our officers. Nothing could go wrong. Most of the men expected to be back within a couple of days, to continue the Christmas celebrations.

But Helmut Backhaus, a signaller who was soon to climb to the foretop, had a strange premonition. 'As I put on my winter clothing, I saw my identity disc hanging on the peg. I had never put it on before. Now I hung it round my neck.'

On board *R 56* and *R 58* Maclot and Hauss were still awaiting new orders.

Slowly the two tugs start to turn the giant steel hull, one at her bow, the other at her stern. The engine-room telegraph rings again, the tugs cast off the towing hawsers, the battlecruiser's propellers churn the water. . . . Little by little the battleship swings to port and heads out of the fjord. . . . The men on the bridges watch in silence, overawed by the spectacle. Gradually the long, graceful ship picks up speed and glides silently past them, not a light showing: a sleek, dangerous predator stealing forth from its mountain lair in search of prey.

Destroyer *Z 38* stationed herself 1,200 metres ahead of the *Scharnhorst* as the two ships sailed towards the boom, the other four accompanying vessels following in her wake. Not until 20.37, more than three-and-a-half hours late, did the *Scharnhorst* pass the anti-submarine net at the head of the fjord, round Klubbenes Point and set a course westwards through Stjern Sound, bound for the open sea. Speed was increased to 25 knots. In the sound the squadron came up against the full force of the gale that was blowing. The wind came howling down from the mountains round about, buffeting masts and rigging. The battlecruiser's foredeck disappeared beneath the towering masses of water until her clipper bow shook itself free, to cleave its way through the next wave. No one seemed to spare a thought for the two minesweepers, which, with a top speed of only 16 knots, lagged further and further astern. The eyes of Werner Hauss on board *R 58* were glued to his binoculars, but there was nothing to be seen. 'The six dark shapes I had just been able to make out against the blackness of the mountains only a short time ago were gone for good.'

Hauss was not the only one to observe the squadron's precipitate departure. High up on the mountainside, on the eastern shore of the Lang fjord, Johan Digre and his family were enjoying their Christmas dinner. Digre was one of the Ida Group's contacts, so it was only to be expected that, commanding as he did a panoramic view of the mouth of the fjord, he should have followed the afternoon's traffic through the boom in both directions with more than casual interest. His son, Per, who was ten at the time, recalls what happened. 'I remember that we were all gathered outside the house when we suddenly saw the *Scharnhorst* glide by, a black shadow against the mountains on the far side. It was travelling at high speed – its bow wave was so strong, in fact, that we had to send people down to the shore to rescue our rowing-boat. Next day we found Christmas trees floating in the fjord; they had been dumped overboard.'

When Johan Digre phoned his contact in the Kå fjord, Harry Pettersen, ostensibly to wish him a happy Christmas, he used an agreed code. 'I shall be home at Christmas, but Grandma has just gone away on holiday.' Pettersen knew immediately what Digre was saying. 'Grandma' was the codename used by the Ida Group to denote the *Scharnhorst*. He recalled: 'I got in touch with Torstein Råby and Karl Rasmussen, who were spending Christmas in the Tverrelv valley. It was they who operated the transmitter hidden beneath the floor of the Highways Department hut.'

Sigrid Rasmussen, by then heavily pregnant, opened the door to the messenger. 'There was a man outside from the neighbouring farm. He said that there was a telephone call for Kalle and his friend Torstein. My father was angry when they made their excuses and left the table. But the *Scharnhorst* had gone out. They couldn't say that they had to try to get a wireless message to London.'

In the meantime, to the north in the Barents Sea, the weather had gone from bad to worse. Since the convoy had passed over *U 601* at about half-past eight that morning, Otto Hansen had made several desperate attempts to maintain contact with it. But a Force 8 south-westerly gale was blowing, accompanied by rain and snow showers, and the U-boat was tossing and pitching wildly. 'There is a heavy sea running, visibility is down to 100 metres, and the conning-tower is continually under water,' Hansen wrote.

For the men on watch in the conning-tower it was an exhausting morning.

It is pitch-dark. 'Look out!' cries the officer of the watch. The boat heels badly. We cling on for all we're worth. A wave comes racing over us, cold seawater washes over our faces and shoulders, taking our breath away and pouring into the tower. . . . We are surrounded by a sea that in its ferocity is beautiful to behold. . . . The boat cleaves its way through a succession of waves whose crests tower 8 to 10 metres above us. . . . From the conning-tower it is an awesome sight. Rolling black mountains of glistening water. . . . Ragged clouds scud across the sky. In the few seconds available to us we scan the horizon through our binoculars. We are here to search for enemy ships. . . . Again the bow plunges deeply into a wave. The next wave is a big one. Its crest is edged with white. It breaks against the conning-tower with a crash like that of a goods train trundling across a railway bridge. The spume lashes our faces. It is as though someone has thrown a handful of grit at us. For several minutes we can't see a thing. The salt water stings.

From the conning-tower Otto Hansen's lookouts could just discern the dark outlines of the merchantmen ahead of them. At 11.02 he reported: 'A DESTROYER AND A NUMBER OF SHAPES 90 DEGREES TRUE', and at 12.26: 'MORE MERCHANTMEN AND A LARGE DESTROYER WITH TWO FUNNELS.' Hansen kept *Kapitän-zur-See* Peters in Narvik continually informed of developments. But it was a dangerous pursuit in which he was engaged. The destroyers were part of the convoy's close escort: they were monitoring the German wireless traffic and knew that the *Eisenbart* Group was close by. Men stood ready to drop depth-charges.

Half an hour later, at 14.08, the U-boat's lookouts spotted a destroyer only 500 metres distant. The alarm was sounded and *U-601* crash-dived. After another half an hour, at 14.36, Hansen again ventured to the surface to find the storm still raging with undiminished force. But the sea was empty: the convoy had vanished to the east.

A few nautical miles away from *U-601* another newly commissioned U-boat, *U-716*, was likewise battling against the elements. Like Otto Hansen, *Oberleutnant-zur-See* Hans Dunkelberg from Mülheim in the Ruhr was only twenty-five. He had assumed command of the U-boat in April and reached Bergen in mid-December after five months' training in the Baltic. A few days later he had been sent to join the *Eisenbart* Group's other U-boats manning the cordon off Bear Island. Now he and his crew were about to fire their first shot in anger.

'The weather was appalling. But Dunkelberg was a good skipper, cool-headed, steady as a rock and held in high esteem by his men. We were in a shipyard in Hamburg having some repairs done just after the firestorm at the turn of the month July/August. It affected us all. After seeing such terrible destruction it was difficult to believe that the war could still be won,' said *U-716*'s wireless operator, Peder Junker.

The U-boat was to the south of *U-601* when, round about ten o'clock on Christmas morning, it picked up Otto Hansen's report of having sighted the convoy. While the wireless operator struggled to get a fix, Dunkelberg crossed to the north-east with the wind and rain coming in from astern. After enduring five hours of violent pitching and tossing, at 14.58 the lookouts caught sight in the murk of an escorting destroyer some distance ahead. Dunkelberg immediately sounded the alarm and turned the U-boat around. At a range of about 3,000 metres he carried out his first act of war as captain of his own vessel. He fired a T5 Gnat homing torpedo at the destroyer. It was the opening shot of the Battle of the North Cape. After briefly reporting what he had done, he dived deep, while the hydrophone operator waited tensely for the sound of a report. But there was none. Dunkelberg had been over-optimistic. With waves 8 to 10 metres in height, it was almost impossible to hit a destroyer that was approaching head-on.

In the war diary Dunkelberg commented: 'Am being run over by a destroyer. Because of the rough sea a miss was only to be expected. Now the throb of engines and turbines is audible at varying distances. The sounds are all fading away to the east.'

When, at about five o'clock that afternoon, *Generaladmiral* Schniewind received a copy of the wireless signal, he noted with satisfaction: 'Boat No. 2 is

in contact with the convoy. The reported position accords well with the last signal from *U-601*.'

Dunkelberg resurfaced shortly afterwards, but by then he was alone in the raging sea. Worse, the U-boat's sensitive *Gruppenhorchgerät* (GHG) sonar had broken down, with the consequence that her ability to detect sounds when submerged was greatly reduced.

Meanwhile, Otto Hansen on board *U-601* had again caught up with the convoy. At 16.36 he was almost rammed by a corvette which unexpectedly appeared only 300 metres away. Again he was forced to crash-dive. The men waited anxiously for the depth-charges they knew were bound to come, but nothing happened. Because of the wind and darkness, the corvette hadn't seen them.

North of *U-601* a third *Eisenbart* U-boat was in trouble. Her skipper was *Kapitänleutnant* Hildebrandt, whose birthday was on Christmas Eve; he had celebrated his thirty-second birthday south-west of Bear Island the previous day. In common with the other Arctic veterans, he preferred to listen for the enemy under water rather than when dangerously exposed on the surface. In the war diary he wrote: 'We know from experience that it pays to stay submerged at night, as 1) visibility is largely poor anyway because of the heavy sea, 2) sounds can be heard at a distance of 8–10 nautical miles, which is twice as far as one can see, and 3) there is less danger of being surprised by an escort vessel attacking out of the dark horizon.' These were sound reasons, but they made the U-boat Commander in Narvik, *Kapitän-zur-See* Peters, fume. 'Remaining submerged is a decided advantage when listening conditions are favourable,' he wrote, '[but] not in heavy seas. One is blind in any case. Diving deep is the right thing to do only if attack is imminent. Under water captains lose the urge to: Listen! Observe! Attack!'

It was a stinging comment. Despite his long service and the fact that he had two sinkings to his credit in the Arctic, it was clear that Hildebrandt was not liked by Peters. Now, at noon on Christmas Day, he dived to listen for the convoy. There was nothing to be heard. When he resurfaced just over half an hour later, he found that Otto Hansen's D/F signals were coming in loud and clear. 'The strength of the signals suggests that we are very close,' Hildebrandt noted. Shortly afterwards disaster overtook them. The U-boat was engaged in changing course when a heavy wave broke over the conning-tower. Tons of ice-cold seawater poured in through the open hatch and the air intake of the diesel engine. The U-boat listed heavily, the engine stopped and chlorine gas began to filter out from the batteries. Within a few minutes *U-636* was rolling helplessly out of control. Eventually the engine was restarted and Hildebrandt was able to turn into the wind. It was in the nick of time. The U-boat had shipped 15 tons of water and the men on board were already beginning to suffer from the effects of the gas. At 14.50 Hildebrandt wirelessed to Narvik: 'BECAUSE OF THE PRESENCE OF A LOT OF CHLORINE GAS AM ONLY JUST ABLE TO DIVE. AM BREAKING OFF. HAMMERFEST.'

After airing the boat for three hours, Hildebrandt again gave the order to dive. As the tanks were still filling he and the rest of the crew heard the unmistakable sound of surface ships. It was the convoy, passing directly overhead. Not until 22.00, by which time the lingering fumes were becoming unbearable, did Hildebrandt dare to resurface and send the following signal: 'AT 18.00–19.20 IN AB6496 RUN OVER BY EIGHT CARGO VESSELS AND THREE ESCORTS. EASTERLY COURSE, 70 RPM. NO CONTACT. POOR LISTENING CONDITIONS. VISIBILITY 800 METRES.'

He received no acknowledgement; nor did he take the precaution of repeating his signal. For that reason it failed to reach both the Battle Group and *Kapitän-zur-See* Peters in Narvik, who was following developments with increasing anxiety. Peters knew that some of the U-boats off Bear Island were right in the path of the convoy. But in the course of only a few hours in the morning the depression had developed with extraordinary speed. The icy wind whipped the sea into a raging cauldron and the U-boats were tossed about like corks. Their targets were nothing but dark shapes sporadically glimpsed amid the mountainous waves, rendering it virtually impossible to bring their torpedo tubes to bear. Then came the forecast for St Stephen's Day and it was anything but encouraging. The wind was expected to increase to a Force 9 gale and heavy seas and snow showers were coming in from the south-west. At about four in the afternoon the *Luftwaffe* had already recalled the last of the reconnaissance planes that were shadowing the convoy, as icing was becoming a serious problem. It was planned to despatch six aircraft at dawn next day, 26 December, but if the storm continued to rage with unabated fury all reconnaissance flights would have to be scrubbed and there would be no chance of finding a lurking enemy covering force. This would mean that the premise on which a successful attack by the *Scharnhorst* rested would no longer be valid.

Like the other German admirals, in the last few days Peters had alternated between hope and despair, torn between his sense of duty and a sober assessment of the risks involved, between the urge to fight and fear of another defeat. The senior officers knew better than anyone how badly weakened was the *Kriegsmarine*'s fighting capacity. But they were professionals: they were determined to carry the fight to the enemy if only an opportunity were to

present itself. On the other hand they could not send their ships and the men who manned them to certain destruction. An attack could only succeed if the circumstances under which it was carried out were exploited to the full and a clash with the enemy's totally superior forces avoided. As both U-boat Commander and acting Admiral in command of the surface forces, Peters bore a heavy responsibilty. He had intervened shortly before Christmas when Bey appeared to be vacillating, and he felt it was his duty to step in once again, before it was too late. His assessment of the situation in the war diary of *Admirals Nordmeer*, penned late in the afternoon of Christmas Day 1943, left no room for doubt as to his feelings.

> Air reconnaissance of the flanks has to be ruled out. No one knows where the enemy covering force, if it exists, is. The weather has deteriorated faster than had been foreseen, with the consequence that both the speed of the German ships and their firepower will be badly curtailed. The U-boats are unable to keep up with the convoy, so it will not be possible to direct the Battle Group to the target. The element of surprise will have been lost. Instead, it must be assumed that the *Scharnhorst* and her escorting destroyers will find themselves doing battle against the enemy's superior covering force instead of the convoy's weaker escort.

Peters's conclusion was dramatic: the operation would have to be called off. He was, however, careful to cover himself politically by adding the rider, 'I cannot, of course, say whether the general situation demands that an operation be mounted even so'.

At about eight that evening Peters picked up the phone and rang Schniewind in Kiel. 'The destroyers haven't a chance in weather like this. *Fliegerführer* Lofoten reports that there will be no improvement tomorrow. It will not be possible to detect a hostile force in time. I propose that "Operation *Ostfront*" be cancelled.'

Reluctantly, Schniewind had to concur. He phoned Berlin, and at 20.46 set out his reasoning in a teleprinter message at about the same time as the *Scharnhorst* and 4th Destroyer Flotilla met the storm in Stjern Sound. 'CONDITIONS ARE VERY UNFAVOURABLE. SIGNIFICANT RESULTS CANNOT BE EXPECTED. THEREFORE PROPOSE CANCELLATION.'

Half an hour later, at 21.16, Bey put his own oar in. From the bridge of the *Scharnhorst* he elected to break wireless silence: 'IN THE AREA OF OPERATION A 6 TO 9 SOUTH-WESTERLY IS FORECAST. THE DESTROYERS' ABILITY TO BRING THEIR ARMAMENT TO BEAR GREATLY HAMPERED. SPEED REDUCED.'

At the time the *Scharnhorst* and her five escorting destroyers had Sildmylingen Point to port and the mountains of Sørøya Island and the storm-lashed Sørøy Sound to starboard. Ahead of them lay Lopphavet, a treacherous expanse of sea notorious for the fury of the storms that beset it. There the German ships had no protection: the south-westerly gale came howling in from the open ocean with nothing to break its force. Wind and wave collided head-on with local currents, lashing the already choppy water into a boiling cauldron. It was then, at the very moment he emerged into the savage waters of the Arctic Ocean, that it seems to have been brought home to *Konter-Admiral* Bey that 'Operation *Ostfront*' was a hazardous venture that offered little chance of success. The signal he sent from Sørøy Sound was thus in the nature of a plea for help.

The admirals in Kiel and Berlin were already aware that the storm and darkness had combined to diminish the battlecruiser's fighting capacity. When they learned that the destroyers too were fighting a losing battle against the elements, the conclusion was obvious: the operation would have to be called off.

But wireless communication was extremely poor. Because of this, Bey's signal did not reach Berlin until 03.56 the next morning, by which time he had nearly reached the area of operation. Moreover, in Berlin attitudes had hardened. Dönitz was not prepared to recall the Battle Group. He had personally promised Hitler results. He had staked his reputation on retaining the big surface ships; now it was up to Bey to act with resolution and vigour.

On board the *Duke of York*, battering her way at 19 knots towards Bear Island, the atmosphere was more restrained. While Schniewind, Peters and Bey were waiting for Dönitz's final answer, a new Ultra decrypt reached Fraser. It told him that at about twelve that morning Bey had tried to contact the minesweeper *R 121*, which was on its way from Tromsø to the Kå fjord with a party of pilots on board. The signal ordered *R 121* to join the *Scharnhorst* in the Lang fjord, where she was to await further orders.

Fraser still did not know for certain that the battlecruiser had left the safety of the fjord, but the probability that she had seemed greater than ever before.

CHAPTER TWENTY

'I have confidence in your will to fight'

THE BARENTS SEA, SUNDAY, 26 DECEMBER 1943

Punkt Lucie (Point Lucie) was a navigational reference point on the secret XI)
German charts some 15 nautical miles south-west of Fuglen, a precipitous
headland on the seaward side of the island of Sørøya. It marked the boundary
between the German minefields and the open sea. It was also where the
Scharnhorst and her five escorting destroyers caught their last glimpse of land, a
chain of jagged, snow-clad peaks just discernible on the horizon. As soon as it
had passed this vital point at 23.03, the squadron set a course of 010 degrees
due north, at a speed of 25 knots. With wind and sea now coming from astern,
life on board became a little easier. However, with their twin 60-ton forward
turrets, some of the destroyers continued to yaw violently, though their
foredecks and superstructures no longer shipped the tons of water that had
previously been such an encumbrance.

At midnight *Grossadmiral* Dönitz's answer came in. It had been encrypted in
the complicated *M-Offizier* cipher and for that reason a whole hour elapsed
before the Signals Officer could take the decrypt to *Konter-Admiral* Bey's cabin.
It was not the answer Bey had hoped for:

By means of a convoy carrying supplies and munitions to the Russians the
enemy will render the heroic struggle of our army in the east still more
difficult. We must help.

Attack the convoy with *Scharnhorst* and destroyers.

Exploit the tactical situation wisely and boldly. Do not break off the battle with the job half done. Utilize every advantage. [Your] greatest advantage lies in *Scharnhorst*'s superior armament. Her contribution is therefore all-important. Deploy the destroyers as you see fit.

Disengage if you judge that the situation so demands. Break off automatically if heavy [enemy] forces are met with.

Instil this spirit in the ship's company. I have confidence in your will to fight.

Heil Hitler! Dönitz, *Grossadmiral*.

The only concession the German Naval High Command was prepared to make followed in a second signal at 03.00. It stated that if the destroyers were unable to cope with the gale that was blowing, the *Scharnhorst* should attack alone. The decision was Bey's: he was on the spot; the responsibility was his.

Berlin had spoken. Now there was no going back. But the squadron had put to sea in haste, badly delayed. Bey had not even found time to confer with his captains. On the windswept bridge of *Z 29* the Flotilla Commander, *Kapitän-zur-See* Rolf Johannesson, followed the exchange of wireless signals between the flagship and Naval Headquarters in Germany with growing trepidation. In his operation order Bey had expressly laid down that the convoy should be annihilated by the combined efforts of the whole Battle Group. The presence had to be taken into account of 'all kinds of British and American battleships, aircraft-carriers and cruisers'. Despite this, the operation was *not* to be called off even if a concerted attack were to prove out of the question. Instead, the Battle Group was under orders to withdraw pending a renewed opportunity the next morning. It was all very difficult to comprehend. The *Scharnhorst*'s only chance lay in a lightning attack; that was the premise on which all the operational planning rested. What made Bey think that he could survive yet another day in the vicinity of Bear Island if he really believed that there were Allied battleships and aircraft-carriers near the convoy?

In the course of only two hours after midnight the barometer on board *Z 29* fell from 997 to 991 millibars. The Battle Group was approaching the storm centre and many of the men were suffering from seasickness. From the *Scharnhorst* dead ahead a signal lamp began to wink: Bey wished to know Johannesson's opinion of the weather. The Destroyer Commander elected to send an optimistic reply: 'WITH SEA AND WIND FROM ASTERN WE HAVE HAD NO DIFFICULTIES SO FAR. . . . I EXPECT THE WEATHER TO IMPROVE.'

Afterwards, Johannesson wrote: 'I was not willing to provide Bey with an excuse to send us back to base, as long as the British destroyers were coping with the weather.'

By this time the *Scharnhorst* and her five accompanying destroyers were midway between the North Cape and Bear Island.

Blacked out and with the men at action stations, the battleship rolls and lurches northwards with the south-westerly gale coming in on the port quarter. . . . The sky is black, with not a star to be seen, as black as the sea. Visibility is hindered by snow showers, so much so that the destroyers are hardly discernible. Now and again an extra-powerful wave builds up ahead, the spindrift hovering in the air for a second or two before the sea floods in over the foredeck, burying it beneath a torrent of water. . . . The night is icy cold, and ice-cold too is the spume that comes flying right up on to the bridge from the forward triple turret every time a wave crashes against it.

No one knows what *Konter-Admiral* Bey, *Kapitän-zur-See* Hintze and their closest associates talked about at this time. Only the bare bones of Kummetz's original staff were still on board. The Operations Officer, *Kapitän-zur-See* Hansjürgen Reinicke, a highly experienced captain, and his deputy, *Kapitän-zur-See* Fritz-Günther Boldmann, had returned to Germany with Kummetz and had not been replaced. Bey had brought with him his Flag Lieutenant, Kuno Lattorf, and a couple of destroyer staff officers. The rest of his staff were transferred from the *Tirpitz*, among them the young writer Heinrich Mulch.

The long days of waiting and the prolonged discussions that followed had been very exhausting, but now the die was cast. All that remained was the forthcoming battle. All concerned may have felt the same sense of relief as Rolf Johannesson on board Z 29 when he wrote in the war diary: 'Now the course of events is clear. We know what lies before us.'

At a 03.45, just before the watches were due to be changed, the broadcasting system on board the *Scharnhorst* crackled into life. It was Captain Hintze, who was about to pass on the Grand Admiral's exhortation to his men: 'Attention ship's company. This is your Commanding Officer. We have received a wireless signal from *Grossadmiral* Dönitz. "Annihilate the convoy where you find it. You will be relieving [pressure on] the eastern front."'

At the Admiralty in London, at about the same time, 02.17, Lieutenant-Commander Denning was issuing his first direct warning to Forces 1 and 2 that

the *Scharnhorst* had put to sea: 'EMERGENCY. *SCHARNHORST* PROBABLY SAILED 6 P.M. 25TH DECEMBER.'

It had taken the codebreakers at Bletchley Park a good seven hours to decrypt the signal '*OSTFRONT* 1700/25/12' sent to *Konter-Admiral* Bey. One minute later Denning despatched a further signal to say that the *Scharnhorst* had warned a patrol boat at the mouth of the Lang fjord that she would be passing through the boom some time after 18.00.

The final warning signal went out to all Allied ships in the area between Bear Island and the North Cape one hour later, at 03.39: 'ADMIRALTY APPRECIATES THAT *SCHARNHORST* IS AT SEA.'

The nineteen ships that made up convoy JW55B were by this time pitching and rolling eastwards 50 nautical miles due south of Bear Island. The *Duke of York* and Force 2 were more than 200 nautical miles to the west. For Fraser, the situation was far from ideal. He ordered his ships to increase speed to 24 knots, with the option of going even faster. But he was still ten to twelve hours away from his point of interception should the *Scharnhorst* attack the convoy. For safety's sake he ordered JW55B to turn due north to lure the German battlecruiser as far away from the coast as possible; while from the east Burnett and Force 1 were drawing closer with every hour that passed. The trap was in process of being set.

At dawn, which in the Arctic was no more than a grey half-light, the ships' companies were informed of what was afoot. Commander Nils Owren, Gunnery Officer of the Norwegian destroyer *Stord*, described the tense atmosphere on board:

On the *Stord* we follow the signal traffic and deployments with keen interest. Things are hotting up! Everyone is a part of it. This time something will happen, we all feel that. . . . The gale is still increasing in intensity, the sea and excitement similarly rising. The *Stord* lurches violently and the waves wash across her deck. In this atrocious weather we are ordered to increase speed, first to 25 knots, then to 27 knots. Every turn of the screw takes us closer to the enemy.

Lieutenant Bryce Ramsden on board the cruiser *Jamaica*, which was stationed due north of the *Stord*, remembers when he heard the news that the *Scharnhorst* had put to sea. It was broadcast as watches were changing and the hands were having breakfast:

'D'you hear there? This is the Commander speaking. We have just received a signal from C-in-C. The *Scharnhorst* is at sea. Hands will be piped to action stations in five minutes' time. That is all.'

For a second my heart stopped beating, and I tried to digest it. The *Scharnhorst* is at sea. The *Scharnhorst* is at sea. Then it had happened at last. No one said anything much, except for a momentary exclamation at the news. It was too big a thing, this sudden realization of weeks, months of sea-time covering convoys, cruisers plodding away near Norway and Bear Island. Russia to Iceland, Iceland to Russia, hours of patient watchkeeping in foul weather and freezing seas, guarding against the possibility of this one thing. And suddenly, in the middle of one such watch, the news had been flung at us. . . . A sense of the inevitable came over me. I was embroiled in a great machine of movement and purpose. Something big was going to happen.

The German U-boats had spent a frustrating day since, on the morning of Christmas Day, the crew of *U-601* had heard the convoy pass directly over them. Several men had been injured. On board *U-636* the effects of the chlorine gas released when the batteries were swamped by seawater had been so serious that the U-boat was forced to return to the *Black Watch* in Hammerfest to be pumped dry and repaired. *U-354* had lost her breakwater, as a result of which every wave struck the conning-tower with stunning force and threatened to drown the lookouts. Deck fittings were damaged, aerials broken off and most of the U-boats had shipped torrents of water through their conning-tower hatches. The heavy overcast made ordinary navigation impossible, so that the U-boat captains were never sure of exactly where they were. *Kapitänleutnant* Herbschleb on board *U-354* tried to take a sounding south-east of Bear Island and found that the depth there was 140 metres: he was 20 nautical miles off course. *U-277* had failed to establish contact with any of her companion U-boats; nor had her captain been able to hand over the remaining radar detectors. Some of the skippers had caught glimpses of the merchantmen as their craft rose and fell with the waves, others had been near to colliding with heavily armed corvettes and destroyers. They were close to the convoy, but none of them got within torpedo range. Only one torpedo had been fired, and that without success. Since Otto Hansen on board *U-601* had been forced to dive at 16.36 on Christmas Day, only one U-boat had made contact with the convoy. This was Hans Hildebrandt's *U-636*. But Hildebrandt's sighting never reached Narvik, which meant that the position he gave was not entered on the plotting-tables.

'The cause [of these problems] is undoubtedly the poor visibility and bad weather, which deprive the U-boats of an overview and give them no opportunity to use their armaments,' Rudolf Peters, *FdU Norwegen*, noted in the

war diary. Peters believed that the convoy would steer a northerly course and accordingly ordered the U-boats to set up a new cordon due east of Bear Island. 'A course due east will mean that the convoy will have the sea on the beam, which will cause difficulties for the heavily laden ships. I therefore believe [that it will take] a northerly course, as this will give it another advantage. . . . The further north our surface ships have to sail to make an attack, the more time the presumed enemy force will have to cut off their retreat.'

It was estimated that the U-boats would be in position by 06.00 on 26 December. They were under orders not to open fire while the Battle Group was attacking the convoy, but they were permitted to keep it in view and direct the squadron to the target with the aid of wireless fixes.

The destroyers restlessly circling the convoy picked up the wireless signals, but the commander of the escort was prepared to bide his time. Captain McCoy on board the famed destroyer *Onslow* had long felt that there was something big in the offing, and for that reason was determined to hold his escort vessels back in order to stave off the main German attack, which he expected to take place the next day south-east of Bear Island. 'CINC's 241325A confirmed the premonition that I had had for some 10 days that *Scharnhorst* was going to make the attempt to retrieve German prestige. All my future actions were based on this certainty and the certainty that the attack would take place to the south-east of Bear Island,' he wrote in his report.

As the various fleets neared the scene of the forthcoming battle from different directions, a mental game of chess was being played among their commanders. It was important to predict their opponents' next move. McCoy guessed that in all probability the German admirals would steer a northerly course to overtake the convoy. The original plan was therefore to do exactly the opposite. On the night of 25/26 December the convoy's course was to have been changed by 90 degrees to take it due east, which would have sent it straight into the arms of the German Battle Group. But Rear-Admiral Maitland Boucher on board the *Fort Kullyspell* was afraid that if he did that his ships and their cargoes would suffer inestimable damage. Boucher reported:

On Xmas afternoon a SSE'ly gale began to develop (starboard beam), resulting that night in a big sea which caused the ships to roll heavily. . . . (In Commodore's ship alone, one large life-float had been washed away, one lifeboat smashed and a Sherman tank was moving about the deck.) These circumstances may really have been the intervention of Providence for, had the course of the convoy been altered 25° to Starboard (to 90°) that night as planned, it would have led still closer to the positions in which the two actions were fought shortly after 1100 on Boxing Day (26th Dec.)

The *Scharnhorst* too was having a hard time. Many of the men were unaccustomed to being at sea in bad weather and suffered terribly from seasickness; very few were able to snatch any sleep. While the starboard watch had taken the ship out, the port watch had cleared the decks and stowed away 50 tons of potatoes that had just been taken on board. 'We hadn't received any supplies from home for a long time. I was told that four of the five ships carrying them had been sunk. We had fish for breakfast, dinner and supper, but just before Christmas a steamer brought us an enormous quantity of potatoes. We had to remove our hammocks to find room for them. There were potatoes everywhere,' says Helmut Backhaus. The starboard watch had been relieved at midnight and the port watch manned their stations in bitter cold and with a rising sea. They were relieved at 04.00 and barely had time to sling their hammocks. They were just beginning to thaw out when the alarm went. At 06.00 the port watch had breakfast. One hour later Action Stations was sounded, and at 08.00 both watches were ready for action.

On the bridge *Konter-Admiral* Bey had decided on his final plan of attack. At 07.00 he estimated that he was about 30 nautical miles ahead of convoy JW55B. The plan was that his five destroyers should then change course and head west, spreading out in line abreast, and approach the convoy at a speed of 12 knots. The *Scharnhorst* would follow 10 nautical miles behind the destroyers, ready to neutralize the escort and destroy the merchant ships with her 11-inch guns.

The plan had only one drawback. It rested on a sighting of the convoy thought to have been made by young Hans Dunkelberg on board *U-716* at 01.30: 'SQUARE AB6642 FORCED TO DIVE BY ESCORT. SOUTH 7. SEA 6–7. VISIBILITY 1,500 METRES.' This signal had been received on board *Z 29* at 03.27, with a resultant improvement in Rolf Johannesson's humour. 'According to this the enemy is about 30 nautical miles further west than assumed (course 60 degrees, speed 9 knots). This is good news for us. The convoy's course is confirmed. Because we are delayed this is very welcome news,' he wrote.

It was a strange signal altogether. According to the war diary, Dunkelberg was heading east at full speed. He had not used his wireless transmitter when the signal was reportedly sent; there was no record of it in *U-716*'s war diary. No other U-boats heard the signal, nor did the watchful U-boat Commander's headquarters in Narvik. Had the Battle Group been deliberately misled?

Was the signal spurious, designed to sow confusion? If so, it definitely achieved its object. At 04.01, half an hour after Dunkelberg's supposed signal had cheered up the men on board *Z 29*, Admiral Bruce Fraser took a hand in the game. He ordered the convoy to change course and sail due north. Three hours later, at 07.00, Bey turned west. Had the original plan been adhered to and the position given by Dunkelberg been correct, at about 09.00 the Battle Group would have been in the midst of the Allied escort vessels and merchantmen. None of them could have stood up to the battlecruiser's heavy guns. In a few minutes the convoy would have been reduced to a blazing inferno of sinking ships. Bey would have brought off what might arguably have been the *Kriegsmarine*'s most resounding victory. The convoys would have had to be discontinued for a second time, with dramatic consequences. Allied warships would have been tied up in the north and the war might well have been prolonged as a result. And Bey would have been able to present Dönitz with the triumph the Grand Admiral had promised Hitler.

But just as gradually and imperceptibly as the day before, things continued to go wrong for Bey. Hildebrandt's signal at 22.00 had not been heard. Dunkelberg's supposed position was no longer correct. Before 09.00 the convoy had put behind it some 15 to 20 nautical miles and was far to the north. Even Bey's first order to turn west and start the hunt for JW55B had been clumsily formulated and was in consequence misconstrued. 'In terms of signalling procedure the order was erroneously worded . . . and very complicated to carry out in the dark and in a heavy sea. . . . On board *Z 34* all the wireless operators were seasick. They failed to take down the signal correctly. The ship sailed on by instinct. As I could not see the destroyer, I could not take control . . . and the operation order prohibited use of radar,' wrote Rolf Johannesson. Bey was still counting on surprise. Like many German naval officers, he distrusted radar, which was primarily a British invention. He did not want the Battle Group to disclose its presence by emitting signals of any description, for which reason its ships continued to grope their way westwards – blind and without communicating with one another.

What had happened provided further proof of the haste that had characterized the entire operation, combined with flawed communications. The destroyer captains had not had a joint meeting with Bey before putting to sea. *Korvettenkapitän* Karl Hetz on board *Z 34* still laboured under the delusion that two of the destroyers were to remain close to the *Scharnhorst*, as presupposed by the original plan. For this reason he stationed himself far to the north and spent the rest of the morning trying to regain his appointed station. *Z 33* strayed much too far south and never regained contact with the rest of the flotilla. *Z 38* also had problems, likewise wandering off course and being identified by the other destroyers as an enemy vessel. 'Ah, the convoy!' Johannesson noted triumphantly in the war diary before the error was discovered. He subsequently added: '*Z-38* headed for an incorrect position in the reconnaissance formation, which later resulted in confusion between friend and foe. I am sure that the captain will not make an error of this kind ever again in his career.'

It was intended that Bey in the *Scharnhorst* should remain 10 nautical miles astern of the destroyers, ready to move in as soon as the convoy was found. But the battlecruiser abruptly turned aside and disappeared from view. No explanation of this manoeuvre was given to the Flotilla Commander, who was searching to the west, far south of the convoy; and the weather, far from improving, had worsened. 'Sailing as they are almost directly into the wind, the destroyers are beginning to pitch violently. They are shipping a lot of water. . . . Most of the untried ships' companies are seasick.'

He was still ignorant of the fact, but Rolf Johannesson and the destroyer flotilla were actually sailing further and further away – both from the convoy and from the *Scharnhorst*.

CHAPTER TWENTY-ONE

What was in the Mind of Konter-Admiral *Bey?*

THE BARENTS SEA, 08.40–12.40, SUNDAY 26 DECEMBER 1943

In the meantime the three cruisers of Force 1 had continued to race south-westwards towards the North Cape. Late in the morning of Christmas Day they turned north, heading straight for the convoy.

At 08.40 the alarm sounded on board Vice-Admiral Robert Burnett's flagship, the *Belfast*. One of the operators on the forward type 273 surface radar had picked up an unmistakable echo 32 kilometres dead ahead – in other words, between the cruisers and the convoy. It was as though an electric shock had run through the ship. The situation would be critical if the flickering blip on the radar screen proved to be the *Scharnhorst*. Poring over the plotting-table Burnett saw immediately that the battlecruiser, if such it was, was only an hour's sailing from the convoy. Provided he interpreted the circumstances correctly, Bey was ideally placed to launch a successful attack. Some nerve-racking minutes were to pass before Burnett could once again afford to breathe easily. To his relief the blip was moving south, *away* from the convoy. It was clear that Bey was unaware of how close to success he had been. Interviewed after the war, Burnett said: 'The part that the cruisers had to play in this action was from my point of view a fairly simple one. I dare to say that I had certain experience in these waters. I knew exactly what our Commander-in-Chief wished us to do. I was completely confident that the captains serving under me knew what was in my mind, and would carry on as I wished them. . . . We found the *Scharnhorst* and turned her away from the convoy.'

At a speed of 24 knots Burnett's three cruisers continued on their north-westerly course, the *Belfast* in the lead, followed by the *Sheffield* and *Norfolk* in that order. Now Burnett had to turn the tables: his duty was to protect the merchantmen. To that end he set out to station his cruisers between the *Scharnhorst* and the convoy instead of the other way round, which had been the case a short time earlier. There was a heavy sea coming in from the beam and the ships rolled violently. Writing under the pen-name of 'Banderillero', a young Ordinary Seaman who had spent the night in A shellroom described the scene when the order 'Stand By' was given: 'Everybody gets up, deflates and puts on their lifebelts which they have been using as pillows, the shellroom's crew start unshipping the bars which hold the shells in place in the trays. The magazine and handling-room men go down to their respective stations and the hatches are closed on top of them. Everyone is tensed for us to open fire . . .'

For forty minutes the three cruisers raced north-westwards. On their radar screens the operators could see how Bey was facilitating their task by unaccountably maintaining a steady course south. *He* was drawing further and further away from the convoy while *they* were approaching it ever more closely. At 09.21 a lookout on the *Sheffield* obtained a sighting. Through his binoculars he saw the *Scharnhorst*, a grey shape to the south-west, sailing past on a reciprocal course: 'ENEMY IN SIGHT. BEARING 222. RANGE 12,000 METRES.'

When the cruisers were a good way past the battlecruiser Burnett gave the order to open fire. He was now exactly where he wanted to be. He had barred the way to the convoy and changed course, first to the west, then to the south. The *Scharnhorst* had lost her chance: if she were to attack the merchant ships, she would first have to take on and defeat the three cruisers.

The *Belfast*'s first star-shell burst high in the sky, the burning phosphorous bathing the storm-lashed ocean in a greenish-yellow glare. Shortly afterwards the *Norfolk* opened fire with her 8-inch guns. As there was no flashless cordite on board the ship, the gunners were dazzled by every salvo, but their firing was none the less both rapid and effective. In nine minutes the *Norfolk* fired six full broadsides. Neither the *Belfast* nor the *Sheffield* could bring their guns to bear, however, as the *Norfolk* lay between them and their target. As the *Norfolk*'s captain, Donald Bain, said, 'We were the first to sight the enemy. We were the first to open fire, and we were the first to score a hit.'

'Banderillero' on board the *Belfast* heard gunfire to starboard. 'We can feel our 4-inch guns firing star-shell. We all look at one another and ask, "Why aren't our 6-inch opening up?". . . The firing lasts a few minutes and we are all very impatient to know what has happened. Then comes the Commander's

Left hand

voice: "After a few broadsides from the *Norfolk* the enemy, whoever she may be, has turned away and we are now chasing her."'

The *Scharnhorst* and her five escorting destroyers had put to sea in highly unpropitious circumstances. Their task was difficult enough from the outset, and the gale that was blowing made it almost impossible to complete it successfully. Moreover, *Konter-Admiral* Bey had shown considerable indecision before the squadron set out – and the surprise attack to which he had just been subjected can have done nothing to bolster his self-confidence. He had despatched his destroyers westwards and was expecting them to report at any moment that they had found the convoy. Instead, the battlecruiser's radar detector had picked up a series of echoes from almost the opposite direction, south-east. Bey did not hesitate. From his position 10 nautical miles astern of *Z 29* he had turned south to investigate the source of the blips, and in so doing forfeited his first big chance of destroying convoy JW55B. At the time he had been less than an hour's sailing from the convoy. Now, although he did not know it, he was sailing further and further away from his quarry. For some unfathomable reason he neglected to inform the commander of the destroyer flotilla why he had so suddenly changed course, which meant that he left the formation without taking the precaution of safeguarding himself from enemy torpedo attack. In the event, the delay in putting to sea was to cost him dear. Had Bey left the Lang fjord at the appointed hour, Force 1 would never have found him. As it was, Burnett had turned up at precisely the right moment, in time to distract Bey from the task in hand. It seemed that the *Scharnhorst*'s legendary luck had begun to desert her.

Petty Officer Wilhelm Gödde, a staid, religious man, who was stationed on the port searchlight platform, level with the bridge, was the oldest of the *Scharnhorst* survivors. Through his earphones he could follow all the reports passed to the Command Centre. The British attack took him by surprise. 'All of a sudden I saw three spouts of water shoot high into the air a few hundred metres away. They were caused by heavy shells. I couldn't see the ship that was firing at us, all I saw were the orange flashes every time a new salvo was fired.'

Another survivor, Günther Sträter, a loader on the 15-cm port battery, said much the same thing: 'Three 20.3-cm [8-inch] shells 500 metres abeam of us to port. Alarm! Of the enemy, only the muzzle flashes could be seen, bearing 245 degrees.'

Based as it was on drills they had perfected over several years, the response of the Command Centre staff was automatic. The men knew exactly what to do. Many of them had been on board since 1939, when the *Scharnhorst* was first

commissioned. Few ships' companies had taken part in more engagements, so it took only a few seconds for the battlecruiser's 10-metre optical range finder to calculate the range of the *Norfolk* and for C turret to reply. Speed was increased to 30 knots, course changed and a smokescreen put down. At 09.40 the engagement came to an end. It had lasted for less than ten minutes, but in that short time the *Norfolk* had scored two hits. One shell landed on the deck and penetrated to the engine-room mess without exploding; the fire it caused was quickly put out. The other shell did far greater damage.

'That shot was a lucky one. I was at my post on the upper platform and felt the draught when the shell whistled right over me. One man was killed, a lieutenant lost a foot and several men were lightly wounded. When I struggled to my feet, I saw what had happened. The shell had carried away the radar's large mattress aerial. The forward radar was totally destroyed,' says Signaller Helmut Backhaus, who was 38 metres above the deck when the shell struck and was thus able to see all that was happening.

With her new *Seetakt* radar gone, the *Scharnhorst* was to all intents and purposes blind. The British radars could detect ships at anything up to a distance of 40 to 50 kilometres. The battlecruiser had, it is true, an extra radar it could fall back on, but it was mounted on the range finder aft and had a range of only 8 to 10 kilometres. A lucky shot had severely reduced the *Scharnhorst*'s fighting capacity.

On board the German destroyers there was considerable surprise when, at 09.30, the lookouts saw the glare of star-shell against the storm clouds and heard the sound of gunfire some 15 to 20 kilometres away to the east. Again a strange thing happened: Bey did not signal the destroyers to come to his assistance and Rolf Johannesson, for his part, made no attempt to do so on his own initiative. Instead of turning to help the *Scharnhorst*, Johannesson continued his search to the south-west, which was the wrong direction.

In all probability Bey had not been using the *Scharnhorst*'s own radar when it was destroyed. For this reason his first wirelessed signal at 09.55 referred to only one cruiser: 'AM IN AC4133 BEING SHELLED BY PROBABLE CRUISER WITH [THE AID OF] RADAR.' The *Sheffield* and *Belfast*, neither of which opened fire, remained undetected.

The grid reference Bey gave, AC4133, was far to the north-east and caused considerable confusion. 'The position is incomprehensible. What is the *Scharnhorst* doing more than 50 nautical miles north-east of its reconnaissance area?' wondered Rolf Johannesson irritably in the war diary. He was not to know that a mistake had been made in encrypting the signal. Instead of

AC4133, the grid reference should have been AC4199, which would have cast an entirely different light on the situation.

The Battle Group had now been in the area of operation for nearly three hours, and most of what might have gone wrong had done so. The gale was blowing with increasing strength and the *Scharnhorst*'s accompanying destroyers had been sent off on a wild-goose chase. Two of them had misconstrued Bey's order and had strayed far off course; the others were battling head-on against wind and wave and shipping an enormous weight of water.

'Visibility was down to only 300 metres. The bulky gun-mountings on the foredeck aggravated the situation. Speed was reduced to 15 knots, but waves continued to break over us. Depth-charges were swept overboard and the anti-aircraft gun had to be abandoned, otherwise the gun crew would have been drowned,' said Hans-Dietrich Lau, an able-seaman serving on board *Z 38*. The *Scharnhorst* herself had been engaged in a gunnery duel with unidentified cruisers and had lost her forward radar. Contact with the destroyers had been lost. The mutual trust and communication between Bey and Johannesson were in danger of breaking down altogether. The Destroyer Commander no longer knew exactly where Bey was; nor did he know what Bey had in mind. He himself lacked either the imagination or the courage to act on his own initiative. Writing later, Johannessen said: 'At about 09.30 we saw star-shell astern at a distance of some 12 nautical miles. Bey reported that he was under fire from a cruiser. I did not feel justified in breaking off the reconnaissance patrol without a direct order. Bey had the best wireless and radar equipment and was therefore better informed, though naturally I was worried about the turn events had taken.'

It was at this critical juncture, at 10.02, that the first positive sighting of the day reached the *Scharnhorst*. *Korvettenkapitän* Robert Lübsen, skipper of *U-277*, who was on his fourth patrol, had that same morning set a course for Bear Island with the intention of checking his position by dead reckoning. At 09.25 he chanced upon a fleet of ships which, because of the storm and danger of collision, were burning navigation lights. 'Came suddenly upon the convoy, true 30, range 3,000 metres. Convoy burning lights. Estimated course 90 degrees,' he noted in the war diary.

Again a fatal error was made. Lübsen knew that he was 40 to 50 nautical miles off course, but despite this he swiftly reported his position without saying that it wasn't exact: 'CONVOY SQUARE AB6365'. Not surprisingly, he assumed that he had stumbled upon the convoy, but it is more probable that he had sighted the four ships of the 36th Destroyer Division under the command

of Commander R.L. Fisher, on board the *Musketeer*, which had joined the convoy the previous day. 'We spent a difficult night floundering about in a following sea and snow flurries, trying to keep station on a convoy making good about 6 knots. I was some 5 miles astern putting down a shadowing U-boat when my division was again detached to join Bob Burnett's cruisers after their first brush with the *Scharnhorst* and ran north with him at high speed in appalling weather with the sea astern.'

Lübsen saw the lights go out on the Allied ships, then suddenly found himself under fire. But the 27-year-old U-boat captain from Oldenburg refused to be panicked into diving. Instead, he turned away and released two Aphrodite hydrogen balloons carrying aluminium foil to confuse the enemy radar. When, a few minutes later, he again turned north-east, the four shadowy shapes he had seen had disappeared. Both on board the vessels of the German Battle Group and at the Command Centre in Narvik Lübsen's signal was taken at face value. But Lübsen himself knew that the grid reference he had given could not be correct. Seemingly prompted by a desire to express his doubts, in his next signal, sent at 10.25, he did make a reservation, saying: 'HAVE ENCOUNTERED CONVOY. CONVOY BURNING LIGHTS. POSITION UNCERTAIN.' At 11.45 he signalled further information: 'FOUR SHADOWS, FOUR DESTROYERS, ASSUME PART OF CONVOY, EASTERLY COURSE, FORCED AWAY, FOLLOWING.'

To the recipients of Lübsen's three signals it appeared that he had maintained contact with the convoy for several hours, ever since he first saw the ships' navigation lights at 09.25. Throughout the morning *Kapitän-zur-See* Peters had repeatedly urged him to transmit a signal to enable the Battle Group and the other *Eisenbart* U-boats to obtain a fix on him, but Lübsen chose not to do so. 'As I have lost contact, am transmitting no further fixes,' he noted in the war diary at 13.00.

It was not until about nine that same evening that Lübsen provided further information in the shape of a new signal: 'IN SHORT SIGNAL 09.45 READ AC4421.' In so doing he acknowledged unequivocally that the first position he had given was some 50 nautical miles out. By then, however, it was too late: nothing could be changed.

What was interesting about Lübsen's sighting was that it correctly placed the convoy *north-west* of the Battle Group. Had Bey been made of sterner stuff, he could still have changed the course of events. He was, after all, within range of the convoy, so he could have turned about, taken his chance of defeating the cruisers and, within an hour, caught up with the convoy. In a harshly worded criticism of *Konter-Admiral* Bey, Dönitz later wrote:

The *Scharnhorst* was far superior to the cruisers in armour, seakeeping properties and, above all, firepower. Against the relatively lightly armed cruisers she had her heavy 28-cm [11-inch] guns, in addition to her secondary armament. In the light of her superiority, there is every reason to maintain that the battle should have been fought to its conclusion when contact was made in the morning. Once the British cruisers had been destroyed or badly incapacitated, the convoy would have fallen like ripe fruit into the hands of the *Scharnhorst*.

In the event, Bey adopted different tactics. He withdrew and wheeled eastwards and northwards in a wide sweep. In all probability he had in mind discussions he had had with Peters and Schniewind on light in the Arctic and the use of heavy guns. It had been ascertained that at that time of year there was most light at 73 degrees North between 11.22 and 12.07. Had Bey attacked from the north at this time, he would have had the enemy ahead of him, silhouetted against the southern horizon. This would have enabled him to bring the *Scharnhorst*'s heavy guns effectively to bear – even without radar. On paper it was a good plan, but Bey again failed to inform Johannesson of his intentions.

At 10.09, seven minutes after Lübsen's convoy report reached him, Bey signalled to the 4th Destroyer Flotilla: 'REPORT ON SITUATION.' Johannesson answered: 'HEADING AS PLANNED FOR SQUARE AC4413. COURSE 230 DEGREES. SPEED 12 KNOTS.'

A few minutes later Lübsen again confused the issue by saying that he was uncertain of his position. This notwithstanding, both Bey and Johannesson now assumed that the German destroyers had wandered much too far south.

The Flotilla Commander wrote: 'Upon receipt of Lübsen's signal it would have been natural for me, as Flotilla Commander, to order a change of course. I considered taking the matter into my own hands. But as Bey knew just as much [about the situation] as I did, I saw no reason to act on my own.'

Not until 10.25, after battling for more than three hours against the gale, were the destroyers ordered to change course: '4TH DESTROYER FLOTILLA. 70 DEGREES. 25 KNOTS.'

It was a strange order. The convoy was thought to be to the north-west, but this order sent the destroyers north-east, back to their starting-point. 'It is not possible to understand what the Commander-in-Chief has in mind. Presumably he possesses information about the position of the convoy that is unknown to us,' Johannesson wrote.

Korvettenkapitän Karl Lampe on board *Z 30* hazarded a guess, writing: 'Bey's intention with this order is unclear at present. Possibly he wants the destroyers to close him so that the convoy can be subjected to a combined attack as presupposed by the operation order.'

To and fro to no purpose. Together with *Z 30* and *Z 38*, the lead destroyer, *Z 29*, turned about and set a course that would take the three of them back to where they had come from. The flotilla's other two destroyers, *Z 33* and *Z 34*, were nowhere to be seen. As an operational unit, the 4th Destroyer Flotilla had disintegrated. The change of course did, however, have one advantage: with the sea now abaft, the destroyers' seakeeping properties improved, although visibility remained poor. Johannesson wrote: 'The day is unusually dark, even for this latitude and time of year. [My] hope of an improvement in the weather has not been fulfilled. But the ship is steadier. The youthful faces of the men have regained a spark of life.'

Some distance north of the German destroyers, Vice-Admiral Robert Burnett was also having trouble. When the *Scharnhorst* turned first east, then north, he was in a quandary. Ought he to follow her or should he close the convoy? After a moment's thought he chose the latter course. He broke off pursuit and ordered the flotilla to steer north-westwards, and at 10.20 the last blip that was the *Scharnhorst* vanished from the cruiser's radar screens. He had committed what was, in the eyes of the Royal Navy, a sin of the first order and a contravention of his orders – he had voluntarily relinquished an assured opportunity to maintain contact with the enemy. In his defence Burnett pointed out that, the weather being what it was, the *Scharnhorst* was doing 4 to 6 knots more than the cruisers (30 knots, as compared with 24). 'I was convinced he was trying to work round to the northward of the convoy and in view of the limit on my speed imposed by the weather I decided to return to place myself between him and the convoy,' Burnett wrote in his report after the battle.

At 10.35 Burnett signalled the flagship: 'HAVE LOST TOUCH WITH ENEMY WHO WAS STEERING NORTH. AM CLOSING CONVOY'. But far to the west Fraser was tense: this was the crunch! The *Duke of York* and Force 2 were still much too far off to intervene. To have lost contact with the *Scharnhorst* was unforgivable. Now anything could happen. Making no attempt to conceal his misgivings, at 10.58 Fraser signalled: 'UNLESS TOUCH CAN BE REGAINED BY SOME UNIT THERE IS NO CHANCE OF MY FINDING ENEMY.'

For Vice-Admiral Burnett there was no going back. He had made contact with the convoy, but he had also precipitated a crisis. By this time it was past eleven. The cruisers took to zig-zagging 8 to 10 nautical miles ahead of the merchantmen, screened by the four destroyers *Musketeer*, *Matchless*, *Virago* and *Opportune*.

Burnett's Flag Captain and friend, Captain Frederick Parham, was at the centre of events:

When he'd taken his decision and settled down to keep with the convoy, he sent for me. He was down in the chart-house one deck below the bridge. He himself worked entirely from the plot. I don't know that he ever came to the bridge at all. There was nothing to be *seen* from the bridge, it was pitch-dark all the time. . . . I went down and he'd cleared the chart-house of everybody else.

He said to me, 'Freddie, have I done the right thing?' I said to him, 'I'm absolutely *certain* you have.' Shortly after that we had a fairly *snorting* signal from the C-in-C which said, roughly speaking, 'if nobody keeps their eye on the *Scharnhorst*, how the *hell* do you think I'm going to bring her to action,' or words to the effect.

Poor old Bob, he was a terribly emotional chap, he was jolly nearly in tears about it. I was able to reassure him. And afterwards of course his judgement was proved utterly correct because the *Scharnhorst* turned up again to look for the convoy and ran straight into us.

The minutes ticked slowly by. On board the *Duke of York* gloom prevailed. The game of chess, with convoy JW55B as the prize, was entering its final phase. The convoy had been discovered and the *Scharnhorst* induced to put to sea. The trap had been very near to closing, but at the last moment the battlecruiser had seemed to sense the danger she was in. And now she had been lost! Again Fraser's nerve looked like failing him. He took a decision that might well have spelled disaster: he reduced speed to 18 knots and reversed the course of Force 2. If the *Scharnhorst* chose to break out to the west, into the North Atlantic, Fraser would find himself south of her and on a parallel course. But with every minute that passed, the gap between him and the convoy widened.

In the meantime a number of disquieting items of news had reached the German admirals in northern Norway and Kiel. Before aerial reconnaissance had had to be called off on Christmas Day, the *Luftwaffe* had reported that they had not been able to locate any enemy covering forces within a radius of 80 kilometres of the convoy. Although that was less than the 300 kilometres Peters had asked for, it was better than nothing. Now the German D/F stations in Kirkenes, the German Bight and Hjørring in Denmark began to report an increase in high-frequency wireless traffic in the Barents Sea. A unit designated JLP was in continual contact with Scapa Flow and an unidentified unit using the call-sign DGO. Some time between 11.00 and 12.00 *Generaladmiral* Schniewind noted in the war diary: 'Signals from one British unit to another may be from a cruiser to the convoy or to own flagship. But signals may also be designed to keep the assumed heavy covering force informed.' His observation was quite correct: JLP was Burnett, DGO Fraser.

Despite the storm that was raging and the danger of icing, three six-strong aircrews volunteered to undertake new reconnaissance flights in the morning of 26 December. At 09.11 three flying-boats took off from the main base of *Seefernaufklärungsgruppe 130* (Long-Range Reconnaissance Group 130) on Skattøra near Tromsø. One of them was piloted by *Leutnant* Helmut Marx, who set a course due north beneath the low cloud ceiling. Although it was day, this was in effect night flying of the most extreme kind, and it demanded a lot from the pilots. 'In a blinding snowstorm and with visibility near nil they had to fly between the mountains with their eyes glued to the second-hand of the stopwatch to reach the open sea in the Arctic darkness,' wrote Frank de Haan, who was on standby with *1. Staffel* (1st Squadron) in Tromsø.

When Marx reached a position some 60 nautical miles north-west of Sørøya Island, his *Hoentwiel* radar began to pick up echoes. At 10.12 Marx sent his first signal: 'POSITION NORTH 72 EAST 22.5. SEVERAL VESSELS LOCATED.'

The course Marx had flown had taken him straight to the *Duke of York*, *Jamaica* and the four Allied destroyers. For the next hour and a half he continued to shadow them.

'I can remember seeing the brute, lurking about in the mist, circling round, not out of range. We didn't fire at it, because what was the sense? We probably wouldn't have hit it, and maybe the *Scharnhorst* would have seen the flashes, and people would have got alarmed. So Bruce Fraser just sat there, smoking his pipe, and said, let it go round and round,' recalled Lieutenant Richard Courage, who was serving on board the *Duke of York*.

The *Hoentwiel* was a rather primitive radar set which operated on a wavelength of 53 centimetres. On board the 'Flying Clog', the name by which this type of aircraft was jocularly known, rocking and shaking with every gust of wind, it was no easy matter to distinguish between the cluster of blips on the radar screen, but Marx refused to admit defeat. 'The captain of the German flying-boat was not satisfied with what he had achieved. Despite the storm and snow showers he flew over the ships and requested an identification signal. He reports that he actually received a response from a destroyer. The signal was incorrect.'

At 11.40 Marx felt sufficiently sure of his sighting to transmit a second, and more detailed, report to the main base at Bardufoss: 'MAINTAINED CONTACT 10.12–11.35. JUDGING BY RADAR IMAGE THERE MUST BE ONE LARGE AND SEVERAL SMALLER VESSELS. PROBABLY PROCEEDING AT HIGH SPEED ON SOUTHERLY COURSE.'

An inconceivable error was then made by one of the most experienced German airmen in northern Norway, the *Fliegerführer* Lofoten, *Generalmajor* Ernst-August Roth. Not until 13.06 – three hours later – did Roth pass on Marx's first sighting to the admirals in Narvik and Kiel. Marx's second and more detailed signal, which spoke of 'one large and several smaller vessels', was held back until well into the next day. The reason was that Roth had no faith in Marx's reported sightings, and he was not prepared to pass on suppositions, only facts.

In Narvik, where it occasioned serious misgivings, the signal was logged at 13.41. 'This report is most unwelcome, as in my opinion it can only relate to an enemy force which is out to cut off the Battle Group's retreat. The Commander of the Battle Group must be in a position to form a clear picture of the situation, as he has received this report via FVLM [the wireless link between the *Luftwaffe* and *Kriegsmarine*] and furthermore knows where his own destroyers are,' wrote *Kapitän-zur-See* Peters.

The thought of a hostile force had troubled Peters day and night since long before Christmas. Nevertheless, he refrained from sending out a general alarm because he felt assured that Bey had received the same signal. In the light of subsequent events this passive attitude on the part of the U-boat Commander is puzzling. On board *Z 38* the signal was not handed to *Korvettenkapitän* Brutzer until 14.45. Brutzer immediately wirelessed it to *Kapitän-zur-See* Johannesson on board *Z 29*, whose Wireless Room did not monitor traffic between the Navy and *Luftwaffe* on Channel FVLM. That channel had been closed down and was instead used to listen out for D/F signals from the *Eisenbart*'s U-boat fleet. Brutzer set out his reasoning in the war diary: 'This signal suggests the presence of an enemy force whose purpose is either to intercept the Battle Group or to attack it from the rear. Late receipt of the signal (4½ hours after the sighting) may have serious consequences.'

Johannesson, on the other hand, said nothing about the signal from Brutzer in *his* war diary. Nor did he make any attempt to contact the *Scharnhorst*, although *after* the battle he wrote: 'My Flag Captain and I had a thorough discussion in the same vein. It was strange that the flying-boat was unable to amplify this crucial report by visual observation.'

Far to the north, *Konter-Admiral* Bey was blissfully unaware of the straws in the wind that were gradually building up to become a dangerous threat. He had with him on board men from the German *B-Dienst* who continually monitored the British frequencies. According to Rolf Johannesson, the presence of American battleships and aircraft-carriers was Bey's 'personal hobby-horse'. Whether it was or not, Bey did nothing to suggest that he was afraid of being cut off. The admiral who, against his will, had been sent to the Arctic, sailed straight into the jaws of death without doing anything to avert disaster.

Between 11.30 and 12.00, by which time he was not far from the edge of the polar ice, Bey turned the *Scharnhorst* about and set a course south-westwards, heading straight into the gale. At 11.58 he finally sent Johannesson a signal the Destroyer Commander could understand: 'OPERATE TOWARDS SQUARE AB6365.' Now Bey's intention became clear: he was preparing to attack the convoy from the north and intended that the destroyers should do the same from the south.

Johannesson's comment in the war diary just about says it all: 'The Commander-in-Chief has thereby given the Flotilla a free hand to act independently. *Dank sei Gott!*'

Square AB6365 was the spot from which Lübsen had first reported having sighted the convoy that day. By this time the report was nearly three hours old – and the Destroyer Flotilla Commander's heartfelt thanks to the Almighty failed to result in inspired action. Having told the other two destroyers to close on him, he then chose the wrong course – 280 degrees, which would take them almost straight to the erroneous position given by *U-277*. Meanwhile, the convoy had made another hurried change of course and was now heading north. This meant that for the second time that fateful morning Johannesson was destined to pass south of the merchantmen he was hunting. To make matters worse, with the gale coming in on the port bow, the destroyers were having a very hard time of it. '[To proceed at] more than 15 knots is unjustifiable with the sea from forward. The ship is vibrating badly,' wrote Karl Lampe on board *Z 30*.

Nearly an hour and a half had passed. On board the two British flagships, the *Duke of York* and *Belfast*, the atmosphere remained tense. The *Duke of York* and Force 2 were now heading westwards, away from the convoy. The *Belfast* and Force 1 were on a line some 9 nautical miles ahead of the convoy and sailing eastwards. Again it was a radar operator on board the *Belfast* who, at 12.04, came up with the news everyone was waiting for: 'UNKNOWN RADAR CONTACT, BEARING 075, RANGE 13 MILES.' When this report reached the

Duke of York a minute later, the relief was almost tangible: 'It was an electrifying moment,' said the ship's Signals Officer, Lieutenant Courage. Admiral Fraser himself wrote: 'I knew now that there was every chance of catching the enemy.'

The operators in the Command Centre could see that the *Scharnhorst* was on what was almost a collision course with the cruisers. At a speed of 20 knots she was approaching them ever more closely, seemingly oblivious of what lurked in the darkness ahead. In the course of the next seventeen minutes the distance between the ships shrank from 26,500 to only 10,000 metres. In the half-light the shadowy shape of the battlecruiser grew ever larger until, without warning, star-shell again lit up the sky above her. The time was 12.21. From the bridge of the *Belfast* Captain Frederick Parham was at last able to get a clear view of the enemy. '[S]he looked *extremely* large and *extremely* formidable,' he said. For Vice-Admiral Burnett it was an exhilarating moment. He had made a controversial decision, but now he felt vindicated; circumstances had proved him right. For the second time he had placed his ships between the convoy and the *Scharnhorst* and in so doing had barred the German battlecruiser's path to her quarry.

Eye-witness accounts from *Scharnhorst* survivors are both sparse and ambiguous. Both the ship's company and Hintze himself appear to have been taken completely by surprise – despite the many wireless signals they had received and despite the weeks of deliberation and the knowledge that strong enemy forces were likely to be at sea.

Able-Seaman Günther Sträter, who was repatriated as early as the summer of 1944 under a prisoner-of-war exchange scheme, prepared a reconstruction of the sequence of events for the *Abwehr* that same autumn. According to him, the men had remained at action stations throughout. *Kapitän-zur-See* Hintze had personally briefed them over the *Scharnhorst*'s broadcasting system, saying, 'There has been a lull in the fighting. We are trying once again to get through to the convoy.'

Wilhelm Gödde remembered in 1948 Hintze's briefing as having been more detailed. 'From the Captain to all stations. Situation report. As expected, this morning we encountered the convoy's covering force, three cruisers of the Town class. We have changed course and are endeavouring to attack the convoy from the opposite side, from the north. We have shaken off the cruisers.'

Just before the *Belfast* opened fire, the first warning voice came from the bridge of the *Scharnhorst*: 'Keep a good lookout!' Shortly afterwards the shadowy outlines of the British ships came into view. 'Alarm! Turrets A and B fired to

starboard. After a change of course C turret followed suit. In the course of the engagement all stations were informed that powerful explosions had been registered on the enemy. An hour later there was another lull. The wounded were taken below. Some time later we were told that our armour had held up once again,' Sträter declared in his reconstruction of the engagement.

Gödde was more restrained in his account:

Shortly before 12.30 several lookouts, myself included, observed and reported three vague shapes ahead. The alarm had already been sounded on the strength of a radar contact. Before our own guns had time to fire, the first star-shells were hanging above the *Scharnhorst*. Enemy shells began to fall pretty close to the ship. The first salvoes from our own guns bracketed the targets. I personally saw that after three or four salvoes a raging fire broke out close to the after funnel of one of the cruisers and there was a lot of fire and smoke both forward and aft on another cruiser. After further salvoes I saw that also the third cruiser had been hit forward. For a brief moment a bright flame was visible, but it was rapidly extinguished. There was a lot of smoke, which suggested that the ships were on fire. The enemy's firing became more sporadic. While we were changing course, the cruisers turned away and vanished from sight in the rain and snow showers. In the course of this engagement the enemy was visible ahead and on both sides. Both our A and B turrets fired, as did the two forward 15-cm batteries. No hits on the *Scharnhorst* were reported, either by phone or by other means. During the first engagement the enemy had hardly been visible at all. [This time] in the grey light of noon their silhouettes were clearly discernible. Besides, the range was considerably shorter than it had been in the morning.

Gödde was correct in saying that the range was much shorter. At the closest point the *Scharnhorst* passed only 8,000 metres from the cruisers; at a speed of 30 knots, it was a breathtaking sight. Fisher's destroyers, which were attempting to mount a torpedo attack, were even closer, being a mere 4,000 metres distant. However, Gödde was somewhat over-optimistic in his assessment of the battlecruiser's shooting. True, one salvo had landed close alongside the *Sheffield*, sending a rain of red-hot splinters on to her deck. Some weighed as much as 10 to 15 kilos. They tore through the bulkheads but, incredibly, no one was injured.

It was the *Norfolk* that bore the worst of it. A 28-cm (11-inch) shell knocked out X turret aft and another landed amidships, to explode beneath the main deck. A member of the damage-control party, a stoker named Moth, has given a vivid description of the scene: 'In the next two or three minutes there was inevitable confusion. Lights went out and one of my mess-mates standing with his back to the communicating door was thrown across the deck by the blast from the explosion.' Seven men were killed outright and five badly wounded, two of them dying some time later. Despite extensive damage amidships, the *Norfolk*'s fighting capacity was unimpaired. Shell splinters had showered the engine-room staff, but the men continued to keep the cruiser going at top speed for a further six hours. They even managed to squeeze a little extra from the engines. 'The men in the engine-room continued to give *Norfolk* more knots than she had ever had before and, instead of dropping back, we were there in the final phase of the action,' said Captain Bain.

The second engagement of the day lasted for only twenty minutes, after which the *Scharnhorst* made off at top speed in a southerly direction. Apart from a dud that landed on her afterdeck, she was unharmed. In view of Gödde's report, the men on board the battlecruiser must have believed that the enemy ships had suffered greater damage than they actually had. This not-withstanding, Bey showed no inclination to continue the battle at close quarters. Although his course took him a mere 12 to 15 nautical miles ahead of the convoy, he did not attempt to break through to get at the merchantmen.

Grossadmiral Dönitz made no attempt to conceal his disappointment at Bey's dispositions.

This time the *Scharnhorst* was in what was, tactically speaking, a much more favourable position. The enemy were silhouetted against the lighter south-west horizon, whereas the *Scharnhorst* had behind her the darkness of the northern sector. What she should have done was to have continued the battle and destroyed the weaker British force, especially as it was obvious that they had already been hard hit. Had that been done, it would have created an excellent new opportunity to attack the convoy.

Bey failed to exploit his tactical advantages. Instead, he continued to race south-east at a speed of 28 knots, making a bee-line for the coast of Finnmark. The explanation is, perhaps, to be found in the signal he sent to the Fleet Commander at 12.40: 'SQUARE 4133 IN ENGAGEMENT WITH SEVERAL OPPONENTS. AM BEING SHELLED WITH [THE AID OF] RADAR BY *HEAVY UNITS* [Author's italics].' But Hintze had himself announced over the ship's broadcasting system that the close escort consisted of three cruisers — and at a

distance of only 8,000 metres the lookouts could clearly see the outlines of the enemy ships. Understandably, on receiving Bey's signal at 13.52 the Fleet Commander, *Generaladmiral* Schniewind, concluded: 'Because of his advanced technology the adversary is able to fight with the aid of radar. *Scharnhorst* has no equivalent equipment. As he is under radar-directed fire by heavy units, in accordance with his orders the Battle Group's Commander has broken off the engagement.'

Bey waited for a whole hour before ordering the destroyers to make for the Norwegian mainland. The signal he sent at 13.40 was brief and to the point: 'BREAK OFF.'

Johannessen, the Flotilla Commander, had wasted a further two hours in a vain attempt to find the convoy himself. He was disappointed at being recalled, but was reluctant to give up. To play for time, he sought Bey's confirmation, wirelessing, 'I REQUEST AN OPERATIONAL ORDER'.

The answer, received at 14.26, was as brief as the original signal: 'RETURN HOME.' Operation *Ostfront* was definitely over. The Battle Group was under orders to return to the Kå and Lang fjords. The attack had been an abject failure and no one was looking forward to the settling of accounts that was bound to follow.

But further to the north Vice-Admiral Robert Burnett had rallied after the exchange of fire. The three cruisers, the *Belfast*, *Sheffield* and *Norfolk*, accompanied by the destroyers *Musketeer*, *Matchless*, *Opportune* and *Virago*, took up the chase. Speed was increased to 28 knots. The ships were some 13 to 20 kilometres astern of the *Scharnhorst* – out of sight, but in radar contact. Hastening in from the south-west came the *Duke of York* and Force 2, guided to their target by wireless signals from Burnett.

Through a combination of bad luck, inadequate preparation and lack of resolution, Bey's plan had failed. Fraser's, on the other hand, had worked perfectly. The showdown was fast approaching.

CHAPTER TWENTY-TWO

Defeat

OFF THE NORTH CAPE, 15.00–21.00, SUNDAY 26 DECEMBER 1943

After the dramatic events of the morning, to a greater or lesser degree most of the men on board the *Scharnhorst* experienced a nervous reaction, though all remained steadfastly at their posts. 'I was in the foretop. The wind howled through the stays. It was bitterly cold and black as pitch. There wasn't a thing to be seen,' said Helmut Backhaus. Some of the men curled up and tried to sleep; others went to get a bite to eat. But in many places the steaming containers of pea soup were left untouched. Heading as she was straight for Nordkyn, the battlecruiser had the gale coming in athwart on her starboard bow. This kept the steel giant lurching and rolling, and even the most seasoned sailors found staving off seasickness more than they could manage.

The morning's engagement had been different from the others the ship's company had taken part in. When the *Scharnhorst* was raiding in the Atlantic in the early years of the war, chivalry had been more to the fore. Merchantmen had been made to heave to and their crews 'persuaded' to abandon ship, whereupon the ships and their cargoes had been sent to the bottom with a few well-directed salvoes on the waterline. But the Barents Sea in November was no place for gentlemen: the *Scharnhorst* had sought out the convoy with the avowed intention of inflicting upon it death and destruction. Admittedly, in the event she had failed to get through to the defenceless merchant ships. But the men on deck had seen the fires on the enemy cruisers caused by their shells and no one was downhearted. Although the enemy convoy had not been destroyed, they had given a good account of themselves. Their reaction was more in the nature

of listlessness resulting from lack of sleep and a sense of relief, sustained by a historically founded sense of pride. The *Scharnhorst* was known to be a lucky ship – and unsinkable to boot. Three or four hours' sailing at full speed, as now, and the Norwegian coast would be in sight. By midnight they would be safely at anchor. Says Helmut Feifer:

> One of my friends on board was going on leave to Wesermünde after Christmas. He had been worried when the order came to put to sea. 'If we have to attack a convoy,' he said, 'we're doomed.' My reply was that the *Scharnhorst* had twenty-one watertight bulkheads and there was no way she could sink, so there was no reason for him to be afraid. 'No,' he said, 'we shall die.' I remember that conversation as though it were yesterday. But he was an exception. The majority of the men did not believe that anything could go wrong. We felt certain that we would soon be back at our anchorage all safe and sound.

The British report based on exhaustive interrogation of the thirty-six survivors in the weeks following the battle says:

> After this second engagement with the British cruisers . . . relative calm settled down on board. A considerable number of the men took advantage of the opportunity to catch up on some much-needed sleep and the sudden sounding of the alarm about 1600 came as a shock, as they had imagined that it was merely a question of maintaining their speed of about 30 knots in order to make base and safety and renew their interrupted Christmas.

The senior officers on the *Scharnhorst*'s bridge can hardly have been as sanguine. Bey knew that he had failed disastrously. Dönitz had sent him out to redeem the honour of the High Seas Fleet by dealing the convoys a crushing blow, yet he had not succeeded in getting anywhere near the merchantmen. The Navy would be overwhelmingly disappointed. No honours awaited him when he got home, only Hitler's and the Grand Admiral's wrath. He must have wondered whether, like Kummetz, he could explain away his failure by pointing to the vagueness of his orders or if he could invoke the bad weather as an excuse. He must have wondered, too, whether he would be dismissed from the service, court-martialled or humiliated in some other way.

The bombardment had ceased at 12.41 when the three cruisers turned away and were lost from sight. But only a quarter of an hour later the men monitoring the British frequencies on board the *Scharnhorst* and at bases ashore in Kirkenes, Jutland and the German Bight picked up another wireless signal: 'JLP TO DGO. ENEMY COURSE AND SPEED 115 DEGREES 28 KNOTS. AM SHADOWING.' With ominous regularity the signals continued to come in at brief intervals – 13.01, 13.12, 13.19, 14.25, 14.45, 15.00, 15.58 and on throughout what remained of the afternoon. The Germans were unable to decrypt all these signals, nor did they know for certain that JLP was Vice-Admiral Burnett on board the *Belfast* or that DGO was Admiral Fraser on the *Duke of York*. But it was clear to all concerned that the signals were coming from one of the cruisers north of the *Scharnhorst* and that they were intended for a British unit close by, in all probability the strong force that had been foremost in the minds of everyone for several days. It didn't take much to realize that the battlecruiser was being shadowed by JLP, which was continually reporting her position to DGO.

At 15.19 Peters commented: 'Continuous contact is being maintained with the *Scharnhorst*. It is clear that the Commander of the Northern Group is on board the unit JLP.' He followed this up at 15.35 by saying: 'The enemy's Northern Group is maintaining steady contact with the *Scharnhorst*. The situation is critical, as like this the enemy will be able to direct the Southern Group to the target.'

Although they had summed up the situation correctly, neither Peters nor Schniewind saw any reason to alarm Bey. In both Narvik and Kiel the commanders seem to have lulled themselves into a state of wishful thinking and misplaced optimism. When, at about three in the afternoon, Schniewind was notified of Marx's sighting of 'several vessels' off Sørøya, he noted: 'The grid square is some 60 nautical miles off Ll [Point Lucie], which is an aiming-point for entry to [the expanse of sea known as] Lopphavet. They may be our own destroyers on their way back. However, they may also be an enemy force, which would be a danger to the Battle Group.' Instead of making an all-out effort to assure himself that Bey was aware of the danger he was in, Schniewind instructed Peters to find out where the destroyers were at the time of Marx's sighting, a process which, because of poor wireless reception, would take hours.

No one knew quite what signals the *Scharnhorst* had received. The battlecruiser's aft radar, at least, was intact, and so, perhaps, was her radar-warning system, which could detect hostile emissions at a range of more than 40 kilometres. If this assumption was correct, Bey and Hintze must have realized that they were being shadowed and that regaining the safety of the coast would not be as easy as the ship's company appeared to believe. On the other hand the battlecruiser had signalled that she was being engaged by *heavy*

units, which would have made it logical for the Admiral and Captain to assume that these shadowers were the dreaded covering force. That would have given them a tremendous sense of relief: they had seemingly escaped the clutches of a superior adversary. They thus had no reason to believe that there was still another force in the vicinity, nearer to the coast.

Some time around about three in the afternoon the *Scharnhorst*'s wireless operators must have picked up the signal from *Fliegerführer* Lofoten: 'SEVERAL VESSELS SIGHTED WEST OF NORTH CAPE.' Bent over the plotting-table, Bey and Hintze must finally have realized the gravity of their position: despite their efforts, an enemy force had managed to station itself between the *Scharnhorst* and her home base.

Nevertheless, as late as 15.25 a signal from Bey to Peters in Narvik revealed no trace of anxiety: 'APPROACHING GAMVIK VIA SG1 AND SG2. MY POSITION AC4526. SPEED 27 KNOTS.' At about the same time, in response to an enquiry from Peters as to whether the destroyers were still with the *Scharnhorst*, Bey signalled: 'NO'.

The alarm must have sounded immediately afterwards. Eight months after the battle Günther Sträter recalled the sequence of events:

At 14.30 a message came over the phone to say that we were on our way back to Norway. At 15.00 the First Officer instructed all stations: 'Collect food by stations.'

At 15.20 he ordered all stations: 'Report as soon as meal is over. Keep a sharp lookout.' The sea was still running high. It was pitch-dark. The first men to succumb to seasickness were stretched out on the floor of the turret.

About 15.30 to all stations: 'Report from *Luftwaffe*. Reconnaissance aircraft reports an enemy force 150 nautical miles to the west. Continue to maintain a good lookout.'

Wilhelm Gödde described what happened next:

At about 15.45 we were again placed at readiness for instant action. At 16.00 the alarm sounded. The Captain himself came in on the gunnery phone and said something to the effect that we were still not out of danger and exhorted us to keep a sharp lookout. 'You know that ever since midday we've had a pursuer astern who we've not been able to shake off, and our radar tells us that there are more targets to starboard. Keep alert, we shall soon be in the thick of things again.'

Hintze's last address to the ship's company revealed that the gravity of the situation was still badly underestimated. In reality Forces 1 and 2 were preparing to close the trap that had been set over the last four days, ever since the *Luftwaffe*'s first sighting of convoy JW55B west of Trondheim.

On board the *Duke of York* the mood had changed. Gloom and uncertainty had given way to a near-overweening self-confidence that increased with every signal received from Burnett. His signals showed that Bey and Hintze were taking the *Scharnhorst* straight into the arms of Force 2. The German commanders were like two farmers taking an ox to the slaughter. What lay ahead was an execution, pure and simple.

Lieutenant Vivian Cox remembers how that afternoon was 'really the time the Commander-in-Chief, Admiral Fraser, was simply dominating the whole ship. He wore no naval uniform, as such, he just wore old trousers and a polo neck shirt – polo neck sweater – and a rather battered Admiral's hat and with his pipe belching sparks and flame he moved among us all being extremely confident and quiet and delightful. . . . It was a real triumph of a single personality dominating a ship's company.'

The *Duke of York* ploughed on eastwards some 60 nautical miles north of the North Cape. By extrapolating the courses of the two ships it was easy to calculate that the *Scharnhorst* would be intercepted some time between four and five o'clock that afternoon. Charles Heywood, a gunner on board the *Duke of York*, said that Fraser asked over the ship's loudspeaker system whether they should sink the *Scharnhorst* 'before or after lunch', then answered the question himself ten minutes later by announcing that corned-beef sandwiches and hot cocoa would be handed out – an announcement that was greeted with loud cheers.

For most of the men it was a cold, grim wait. Dennis Welsh, who manned one of the after guns on the destroyer *Matchless*, put it like this. 'We were all very young, we were only about nineteen, I don't think it entered our heads [to be frightened]. . . . We were on a kind of high and when we were ordered in for a torpedo attack, it was just excitement, I suppose adrenaline. It wasn't until after the action had completely finished that we realized what had happened.'

The weather imposed great strain on all concerned. Bjørn Hagen, who was in charge of the *Stord*'s forward 12-cm gun, said: 'The weather was foul. It was blowing a gale practically all the time. For us in the turret on the foredeck it was all we could do to cling on. The spray drenched us and turned to ice.'

On board the *Scorpion*, the *Stord*'s sister ship, Signaller John Wass had much the same experience. '. . . we were travelling at speed . . . bouncing about all over the place, and water was coming over the top and down through the

ventilation ducting and we got sort of two inches of water slewing around on the mess deck, so it wasn't a very pleasant experience, especially as the ship was rolling badly, as you might imagine.'

Most of the close on 8,000 young men on board the thirteen Allied ships making for the *Scharnhorst* were shut in at their battle stations, encased in bare steel. They felt and heard the hull strain and moan as it crashed through every breaking wave, but they neither saw nor heard what was going on outside. Only the officers had a little more of an overview.

> . . . our fear at that point really was that somehow we would miss the enemy. Time and again we had swept out, gone off, acted as deep cover for various convoys against the enemy coming out, and he never did. This time . . . we were a bit despondent on Christmas Day, because there was so much uncertainty, but once we got Admiral Burnett's enemy reports, then we knew that he had come out and therefore we thought that we were in with a chance and we reckoned that we wanted to meet up with the enemy, because we thought we were better than him.

So said Admiral Sir Henry Leach, who at the time was one of the *Duke of York*'s youngest gunnery officers. Lieutenant Bryce Ramsden on board the cruiser *Jamaica* wrote:

> 'Boxing Day, bulletin number 12,' piped the First Lieutenant. 'Belfast reports *Scharnhorst* making 28 knots on the same course. We are closing her rapidly and are now 20 miles away.' Time was about half-past three, and at last it appeared that we were bound to meet her unless something drastic went wrong. Although the tension increased a little I was becoming resigned to the inevitable. Then, at about four o'clock the order came through – 'Lookout bearing Red Five 0'. As I gave the order to start the motor and told the control position below to stand by, my heart beat faster. . . . The director was now trained into the biting wind, and our bows were dipping into the seas. I strained my eyes through the binocular sight, and saw nothing save a black, empty horizon. . . . My brain was working overtime on singularly dramatic thoughts. Seconds lengthened into an age.

At precisely 16.17 the *Duke of York*'s radar operators picked up the first weak echo from the *Scharnhorst* at a range of almost 42 kilometres. The battlecruiser made no attempt to change course; instead, she drew ever closer. By 16.23 the distance between the two ships had narrowed to 37 kilometres, and it continued to decrease: 24 kilometres at 16.36, 15 kilometres at 16.43. On the battleship's bridge tension mounted. The ten heavy 14-inch guns were loaded and swung into position. Fraser's plan was to wait until the *Scharnhorst* was so close that she would be unable to escape despite her superior speed. But the flagship's captain, Guy Russell, who was beside Fraser on the bridge, was doubtful of the wisdom of this course. 'You know you can open fire any time you like now, sir,' he ventured. 'No, no. We'll wait,' Fraser replied, unperturbed and puffing his pipe. 'While the enemy doesn't know we're here, the closer we get, the more certain we'll be.'

At last, at 16.47, when the range was down to little more than 12 kilometres, the *Duke of York* and *Belfast* fired simultaneous star-shell salvoes. None of those who witnessed the sight would ever forget the moment the shells burst and the Arctic darkness to the north-east was abruptly rent by a blinding light. There, in full view, was Hitler's last remaining battlecruiser creaming her way through the towering seas at full speed, foaming water swirling in over her sharp clipper bow.

Vivian Cox, who was on the *Duke of York*'s flag bridge, described it as 'the most incredible sight; the *Scharnhorst* looking like a marvellous fish – a huge salmon – coming dead towards us.'

'Four star-shell, and there she was, guns still fore-and-aft. *It was terrific* – I can still see that illumination now,' wrote Admiral Fraser.

To the *Duke of York*'s Gunnery Officer, Lieutenant-Commander James Crawford, peering through his binoculars, 'To see this incredible sight about seven miles away, like a great silver ghost coming at you. . . . It was a gunnery officer's dream.'

On board the *Jamaica*, which was following in the *Duke of York*'s wake, Lieutenant Ramsden was in the front row of the action: '. . . the *Duke of York* fired her 14-inch, and even to us, now a thousand yards astern, the noise and concussion were colossal, and the vivid spurt of flame lighted up the whole ship for an instant, leaving a great drift of cordite smoke hanging in the air.'

Every shell had an armour-piercing nosecap of hardened steel and contained several hundred kilos of high explosive. While Ramsden was watching the tracers, a full broadside was on its way. Over 7 tons of steel and explosive were heading straight for the *Scharnhorst*.

Almost as soon as she could be seen, there was a deafening crack and a spurt of flame as we fired our first full broadside of 6-inch. The concussion momentarily deafened me, and my vision was blurred by the shaking of the

director and the sudden flash out of the gloom. We could see the tracer shells coursing away like a swarm of bees bunched together, and could follow them as they curved gently down towards the target.

On the battlecruiser's armoured bridge Bey and Hintze had known for several minutes that they might soon find themselves in action again. In a wireless signal transmitted shortly before half-past four they had said, 'SHADOWER (NAVAL) KEEPING PACE. MY POSITION AC4595.' Despite this, it seems that, for the third time that fateful second day of Christmas 1943, the *Scharnhorst* had been taken by surprise when, at 16.50, the *Belfast* and *Duke of York* opened fire from different directions. As Admiral Fraser observed, her guns were still aligned fore-and-aft, which meant that some time elapsed before she could bring them to bear and return the enemy fire. Some 38 metres above the battlecruiser's deck Helmut Backhaus had a most unpleasant time. 'I was standing on the platform, as I had been pretty well ever since we left the Lang fjord. Suddenly there were flashes of light to the south-west and north. We were bathed in light, it was like midday. Enormous spouts of water rose on both sides – unpleasantly close. They towered above me! I was drenched in spray.'

Bootsmann Wilhelm Gödde was in charge of the port searchlight. 'It was one thing after another. Ship and men alike were caught up in a maelstrom. The alarm sounded. A few minutes later the first star-shells were hanging over the ship, and before long heavy shells were whining their way towards us.'

The British *Interrogation Report* states:

The report of 'Schweres Mündungsfeuer' (heavy gun flashes) from a completely new direction over the broadcasting system caused a rude awakening. It is not clear at what time the ship's company became aware that they were in contact with a British heavy unit and they seem to have been under the impression for some time that they still only had to deal with cruisers. However, the order to load armour-piercing shells in the main turrets soon gave an indication to the gun crews of the nature of their opponent.

Bey's first reaction was more or less instinctive. He ordered hard a-port and turned the *Scharnhorst* on to a reverse course. But to the north, too, the night sky was rent by belching flames. They came from the muzzles of the *Belfast* and *Norfolk*'s heavy guns. 'It was a terrifying sight. We were under fire from every direction. We seemed to be surrounded by enemy ships,' says Backhaus The only way of escape was to the east. Bey wheeled again and exhorted

Right hand
Port = left hand

the engine-room staff to do miracles. At 16.56 he sent the following Top Priority signal to base: 'SQUARE AC4677. HEAVY BATTLESHIP. AM IN ACTION.'

Günther Sträter told the *Abwehr*: 'The alarm sounded. "To all stations: We are turning eastwards." Our adversary opened fire on our starboard side. . . . We were on the port side and were able to open the turret hatch. Right above us hung the enemy's star-shell.'

Five precious minutes were to pass before the *Scharnhorst*'s guns could retaliate – first against the *Duke of York*, then in the shape of two ineffective salvoes directed at the cruisers to the north.

According to the official report based on survivors' accounts, it seems almost certain that the *Scharnhorst* was forced to rely exclusively on visual range-finding for all her armaments during the remainder of the action. As one survivor put it: '*Scharnhorst* was by now ringed with star-shell, which dazzled the range-takers and made their work extremely difficult. The 20 mm. and 37 mm. armament was ordered to shoot down star-shell whenever possible and *Scharnhorst*'s own star-shell firing seems to have been inaccurate and unsatisfactory, illuminating only bare expanses of water.'

The *Duke of York*'s first salvoes were right on target. Wilhelm Gödde witnessed the first hit:

About a quarter to five there was a violent explosion on the starboard side of the forepart of the ship, level with A turret. I was blown to the floor by the shockwave and struggled to recover my breath in the thick smoke. Hintze came out from the bridge. He wanted to see what the situation was and at that moment you couldn't see out of the windows on the bridge. He helped me up and asked if I was hurt. I said I wasn't and he said, 'Stay at your post. It's very important that we should not be surprised on this side too.'

The rain of splinters had smashed the lenses of the ingenious periscopes on the bridge, but no one had been hurt. Things were worse forward. The explosion had blown A turret askew and killed several members of the gun crew. A nasty fire broke out which rapidly spread to B turret's magazine and generated a lot of smoke. To avert catastrophe, both the forward magazines were partly flooded. 'We struggled about in the icy water and tried to save as much of the ammunition as possible. A few critical minutes passed before the water was pumped out and B turret rendered serviceable again,' said Rudi Birke, who served on Bruno turret's gun crew.

Wilhelm Gödde noted: 'A turret was jammed facing starboard and could no longer be rotated. Later I heard on the guns phone that there was no sign of life in the turret. Because of the fire and dense smoke it could no longer take part in the battle.'

Another shell struck just above the waterline on the starboard side and exploded on the 'tween deck. By strenuous effort the damage-control party managed to weld a metal plate over the breach. 'The water-entry was a source of inconvenience to the welders rather than a danger to the ship and no vital installations were damaged,' said an able-seaman who helped with the repair work.

Shortly before five o'clock Günther Sträter again felt the ship lurch and shudder:

I guessed that we had been hit amidships, perhaps on the port side. . . . Smoke was reported coming from the magazine. . . . The commander of the gun crew, Wibbelhof, ordered us to put on our gasmasks. . . . A little later the first 15-cm gun crew on the starboard side reported that a shell had penetrated the magazine and that the gun was out of action. The men in the magazine were killed. The survivors were told to make their way forward to their assembly point.

A critical fifteen minutes had passed. A radar-controlled hail of fire from two directions had caused extensive damage to the battlecruiser, but the ship was still afloat – and she still possessed an important advantage, her speed. Deep beneath the armoured deck the engine-room staff under the command of *Korvettenkapitän (Ing.)* Otto König were working all out. Everything depended on them. Boilers and turbines alike were pressed to maximum output. With wind and sea on the starboard quarter the *Scharnhorst* continued to speed eastwards and was soon probably doing over 30 knots, which was more than she had managed during her trials in Varg Sound at the end of November.

'By 17.08 *Scharnhorst* was steady on an easterly course and engaging *Duke of York* and *Jamaica* with her main armament. Her tactics were to turn to the southward, fire a broadside and then turn end on away to the east until ready to fire the next, making *Duke of York*'s gunnery a difficult problem,' wrote Admiral Fraser.

The *Scharnhorst*'s first salvoes had been well off target, landing 2,000 or so metres from the *Duke of York* and *Jamaica*; but little by little they crept closer until they were regularly straddling the targets. Two 28-cm shells tore through the *Duke of York*'s rigging, bringing down stays and aerials. Lieutenant Ramsden wrote:

> The star-shells burst, two or three together, with intense white flares which hung in the air above us. In their light the sea was lit up as by the moon very brightly, and I remember thinking that we must have been visible for miles. I felt as if I had been stripped stark naked, and had to resist the natural urge to hide behind something away from the light, as if it would have mattered! After what seemed like an age her star-shell dimmed and guttered out in a shower of bright sparks, which fell down to the sea for all the world like stubbing out a cigarette or knocking out a pipe at night.

Although the battlecruiser's star-shell eventually burned out, leaving the *Jamaica* once again in darkness, there was more to come, as Lieutenant Ramsden so vividly recalls:

> Just as we had again been plunged into the comforting gloom I saw the angry white wink of her first 11-inch broadside, and said to myself, 'She's fired'. . . . Thank God we couldn't see her shells coming as we could see ours going. The waiting for their arrival was bad enough, but to see them coming all the way would have been far more grim. There was a vague flash off the port bow which I caught in the corner of my eye as I gazed through the binoculars, and then – crack, crack, crack, sharp like a giant whip, and the drone and whine of splinters passing somewhere near.

Robin Compston, an RAF officer on Fraser's staff, said:

> We hadn't long to wait before the enemy's reply came, the shots short at first and then suddenly the most perfect straddle of our forecastle. Had one of those 11-inch shells scored a lucky hit inboard, how different might have been the outcome of the battle. Shortly after the straddle a salvo pitched in the sea just ahead of us and the *Duke of York*'s stem ran through the swirl some seven seconds after the spurts of water had subsided.

Just before opening fire, Admiral Fraser had formed the destroyers up in two sub-divisions, with the *Savage* and *Saumarez* on the battleship's port beam and the *Scorpion* and *Stord* on her starboard beam. The Divisional Commander,

Commander Michael Meyrick on board the *Savage*, was ordered to 'take up the most advantageous position for [a] torpedo attack'.

The running battle continued eastwards at a hair-raising pace – at times some of the ships were doing more than 30 knots. With wind and sea astern, the destroyers yawed violently and there were times when they looked like boring their way under for good. Said the *Stord*'s captain, Skule Storheill:

> The impression a salvo from a 14-inch gun battery makes on one's sight and hearing, and the knowledge that it is being fired in anger, is something one never forgets. The sea was very rough – it was like surfing – and on the *Stord* and other destroyers we were prepared for the same surprises that are a part of that sport. The engine-room staff did a wonderful job and coaxed the maximum out of the turbines. We couldn't see the *Scharnhorst*, all we could see were the muzzle flashes every time she fired a new broadside.

Try as they might, neither the *Duke of York*, the cruisers nor the destroyers could get much closer. It seemed that the *Scharnhorst*'s luck was still holding. With enormous pressure from her boilers the battlecruiser sped south-eastwards, increasing the gap between her and her pursuers with every passing minute. Even another hit amidships seemed to have had no effect. The heavy shell landed beside the funnel and started a savage fire in the aircraft hangar. 'The anti-aircraft crews were sent to put it out. There was aircraft fuel in the hangar and the heat was overpowering. It looked very dangerous until we got it under control,' says Backhaus. The men were heroic in their endeavours to extinguish the fire and several lost their lives, among them the commander of the 10.5-cm batteries.

As long as the fire raged, the range-takers on board the *Duke of York* had a clear target at which to aim. When it died out at about a quarter past five, they had to rely on the muzzle flashes, 'great deep orange flashes in the Arctic darkness'. From 17.17 onwards the *Duke of York* was compelled to rely on radar for firing. At that time the range was still only 12,500 metres, but it continued inexorably to increase for the next hour – to 16,500 metres at 17.46 and 19,500 metres at 18.24. That may explain the devil-may-care signal Bey sent Dönitz and Schniewind at 18.02: '*SCHARNHORST* IMMER VORAN', which the British translated as '*Scharnhorst* will ever reign supreme' instead of '*Scharnhorst* ever onwards'.

Subsequent investigations reveal that at this time the battlecruiser was travelling almost 3 knots faster than the *Duke of York*. She was on the verge of

See Menace, Kennedy p. 139

escaping and, under cover of darkness, would have been able to slip into the
Tana fjord or one of the other inlets along the northern coast of Norway, where
she would be protected by the *Luftwaffe* and coastal batteries. Henry Leach, who
was at his post in the gun turret, remembers how 'steadily, gallingly the range
counters clicked up as the enemy drew away. I cannot adequately describe the
growing frustration of those few who were in a position to realize what was
happening; to have achieved surprise, got so close, apparently done so well, and
all for nothing as the enemy outpaced us into the night.'

The senior officers in Narvik and Kiel, who had reluctantly initiated the
foolhardy attack on the convoy, were becoming increasingly worried. Rudolf
Peters's U-boats had had a disappointing day; since Robert Lübsen's report at
12.38 of 'four shadows', little had happened. True, *Kapitänleutnant* Rudolf
Büchler on board *U-387* had caught sight of two destroyers at 14.05. He had
tried to slip away to the west, but the wind was too strong and the U-boat was
unable to make more than 13 knots. For this reason he deemed the wisest
course was to dive. When, an hour and a half later, he resurfaced, there was
nothing to be seen. Not only the destroyers but the convoy itself had
disappeared and contact was never regained. The Group Commanders in Narvik
and Kiel were beside themselves with frustration. There was no coordination
between the various flotillas and groups, no understanding of the true nature of
the situation. The youngest of the *Eisenbart* skippers, *Kapitänleutnant* Gerhard
Schaar, Captain of *U-957*, was only twenty-four. He had arrived off Bear Island
direct from Kiel. As a young *Oberleutnant-zur-See* (Sub-Lieutenant) in Narvik in
the spring of 1940 he had seen the destroyer *Erich Giese* shot to pieces by the
British battleship *Warspite* and her attendant destroyers after a heroic stand. In
1944 Schaar was awarded the Knight's Cross for his deeds in the Arctic, but on
this occasion he does not seem to have grasped the realities of the situation. At
16.17 he noted in the war diary: 'Have not yet been able to pick up any D/F
signals. The reckoning is uncertain and will only provide an indication of where
the enemy is. Büchler is clearly the only one in the neighbourhood, with the
exception of the surface vessels, which are operating independently of us. I am
wondering whether to suggest that they be ordered to direct us to the convoy.'

At this juncture several of the U-boats heard the sound of distant gunfire.
But the lookouts could see nothing: the sea was empty.

At 17.24 Bey again wirelessed base: 'AM SURROUNDED BY HEAVY UNITS.'
The Fleet Commander, *Generaladmiral* Schniewind, received this alarming
signal three-quarters of an hour later. Though still in two minds as to what
action to take, he requested that wireless contact be established with the

Commander of the Destroyer Flotilla, Rolf Johannesson. 'If this signal is correct
. . . we must endeavour to direct 4th Destroyer Flotilla to the scene of action.'
He also took steps to find out whether the *Luftwaffe* was prepared to send
aircraft to the scene. The answer was negative: the weather was still too bad.

As Fleet Commander, Schniewind was in a tight spot. Although, at Peters's
behest, he had tried to recall the Battle Group at the last minute, the operation
was his responsibility. In the darkness, and with a gale raging, all his
forebodings had been realized. After a day of nervous waiting the worst had
happened. The *Scharnhorst* had fallen victim to a perfect ambush. Schniewind
himself seems to have had little understanding of the tactical situation. He
had, for example, no idea of where the destroyers were, nor was he aware of the
extent of the breakdown in coordination between Bey and Johannesson. Both
the decision-making process and communication continued to proceed at
snail's pace.

When he asked about the destroyers, then pitching and tossing far to the
west, they were heading for the coast at a speed of 24 knots. On board *Z 29* the
Scharnhorst's first intimation that she was surrounded by heavy units was received
at a quarter to six, almost an hour after it was sent. Johannesson did not change
course but noted in the war diary, as though it had nothing to do with him:
'This signal is revealing of a deplorable situation. Ninety nautical miles to the
east, without his destroyers, the Commander-in-Chief has run straight into the
arms of the enemy force which, without being observed, has placed itself
between us and the coast. Will he manage to escape, considering that the enemy
can track him by radar at a range of more than 33 nautical miles?'

Kapitän-zur-See Peters in Narvik was the first to take appropriate action.
When, at 17.17, he received Bey's signal to the effect that the *Scharnhorst* was in
action against a heavy battleship, he noted: 'This report is very disturbing.
Either the Northern Group has caught up with the *Scharnhorst* or, thanks to the
bearings, the Southern Group has reached her.' When, a quarter of an hour later,
he learned that Bey was surrounded, he added: 'I am afraid that the fate of the
ship is sealed.'

At 18.15 Peters alarmed the *Eisenbart* Group, signalling: '*KRIEG! KRIEG!*
STEER AT TOP SPEED FOR AC4930.' Those U-boats that happened to be on the
surface and received the signal immediately changed course accordingly.

Meanwhile, in Kiel, Schniewind had also come to the conclusion that the
Scharnhorst was in a very serious situation indeed. Despite this, his comment in
the war diary was strangely at odds with the reality of the situation: 'The
question is whether it is correct to uphold the order to the destroyers to close

the *Scharnhorst*. I am inclined to answer in the affirmative. The only battleworthy heavy ship is engaged, possibly against a superior enemy. This makes it essential to go to her aid regardless. Measures directed at the convoy must be subordinated to this by the destroyers as well as by the U-boats.'

Before the order to make for the *Scharnhorst*'s last known position reached Z 29, Johannesson – for the first time that December Sunday – had plucked up the courage to act on his own initiative. With the wind abaft, he set a course eastwards. 'Whether it will be possible to help the *Scharnhorst* in what is obviously an unequal battle it is impossible to say. No order has reached the Flotilla, but this calls for action.'

This was self-justification on Johannesson's part. It was already half-past seven and the end was near. Both the destroyers and the U-boats were much too far away.

After an hour and a half's running battle, at 18.19 a new signal from the stricken battlecruiser reached the admirals in Narvik and Kiel: 'THE ENEMY IS FIRING BY RADAR AT A RANGE OF MORE THAN 18,000 METRES. POSITION AC4965. COURSE 110 DEGREES. SPEED 26 KNOTS.'

A moment later heavy shells again struck the ship. 'I can no longer say exactly when different things happened. The violence [of the explosions] was too great,' said Wilhelm Gödde:

One shell ripped up the forepart of the ship and I was again thrown on to the deck by the force of the explosion. *Kapitän-zur-See* Hintze, who emerged from the Admiral's bridge to survey the damage, was wounded in the face by splinters, but it did not stop him from coming over to me and helping me to my feet. For a second time he asked if I was hurt, but again I'd been lucky. He then sent me over to the starboard range-finder to find out why the men were not answering calls. They were all dead. The range-finder had been blown to bits.

Only five minutes later, at 18.24, the *Duke of York*'s fire-control radar broke down. By then the range had increased to almost 20,000 metres. The battleship ceased fire; to have continued firing would only have been to waste ammunition. 'A distinct atmosphere of gloom and disappointment was felt at the order to check fire, when it appeared that despite undoubted hits the enemy would escape with her superior speed,' says her Gunnery Narrative.

Suddenly a strange silence fell over the field of battle. Not a shot was fired. The only sound was the howling of the wind and the anguished cries of the wounded.

No one knew at that point that one of the *Duke of York*'s concluding salvoes – it may have been the very last – had hit a vital spot. A shell had penetrated the *Scharnhorst*'s No. 1 boiler-room, severing a steam-pipe that fed the turbines. 'I glanced at the speed indicator. It was down to about 22 knots. What had happened? The situation was desperate. I knew that unless we could make top speed we'd never be able to get away,' says Backhaus.

Wilhelm Gödde was closer to the centre of events. 'The third turbine ceased to function because of a failure in the steam supply. The engine-room staff worked desperately to repair the damage. The Chief Engineer reported that he hoped the break would be repaired within twenty to thirty minutes. I heard Hintze say, "Well done, Engine-room. Officers and men, thank you for what you are doing!"'

On the devastated bridge Hintze remained calm. But the signal he immediately dictated and sent to Adolf Hitler at 18.25 revealed his true assessment of the situation: 'WE SHALL FIGHT TO THE LAST SHELL.'

Inexorably, the *Scharnhorst*'s speed fell, but it still took nearly a quarter of an hour for the radar operators and range-takers on board the Allied ships to realize what a dramatic turn events had taken. As late as 18.40 Admiral Fraser sent a bitter signal to Vice-Admiral Burnett on board the *Belfast*: 'I SEE LITTLE HOPE OF CATCHING *SCHARNHORST* AND AM PROCEEDING TO SUPPORT CONVOY.' Yet again Fraser had ordered the abandonment of the operation – and yet again he was saved by the bell. Before the order could be implemented, the first excited reports came from the Plotting Room. Something unexpected was happening. 'Quite suddenly the range steadied, then the range counter started to tick down, it was almost like waking from a bad dream, you realized as it went on like that that you were catching him again,' said Henry Leach.

On the bridge of the *Savage* Commander Meyrick had a similar experience. 'We only had a little speed in excess of the *Scharnhorst* and to catch up was going to be quite a business. After a time I had a shout from the officer in the plot who said he was sure we were getting much nearer . . .'

Upon learning the news, Fraser didn't hesitate. He immediately cancelled his last order. 'I had already decided to turn towards the Norwegian coast, hoping the enemy would also lead round and so give my destroyers a chance to attack. When, however, I saw the speed reduction, I turned in straight at the *Scharnhorst*,' he wrote.

On board the *Stord* Skule Storheill had similarly discovered that the *Scharnhorst* was gradually losing speed:

The *Stord*'s engines were pressed to their maximum to get us into a position from which we could attack from the east. It was no easy matter as, the weather being what it was, the *Scharnhorst* was doing about the same speed as ourselves. . . . The distance between us was 10,000 metres when we found that the *Scharnhorst*'s speed had fallen, probably because of a lucky hit by a shell from the *Duke of York*. We changed course. We had to get in close to fire our torpedoes.

On the *Scharnhorst* many of the men were in a state of shock. The steel plating of the deck and superstructure had been gashed and torn up by the heavy shelling. Dead and wounded lay everywhere. The stretcher-bearers had a horrible job making their way through the chaos to get to the first-aid stations. Blood and seawater swilled about in the passageways. Some of the men who had been on deck had been blown to bits. No one had time to dispose of the torn limbs and body parts.

Among the survivors, impressions vary considerably. Nicolaus Wiebusch, a 21-year-old from Cuxhaven, was one of the men manning the 37-mm anti-aircraft battery on the starboard side aft. 'Our guns had a range of only 4,800 metres, so there was nothing for us to fire at. We had earlier been ordered to remain under cover, so we saw little of what happened.'

One of the most experienced engine-room artificers, 24-year-old Rolf Zanger from Wetzlar, had trained as a motorman at the Marineschule Wesermünde. After first serving on board the destroyer *Karl Galster*, he had joined the *Scharnhorst* early in 1941. He went off watch at *Kraftwerk 3* at 16.00, then joined a damage-control party on the 'tween deck.

I'd no life-jacket, only a leather jerkin and trousers. They were specially designed to protect us against steam if a shell should penetrate the engine-room. The *Scharnhorst*'s engines were fantastic, but the steam circulated under pressure and at a temperature of close on 500°C. If steam escaped, it would go through pretty well anything. Quite early on a nasty cable fire had broken out on the port side. Fires like that were very hard to deal with. We had great difficulty in putting it out.

Twenty-year-old Franz Marko had also signed off watch in the engine-room earlier in the day. When he hastened off to fetch his life-jacket, he saw many dead and wounded. 'I passed one of the light guns. The gunner was still in his seat, but his head had been sliced clean off.'

At this time heavy shells from the *Duke of York* were no longer raining down on the *Scharnhorst* and her own guns were likewise silent. But the respite lasted for only a few minutes. At 18.45 reports came in of dark shapes both astern and to starboard. The destroyers were closing in for the kill.

Confusion and disagreement now reigned among the gunnery officers. Earlier in the afternoon *Korvettenkapitän* Bredenbeuker had sent many of the men manning the battlecruiser's secondary armament below, reasoning that as long as the guns could not be used, unnecessary casualties should be avoided. Some of the medium and light batteries had in the meantime been destroyed and the remainder were unmanned. To quote the British *Interrogation Report*:

> It was about 18.30 when 'shadows' were reported on either beam of the *Scharnhorst*. The Gunnery Officer is said to have remarked that he couldn't fire on shadows and that he required targets. However, as more than one survivor plaintively remarked, 'The shadows were tangible enough to pump us full of torpedoes.'
>
> At about 8,000 yards the 'shadows' materialised into destroyers. There was such a heavy sea running that it was almost impossible to see them from the upper deck and in a desperate attempt to illuminate the targets the 20 mm. and 37 mm. guns received orders to fire tracer bullets.

On board the *Stord* Bjørn Hagen, the forward battery commander, watched as the battlecruiser loomed ever larger. 'We opened fire at about 6,000 metres. I could see our shells hitting the superstructure.'

When the *Scharnhorst*'s lookouts finally realized that a torpedo attack was imminent, the battlecruiser made a sudden turn to the south. This brought her on to a near-collision course with the *Stord*, but Storheill's nerve held and he refused to turn aside. The destroyer yawed violently in the heavy sea, her hull leaping and shuddering with every oncoming wave. Nils Owren wrote:

> We closed at high speed. . . . Suddenly we were surrounded by towering columns of water – the first shells from the *Scharnhorst*. We were under fire.
>
> The gunner rushed to ready the torpedo tubes. The range grew shorter at terrifying speed: 3,000 – 2,500 – 1,900 – 1,800 metres. I could hardly believe my eyes. There, right in front of me, lay that awesome steel giant. It was so big that there was room for only half of it in the battery commander's binoculars!

Rex Chard, Navigation Officer of the *Scorpion*, was standing ready for action beside one of the destroyer's 4.7-inch guns.

[We] went up to full speed and immediately turned in towards her, and just as we did that there was an outbreak of firing from the *Scharnhorst* . . . and star-shell [from the *Saumarez* and *Savage*] was falling between the *Scharnhorst* and us. We couldn't see beyond the star-shell. So we were really blind then. . . . The range was closing very rapidly and it was obvious she had turned towards us and we were approaching one another very rapidly. I was ordered to fire a star-shell, which I did, and we could then see her coming straight at us. She was bows on and we were totally out of position to fire torpedoes at her. . . . [F]ortunately she turned away, she turned to starboard and presented her port beam, so that by the time we got in to about 2,000 yards we had a good shot at her with torpedoes, almost a perfect shot.

At one-minute intervals the *Scorpion* and *Stord* fired eight torpedoes each at the battlecruiser. At 18.55 the first sixteen torpedoes were on their way towards her at a range of less than 2,000 metres. Captain Storheill of the *Stord* said:

When we yawed, a heavy wave came in and washed over the stern, with the tragic result that one of the torpedo-men was carried overboard and drowned. A torpedo tube was distorted and the port rail and depth-charge launchers, complete with depth-charges, were also washed overboard. As we yawed, black smoke poured from the funnel, but as this seemed to have caught the enemy's attention, the order to make smoke was immediately cancelled.

'There was a nerve-racking wait,' wrote Nils Owren. 'Then suddenly we heard a succession of underwater explosions. Some thought they heard three, others four. There were also some who thought they heard six and seven.'

The great speed and heavy sea made the *Scharnhorst* a difficult target. The *Scorpion* reported only one hit, whereas Storheill had to acknowledge that none of his torpedoes had found their mark – despite the claims of the crew.

On the other side of the battlecruiser the *Savage* and *Saumarez* had attracted her attention and were in a far worse plight than their sister ships. The two destroyers came under fire both from small-calibre guns and the heavy guns of C turret, but they were soon so close that many of the shells passed harmlessly overhead. 'As we closed *Scharnhorst* she did her best to drive us off with gunfire, but thanks to the captain's manoeuvring no one

was hit on the way in, although there were plenty of shells flying about,' said Lieutenant Dennis.

Through his binoculars Commander Meyrick could see that the *Scharnhorst's* desperate southward manoeuvre was gradually presenting him with a perfect target. He had been directly in the battlecruiser's wake, and now he had before him the whole of her starboard side. 'I could not believe my eyes as I focused on the starboard side of a huge ship just a few hundred yards away. . . . My first impression was how beautiful the *Scharnhorst* looked – all silver in the cold Arctic light. I could see men on her upper deck very clearly and they seemed so close that I felt that I could almost reach out and shake hands with them!' wrote George Gilroy, an able-seaman serving on board the *Savage*.

At 18.56 the *Savage* fired a full salvo of eight torpedoes at a range of 3,500 metres, then turned away. Her sister ship, the *Saumarez*, was by no means as fortunate. An 11-cm shell went through her director, killing ten men outright; two more were mortally wounded. Another exploded close alongside, sending a hail of splinters across the deck and damaging the forced lubrication system. The destroyer's speed dropped to 10 knots and she was able to fire only four of her torpedoes before, severely damaged, she limped away.

The attack mounted by the four destroyers has gone down in the annals of naval warfare as one of the boldest and most successful ever. 'This gallant attack was practically unsupported and carried out, particularly in the case of the first subdivision, in the face of heavy fire from the enemy,' Admiral Fraser wrote afterwards.

To those of the *Scharnhorst's* company who were still alive the destroyer attack was yet another nightmare. 'Through my headphones there came a stream of reports. There was the sound of approaching torpedoes. Then came the explosions. A tremor ran through the ship and she gave a great heave – it was like an earthquake. A short time earlier Chief Engineer König had reported that he could still make 22 knots. After the explosions our speed fell dramatically, right down to 7 or 8 knots. We no longer had a chance,' said Helmut Backhaus.

One torpedo struck well aft, in Division 3, where Helmut Feifer was still playing his mouth-organ. Recalling the incident, he said:

I was a messenger and was sent to deliver a message. I felt the ship give a violent jolt. The lights went out. It was pitch-black. I'm not sure, though, whether the jolts came from our own guns or whether they were caused by hits from enemy shells and torpedoes. Only when I got back did I realize what had happened. There had been a bloodbath in my division: all my pals were dead – only one was still alive. He was sitting on a crate of potatoes, leaning with his back to the wall, but his clothes were on fire and his hair was a blazing torch. I put out the flames and called for help. Men came running from C turret and together we carried him out. His sufferings were beyond description. Even today I cannot find words.

An extra party was quickly formed to ascertain the extent of the damage to the stern. Torrents of water were pouring in. It was impossible to get to the aftermost areas, so a dramatic decision was taken. The watertight doors were closed, sealing off the whole after section of the ship. More than twenty-five men of the engine-room staff were still alive. They were left to their fate.

The British report compiled from interrogations of survivors says:

Survivors have described fierce arguments between the first and second Gunnery Officers, *Korvettenkapitän* Bredenbeuker and *Kapitänleutnant* Wieting. At one point Wieting ordered the 150 mm. port mountings to load star-shell, but the order was countermanded by Bredenbeuker, the crews being ordered to unload and reload with armour-piercing shells. . . . Survivors were amazed at the relentless manner in which the destroyer attack was carried out. Coming in at full speed to within 1,800 yards or less, they fired full salvoes of torpedoes. The hydrophones gave due warning of their approach, but there were too many torpedoes coming from too many angles and at least three hits were scored. During this attack the 105 mm. guns' crews remained under cover and survivors have never ceased to bewail this error and utter violent threats as to how they would deal with the Gunnery Officers if they were only able to lay hands on them. They ascribed the ultimate loss of the vessel to this attack and contend that if the 105 mm. guns had fired the destroyers could have been kept at a distance which would have rendered any torpedo attack innocuous.

On the bridge wing Wilhelm Gödde witnessed the disastrous turn of events:

After about twenty minutes, getting on for seven o'clock, a torpedo struck, bringing the ship to a momentary standstill. Then we were hit by a small-calibre shell that blew the range-finder off its mounting. I was standing just behind it and both leads of my headphones were cut, but I myself was still unhurt. A helmsman sent by Hintze to assess the damage told me to make my way up to the bridge. There was no point in remaining at my post. I went

with him and for that reason we were both witness to the shocking and final act of the battle between our ship and a numerically superior opponent.

At about the same time as Gödde reached the badly damaged bridge and, for the first time, saw Bey and Hintze together, the vague shapes of the *Duke of York* and *Jamaica* were visible to the south-west. At precisely 19.01 both reopened fire with their main armaments, to be followed by salvoes from the *Belfast* to the north. Says Rex Chard, who, from the deck of the *Scorpion*, had a grandstand view of the unfolding drama: '[W]e drew back to station ourselves on the cruiser *Jamaica* and . . . the *Duke of York* came up and started pounding her [the *Scharnhorst*] again with her heavy guns and we could actually see the damage that was being caused . . . fires everywhere, and explosions . . . By that time I think the *Scharnhorst* was only turning very slowly in a circle, probably only doing about 8 or 9 knots.'

Lieutenant Bryce Ramsden on board the *Jamaica* wrote:

We turned to starboard, the turrets following round so that both ships presented a full broadside. . . . I think I yelled 'Stand by again!' over the telephones, but my words were drowned by the deafening crash of gunfire. . . . Suddenly – a bright-red glow, and in it the enemy was to be clearly seen for a brief moment. 'She's hit! My God, we've got her!' . . . All over the ship a cheer went up. I had risen half standing in my seat as the wild thrill took hold of me. Again the dull glow, and in its light the sea was alive with shell-splashes from an out-pouring of shells. Great columns of water stood out clearly in the brief instant of light, and I could see smoke hanging over her.

In the course of the next twenty-seven minutes the *Duke of York* pumped more than two hundred heavy shells at the *Scharnhorst* from distances as short as 4,000 metres. Strangely, only seven or eight of them appear to have scored hits, but for Bey and Hintze that was more than enough. Despite the havoc that had been wrought, the men still did not seem to have grasped the gravity of the situation they were in; only the senior officers realized that it would take a miracle to save the ship. The *Interrogation Report* says:

All but four of the survivors were stationed under cover or below decks and very few of the prisoners seem to have been able to distinguish between the explosion of the torpedo hits, the impact of the heavy shells and the detonations of their own main armament. In spite of the serious damage which *Scharnhorst* had suffered, no inkling of the seriousness of the situation seems to have become general among the ship's company. A report over the inter-communication system from the Engineer Officer to the Captain said, 'I can maintain 22 knots, we will make it even yet,' to which the Captain replied, 'Bravo, keep it up.' All the lights were still burning and continued to do so up to the end, the two remaining engines were functioning smoothly and a large part of the armament was still in action, but from the moment of *Duke of York*'s re-engagement *Scharnhorst* began to take a terrible pounding.

A turning point was reached when a shell knocked out the ventilation system of B turret. Every time the breeches were opened the turret filled with black smoke. Despite the powerful lights it was impossible to see anything and the poisonous fumes threatened to choke the men. Moreover, they were running short of ammunition. The order was given to evacuate the turret.

Wilhelm Gödde well remembered that dramatic moment: 'Then came the depressing report from the heavy-gun crews that they were almost out of ammunition. B turret had three shells left, C turret none. We were ordered to take ammunition from A turret's magazine to C turret's, but before the order could be carried out Hintze had sent his last signal to the *Führer*: 'WE SHALL FIGHT TO THE LAST SHELL. LONG LIVE GERMANY. LONG LIVE THE *FÜHRER*.'

Günther Sträter's 15-cm gun – No. 4 on the port side of the ship – was at last in action. Several of the other guns had, however, been destroyed by enemy fire. 'The medium-calibre guns on the port side now joined in the battle. The aiming-point was the enemy muzzle flashes obliquely ahead of us. We fired at six-second intervals. . . . Some time between 19.00 and 19.30 Hintze gave us a direct order. "Now it's up to you," he said. "The heavy guns have been knocked out."'

Towards the end some officers made suicidal attempts to stave off the final catastrophe. *Luftwaffe* pilots tried to take off in the one Arado that was left, but were unable to do so as there was no compressed air to operate the catapult. The Torpedo Officer, *Oberleutnant* Bosse, fought his way to the port torpedo tubes. Amid a hail of shell splinters he brought the triple battery of torpedoes on to their aftermost bearing and fired a full salvo in the hope of scoring a lucky hit. It was a brave attempt, but it failed. Two of the torpedoes flew across the deck and disappeared into the depths; the third stuck halfway out of the tube, where it remained until the *Scharnhorst* sank.

'Suddenly there was a deafening crash from the bow. I looked up and saw that one of the anchor-chains was running out. The boatswain, a stalwart fellow if ever there was one, made his way across the deck to see what had happened. At that moment a breaking wave swept across the foredeck, and the next time I looked over the coaming, he wasn't there,' says Backhaus.

The time was now nearly half-past seven and the announcement was made that Hintze had taken command of the ship. He sounded perfectly calm when he again spoke over the broadcasting system to what was left of the ship's company. The order he gave was, 'Take Action No. 5'. That was the initial phase of our emergency procedure and meant that the watertight doors were to be closed to prevent the ship sinking too fast. It was intended to give as many men as possible a chance to get clear.

But time was running out. Already at 19.19 Fraser had ordered the *Jamaica* and *Belfast* to sink the battlecruiser with torpedoes. '. . . [B]y the time the final torpedo attacks came resistance was practically at an end,' he wrote in his final report. At 19.25 the *Jamaica* fired three torpedoes, and three minutes later the *Belfast* three more. Directly astern of the cruisers Commander Fisher's destroyers, the *Musketeer*, *Matchless*, *Virago* and *Opportune*, had finally caught up. In the course of three lethal minutes between 19.30 and 19.33 three of the destroyers fired no fewer than nineteen torpedoes at the *Scharnhorst*, which, as Fraser wrote, was 'steering an erratic course, was altering around from the north-east to the south-west . . . and almost stopped'. Seven torpedoes slammed straight into the stricken ship, which rapidly developed a strong list to starboard. A merciless but effective crescendo, it was rounded off by a further three torpedoes from the *Jamaica* at 19.37. By then 'the enemy [was] broadside on and almost stopped. Two hits were claimed but were not observed as the target was completely hidden by smoke; they are considered probable as underwater explosions were felt after the correct interval.'

When the last devastating attack commenced, *Kapitän-zur-See* Hintze broadcast to the ship's company for the last time. 'I am saying goodbye and shaking you all by the hand for the last time. I have signalled to the *Führer* and declared that we intend to fight to the last shell. *Scharnhorst immer voran!*'

Some of the emergency procedures had long since been put into effect. Writer Heinrich Mulch and the rest of Bey's staff were frantically destroying cipher machines and secret documents.

Wilhelm Gödde was an eye-witness to the concluding phase of the drama:

More torpedoes followed. The whole ship quivered and it began to list to starboard. Then came the order, 'Prepare for sinking!' One after another reports came in from the various stations. More torpedoes struck the ship, all on the starboard beam, and the list increased. Our last position was wirelessed in clear. Then came the Commander-in-Chief's last order: 'Abandon ship! All hands to the upper deck. Put on life-jackets. Prepare to leave the ship.' Hintze exhorted us to think of ourselves and leave the bridge. There were about twenty-five of us there still alive.

The last signal from the *Scharnhorst* was transmitted to Narvik and Kiel at precisely 19.25. 'STEERING FOR TANA FJORD. POSITION SQUARE AC4994. SPEED 20 KNOTS.'

Only a few minutes later a torpedo tore its way through the steel hull, causing severe damage to the engine-room. Boiler Room No. 2 was flooded and speed fell to not much more than 12 knots.

Günther Sträter's gun was one of the few still firing. His account of the battlecruiser's last few minutes says:

At about 19.30 the order came from the bridge to leave the ship. There were more powerful explosions. The ship was listing faster and faster to starboard. By the time the end came only the port 2-cm gun of the main anti-aircraft station in the foremast and our 15-cm turret were still in action. There were no problems in the turret until the list caused the ammunition hoist to jam in the shaft. The men in the magazine couldn't get out on to the deck; nor could any of the others in the compartments far below deck. When I left the turret there were only dead and wounded on the upper deck. The two men in charge, Wibbelhof and Moritz, refused to leave their post. 'I'm staying here, where I belong,' Wibbelhof said. Moritz said that he was staying in the turret. Wibbelhof insisted that we should leave our posts. As a last farewell, he shouted to us, 'Long live Germany! Long live the *Führer*!' We answered with the same words. Then he lit a cigarette and calmly sat down in front of the gun sight. He and Moritz went down with the ship when she capsized.

Rolf Zanger and the rest of the damage-control party were still struggling to do something about the glowing cables on the 'tween deck.

I was standing there when the Chief Engineer, *Korvettenkapitän* König, came rushing by with a party of men. They were on their way to the starboard side

of the ship to see if they could do anything to save her. I must have been one of the last to see him alive. I still remember when the order came to abandon ship. Close to us there was an open hatchway leading from below. A man stuck his head out. Someone shouted to him, 'For God's sake come on out, we're abandoning ship!' But the chap only shook his head. 'No thanks,' he said, 'the Barents Sea's too cold for me.' Then he closed the hatch cover and disappeared below.

Many men found themselves trapped: 'One of the torpedoes put paid to B turret for good. . . . The shock of the explosion knocked out the elevation and rotating mechanisms. The men in the magazine climbed up into the turret, only to find that the doors were jammed tight. After a desperate struggle they managed to get one of them open. The *Scharnhorst* was already sinking and the turret was becoming flooded from below. Only one man made it.'

Evacuation of C turret proceeded in orderly fashion, according to a mechanic who was there, Ernst Reimann. 'We hadn't been hit, and fought to the last – until all the ammunition brought aft from A turret had been expended. I remember the Gunnery Officer giving his last order: "Load the middle gun." The last shot was fired. By then the *Scharnhorst* was already listing to starboard. We shut down all the machinery and brought up the last men from the magazine. Then we climbed out through the hatch, one by one.'

Helmut Feifer was not a member of C turret's regular crew. He had made his way there from the 'tween deck after he had carried his badly wounded friend to the first-aid station. 'I was sitting on an empty shellcase when a man came dashing past. "What're you doing here?" he asked. "Remember me to everyone back home," I said. "I haven't a life-jacket, so I don't have a chance anyway." "Don't be daft," he said, and bundled me out of the turret.'

On the bridge Bey and Hintze were still urging the remaining men to abandon ship. Wilhelm Gödde wrote:

Most of them were reluctant to leave their posts without their Captain and Admiral. One young Able-Seaman said simply, 'We'll stay with you.' In the end, though, the two of them managed to persuade us to go out on to the bridge wing. Through his loud-hailer Hintze told the men on the upper deck to jump overboard. Torpedoes were still striking the ship. The list continued to increase. On deck, everything was orderly and disciplined; hardly anyone raised his voice. Towards the end the First Officer, *Fregattenkapitän* Dominik, had also made his way to the bridge and he now joined us on the wing. I later saw his tall figure below us, on the upper deck, where he was helping the hundreds of men there to clamber over the rail. The Commander-in-Chief again checked our life-jackets. Then he and the Admiral said goodbye to each one of us and shook us by the hand. 'If any of you get out of this alive, you must give our regards to those at home and tell them that everyone did his duty to the last.'

Our proud ship slowly heeled over to starboard. Boatswain Deierling from my division helped me with my life-jacket and reminded me to blow it up. That was his last endearing, friendly gesture towards me.

On the lookout platform high above the bridge only Able-Seaman Backhaus was left alive:

The ship was still under way, but the list was worsening. The wind had died down a little, but the sea was still running high and coming in on the starboard beam. I remember a friend of mine coming through on the intercom. 'Tell me honestly,' he said, 'How serious is it?' I told him to drop everything and that we were abandoning ship. He didn't believe me. 'You're mad,' he said. But the *Scharnhorst* was by then almost horizontal in the water. Men were jumping overboard wherever you looked. Some were struggling with the rafts, but many rafts had been damaged by shell splinters. I remembered the advice of a friend in Narvik: 'If the ship goes down, you have to get rid of your clothes, otherwise you'll be dragged under.' I tore off my fur jacket and boots. When I clambered up onto the big searchlight I was already up to my knees in icy water. Like a swimmer, I just dived in. I threw myself in to the sea and fought to get away from the undertow.

Forward, Hintze was warning men against trying to get off the ship on the starboard side. He urged them to climb over the port rail so that they could slide down the sloping hull into the water. Gödde grasped his boatswain friend Deierling's hand, but the ladder was so crowded that they were unable to get through and were forced to make their way to the other side of the ship.

We hadn't got far before the bridge was already level with the water and waves were breaking over the foremast. Suddenly we lost our footing and the sea engulfed us. I found myself in a swirling mass of water and was sucked under. When I broke surface, Deierling was gone. I never saw him again. Gasping for air, I struggled to get clear of the ship.

Ahead of me there was a man sitting on a float that was used to sweep mines. It capsized when I tried to climb on to it and we both fell into the water. I kept on swimming through a sea of oil. . . . Terrible scenes were being enacted all about me, illuminated by the enemy's star-shell and a flare on board a raft crowded with men. . . . I saw a lieutenant get to his feet on the raft. He shouted, 'Comrades! Our sinking ship, our proud *Scharnhorst*! Hurrah! Hurrah! Hurrah!' Echoed by the men floundering in the sea, three more cheers rang out across the water. A seaman on the same raft shouted, 'Our loved ones! Our homes! Hurrah! Hurrah! Hurrah!' All those nearby joined in. It was a heartrending moment for all who experienced it.

When Helmut Backhaus had succeeded in distancing himself from the sinking ship, he turned to look back. 'I could see the keel and propellers. She had turned over and was going down by the bow. Shortly afterwards there were two or three violent underwater explosions. It was like an earthquake! The shockwaves left me gasping for air.'

He continued swimming, forcing his way through a sea of wreckage. Empty cases, wooden crates, potatoes, lengths of planking, clothes – and in the midst of it all, dead sailors floating face-down. The first raft Helmut got to was over-full and the men on board refused to let him on.

Strangely enough the sea was reasonably calm; it may have been because of the oil. I swam on and caught sight of another raft. There, there was room for one more. Someone helped me on to it. I lay flat out, completely exhausted. Then I saw a young officer get to his feet. 'There's no point in this,' he said, and jumped overboard, to disappear immediately. There was nothing we could do. I had hurt my hand. We just sat there, indifferent. From far away came the sudden thunder of gunfire. 'Are the British firing at us in the water?' someone asked. They weren't, they were simply out to prevent the guns seizing up in the cold.

The young lieutenant was not the only officer to choose death. The Gunnery Officer in charge of the anti-aircraft guns is also reported to have committed suicide, shooting himself in his cabin in front of a photograph of his family. None of the battlecruiser's fifty officers and thirty-five officer cadets was saved, though the survivors were not sure what had happened to them. 'I was told that the officers had resolved to go down with the ship, that's all I know,' says Franz Marko. Considerable confusion surrounded the fate of *Konter-Admiral*

Bey and *Kapitän-zur-See* Hintze. In the report compiled immediately after the battle on the basis of interrogations of the thirty-six survivors, it was claimed that the senior officers shot themselves on the bridge after saying goodbye to the men nearest to them. However, this report was to some extent contradicted by the evidence of other British witnesses. Lieutenant-Commander Clouston, Captain of the *Scorpion*, later reported that Hintze had been seen in the water close by, together with Dominik, and that both men were badly wounded. Hintze was said to have died before he could be reached, but Dominik had actually managed to grasp a line, only to slip away out of reach, never to be seen again.

Gödde wrote: 'As to speculations about whether the Admiral and Captain committed suicide, I can but refer to what I myself heard while I was in the water. The Captain, the First Officer and Admiral Bey jumped together from the bridge fifteen to twenty minutes after the rest of us. All I can say is that I believe speculations on the part of the British result from wishful thinking pure and simple.'

Aft, both Helmut Feifer and Ernst Reimann were washed overboard by a breaking wave. 'Every gleam of light disappeared, leaving me in darkness. I was all alone in the sea, but my life-jacket kept me afloat. After a while I saw a raft and was hauled up over the edge,' said Reimann.

Feifer had an even more terrifying experience. When he was dragged on to a raft, his clothes were found to be soaked in oil, blood and water. 'I heard someone say, "He's wounded. He's covered in blood!" For a moment I thought they were going to throw me back into the sea to make room for someone who hadn't been wounded and thus had a better chance of survival. I said, "It's not my blood, it's my friend's." I explained how I had taken him from the 'tween deck to the first-aid station. I was frozen stiff, but I was unhurt.'

Franz Marko was a good athlete and swimmer and managed to make his way to a rubber dinghy in which a number of men were striving to keep their hold. 'One man couldn't get on to it and was lying in the water. I grabbed hold of him and held on to him. After a while I began to shiver uncontrollably – but I didn't let go.'

Rolf Zanger, without a life-jacket, was in an even more desperate plight. 'I was kept afloat by my leather jacket, which was tight round the wrists and full of air. The problem was the collar, which was loose-fitting. I held it tightly to my throat with one hand to keep the air in and paddled away from the ship with the other. It was an awful moment when I felt the shockwaves through the water and realized that the boilers had exploded.'

According to Wilhelm Gödde very few of the *Scharnhorst*'s rafts were intact. Most of them had been holed or blown to bits in the shelling; those that were still afloat were crowded with men.

> Once again I saw our ship. The superstructure was lost to sight. She had capsized and was floating keel uppermost. I could see men on the keel. Among them was one of our artificers, Johnny Merkle. He remained sitting on the keel until an empty raft drifted past. Then he plunged into the water, hauled himself on to the raft and dragged several of the other men on with him. It was bitterly cold and there was snow in the air. My strength failed me, but by a miracle of God I drifted towards the raft. Merkle helped me so that I was able to get the upper part of my body on to it. A short time before I had seen the *Scharnhorst* for the last time. By then only her stern was visible, then the sea swallowed her. She had carried us over many an ocean. No one who did not experience it for himself can know what a sad moment it was.

The *Duke of York* had ceased firing as early as 19.30 and had withdrawn from the battle. 'Three cruisers and eight destroyers were now in the target area and *Duke of York* steered to the northward to avoid the melee. All that could be seen of *Scharnhorst* was a dull glow through a dense cloud of smoke, which the star-shell and searchlights of the surrounding ships could not penetrate,' Fraser wrote. There was little jubilation on board. The tension had been relieved and everyone realized how tired they were. Many found time for reflection. 'I felt enormous relief that it was all over,' says Henry Leach, 'and, frankly, sad because this very fine ship, and she *was* a very fine ship, had been completely blown out of the water.'

As, one by one, the ships ringing the doomed battlecruiser called off their attacks, they too drew away. When, at 19.47, the *Belfast*, the last to do so, turned to fire her last three torpedoes, her target had disappeared, leaving the sea covered with oil and wreckage. The *Scharnhorst* was no more. 'No ship therefore saw the enemy sink, but it seems fairly certain that she sank after a heavy underwater explosion, which was heard and felt in several ships about 19.45,' Fraser wrote.

In the *Duke of York*'s radar room Lieutenant Vivian Cox watched as the blip that was the *Scharnhorst* gradually diminished in size until it was nothing more than 'a little golden streak'. But Fraser was not satisfied. He paced to and fro on the bridge, riled by the fact that no one had actually seen the German battlecruiser go down, thus making it impossible to confirm that she had indeed been sunk. A stream of wireless signals went out to the Allied ships.

19.46: 'ALL DESTROYERS JOIN ME.'
19.48: 'DESTROYER WITH SEARCHLIGHT ILLUMINATE TARGET.'
19.51: 'CLEAR AREA OF TARGET EXCEPT FOR SHIP WITH TORPEDOES AND DESTROYER WITH SEARCHLIGHT.'

The only destroyer in the neighbourhood equipped with a searchlight was the *Scorpion* and the only one with any torpedoes left was the *Matchless*. A breaking wave had knocked her torpedo tubes out of kilter when she first went into the attack, forcing her to abort. When she returned to the fray, the *Scharnhorst* was no longer there. In consequence, the net result of Fraser's signals was that only two destroyers returned to the spot where the *Scharnhorst* had last been seen, the other eleven vessels all withdrawing. No specific order was given to pick up survivors – Fraser's foremost priority was to assure himself that the *Scharnhorst* really had gone to the bottom. When the *Stord* requested permission to join in the work of rescue, she received no reply.

At 19.51 the first signal from the *Scorpion* was received on board the flagship: 'A LOT OF WRECKAGE ON SEA. AM CLOSING NOW.'

Able-Seaman John Baxendale was stationed on the *Scorpion*'s upper deck, from which a scrambling-net had been draped over the side. 'We were the only ship there with a searchlight, so we swung round and came back . . . switched the searchlight on and there they all were, floating all round, everywhere. . . . It was terrible, they were all like bloody seagulls, bobbing up and down in the water on rafts.'

From their raft Helmut Backhaus and his shipmates saw the searchlight suddenly probe the darkness of the night like a ghostly finger. 'A couple of chaps on the raft had flashlights. We signalled [with them] and called for help. They saw us and drew nearer. But we were frozen to the marrow and many of us were unable to keep a grip on the ropes thrown down to us. I tied the end of a rope round my waist and was hauled up. Two men hung on to my legs, wanting to be hauled up with me, but they were unable to hold on. Both fell back into the sea and disappeared.'

Helmut Feifer was too exhausted to tie the rope lowered to him. 'I lost consciousness. Then one of the British [sailors] climbed down on to the raft and tied the rope round me. I didn't regain consciousness until I came to in the sickbay.'

Like Marko, Zanger and Wiebusch, Wilhelm Gödde was saved by the *Scorpion*. 'One destroyer carefully edged towards us, so that the raft was in her lee. There was a stout net hanging over her side. Ropes were thrown down to us, but I couldn't keep my grip. I fell back into the water four times. On my fifth try I sank my teeth into the rope and was hauled up and dragged over the rail by a pair of strong hands.'

When he got back to Germany in 1944, Günther Sträther gave a more sober-minded description of the rescue work. 'We finally drifted towards an English destroyer which was hove to. We got on to the deck with the aid of a scrambling-net. Those who couldn't make it on their own received no assistance. Because of that, three men on our raft drowned.'

It should be noted, however, that Sträter was one of those who also claimed that the men sang when the *Scharnhorst* went down. 'All three propellers were still turning when they rose above the water, and quite fast at that. To the very end the ship was under way. The men in the water tried to climb on to the rafts. Those who succeeded sang two verses of the song '*Auf einem Seemannsgrab, da blühen keine Rosen*' ['On a sailor's grave, no roses bloom']. I heard no cries for help. Everyone remained calm and there was no panic.'

Helmut Backhaus saw things differently:

I heard nothing, nothing at all. *I* didn't sing, at any rate. It is tempting to believe that someone has wished to dress the story up a little. To say that everyone sang – I mean to say, after all . . . We were close to our last moment, and we were fighting for our lives. First in the sea, then on the rafts, where we just waited apathetically, not knowing whether we would be saved. Then suddenly the destroyer appeared, awakening our instinct for survival. You'd never believe how quickly everyone perked up. We wanted to save ourselves – understandably.

John Baxendale agrees with Backhaus. '. . . some of the survivors will tell you they were singing. They weren't singing, they were bloody shouting out for help.'

At 20.15 the *Scorpion* signalled: 'AM PICKING UP GERMAN SURVIVORS.' But Fraser was still not satisfied. At 20.16 he signalled: 'PLEASE CONFIRM *SCHARNHORST* IS SUNK.' Three minutes later, at 20.18, the *Scorpion* signalled the C-in-C: 'SURVIVORS ARE FROM *SCHARNHORST*. And finally, at 20.30: 'SURVIVORS STATE *SCHARNHORST* HAS SUNK.'

At about the same time Vice-Admiral Burnett on board the *Belfast* chimed in, signalling: 'SEVERAL SURVIVORS SAMPLES BEING TAKEN. SATISFIED THAT *SCHARNHORST* IS SUNK. WHERE SHALL I JOIN YOU?'

A few minutes later Admiral Bruce Fraser ordered the whole squadron to accompany him to Murmansk. When the *Scorpion* pulled away, several hundred men who had survived the sinking were still floundering in the water.

John Baxendale says: '[T]here were only eight of us pulling survivors out, because everybody was still in action stations. . . . I was just about to pull another guy out when we got the buzz that the U-boats were arriving. Well, naturally, the Captain ups and out, so we had to leave them all there, we were nearly crying.'

The *Matchless* was actually sweeping in to fire her torpedoes when she came across a raft with six men on board. She found time to pick them up before the order came to leave the area. Able-Seaman Dennis Welsh says:

[W]e were sent round again and when we got to where the *Scharnhorst* was, all there was were men floating in the water. . . . We couldn't bring them all in, they were sliding back in the water . . . We managed to get six aboard and then we were given orders to rejoin the fleet and we left the scene with many more we could have saved . . . We turned off all the lights, all the searchlights off on the ship. I think it was so they wouldn't lose hope . . . we didn't want them to see that we were going away.

Admiral Fraser ascribes his decision to leave the scene so precipitately to his fear of German U-boats. But the *Eisenbart* Group had spent the whole day vainly trying to catch up with the convoy ploughing its way eastwards more than 100 nautical miles further north. It was not until 18.15 that the U-boats were ordered to make for the scene of the battle, an order which most of them received too late. Schaar, on board *U-957*, did not acknowledge receipt of the signal until 20.10; Lübsen (*U-277*) sent his acknowledgement at 21.57 and Herbschleb (*U-354*) at 22.42. By then, almost three hours had passed since the *Scharnhorst* had sunk. The U-boat closest to the scene was 70 nautical miles away. After a short-lived lull the wind had again risen to gale force. Herbschleb noted in the war diary: 'Sailing course 163 at top speed. The sea is crashing violently against the conning-tower. Loose fittings are being slammed against the hull. . . . The bilge pump cannot cope with all the water that is getting in. Speed will have to be reduced.'

Further signals made it clear that it was no longer a matter of an offensive supporting operation but of a search for survivors north-east of the spot where the *Scharnhorst* was thought to have been lost. Radio beacons from Ingøy in the west to Vardø in the east were switched on to facilitate navigation. When, late

that night, the first U-boats reached the northern perimeter of the search area, the gale was blowing with renewed fury. Many U-boats suffered further damage and it was almost impossible to search the area properly. 'Poor visibility and the raging sea with its mountainous waves make searching very difficult. Visibility varies from 100 to 300 metres,' Herbschleb noted in the war diary at dawn on 27 December. After *U-277* had battled the gale for twelve hours without seeing any sign of life, Lübsen wrote, 'Searching appears to be futile. No one is likely to remain alive in this heavy sea.'

Early in the morning of 27 December *U-314* observed a patch of oil far to the north-east of the scene of the sinking. It was all that was left: the *Scharnhorst* and the men who manned her had vanished without trace.

On board the vessels of the convoy the officers had followed the drama from hour to hour. Rear-Admiral Boucher wrote:

At 19.30Z/26th Dec., a V/S signal from the escort stated: '*SCHARNHORST* NOW STOPPED AND BURNING. WE ARE SURROUNDED BY U-boatS AND ATTACK IS CERTAIN.' The wind was on the starboard bow and still very strong, there was a high sea, occasional sleet, it was very dark and prospects looked gloomy. The luck of the U-boats was 'in'. With surprising speed, however, these conditions suddenly changed. The wind and sea became much calmer. The sky cleared, and the most extraordinary Northern Lights ever seen during the voyage illuminated the whole sky for some hours. Broad, sinuous ribbons of very bright light streamed right across the sky from horizon to horizon. Sometimes three or more together lighting up the whole sea. It seemed like supernatural aid in our favour for a second time, for it quite reversed the conditions for submarine attack, and may have saved the convoy.

Only a few minutes after the Fleet Commander in Kiel, *Generaladmiral* Schniewind, had grasped the fact that the *Scharnhorst* was irretrievably lost, *Kapitän-zur-See* Rolf Johannesson and the 4th Destroyer Flotilla were ordered to abandon their attempt at rescue. At the time they were still ten hours' sailing from the scene of the battle. In Narvik and Kiel the admirals were afraid that the British had stationed yet another covering force near the Norwegian coast, for which reason Johannesson raced at full speed for the mainland for fear of sharing the battlecruiser's sad fate. But the British force was by then on its way to the Kola peninsula and had no interest in the destroyers. At 05.00 the entire destroyer flotilla anchored safely in the inner reaches of the Kå fjord. Following internal discussions at Fleet Headquarters, the next morning it was decided not to send the destroyers out again 'to search for survivors'.

It had been a dark day for *Kapitän-zur-See* Johannesson. Many years later he was to write:

> I can't say what I did wrong. The worry has gnawed at me ever since. . . . The time spent in Alta afterwards with the *Scharnhorst* gone was dreadful. I do not blame myself for lack of courage or reluctance to make a sacrifice. But did I exploit the tactical opportunities available to the full? It is an open question. There was only one bright spot, one that I kept locked deep in my heart – not of a heroic, but of a human, nature: I brought all my men back.

While the U-boats and destroyers were still battling their way through the heavy seas on the evening of 26 December 1943, two wireless signals were transmitted from Germany. One, addressed to the *Scharnhorst*, was from Hitler's bunker in East Prussia. It read: 'THE GERMAN PEOPLE THANK YOU IN WHAT WAS FOR YOU SUCH A GRIEVOUS MOMENT.' The other was from *Grossadmiral* Karl Dönitz and was addressed to the whole Battle Group. It read: 'YOUR HEROIC BATTLE FOR GERMANY'S VICTORY AND GREATNESS WILL BE AN EXAMPLE FOR ALL TIME.'

Hitler and Dönitz had spoken. It was they who had ordered the *Scharnhorst* to sea and it was they who, in the final reckoning, were responsible for the battlecruiser's loss. Of the *Scharnhorst*'s complement of 1,972 men, only 36 were saved; their average age was twenty-two.

CHAPTER TWENTY-THREE

Found!

HAMMERFEST, TUESDAY 26 SEPTEMBER 2000

The town of my birth was again enshrouded in the darkness of autumn, a soft, violet cloak that slowly enveloped and blotted out the landscape. A light rain was falling over the docks, which were bathed in the orange light of sodium lamps. Moored alongside the dock was the research vessel *H.U. Sverdrup II*. Not long before, through the window of the Harbourmaster's office I had seen my friend Captain Arne Jensen poring over his logbooks. I hurried across the rain-washed expanse of concrete to say hello. I wanted to tell him that we were about to set off for the position he had pointed out to me, twenty-three years earlier, on a tattered chart in the wheelhouse of the trawler *Gargia*, the place where the wreck of the *Scharnhorst* was thought to lie. But when I reached the office, the light was out; Arne had gone home.

Was that a good omen or a bad one? I wondered. I was lacking in self-confidence and my nerves were badly frayed. For almost three years I had waited and worked to mount this expedition. Now the moment had come: this was my great – and only – chance of finding the wreck of Hitler's last battlecruiser. I needed all the encouragement I could get. But the office was closed and there was no more I could do. Standing on the afterdeck of the *Sverdrup*, watching the lights of Hammerfest fade and disappear astern, I felt very much alone and abandoned. I was near to despair. We passed the jetty where the *Black Watch* and the German U-boats had lain so long ago. A few hundred metres away was my childhood home, standing on the very edge of the cold Arctic Ocean. Not a few Jeremiahs had emphasized how vast the ocean was, how enormous the area I intended to search. 'You'll never find the *Scharnhorst*,' they said. But I'd dug my

heels in and refused to be diverted from my purpose. I wouldn't give up and was determined to complete the task I'd set myself. Now I had all the information I could possibly need, carefully marked on a chart in the shape of hundreds of tiny dots. One of those dots was the *Scharnhorst*. The problem was, which one?

To starboard I could see the red-and-green flashes of Fuglenes Light. It brought to mind another evening, another setting, that too more than twenty years in the past. I had been standing on a bare, rocky hilltop. Around me stretched the Finnmark plateau; a vast expanse of mountain moorland, it closely resembled the surface of the moon. Down in the valley I could hear the sonorous clang of bells on reindeer stags. The temperature was -35°C and I was numb with cold. Miles away from the nearest human settlement, I was there to cover the annual migration of the reindeer herds for my paper. Deep in the valley my Sami companion, Mikkel, had erected his tent. I could see a thin spiral of smoke curling from the vent at the top. There would be strong coffee and dried reindeer meat for supper. Suddenly a bluish-green flash of light lit up the spring sky. Mikkel looked up. A true child of nature, for a long time he remained silent. Then he turned towards me.

'What do you think?' he asked. 'What do you think that means?'

I was in my mid-twenties and not at all superstitious, though I knew that in that desolate wilderness anything could happen. But I was young, strong, well-built and brimming over with a zest for life. Just then, however, I was tired and I couldn't feel my toes because of the cold. None the less I made an effort and said in as cheerful a tone as I could muster: 'It was a shooting star, Mikkel. It means good luck.'

Beneath my feet I felt the deck vibrate as Captain Jan Loennechen increased speed and the 2,000-hp diesel engine began to throb as it neared full power. The white-leaded hull heeled over. There was quite a wind blowing, so I knew we were in for a rough night. But my thoughts were on the shooting star over Mount Laksefjell and I resolved to look on the bright side. There had been too many setbacks. This time, I felt, the Almighty was on our side.

I had had the good fortune that attends hard work; that, at least, was what I told myself. Thanks to Commander Marcus Osen and retired Rear-Admiral Kjell Prytz, my acquaintanceship with Jarl Johnsen and the Defence Forces Research Institute, of which he was the head, had yielded a highly positive result. The Department of Submarine Warfare had for some years been engaged in a comprehensive and largely secret military mapping project. But there had been no secrecy about one aspect of the project, the Institute's meticulous survey of

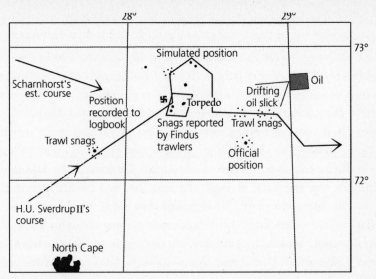

On the basis of his analysis the author plotted a course for the research vessel *H.U. Sverdrup II* which took her through the most promising search areas. The side-scan sonar revealed the presence of a variety of objects on the seabed. The most likely position of the wreck lay close to the 'Findus snags' and is marked here with a swastika.

the seabed in the Norwegian and Barents Seas conducted in the interests of Norway herself and of her allies. The purpose of the survey was also public knowledge: accurate charts of the seabed were needed to facilitate underwater navigation. It was the submarine service which would, in the final instance, incorporate the new charts in its navigational and command computers. It was a long-term project and the work was demanding, necessitating as it did use of side-scan sonars and multiple-beam echo sounders. I guessed that the military versions of the charts would have a resolution down to a few metres and that they were never likely to become accessible to the general public. But other and rather less precise versions would be made available for civilian purposes. For the first time the seabed would be accurately surveyed, with all that meant for the fisheries, the offshore oil industry and shipping in general.

In the summer of 2000 the Research Institute embarked upon a major programme of exploration. The sophisticated ten-year-old 1,400-ton research vessel *H.U. Sverdrup II* was going to survey areas of the ocean floor in the Barents Sea and, in addition, test a new low-frequency sonar with a range of more than 5,000 metres. It was a tight programme and a demanding one into the bargain, and would take the ship a long way east. Despite this, Johnsen and his associates had generously agreed to the proposal I had put to them. I had

drawn a line through five of the six priority areas between 72° and 73° N. At a towing-speed of 6 to 8 knots, with her new side-scan sonar the *Sverdrup* would make a wide sweep to the north-east and in so doing cover, within the course of sixteen hours, 80 per cent of the search area I had singled out, thus killing two birds with one stone. I would solve most of my problems and they would be enabled to carry through their programme without untoward delays.

I spent that summer cycling along the coast of Jutland in Denmark, with sand dunes on one side and the blue of the sea on the other. But my thoughts were elsewhere. Somewhere north of the North Cape the *H.U. Sverdrup II* was working her way eastwards through the area that had been uppermost in my mind for the last three years. What would they find? The same as we had, a bare, flat expanse of sea floor? I shook off such gloomy thoughts and cycled on. And at last, one scorching July day, in the shade of Skagen lighthouse, I received a phone call. They had found something! They had logged some interesting echoes, but were uncertain of what they portended. The information had first to be processed by computer. But it looked promising. At least nine of the echoes deserved to be studied more closely. I was elated, and showed it. I'm sure the Danes put me down as yet another crazy Norwegian, but I didn't care. I threw myself down and rolled over and over in the sand!

In August I had several meetings with specialists from the Research Institute. On the compressed sonar printouts the echoes to which they had referred were mere flyspecks, tiny, shapeless black dots. Together we studied the charts and discussed dark shadows and angles. Because of the activity surrounding the wreck of the Russian submarine *Kursk*, the *Sverdrup* had been compelled to concentrate on an area further west, and as a result had gone over the area several times, using both sonar and a multi-beam echo sounder. One echo in particular attracted our attention, that from a large, irregularly shaped object on the seabed 66 nautical miles north-east of the North Cape. When it had been processed and magnified, it was decided that it might well be a ship — but was it a ship of the right size? The *Scharnhorst* measured 230 metres from stem to stern, whereas the echo was a mere 120 metres in length — 150 at a pinch. The biggest Liberty ships torpedoed in the same area during the war were well over 100 metres overall. Could it be one of those, so blown apart and mangled as to make the echo seem bigger than the ship that caused it? Or was it the wrecks of *U-28* and the *Olive Branch*, which had gone to the bottom more or less side by side in the First World War? I didn't know what to think. 'What it is,' the sceptics said, 'is an underwater rock. A solid chunk of Norwegian granite, 300 metres below the surface of the sea — Alf Jacobsen's money mountain.'

What intrigued me, however, and aroused my hopes was the position of the object: 72°31'N, 28°15'E. The *Duke of York*'s logbook gave the position as 72°29'N, 28°04'E. The torpedo had been found at 72°33'N, 28°20'E. It was almost too good to be true! The positions were only a few nautical miles apart. I showed Jarl Johnsen the old charts on which the same area was shaded in red and marked 'very bad!'. 'It must be right!' he exclaimed. 'Fishermen give that area a wide berth. We know there's something big there. I think we're on to something.'

Now we were on our way to find out – my television crew, Kjell Prytz, Kjetil Utne and Petter Lunde, together with two engineers, Rolf Kristensen and Arnfinn Karlsen from the Defence Research Institute.

I hardly slept that night. There was little wind, but in from the north-west came a gentle swell that kept the ship rolling slowly from side to side. My mind went back to that fateful, stormy December night in 1943 when fourteen fighting ships had set a course for the same area of ocean, not to leave it until the darkness was lit by flame, the surface of the sea obscured by oily smoke and the night rent by despairing cries for help. I had got to know some of the German survivors quite well and had had many prolonged conversations with them. But even now, almost sixty years after the event, they remained taciturn, guarded, almost as though they were determined to keep to themselves the truth of what had actually occurred. I thought I understood why they wished to protect themselves and their memories. There were, after all, only thirty-six of them. *They* had survived, a select handful plucked at random from among almost two thousand men. Why had God's finger rested on them? Why had they, and they alone, been dragged from that merciless, ice-cold sea? One would have thought that their having been rescued would have given them renewed vitality and appreciation of life, but I sensed the opposite. It was a feeling with which I was myself very familiar. I found among them no spontaneous joy but rather a lurking sense of guilt. One question continued to gnaw at them: Why me, exactly, and not the others?

Late in the afternoon Captain Loennechen reversed the engines. The strength of the current, temperature and salinity on the sea floor were measured and the computers carefully adjusted. From the head of the echo sounder beneath the keel 111 narrow beams of sound pulsated in a fan pattern into the depths. As though by magic, on the monitors there appeared a picture of the seabed, black as night, 300 metres beneath the ship. It was like using a set of fine brushes to expose, metre by metre, the contours of the sea floor – traces left by retreating glaciers thousands of years ago, the drag-marks made by trawls, a rock or two and, here and there, shallow depressions. Mostly, however, all that was to be

seen was an expanse of ocean floor, flat and featureless – not so much like a dance floor but more like a newly ploughed field.

A voice came over the intercom: 'Here's something!' We stared at the screen while Loennechen gently eased the *Sverdrup* into position over Target No. 5. It was a never-to-be-forgotten moment as the first dark object came into view and slowly grew into an oblong shape as the scanner advanced. Within a radius of several kilometres the seabed was uniformly even, a grey carpet with nothing to break the monotony. But immediately below us lay a large, solid object. Shaped like the hull of a ship, in some places it towered a good 15 to 20 metres above the sea floor, but its outline was irregular. Moreover, whatever it was, it was in two parts. The larger of the two was 160 metres long; at right-angles to it, stretching away to the south-east, lay the remainder, a 60- to 70-metre-long appendix. We had found something, but what? Was it really the wreck of Hitler's battlecruiser or merely an underwater promontory of about the same size?

I asked the Navy's and Research Institute's experts for their opinions. None of them was absolutely sure, but the consensus was that in all probability Target No. 5 was what we were looking for. Final proof would not be forthcoming until a Remotely Operated Vehicle (ROV) had been lowered and the object filmed. But there was no ROV on the *Sverdrup*; only the Navy's diving vessel KNM *Tyr* carried such advanced equipment.

Petter Lunde put into words what we all were thinking: 'No matter what it is, it looks as though it's had a pretty rough time of it.'

I went below to my cabin to think. I needed to be alone. I had the option of chartering the *H.U. Sverdrup II* for a further three days. If I did that, we would be able to cover the rest of the search area with the multiple-beam echo sounder and investigate the other finds more closely. That would be playing safe, as it would enable me to rule out all other alternatives. Or I could gamble. I could declare myself satisfied with the *status quo* and stake everything on Target No. 5 being the *Scharnhorst* and stop there. That would save both time and money. The choice was mine. Again I felt that familiar knot in my stomach. I was in a cleft stick: I knew that I had just this one chance. If I took the wrong decision, there would be no question of a second try.

I spent half an hour alone, thinking things over. For some unaccountable reason I gradually began to feel easier in my mind. I said to myself, 'Heed your instincts. They're telling you what to do.' Then I returned to the bridge. 'OK,' I said, 'we'll take a chance. Let's make for the North Cape.'

Meanwhile, the *Tyr*, a converted supply ship, had been engaged in an underwater search for a lost practice torpedo in the Lyngen fjord. This was

Wednesday evening. By rights we should have transferred from the *Sverdrup* to the *Tyr* and set out from Hammerfest late on Sunday evening. Instead, we phoned and asked whether it would be possible for the diving ship to do the job before the weekend. The *Tyr*'s Captain, a distinguished sailor, officer and musician, Lieutenant-Commander Arne Nagell Dahl Jr, agreed immediately, which suggested that the ship's Lyngen assignment had been satisfactorily completed. Dahl and his crew wanted to be finished with the Barents Sea as soon as possible. Accordingly, we agreed to meet in Honningsvåg early next morning.

The autumn sun had just disappeared below the horizon and above us the evening sky was a glowing tapestry of purple and gold. The weather was surprisingly good, but no one knew what the morrow might bring. It was 70 nautical miles to the North Cape. A trough of low pressure might well appear from nowhere and spoil everything. I thrust the thought from me. Instead, I curled up on my bunk and immediately fell into a deep sleep.

At five next morning we were again on our way to the search area, this time on board the *Tyr*. Stretching away ahead of us was the open sea, slate-blue and majestic, while to the west loomed the beetling brow of the North Cape.

Arne Nagell Dahl Jr, a fair-haired forty-year-old from Voss, commands a 100-per cent professional and warm-hearted ship and crew. Over the years he and his men have become a familiar and respected sight along the Norwegian coast, always willing as they are to help search for missing ships and to take part in rescue operations. Thanks to long and varied experience of subsea searches, the *Tyr*, with her powerful Scorpio ROV, has done sterling work both for the military authorities and for society at large. When there was talk of budgetary cutbacks and the Navy threatened to lay the ship up, there was a public outcry. Couldn't the Navy of a maritime nation of Norway's standing, with one of the world's longest coastlines, afford to maintain a single diving vessel? It didn't bear thinking about – it would be too embarrassing for words. Finally, even the bureaucrats tied to their desks in faraway Oslo came to the same conclusion, and the *Tyr* was saved.

I was as naïve as ever. I had thought that I had conquered my fears, though I was well aware that the last two hours are always the worst. Slowly we neared our objective. The sea was calm, the colour of pewter. To the north-east clouds were gathering. 'What does that mean?' I ventured to ask. 'Wind? Bad weather?' I was so very, very near my goal. Only a few nautical miles more and we'd be there. But at a depth of 300 metres margins are small. If the wind rose to much more than a fresh breeze the ROV would have to be recovered, and for preference the waves should not be more than a metre high.

I returned to my cabin, shut the door behind me, sat down on my bunk, closed my eyes and offered up a silent prayer. 'Dear God, not bad weather, not now. Just a few hours more. Please!' That was all we needed. We didn't intend to anchor up. The ROV would be on the seabed in half an hour's time. A few pictures would provide the proof we needed. Four or five hours would be ideal, however. I do not recall my exact words, but I do remember saying in that silent prayer that I knew I didn't really deserve special consideration, nor could I promise to improve. I admitted that I was a weak vessel, but even so . . . Four or five hours of calm, that was all I was asking for.

When we slackened speed, I breathed a silent thank you and made my way back up on to the bridge. To my immense relief the sky had brightened again. The sea looked as though it had been smoothed by a large and helpful hand.

There was room for us all in front of the monitors, on which we could follow the ROV on its descent into the depths. Excitement rose when the depth-gauge passed 270 metres and the bubbles of air on the screens gave way to something quite different, a rust-brown shape. The pilot, Roger Andersen, adjusted the controls. 'It's steel,' he said. 'It's a hull. We're bang on!'

Slowly the ROV worked its way along the length of the keel. The metal gleamed dully in the beam of the vehicle's searchlight. There was little sign of corrosion; it looked fresh from the foundry. No one raised his voice or danced with joy. But, deep down, I knew that we had found what we were looking for. That steel just had to be Krupp steel, and not ordinary steel either. It was hardened Wotan steel, cast to armour-plate the heavy battleships of the *Kriegsmarine*. What we were seeing on the monitors was something that had been hidden from human eyes for more than fifty-seven years – the *Scharnhorst*.

Roger raised the ROV and steered it away from the wreck before going in for another look. We passed a verdigris-green shellcase and an overturned gun mounting. I recalled something Helmut Feifer had told me: 'We threw empty shellcases overboard. If you turned them upside-down in the water so that the air couldn't escape, you could use them as floats. It wasn't easy, but it was better than nothing.'

Before us lay the vault of the hull, a gigantic greyish-brown shell. The battlecruiser had capsized and lay bottom-up on a north-east/south-west axis. The ROV moved slowly along the keel to reveal an inch-wide crack. The steel hull had split all the way round, perhaps when the sinking giant struck the seabed. 'When 30,000 tons of steel hit the bottom at 30 kilometres an hour, anything can happen,' said Dahl.

The ROV moved further aft and we saw the two rudders and three propellers with their graceful 5-metre-long blades, built for high speeds. What was it Gödde had said? 'They had carried us over many an ocean.' During that last desperate flight, the Chief Engineer, Willi König, had set them turning faster than ever before, but it hadn't been fast enough. The propellers were undamaged: they had still been turning when the ship plunged beneath the waves. It was just that earlier they hadn't been turning as fast as they should have been – because the engine-rooms had slowly filled with water. A steam-pipe had burst and the boilers had gone out. When she went under, the *Scharnhorst* had been doing only 4 or 5 knots.

The question was, what had caused her to lose speed in the first place? What had reduced her speed from close on 30 knots to a mere 22? That sudden reduction had enabled the British destroyers to catch up with her in the space of only fifteen minutes. That had really been the beginning of the end. We could see gaping holes in the hull, holes probably caused by armour-piercing shells. But we could see something else too: just behind the rudders, the whole stern had been blown clean away. All that was left aft was a gaping void from deck to keel. Ice-cold water must have poured in, ton after ton, in the space of only a few seconds. I remembered what the official report said: the water had flooded the stern compartments, preventing the auxiliary damage-control party from getting in. And then the watertight doors had been closed. The twenty-five men of the engine-room staff had been sealed off. 'But it wasn't that that made her sink,' Prytz said. 'That only explains why she stopped.'

Arne and Roger cautiously piloted the ROV aft, along the port side of the hull. In some places there was a metre or two clearance between the upper deck and the seabed. We could see guns – the twin 10.5-cm guns and the single 15-cm gun – and the torpedo tubes that had been swung out at the last moment. But we could also see something else. The secondary armament was directed aft, as if it had not been in operation. Again my mind went back to the official report. The Gunnery Officers had disagreed fiercely among themselves and the gun crews had been ordered below. The most effective close-combat weapons had never been in action, which was one of the reasons why the destroyers had been able to get as close as 1,800 metres.

And there were the torpedo tubes which, amid a hail of shell splinters, Lieutenant Bosse had brought to bear with his last remaining strength – to no avail. Of the three torpedoes he had fired, two were reported to have splashed harmlessly into the sea and one to have remained jammed in the tube. But we could clearly see that there were *two* torpedoes still in their tubes, so either the

report was wrong or Bosse had managed to reload and fire another salvo, which seems unlikely. We shall never know.

But the most dramatic images were still to come, when we moved to inspect the bow and approached the bridge. Arne Dahl was the first to spot it. 'If you look,' he said, 'you'll see something strange. The rest of the hull's missing.'

He was right. The *Scharnhorst* had broken in two just forward of the bridge. The foremost 60 metres of the ship were simply not there. In fact, the entire foreship had been destroyed and lay like a heap of scrap iron at an angle of 90 degrees to the rest of the hull. Again I remembered what Backhaus and Boekhoff had said about when they were in the water. They had felt two or three powerful explosions – like an underwater earthquake. They had also felt enormous pressure on the lower part of their bodies. Backhaus thought it was the boilers exploding. But it wasn't, it was the whole of the foreship. A salvo of torpedoes must have struck forward of the bridge and set off a chain reaction. Perhaps it was the magazine of A turret that had caused the explosion that had sent the *Scharnhorst* to the bottom. She had been a lucky ship, but even a lucky ship could not withstand an explosion of such magnitude.

It was a terrible sight. The hull was gashed and mangled as though it were tin, its 32-cm-thick armour steel reduced to fragments. Of the bow, only bits of the anchor chain were to be seen, together with the foremost part of the keelson. The destruction was horrifying. It was like watching a silent film of Armageddon.

The ROV then moved northwards. We found the aft mast, which had been broken off, the crow's nest a blind observation post in the stygian darkness. Upside-down, a short distance away, lay the 10-metre range-finder, its two outriggers, like arms, still extended as though in a desperate cry for help. But the image on the screen gave a false impression. When the *Scharnhorst* sank, not one of the range-takers was still alive.

Still further to the north lay what was left of the superstructure, which was where Heinrich Mulch had spent his last hours. We could see the ladder, the ladder up and down which hundreds of men had climbed during four years of war. Affixed to its outer side was a fire hose. Never used, it was still neatly rolled up in its housing. Further away still was the shot-away stern, the joins between the oak planks still clearly visible, cut through as though by a blowtorch.

And finally, like an enormous, glazed eyeball staring vainly upwards towards the surface of the sea, was the big searchlight on the Admiral's bridge, the glass still intact. I remembered Helmut Backhaus telling me that he had clambered up on to that very searchlight.

We saw no trace of human remains. There was nothing to indicate that the ship had once been home to nearly two thousand men. Bey, Hintze, Wibbelhof and all the others were still encased in their steel sarcophagus. Those who had been helped overboard by Hintze and Dominik had been swept away by wind and wave; they too were now at rest in the Arctic Ocean, together with the thousands of others who had been engulfed by that unrelenting sea.

Reverently we continued to explore the wreck, awed by what we saw. We touched nothing. The *Scharnhorst* was a war grave. Most of those who had served and died on board her were young men: victims of the ineluctable logic of war, they had done their duty and in the doing, died.

By this time it was nearly ten o'clock. I stood on the bridge wing and watched as the light of the ascending ROV grew ever stronger, a splash of yellow against the dark-blue surface of the sea. The wind had dropped, but there was rain in the air. Around us darkness reigned. I had an enormous feeling of relief, but it was relief tinged with sadness. Because of my upbringing I felt that I could understand something of the fear and much of the sense of duty that had imbued the men of the *Scharnhorst*. If that sounds conceited, so be it. I had plumbed the depths and seen what they held. What I found there hadn't made me happy, but it *had* set my mind at rest. I felt that I now understood a little more and, in consequence, could find it in my heart to forgive more.

I tossed my cigarette end over the rail and followed its glowing descent until it was extinguished by the sea. What was it Wibbelhof had said? 'I'm staying here, where I belong.'

I thought that now I knew what he meant. But his world had been a different world, a world with a different logic.

'Let's leave it now,' I said. 'Let's leave it and get back home.'

V

CHAPTER TWENTY-FOUR

The Intelligence Riddle

WESTERN FINNMARK, CHRISTMAS 1943

It was a Tromsø man, Egil Lindberg, who first claimed that the news of the *Scharnhorst*'s departure from the Lang fjord on Christmas Day 1943 was conveyed to London by Norwegian agents. In an account written as early as 9 June 1945, when the events were still fresh in his mind, Lindberg said: 'I used to gather information I thought would be of interest and pass it on to Nikolai. On 20 December 1943 I was warned of the *Scharnhorst*'s impending attack on the convoy to Russia and sent Torbjørn hurrying off to inform Nikolai.'

Nikolai was the name used as a cover by Einar Johansen, one of the Norwegian SIS agents landed by submarine in the summer of 1943 (see chapter 9). At this time he was operating the Venus transmitter from the cellar of Finnsnes Dairy. Torbjørn was Einar's younger brother. It was Torbjørn who, in August that year, had gathered intelligence on a bicycle ride from Alteidet to Kåfjord and back. Now Torbjørn took the coastal-express steamer to Finnsnes, whence Einar transmitted the report to London.

In a well-splashed series of interviews published in the weekly magazine *Aktuell* in September 1958, Torstein Pettersen Råby gave a rather different version of the course of events.

We didn't need to keep watch on the *Scharnhorst* for more than four months. In all that time she left her moorings only once. That was when she sailed out of the fjord and through a sound into the Bur fjord, then came back. We set off to look for her, and found her, too, and reported her movements to England. But just before Christmas 1943 there was a sudden burst of activity in the

Lang fjord. A German supply ship came in – it was on Christmas Eve, I seem to remember – and all leave was cancelled. We realized at once that something big was pending. We set up the transmitter and reported to England that it looked as if the *Scharnhorst* was preparing to sortie. When she sailed, we immediately reported it – the British stations were by then listening out for us around the clock. Another two agents, Lasse Lindberg and Trygve Duklæt in Porsa, had also learned that the *Scharnhorst* had left her anchorage and reported it, so the British received three reports of her departure. It later transpired that they had taken steps to intercept her. Two days after she left the Lang fjord, the *Scharnhorst* was sunk north of the North Cape.

In 1962 the British author Michael Ogden published an account of the action in his book *The Battle of North Cape*, an account which Rear-Admiral Skule Storheill, who had captained the destroyer *Stord* in the battle, commended as 'a truly accurate military account of the course of events', adding, 'It is particularly satisfying to see officially confirmed the rumour we heard in England during the war that it was the [Norwegian] Home Front that warned the Admiralty that the *Scharnhorst* had put to sea.'

Ogden was not an official historian, however. He was an author who had served in the Royal Navy during the war. The official account of the incident was not published until twenty-two years later, when it appeared in Volume III of the five-volume work *British Intelligence in the Second World War*. Written by F.H. Hinsley, a professor of history at Cambridge University, it was published by the British government in 1984.

But Hinsley did not confirm that it was 'the Home Front' that had warned the Admiralty. On the contrary, he seemed to have deliberately set out to dismiss the Norwegian agents' contribution as pure hearsay, writing:

> In assessing the part played by intelligence in bringing about her [the *Scharnhorst*'s] destruction, however, it is not wise to dwell too much on the failings of the Germans. These would not have been crucial unless the British forces had been in a position to take advantage of them; and the fact that the British forces were so placed was due to the high quality of British intelligence. It was a tribute in particular to the value of the Sigint, the *only* source which had contributed . . .

In a footnote he added: 'The SIS agent in Altenfjord had not reported the *Scharnhorst*'s departure; his base opposite Kaafjord was a long way from her berth in Langfjord.'

The official Norwegian historian, Ragnar Ullstein, accepted Hinsley's version. In Volume II of *Etterretningstjenesten på Norge 1940–45* ('The Intelligence Service in Norway 1940–45') he wrote: 'The *Scharnhorst* put to sea without [her departure] being reported by the SIS stations.'

Not surprisingly, those agents who were still alive greeted Hinsley's and Ullstein's categorical denial of the contribution made by Norwegian agents with righteous indignation. One of them, the former head of *Forsvarets Fellessamband* (The Defence Forces' Joint Signals Organization), Colonel Bjørn Rørholt, was particularly incensed. At risk to his life, Rørholt had kept close watch on the movements of the German battleship *Tirpitz* in the Trondheim fjord during the first three years of the war, and had been highly decorated by the British for his gallantry. He was also a close personal friend of Torstein Pettersen Råby, whom, towards the end of the 1950s, he had put in charge of the wireless station on the island of Jan Mayen. By that time Råby, who had been a member of Thor Heyerdahl's *Kon-Tiki* expedition, was beginning to show signs of the hard life he had led and his over-indulgence in alcohol.

'I think the British are wrong, and I intend to prove it,' Rørholt said to me when I met him for the first time in the canteen of the Oslo newspaper *VG* in 1987. By then he had already begun to compile material for what he referred to as the definitive account of the two hundred or so Norwegian agents' contribution to the Allied war effort. It was published in 1994 under the title *Usynlige soldater* ('Invisible Soldiers').

By then Hinsley was a Professor Emeritus of the History of International Relations and Master of prestigious St John's College at Cambridge University. During the war he had been a leading figure at the top-secret Government Code and Cipher School at Bletchley Park, where he was closely associated with analysis of the German *Kriegsmarine*'s signal traffic. He also acted as liaison between Hut 4 and the Operational Intelligence Centre beneath the Admiralty in London. It was Hinsley himself who phoned Lieutenant-Commander Denning in the evening of Christmas Day 1943 to inform him of the content of the decrypted wireless signals exchanged between the Battle Group in the Kå and Lang fjords and the German admirals in Narvik and Kiel. According to Hinsley, it was these signals that had kept the British abreast of the dispositions of the Battle Group, the U-boats of *Gruppe Eisenbart* and *Luftwaffe* reconnaissance flights over the Barents Sea, not Norwegian agents.

Not to be intimidated by Hinsley's high standing, Rørholt went to Cambridge and entered into a heated discussion with the professor. Although Hinsley refused to give an inch, Rørholt did discover one important thing.

He wrote to me in the autumn of 1987: 'I spent the morning of Tuesday, 27 October, with Hinsley at the Master's Lodge in Cambridge. . . . He confirmed that the SIS had not allowed him access to their archives, which were still classified.'

Rørholt was of the opinion that Hinsley's own background in signals intelligence blinded him to the value of agents in the field. The obsession of the British government with secrecy was extreme – as it still is. No minor allies were made privy to British codes and communication systems. Nor did any of them know of the existence of Bletchley Park, still less of the results of its activities. Even on board the *Stord* Storheill had to accept a British Signals Officer. The young Norwegians who were landed behind enemy lines in their home country were hand-picked by the British Secret Service and the Norwegian 'E' Office ('E' = *Etterretning* (Intelligence)). But both formally and in practice they were controlled by the British alone. Only some time after news was received from Occupied Norway was the 'E' Office informed of its receipt. Copies of such signals often reached the office late, and it was impossible to know whether the information in them was complete or whether certain items had been held back. The only authority to know all that was going on was the Secret Service (MI6) itself. But MI6 was – and is – a closed organization. Despite the esteem in which he was undeniably held, even Professor Hinsley was not given access to MI6 archives and had to rely on information from other sources. Rørholt thus had good reason to believe that the professor's conclusions were not necessarily correct.

Close study of the professor's footnote (see above) may suggest that Rørholt was right. In his footnote Hinsley appears to allege that the SIS agent concerned did not report the *Scharnhorst*'s departure because he was not living in the Lang fjord area and in consequence had not personally seen the battlecruiser leave. Hinsley clearly believed that the Ida transmitter was operated by only one man, Råby, and that he, all alone, covered the whole of the 100-kilometre stretch of water that separated the Kå fjord from the Lang fjord. This assumption is not calculated to increase confidence in the professor's assessment of the situation. In the first place the Ida Group consisted of two men, Råby and Karl Rasmussen. Furthermore, they had enlisted the aid of many Highways Department employees between Lakselv in the east and Alteidet in the south, plus that of numerous other volunteers, all of whom continually submitted reports.

As Råby wrote in his report of 31 July 1944, only ten weeks after making his escape from Alta to Sweden:

What we needed most, was a man in Kaafjord, and another man in Langfjord. Once a week we had to pay out the workers in Langfjord and Kaafjord, and we could then see with our own eyes what was going on. In addition, if anything special was up, Kalle could requisition a car and drive off to investigate. In Langfjord there was a deputy Sheriff, who had been sacked and was now employed as an office assistant by the Road Authority at Storsandnes [at the mouth of the Lang fjord]. It seemed to us that he would be a useful man since he also had a car. Kalle went over to talk to the man (Jonas Kummeneje) who immediately said he was willing to help. On one of his pay trips, to Hammerfest, Kalle met Chauffeur Harry Pettersen from Kaafjord. He drove cars for the Road Authority in Lakselv, and was a good friend of Erling Pleym [head of the local Highways Department office]. Harry was on holiday and was on his way home to [the village of] Kaafjord. Kalle asked him whether he would join 'The Service', as he used to call it. Harry Pettersen was keen.

Harry Pettersen also had his contacts, among them Jens Digre, a Storsandnes shopkeeper. Hinsley's reasoning was thus wrong from the start. Råby and Rasmussen had no need to live in close proximity to the Lang fjord to be able to keep an eye on the *Scharnhorst*'s movements: they had a network of trustworthy informants on whom they could rely.

The only confirmation of precisely what reports were sent from Norway and received in London would be a complete record of the signals passing between the two, but the relevant files are still closed. The copies received by the Norwegian 'E' office are manifestly incomplete, meaning that an analysis of them at this late date would necessarily be both ambiguous and far from clear.

Egil Lindberg, who first claimed credit for reporting the *Scharnhorst*'s departure, was a key figure in wartime intelligence activities in northern Norway, a seasoned agent who maintained wireless contact with London from Tromsø for five years without detection. At a pre-Christmas party he met a man who was working for the Germans in the Kå fjord area and successfully pumped him for information without, of course, disclosing what he wanted it for. 'The man seemed to be both intelligent and level-headed. He gave me correct information about the anti-torpedo nets and gave a credible account of the attack by midget submarines,' Lindberg wrote.

But the copy of the signal transmitted from Finnsnes to London on 23 December did not reach the 'E' office until six days later, that is, 29 December – and it said nothing about plans for an attack on a convoy. The last paragraph

read: 'Scharnhorst has been moved to Burfjord in Kvænangen. Since the Scharnhorst's arrival at Alta, she has been tended by pumpboats. The pump jet could be plainly seen 1½ kilometres away.'

It was correct that the Scharnhorst had transferred to the Bur fjord, but that had been on 15 December; she returned to the Lang fjord on 18 December. The report that the battlecruiser had received assistance from pumpboats was confusing. If Lindberg was suggesting that she was leaking, it might have led the British to believe that she was not operational. The signal continued: 'Trial gun practice was announced, with heavy artillery in the direction of Enoey [Island] in Kvænangen. Eleven shots were fired from medium guns, then the pumpboat was recalled again.'

Once again the information was substantially correct. On 18 November the Scharnhorst had fired ten shells from the Lang fjord over the intervening mountains to land in the Kvænang fjord on the far side of Alteidet. But it was not the ship's medium-calibre guns that were fired, it was the heavy guns of A turret. Once more there was mention of a pumpboat in the signal – as though the Scharnhorst needed assistance whenever she left her anchorage or her guns were fired. The observer had not seen a pumpboat, however. What he had seen was either the oiler Jeverland or the Harle, an auxiliary vessel that supplied the Scharnhorst with electric power and fresh water.

The last paragraph of this signal stated: 'The ships showed no sign of activity during the last British manoeuvres in the Arctic Ocean. . . . The Scharnhorst's camouflage is mostly of only one colour, dark-grey. Her camouflage has not been changed while the ship has been at anchor in Alta.'

The wording suggests that the agents had been asked questions and had been provided with carefully tailored information by London. 'Manoeuvres' was clearly a reference to the fact that the convoys had recommenced sailing. It was correct that there had not been any special 'activity' on board the Scharnhorst between the time when the ship's company was twice placed in a state of readiness at the turn of the month November/December until convoy JW55B was sighted and the alarm given on 22 December. But where was Lindberg's report that the battlecruiser and her escort of five destroyers were preparing to attack the convoy? Whatever the answer, there was no mention of it in the copy received by the Norwegian 'E' office. The way the signal was worded, it looked as though the opposite was the case, with no activity having been observed and the ship needing the assistance of pumpboats. That hardly suggested that the Battle Group was ready to put to sea and had steam up. How could Lindberg's memory have been so at fault such a short time afterwards? Was he taking credit for something he hadn't done, or was there another signal, one of which the Norwegians had not received a copy? Had the signal been doctored? Were the British afraid that the exiles would be unable to keep the news to themselves? Did they fear that the Germans would call off the attack if there was a leak?

The signal raised more questions than it answered. An examination of the copies of signals transmitted by Ida and Lyra yielded equally discouraging results.

Ida went on the air for the first time on 11 November 1943. But the Ida file contained only three signals from the time contact was first established until New Year 1943. Was that possible? Had Torstein Pettersen Råby, who had spoken of daily contact, really sent only three signals to London in the first two months? Two of these signals had the same date, 13 November, while the third was from the end of December. If the copies reflected the true state of affairs, Ida had been on the air only three times from the day contact was first made, i.e., 11 November; after that, there had been six weeks of silence. Could that be right?

What is more, in the light of what was actually happening at the German base, the contents of the three signals were prosaic, to say the least. One signal merely said that the *Scharnhorst* was moored in Langfjordbotn, that is, at the head of the Lang fjord. The second contained yet another description of the anti-torpedo nets in the Kå fjord, the result of a visual observation. In both cases the British already possessed this information, and it was also augmented by regular air reconnaissance flights.

In the same period the *Scharnhorst* and her attendant destroyers carried out extensive training in the Varg and Stjern sounds. Hintze staged weekly gunnery and radar exercises, concluding with the speed trial on 25 November. If those three signals really were the only ones transmitted to London at that time, Råby had missed most of the action.

Trygve Duklæt and Rolf Storvik in Porsa had been far more active in the same period, but the Lyra file does not seem to be complete either. From the time contact was first established early in July 1943, and for the succeeding four months, no copies of any signals appear to exist. The first recorded signal was transmitted on 5 November and contained sound tactical information to the effect that 'the hospital ship *Posen* has arrived at the U-boat base in Hammerfest with torpedoes'. A copy of this signal did not reach the Norwegian 'E' office until 18 November. Between then and Christmas a further twenty or so signals were sent, ranging from warnings not to attack the replacement coastal-express steamer to rumours that the repair ship *Monte Rosa* had arrived in the Kå fjord.

In the middle of December London appears to have been worried about Ida. A signal sent by Lyra on 13 December, clearly in answer to an anxious question, contained the following assurance: 'We shall get in touch with Ida. Wireless conditions have been difficult for the past 14 days.' This suggests that London had not heard anything from Råby, prompting them to urge Duklæt and Storvik to find out what had happened.

For some strange reason, among the copies of signals that have survived there is no sign that Lyra reported either the *Scharnhorst*'s movements or her departure. Immediately before Christmas four signals reached London from Porsa. One, from Lyra, warned that a convoy of four cargo vessels was passing through Varg Sound. The second said that German troops were being sent home from Finnmark. The third reported that the *Black Watch* was moored inside the mole in Hammerfest, with the torpedo transport *Admiral Carl Hering* alongside. The last signal, transmitted on 22 December, informed London that the *Monte Rosa* was rumoured to have arrived in the Kå fjord. Duklæt concluded with 'Best wishes for a happy Christmas'.

On 15 November the Murmansk convoys again began sailing. The course they chose from Scotland to the Kola peninsula took them close to the Norwegian coast. They were meant to be discovered, in order to lure Hitler's last operational battlecruiser into an ambush. At great risk to the lives of the agents on the spot, the British Secret Service had set up two wireless transmitters near the German base, their primary task being to warn London if the Battle Group put to sea. The presence of these transmitters notwithstanding, there is hardly a word about the *Scharnhorst* in the copies of the signals passed on to the 'E' office. No reports, no observations, no questions, even. It is all very mystifying. Is the explanation simply that the signals relating to the *Scharnhorst* were held back? Is that why there are no copies of them in the Norwegian files? Or was it that the British were not all that interested in reports from agents in the field? Were they receiving better and more accurate information from other sources? Were the agents really being employed to protect those other sources? Was it, perhaps, more important for the British that *German counter-intelligence* should monitor the signals transmitted from Kronstad and Porsa and so be led to believe that Norwegian agents were the main source of information?

All the time the *Scharnhorst* remained in the Lang fjord, that is, from March 1943 until she was sunk on 26 December, the British were monitoring and decrypting wireless signals sent by the Fleet Commander in Kiel to the naval base in Norway. They were also intercepting signals from the *Luftwaffe* bases in Bardufoss and Tromsø, along with those passing between the Commander of the U-boat flotilla in Narvik and the U-boats operating off Bear Island. These signals were encrypted on Enigma machines, in which the Germans had blind faith. But the British cryptologists at Bletchley Park – among them Hinsley – had solved Enigma's secret, and by 1943 were reading German wireless traffic almost like an open book. Commonly known as Ultra, the breaking of the Enigma cipher was the best-kept secret of the Second World War. It gave the British a very good insight into Germany's military thinking and intentions – and it also revealed the Battle Group's plans to attack the Russian convoys.

Throughout the whole of November and December 1943, therefore, Lieutenant-Commander Norman Denning at the OIC in London received copies of many of the orders, reports and views exchanged between Bey and Hintze at the naval base in western Finnmark, Peters in Narvik and Schniewind in Kiel – with only a few hours' delay.

On 11 December, for example, Denning was informed that the *Scharnhorst* had reported that she was preparing to carry out exercises in the Alta fjord on 14 December. On 17 December decrypts revealed that, two days earlier, she and *Z 29* had left the Lang fjord, presumably with the intention of carrying out the planned exercise. On 19 December Ultra revealed that the *Luftwaffe* was planning reconnaissance flights to report on the movements of a convoy that was expected to appear off the coast of northern Norway. On 20 December signals simply poured in. Two U-boats had sighted a convoy near Bear Island. Ultra revealed the areas of attack allocated to each U-boat, the fact that aerial reconnaissance had had to be called off owing to bad weather, and that the men of the *Scharnhorst* had been placed on three hours' notice at 18.23 on 18 December.

And so it went on, from the time convoy JW55B was sighted by a German weather plane in the morning of 22 December until that fateful coded signal 'OSTFRONT 1700/25/12' was intercepted at 18.30 on Christmas Day and handed to Denning in clear a bare seven hours later. On the basis of this signal and collation of all other available information, at 02.17 on 26 December Denning was able to signal Admiral Bruce Fraser on board the *Duke of York* 'EMERGENCY. *SCHARNHORST* PROBABLY SAILED 1800 25 DECEMBER.'

But does this mean – as Professor Hinsley claimed – that Ida and Lyra did *not* warn London that the battlecruiser had put to sea? What about Torstein Pettersen Råby, who maintained that a signal to that effect had been despatched? And what about Harry Pettersen, who was notified of the battlecruiser's departure by Jens Digre and who took steps to ensure that the

news reached the two agents in the Tverrelv valley, where they were having their Christmas dinner?

There is one last, singular document that casts a little more light on the matter. On 29 December 1943 Eric Welsh of the SIS sent the following personal memo to Major Knut Aas, head of the Norwegian 'E' office. 'You may be interested to know that our IDA Station in a message dated the 23rd of December, but not received until the 29th of December, requested us to maintain a listening watch for him every other hour.'

What was it Råby told Jostein Nyhamar, editor of the magazine *Aktuell*, in 1958? 'A German supply ship came in – it was on Christmas Eve, as far as I remember – and all leave was cancelled. We realized then that something was up. We set up the transmitter and reported to England that it looked as though the *Scharnhorst* was preparing to sortie. When she left, we reported it immediately – the English stations were by then listening out for us around the clock.'

The supply ship was the 'potato carrier' which, just before Christmas, supplied the Battle Group with several hundred tons of potatoes. On 22 December the men of the *Scharnhorst* and her destroyer escort were again placed on heightened readiness and preparations for immediate departure put in hand. The following day Råby and Karl Rasmussen asked London to listen out for them every other hour, as something big was in the offing. What else could it have been other than that the two had learned that the *Scharnhorst* had steam up and was waiting for the order to put to sea? The British had clearly received the agents' request that a constant listening watch be kept, as witness the letter from Welsh to Aas. London must have welcomed the request; after all, the situation was critical. It was precisely on 23 December that Admiral Fraser and Force 2 had been standing by in Akureyri, poised to put to sea as soon as they heard that the *Scharnhorst* was out.

At the same time Hinsley and Denning, prompted by the Ultra decrypts, had begun to suspect that Schniewind, Peters and Bey were planning an attack on convoy JW55B. Now they were being offered an opportunity to be kept updated on the course of events, every other hour, by people stationed in the very heart of the area in which the German base was located. Wouldn't they normally have had all operators listening out? And wouldn't they immediately have signalled their gratitude to Råby and Rasmussen and warned them how important it was that they should not let the *Scharnhorst* out of their sight for a moment?

The laconic note from Welsh said nothing of this. The British were at a turning point in the naval war. But no one seems to have reacted to receiving this important signal only after a delay of six days – a signal devoid, at that, of all comment and supplementary information. There is something very strange about it all.

I have devoted a great deal of time and effort to trying to separate fact from fiction. To me, the memo suggests that on 23 December Torstein Pettersen Råby and Karl Rasmussen were preparing to send an urgent signal to London. That being so, and especially in the light of what the British probably sent them in the way of appeals, would they have been likely to call it a day, leave the *Scharnhorst* to her own devices and set about enjoying their Christmas break? Would they have neglected to send a signal after having urged London to maintain a listening watch? I do not think they would. I believe that they did their best to send a warning.

In that case, why is there no trace of any such signal? Why did not their friend and controller, Eric Welsh, comment further on the strange situation that had arisen? Was the explanation simply that reception was so poor that the signal never got through?

Or was it that Hinsley and all the other high-ups in British intelligence relied primarily on Ultra, the existence of which had to be protected at any price? Was it intended that Råby and Pettersen should use their transmitter not only in order that London should pick up their signals, but also that the German D/F stations should do so? That would lead the Germans to believe that information relating to the *Scharnhorst*'s departure originated with agents in Norway, whereas in reality it came from Ultra. The primary source had to be safeguarded at all costs. If that was what really happened, it was a cynical ploy that put the Norwegian agents' lives at risk. On the other hand, cynicism has always been a key factor in intelligence work. Furthermore, it was war, and war has its own brutal logic. What, then, were the lives of a handful of Norwegian agents worth compared with the war's greatest secret? Nothing. They were expendable.

CHAPTER TWENTY-FIVE

Aftermath

THE BARENTS SEA/GERMANY, WINTER 1943/4

Late in the afternoon of Monday 27 December the *Duke of York* and the rest of the Allied fleet steamed into the Kola Inlet and dropped anchor. While the ships were engaged in bunkering 10,000 tons of oil from the tankers that drew alongside, the thirty-six German survivors were transferred from the *Scorpion* and *Matchless* to the flagship. Some were afraid they would be handed over to the Russians, but their fears were groundless. Admiral Fraser had no intention of losing his prisoners and kept them locked up under the watchful eyes of six Royal Marines.

In his diary, the C-in-C of the Soviet Northern Fleet, Admiral Arseni Golovko, made no attempt to disguise his irritation:

> The destruction of a German battleship is undoubtedly a great success for the British. . . . He [Fraser] described the action briefly. . . . It seems that the ship was struck by eleven torpedoes, according to the British, but by eight, according to the prisoners. . . . We are not being told anything more, although it must be clear to Admiral Fraser and his Staff that the information obtained from the Nazis fished out of the water interests us keenly – not, of course, the details of the action, but the situation at Altenfjord and Lang Fjord, which form the pivot of the Nazi naval forces operating against us in the Northern theatre. Hence the annoyance caused by the way the allies on this occasion confined themselves to radiant smiles and lengthy declarations that they and we were allies. Never mind, we will manage on our own information.

With a large fur hat and an all-enveloping fur coat as parting gifts, Admiral Fraser and the rest of the fleet left Murmansk the next day. They set a course for their home base, Scapa Flow, into which they made a triumphal entry on New Year's Day 1944.

Nils Owren, Gunnery Officer of the *Stord*, described the scene when the fleet entered the harbour, battle-ensigns flying:

At the entrance to the anchorage [in Murmansk] we lined the rail and gave three cheers for the men of the *Duke of York* as we passed the battleship. We were ourselves loudly cheered in return. But this recognition of the success of the operation was as nothing compared with that Forces 1 and 2 received on reaching Scapa Flow on 1 January. All Allied ships in the waters round about had been ordered into the harbour and were anchored there in two long lines, and we Arctic seafarers had to run the gauntlet between them. The rails were lined on every ship and everyone cheered us and congratulated us on the operation. Worn out, we stood silently at attention on deck and accepted all these laudations. There is no denying that there were times when we all had a lump in our throats.

Congratulations poured in from every quarter. 'Well done, *Duke of York*, and all of you. I am proud of you,' wrote King George VI, while Churchill telegraphed Fraser: 'Heartiest congratulations to you and Home Fleet on your brilliant action. All comes to him who knows how to wait.' Fraser himself sent a note of congratulation to the Norwegian C-in-C in London.

The action brought the participants a host of honours and decorations. Fraser was awarded the Grand Cross of the Order of the Bath and, by the Soviet Union, the Order of Suvorov, First Class. He was later given a peerage, taking, with the express permission of King Haakon VII of Norway, the title Lord Fraser of North Cape. Vice-Admiral Robert Burnett was made a KBE, while several captains were awarded the DSO. Captain Skule Storheill, who was later to rise to the rank of Vice-Admiral and be appointed C-in-C of the Royal Norwegian Navy, received a bar to his DSC.

The young Germans who had been rescued and taken prisoner were both well and correctly treated. 'The British sailors gave us all the assistance they could and took pains to help us recover. We were suffering badly from hypothermia when we were dragged on board and we'd all swallowed a lot of oil and salt water. Some of us had minor injuries, too,' says Helmut Backhaus. 'It took a long time before we could reconcile ourselves to the fact that we were the sole survivors and that all the others had been lost. To find the deck gone beneath your feet after a bloody battle and then suddenly find yourself in the open sea is a unique experience. One feels infinitesimally small and fragile, a piece of straw, nothing more. I was one of the chosen ones. The only reason is that I had an angel by my side.'

Although the survivors were well treated, one mistake was made while the *Duke of York* was on her way from Murmansk to Scapa Flow. Despite his protests, Lieutenant Edward Thomas, Fraser's Intelligence Officer, was urged – and finally ordered – to conduct a preliminary interrogation of the prisoners. The battleship's officers were eager to find out all they could. '[T]hey were punch drunk with their terrible experience and if ever there was a case for leaving prisoners alone to be competently dealt with in due course this was it,' wrote Thomas, who got little out of them. The British were mostly interested in the *Scharnhorst*'s armaments – the controlling machinery, guns, radar and range-finders; everything, in fact, that could give them an indication of the state of German technology. The intention was to wrest from the survivors as many of Germany's military secrets as possible. 'But we were prisoners of war and for that reason under no obligation to provide more information than was strictly necessary,' says Backhaus, who, on reaching Scotland, was put on a train with the rest of the survivors and taken to London. 'We were subjected to daily interrogation, first by German immigrants, later by British military experts. Questioning lasted for several weeks, but most of us withstood the pressure.'

That this is true is borne out by the report – it runs to close on one hundred pages – compiled on the basis of interrogation of the survivors, which says:

Contrary to expectations, the survivors, all of whom were ratings, presented a front of tough, courteous security-consciousness, and evidence of high morale, which, combined with meagre and limited knowledge, has provided interrogators with a difficult problem.

The task of obtaining reliable technical information and an accurate account of the last action was hindered by evidence of inexpert preliminary interrogation, during which the prisoners apparently received sufficient information on the action from the British point of view to colour their own version and make the extraction of a parallel account most difficult.

The fact that all but four of the survivors were below decks or under cover during practically the whole of the action has proved a major drawback. Most of the remainder were unable to distinguish between the explosion of torpedoes, the impact of the heavy shells and the firing of their

own heavy armament. To many of them, the order to prepare to abandon ship came as a surprise, as they had no idea that *Scharnhorst* had been damaged to that extent.

As noted above, Able-Seaman Günther Sträter was repatriated shortly afterwards under the auspices of the Red Cross. He was the only one. After a brief stay in Scotland, the other survivors were taken to New York aboard the *Queen Mary*. Eight were interned in Canada, the remainder in Camp McCain outside New Orleans.

'After a hard life at sea, we became cotton-pickers in Mississippi. We were paid 80 cents a day – but only if we managed to fill our quota of 80 kilos,' says Backhaus, who still has his tattered diary containing the comments of his fellow prisoners. Some of the men made no secret of their true feelings. 'To be German is to be loyal,' wrote one. Others were more personal. 'We got to know each other in a dire emergency at sea. It is hard to part, but I shall always remember you with gratitude.' Some of the prisoners were repatriated in 1946, but the last of them did not get home until 1948. Said Ernst Reimann:

It was a sad, strange homecoming. In my little town I was the only one who had survived. I went to see the next-of-kin [of my shipmates] who were still alive. But there was so little I could tell them. I couldn't say exactly how the others had died. How could I explain why I was alive, when all the others were dead? For that reason, many of us chose to remain silent. We had to overcome our feeling of guilt and pick up the threads, bit by bit.

In the meantime German U-boats and ever stronger escort groups continued to do battle in the Barents Sea. When the search for survivors from the *Scharnhorst* was finally abandoned in the afternoon of 27 December, the seven remaining U-boats of *Gruppe Eisenbart* set off eastwards at full speed in pursuit of the convoy. But it was too late. By then, all nineteen merchantmen had almost reached their destinations in the Kola Inlet and White Sea. Pawns though they had been in an audacious game, they all reached port unharmed. In Narvik, *Kapitän-zur-See* Rudolf Peters was feeling very dejected and disheartened. He ascribed the setback to the enemy's radar superiority, which had enabled them to locate his U-boats and force them under. 'Taken all round, our U-boats were inferior to the covering forces and were in most cases surprised by the escorting destroyers and other units.' He did not realize that an equally important cause was the many wireless signals he had required his U-boat captains to transmit.

The British intercepted them, took bearings on them and decrypted them, then sent in their destroyers.

The weather was atrocious throughout, making it practically impossible to shadow the convoy. 'Lack of experience among the untried U-boat skippers undoubtedly also played a not insignificant role,' Peters wrote.

The loss of the *Scharnhorst* resulted in Peters at last being allotted the additional U-boats he had begged for for so long. Against succeeding convoys in January, February and March 1944 he was able to despatch ten U-boats to the Bear Island Trench, to be followed by a further fifteen, most of them equipped with radar-warning systems and new type-T5 homing torpedoes. *Gruppe Eisenbart* was disbanded, to be replaced by wolf packs with such stirring mythological names as *Isegrim*, *Werwolf* and *Wiking*.

Despite this massive and sustained onslaught, the U-boats never succeeded in regaining the initiative. The British retained their technological lead and, thanks to their resoluteness and long experience, repeatedly repulsed the attackers. In the course of the next sixteen months only twelve Allied merchant ships were torpedoed. In the same period Germany lost no fewer than twenty-five U-boats, most of them with the loss of all on board.

'In 1944 we found ourselves on the defensive for good. The escorts were incredibly strong. The moment we fired a weapon we were attacked from every direction. We had constantly to be ready to dive,' says Hans-Günther Lange, who, as captain of *U-711*, took part in all major attacks on the convoys up to the spring of 1945.

Only one of the eight *Eisenbart* U-boats survived the war. *U-314* was captained by 26-year-old *Korvettenkapitän* Georg-Wilhelm Basse, whose escutcheon was the Olympic rings; this was because Basse had commenced his training in 1936, in which year the Olympic Games were held in Berlin. His captaincy had not been attended by a great deal of success. In March 1943 he had taken *U-339* to sea on her maiden voyage from Bergen. Only four days later the U-boat was so badly damaged in an attack from the air that it never returned to service. Basse was given a new command, *U-314*. On his very first patrol, at the end of December 1943, he found, the only U-boat skipper to do so, a patch of oil, all that was left of the *Scharnhorst*. Four weeks later, south of Bear Island, he fired a salvo of torpedoes at two British destroyers, the *Whitehall* and *Meteor*. The torpedoes missed, but the depth-charges dropped by the destroyers did not, and *U-314* was sent to the bottom, taking with her the whole of her fifty-man crew. On 25 February 1944 it was Otto Hansen's turn. A Catalina from Sullum Voe caught *U-601* midway between the islands of

Sørøya and Jan Mayen. The U-boat sank in thirty seconds. Surviving members of her crew were seen clinging to scraps of wreckage, but they had no chance of rescue. On 1 May Robert Lübsen, captain of *U-277*, and his entire crew of forty-nine men perished south-west of Bear Island following an air attack. Towards the end of August 1944, under her new skipper, *Korvettenkapitän* Sthamer, *U-354* sank the frigate *Bickerton* and damaged the aircraft-carrier *Nabob* in a highly successful torpedo attack north of Nordkyn. But another frigate, the *Mermaid*, gave chase and didn't give up until she had sent *U-354* to the bottom. Oil continued to rise to the surface for more than twelve hours afterwards. By an ironic stroke of fate, after the war the *Mermaid* was sold to Germany's new *Bundesmarine* and given a traditional name – *Scharnhorst*. On 10 October 1944 *U-957*, skippered by *Korvettenkapitän* Gerhard Schaar, became a total wreck after a collision in the Vest fjord. Schaar had shortly before been awarded the Knight's Cross of the Iron Cross after sinking three Allied ships and raiding a Soviet wireless station east of Novaya Semlja. As the war neared its end *U-387*, captained by Rudolf Büchler, was sunk with the loss of all hands off the Kola peninsula in December 1944, and *U-636* disappeared in the Atlantic in April 1945; *Korvettenkapitän* Hans Hildebrandt, who had not had a very successful war, was no longer on board. On 30 December 1943, following repair of the U-boat's batteries, Hildebrandt had once again put out from Hammerfest and taken part in attacks on the Russian convoys. But his eyesight was beginning to trouble him and his tactical dispositions aroused Peters's ire.

> I cannot accept that on most days the boat remained submerged for long periods; nor can this be excused on the grounds of the Captain's having been ill. The precautions he took in the initial phase are incomprehensible. . . . A skipper who constantly remains submerged at Depth A and who, at the first sound, dives to Depth 2A + 20, can hardly be expected to achieve results. I am not satisfied with the way the assignment was carried out. In the meantime the Captain has been relieved of his command owing to an eye ailment that has greatly impaired his night vision.

Of the eight U-boats that had taken part in the Battle of the North Cape, the only one to survive was Hans Dunkelberg's *U-716*, which in May 1945 was taken over by the British and scrapped. For her, too, it had been a near thing. She scored her first and only success in January 1944, when she sank the brand-new Liberty ship *Andrew C. Curtin* south of Bear Island with the loss of a 9,000-ton cargo that included steel and locomotives. Some weeks later *U-716* was surprised off Jan Mayen by an Allied aircraft, which dropped two bombs. They exploded close to the U-boat and blew the diesel engine off its mounting. The hull took a tremendous pounding. The horizontal rudder wouldn't answer and we continued to sink – down, down, past the tested depth of 100 metres. Only when the tanks were blown and the whole crew ordered forward, did Dunkelberg manage to stabilize us. By then, the depth-gauge stood at 276 metres. They were terrifying minutes. We were millimetres from certain death, but we made it,' said the U-boat's wireless operator, Peter Junker.

In the days following the sinking of the *Scharnhorst*, both the Commander-in-Chief of the Navy in Berlin, *Grossadmiral* Karl Dönitz, and the Fleet Commander in Kiel, *Generaladmiral* Otto Schniewind, did their subtle best to escape responsibility for what had happened. *Konter-Admiral* Erich Bey, who was no longer in a position to defend himself, was singled out as scapegoat. However, as Bey had fought to the last and chosen a hero's death, any criticism levelled at him had of necessity to be indirect and cautiously worded. Dönitz never admitted that Operation *Ostfront* had been a hazardous and badly planned operation from the outset and, the weather being what it was, should never have been mounted in the first place. His contention was that his decision to order the *Scharnhorst* to put to sea had been justified, as she was in a favourable position, but that Bey had made a tragic mistake and 'confused the British cruisers with heavy units'. Had he attacked them, Dönitz told Hitler, it was 'absolutely possible that the first phase would have developed to our advantage'.

In his memoirs, published fourteen years later, Dönitz was still more scathing in his judgement:

. . . [A]t about 1240 *Scharnhorst* turned and steamed on a south to south-east course at high speed towards the Norwegian coast.

Now comes the decisive question. Why, when she turned away, did *Scharnhorst* do so on *this* particular course, upon which both the British cruisers and the destroyers, running with the weather more or less on their beam, could follow her? Had she steered a more westerly course into the wind and sea, the cruisers and destroyers maintaining contact would very quickly have lagged behind, for steaming into the head sea the heavy German ship would certainly have been several knots faster than the more lightly built enemy cruisers and destroyers. In his report on the action Admiral Fraser says that the weather would have given the *Scharnhorst* 'the advantage of a 4 to 6 knots higher speed'.

The Grand Admiral spent the first three days after the turn of the year together with his *Führer* at the Wolf's Lair in East Prussia, after having issued the following inflammatory Order of the Day to what was left of his Navy:

> An iron year lies behind us. It has made us Germans hard as no generation before us. Whatever fate may demand from us in the coming year, we will endure, united in will, steady in loyalty, fanatical in belief in our victory.
>
> The battle for freedom and justice for our people continues. It will see us pitted inexorably against our enemy.
>
> The *Führer* shows us the way and the goal. We follow him with body and soul to a great German future.
>
> *Heil* our *Führer*!

Dönitz had promised Hitler a crushing victory over the convoys. Instead, he had lost his last operational battlecruiser and suffered a humiliating defeat. He had every reason to fear the *Führer*'s wrath, but, in the light of the Grand Admiral's grovelling, Hitler curbed his anger. Admittedly, he inferred that the real reason the big ships had been such a failure was that they had preferred to flee rather than fight – as, in his opinion, they had done ever since the pocket battleship *Graf Spee* was scuttled by her own men in Rio de la Plata in 1939. As Dönitz's biographer, Peter Padfield, wrote:

> Undoubtedly he [Hitler] had won his wager over the usefulness of the big ships, but he made no reference to it now or later, and was content for Dönitz to dispose of the remaining heavy units as he wished. The fact was he needed Dönitz; he needed the support he invariably gave him over the strategy of holding on everywhere until . . . He needed the hopes he embodied of a renewed U-boat offensive with the new types of boat, and he needed the personal loyalty he brought to all questions.

A *Kriegsmarine* spokesman, the ageing *Admiral* Lützow, was chosen to hold the formal memorial eulogy over the German broadcasting network in the evening of Wednesday 29 December 1943. Lützow concluded with the following words: 'We pay homage to our comrades who died a seaman's death in a heroic battle against a superior enemy. The *Scharnhorst* now rests on the field of honour.'

For thousands of people all over Germany, the next-of-kin of the dead sailors, the announcement was greeted with shock and disbelief, most notably in the heavily bombed Ruhr, where most of the men came from. The *Scharnhorst*, that 'lucky ship', had been lost, and with her, it seemed, her entire complement of nearly two thousand men. 'It was a terrible blow to my mother,' says Thomas König, son of the *Scharnhorst*'s Chief Engineer, *Korvettenkapitän* Otto König:

> She was left with two children. I was the younger, I was only six. She returned to her home town of Wetzlar and, warm-hearted and upright woman that she was, devoted herself body and soul to our future. Like thousands of other officers' widows, she received no support when peace came in 1945. It was only many years later, in the early 1950s, that she was granted a small pension. But she bore her grief, her many problems and poverty with dignity. She never remarried. We have her to thank for everything.

Those of the ship's company who had been granted Christmas leave and were in Germany when the battlecruiser was sunk were deeply distressed by the news. One of them was the ship's hairdresser, Karl Ernst Weiss. 'He was paying a family visit,' says his grandson, Oliver Weiss, 'when his brother came in, looking grave, and grasped my grandmother's hand. "I must congratulate you, Gretl," he said, "on the fact that your husband is still alive. The *Scharnhorst* has just been sunk." It was an awful shock to them both. My grandfather never got over it. Fate had taken a hand, so that he had survived, but he found no solace in the thought. He suffered from an overwhelming sense of guilt for the rest of his life.'

In Bad Bevensen, news of the death of *Kapitän-zur-See* Fritz Julius Hintze reached his home only a few weeks after he, a family man to the depths of his being, had bade a last farewell to his nearest and dearest. Looking back, Hintze's niece, *Frau* Karin Woltersdorf, said:

> My uncle was a warm, good man. For all these years the thought of him and the two thousand men who perished off the North Cape has been an integral part of our lives. His early death left behind a void that cannot be filled. The news affected us all equally strongly. He was greatly missed, especially by his wife Charlotte, whom he loved so much. They had no children. She never recovered from the loss of her husband and died not long after the war.

The loss of the *Scharnhorst* was mourned all over Germany, but in Giessen nineteen-year-old Gertrud Damaski felt no cause for anxiety. Her fiancé, Heinrich Mulch, was on the *Tirpitz*, not the *Scharnhorst*, and she was expecting him home on leave and that he would soon be released to continue his studies in January.

When sadness and loneliness overcame her she would take out the verses Heinrich had composed in the shadow of the mountains that ringed the Kå fjord. Full of his love and yearnings, they read, freely translated from the Norwegian version, as follows.

> Alone, as I am, far away in the north,
> where the Man with the Scythe forever stalks forth,
> I need all the love that a young girl can give –
> a dream that beneath southern skies now does live.
>
> I think back with longing, trembling too,
> to ravishing moments,
> carefree and tender,
> spent quietly with you.
>
> My writing hand fails me,
> no words can I find.
> Though war now us parts,
> one moment for ever's engraved in my mind.
>
> That moment our lips,
> touched to reflect,
> the fire in our hearts.
> Gertrud, my darling, don't ever forget.
>
> The ocean divides us,
> yet we are so near,
> good times lie ahead –
> I am with you, my dear.

Gertrud had been hurt by her rejection by Heinrich's family, but was determined not to allow it to cast a shadow over their relationship. She was in love and her future was with Heinrich. But the days passed without any letters from northern Norway. The shock came a week or two later, in January 1944, when Heinrich's sister came to see her.

I couldn't imagine what she had to tell me. It turned out that Heinrich was one of the men missing after the loss of the *Scharnhorst*. In all probability he had gone down with the ship. I protested that Heinrich hadn't been serving on board the *Scharnhorst* but on the *Tirpitz*, but she said he'd been on the Admiral's staff and that he was one of those who had had to accompany the Admiral on that last sortie. He'd been transferred on Christmas Eve. I don't think I really grasped what she was telling me. I seemed to have turned into a block of ice. I tried to come to terms with the fact that the unbelievable had happened. Heinrich, who in his last letter had said that he was coming home, was no more.

Gertrud contacted the German Red Cross. On 27 January 1944 they replied, sending with their letter a copy of an earlier letter to Heinrich's family. It read:

Immediately upon receipt of your request the German Red Cross made the necessary enquiries, but it is regretted that so far nothing new relating to your next-of-kin has reached us. As soon as our enquiries have been completed, you will be informed. Should you yourself in the meantime receive any relevant information, please let us know. The Red Cross asks that you endure the inevitable wait with patience, in the hope that there will be good news later. We share your grief and deeply sympathize with you. *Heil* Hitler!

The shock left Gertrud Damaski numb. Her Heinrich was gone, lost for ever in the endless wastes of the Arctic Ocean. Her dreams for the future were shattered. All she had left were his letters and her memories. 'To keep going I had to repress everything. I was but one of millions at that time who had had their hopes dashed. I was called up for service as a radar operator with an anti-aircraft battery in Regensburg and had to leave Giessen. Things were very difficult, but life had to go on.'

More than fifty years were to elapse before, in 1994, Gertrud again took out Heinrich's letters and tried to find out exactly what had happened to him. 'There was no help to be had. No one talked about those years. Everything had been repressed. I have tried to find an answer, but no one knows precisely what happened. No one knows whether Heinrich died on board or whether he died afterwards, in the sea. He was the love of my youth. He disappeared, but for me he is still alive. I neither can nor will forget.'

CHAPTER TWENTY-SIX

The Reckoning

WESTERN FINNMARK, JANUARY–NOVEMBER 1944

On 2 January 1944 Karl Rasmussen's wife Sigrid gave birth to a baby girl at her parents' farm in the Tverrelv valley. It was a happy moment for the young couple, dreaming as they were of a better and easier life once the war was over. 'The midwife was sent for and came home to us. The birth was straightforward. She was a lovely little girl. We named her Brit. She brought me much happiness and has been a great support and help ever since.'

Sigrid still did not know that for two months her husband had been operating the Ida transmitter together with his friend Torstein Pettersen Råby, who had returned from England to Alta in October of the previous year. But she was fully aware that all was not as it should be, that the man she loved so dearly was engaged in something very dangerous. 'He had changed. There was a tension between us that had never been there before. He urged me not to ask questions. He wanted to protect me.'

While Sigrid was busy caring for her infant daughter throughout the winter of 1944 the importance of Ida and its companion transmitter Lyra in Porsa dramatically increased. The *Scharnhorst* had been sunk and no longer menaced the Russian convoys, but the *Tirpitz*, more formidable still, remained tucked away behind her anti-torpedo nets in the Kå fjord, surrounded by the destroyers of the 4th Flotilla; and *Grossadmiral* Dönitz was continuing to reinforce the U-boat base in Hammerfest. True, the *Tirpitz* had been severely damaged by the midget submarines that had so heroically attacked her in September 1943, but an army of welders and engineering workers from shipyards in Germany had been sent north to make her seaworthy again. It was rumoured that repair work

on the battleship would soon be completed and that she would then be despatched to attack the convoys.

In London, the Admiralty was growing increasingly anxious. The Pacific fleet needed reinforcements, but as long as the *Tirpitz* remained afloat, extra battleships and aircraft-carriers were having to be held back in a state of readiness in the North Atlantic. Ultra provided regular intercepts of wireless traffic between the Kå fjord base and Fleet Headquarters in Kiel, but there were still certain aspects of the situation that were not clear. Direct surveillance by agents behind enemy lines had therefore become of heightened importance, especially from mid-January onwards, when the British began planning a new attack on the *Tirpitz*.

As early as Monday 3 January Råby and Karl Rasmussen sent a signal to London in response to an initial enquiry about the damage sustained by the *Tirpitz*.

I have no definite reports of great damage but will talk to Lyra and investigate. After the attack, the *Tirpitz* had a list to port. Cement was taken on board. The next morning she was righted again. The gun mountings and turret had been badly jarred. No other damage is visible above the water line, beyond what I have reported. Machine ship still lying alongside, continuous work on board. Smoke from the funnels. Welding in the forward turret. A small oil boat on the other side. All cars which pass along the road are stopped twice for control.

In those days Alta was a straggling rural community in which most of what went on was common knowledge; it also housed a number of German detachments. In consequence, danger was ever present and the risk of discovery never far distant. Strong nerves and a cool head were crucial to the success of the operation. In a report he wrote on his return to London in July 1944 Råby described one particularly hair-raising incident:

Once when Kalle and I were out on a pay trip, we were stopped close by the *Tirpitz*. It so happened that Kalle had forgotten his pass. We were ordered out of the car, with machine pistols pointing at our stomachs, and we thought that our last hour had come. The driver, who was half a Quisling, assured the sentry in his excellent German that we were not spies. Kalle explained that we were employees of the Road Authority, out on a pay trip, and that the workers must have their pay before they finished work for the day. Kalle suggested that the driver and I should drive on, while he could remain with the sentry. An Officer came up from the *Tirpitz* and this proposal was agreed to. Kalle was able therefore to stand for half an hour right by the *Tirpitz*, which was of course strictly forbidden.

In the scattering of houses that was Porsa, where it was even more difficult to keep anything secret, Trygve Duklæt and Rolf Storvik were taking equally great risks. Not only were they operating the Lyra transmitter, they were also listening to broadcasts from London and passing on news about the progress of the war to the local population. Their activities often brought them into conflict with the pro-Nazi mayor of nearby Kvalsund, Rolf Arnt Nygaard, who not only worked with Duklæt as an engineer at the local power station but also lived in the same house – which was also where the transmitter was hidden in the cellar. Neither Storvik nor Duklæt knew that, as early as 1942, Nygaard had been recruited by the *Abwehr*. In return for 500 kroner, a bottle of schnapps and 150 grammes of tobacco a month, Nygaard had agreed to report all suspicious incidents to his German 'employers'. It was an ingenious set-up. Nygaard passed on his reports to another local *Abwehr* agent, who had been equipped with a wireless transmitter and stationed in the small community of Fægfjord. His name was Nils Bakken, a 31-year-old Norwegian from Honningsvåg whose cover name was 'Bjarne'. Using Morse, Bakken transmitted Nygaard's reports to a receiving station, Thea, at *Abwehr* HQ northern Norway in Tromsø.

In a recapitulation of events after the war, Rolf Storvik said:

In Porsa there was a Quisling supporter named Rolf Nygaard. He had several times tried to trip me up on different things, and whenever he felt he was on to something, he used to threaten me with the German Security Police. I remember when Hornæs was here in June 1943 [to hand over the Lyra transmitter]. Nygaard phoned the chairman of the Labour Office in Kvalsund to ask if he [Nygaard] was authorized to demand identity papers from strangers, as another had just turned up. My wife ran the telephone exchange and listened-in on the call. . . . It seemed that Nygaard was keeping an eye on non-locals visiting me, and that it was a matter of importance to him. . . . For one thing, he reported my wife to the Norwegian police for sabotaging the exchange, claiming that she had sabotaged his calls by disconnecting his phone on several occasions.

Despite the clash that threatened, all through the winter of 1944 Lyra continued to send a stream of reports to London, often transmitting several in

the course of only one day. They related to ships passing through Varg Sound, fortifications surrounding the U-boat base in Hammerfest and observations passed on from the Kå fjord area which Storvik and Duklæt received from contacts they had on the local steamers, foremost among them Paul Johnsen, First Officer of the *Brynilen*.

A signal transmitted on 10 January, for example, read:

'A raft about 30 metres long with a superstructure has been towed to the *Tirpitz*. It is apparently a raft for divers. A German bosun says that the holes in the *Tirpitz* were filled with cement, but there was a leakage when the guns were fired. A number of floats arrived with *Monte Rosa*, these will be used to raise the *Tirpitz*.'

On 26 January Lyra followed up with: 'Norwegian fisherman reports: Altenfjord mined. Two belts of mines. The minefield is from Talvik to Altnesset. Off Altnesset a 500 metre broad passage from the land seaward. Another mined area further in. No details. The same fisherman says that a large floating crane has been towed in to the *Tirpitz*. This report not confirmed.' At about the same time Ida reported from Kronstad: '*Tirpitz*. Morale on board can safely be described as bad for following reasons. First, the attack on *Tirpitz* and the sinking of the *Scharnhorst*. The bombing of Germany, and the long hours of darkness and other reasons. An ordinary seaman (probably drunk) said, "What else can one do except drink, while one awaits capture?"'

Ten days later, on 6 February, Lyra's information about the floating crane was confirmed. 'Re *Tirpitz*. A twenty-ton crane arrived February 1st. It is erected on a float on the starboard side of *Tirpitz* . . .'

On 9 February Duklæt and Storvik sent another – alarming – report to London from Porsa: 'Our source in Kaafjord has talked with German civilian workers. Amongst these are specialists who took part in the building of the *Tirpitz*. They say she will be ready to leave in March.' This report confirmed the conclusion the British themselves had reached on the basis of Ultra decrypts and earlier reports. The *Tirpitz* would be operational from mid-March 1944. This meant that there was little time left if impending attacks on the Russian convoys were to be nipped in the bud. Fleet Air Arm crews had already begun training for a bombing attack. Using aerial reconnaissance photographs and detailed topographical information, the British had constructed an accurate model of the German base in the Kå fjord. Barracuda bombers came roaring in over Loch Eriboll in Scotland, where the landscape was similar to the fjords and islands of western Finnmark. Ida and Lyra were urged to provide still more detailed information on the defences surrounding the *Tirpitz* – anti-aircraft batteries, smoke pots and D/F stations. As little as possible was to be left to chance.

As a precaution, the British often asked both stations the same questions. On 6 February the *Tirpitz*'s camouflage was described by Ida as follows: '*Tirpitz* is camouflaged only to seaward. The colours are light grey, blue and light yellow alternating in zig-zag patches. The decks are not camouflaged. No nets, only paint. The welding hut and another smaller shed is [sic] erected on after deck, they are unpainted and light in colour. Reliable source.' Three days later Lyra sent a signal reading: 'No change in the pattern of the camouflage of the *Tirpitz* has been observed up here. The camouflage from the sea consists of three cornered and fan-shaped fields in three colours. The hull is painted light grey forward of the first gun turret and aft of the aft gun turret in order to make the ship look shorter. I can confirm that another floating crane has arrived for the *Tirpitz*.'

In the feverish weeks that followed, Ida and Lyra reached their zenith as suppliers of first-class tactical information. If an aerial attack from an aircraft-carrier north-west of Sørøya Island was to have any point, the pilots of the aircraft involved needed to be reasonably sure of finding the *Tirpitz* at her regular anchorage. If she were to succeed in weighing anchor and slipping into one of the narrow fjords that abounded round about, all their training would be in vain. A constant flow of updated eye-witness observations was therefore essential to augment the information the British were receiving from their Ultra decrypts and air reconnaissance flights over the base area.

Ida was first to respond, signalling on 3 March: '*Tirpitz* still at anchor in her old position fired salvos with her two forrard guns at a floating target to-day 3.3.44 at 1000 GMT. Only one U-boat in Kvenvik. Good source.' One week later, on 10 March, a new signal was sent: 'The welding hut on *Tirpitz* after deck was removed yesterday and the tank taken up. There were also a 3,000 ton tanker and a small ammunition ship in the harbour. My source who is reliable is of the opinion she is ready to sail.' Lyra in Porsa gave the final alarm on 14 March by transmitting an ominously worded signal saying: 'Three torpedo boats have done several trips as minesweepers to-day Vargsund. Earlier they have made these trips when large warships were expected. Expecting the *Tirpitz* on steaming trials.'

Storvik and Duklæt's conclusion was absolutely correct and shortly afterwards was confirmed by Ultra. At 10.00 on 15 March 1944 the *Tirpitz* weighed anchor for the first time in six months and sailed out of the fjord under her own steam. 'The entire ship's company was deeply moved as the ship slowly left her anchorage. Once again her bows cleft the waves, while the men on the supply ships and destroyers saluted her. The *Tirpitz* had come back to life.'

In the course of the next two days her captain, Hans Meyer, tested the battleship's engines and armaments. Her speed was registered as 27 knots. Her heavy 38-cm shells exploded accurately in the distant mountains. The *Tirpitz* was again ready for action.

From the Highways Department hut at Kronstad, Torstein Pettersen Råby and Karl Rasmussen transmitted a series of top-priority signals. '*Tirpitz* left Kaafjord at her usual speed. I heard violent gunfire in the fjord at 1600 GMT. Her net is open. The net at Auskarnes is now closed. "Stand by" for goodness sake.' A little later there was another signal: '*Tirpitz* is not to be seen. She is not in Kaafjord. Good source. Observation 1730 GMT Keep constant watch.' Next day, the British at last received the signal they had been waiting for: '*Tirpitz* back again in Kaafjord at 1615 GMT. She nearly ran into her own net. She was out in the fjord all night. She was off Bossekop this morning and at 4000 GMT sailed out towards Seiland.'

On 18 March Bletchley Park intercepted the report of the results of the exercise sent by Meyer to the Fleet Commander in Kiel. The same day Duklæt reported from Porsa, clearly after he or Storvik had personally travelled to Sopnes and back on the local steamer: 'Personal observation of the 17th. In Langfjordbotn 3 destroyers; in Kaafjord at 1430: *Tirpitz, Monte Rosa, Harald Haarfagre, Tordenskjold*, 1 large tanker, *C.A. Larsen* and one destroyer.'

A succession of similar reports followed in the next few days. They convinced the C-in-C of the British Home Fleet, Admiral Bruce Fraser, of the need to act quickly. A force consisting of two large and three small aircraft-carriers under the command of Fraser's Second-in-Command, Vice-Admiral Henry Moore, was despatched, heading for the base. When Ultra revealed that the *Tirpitz* was planning new speed trials for the morning of 3 April, the attack was brought forward.

At 17.00 on 2 April Ida was on the air every other hour with weather forecasts direct from the Kå fjord. But halfway through the operation, there was a near-disastrous hitch:

> At the time electricity was rationed in Alta, so we had to use an accumulator. Without warning it broke down and we were unable to repair it. We toyed with the idea of starting the generator . . . but to start a petrol engine in that little community was asking for trouble. . . . Rasmussen knew the manager of the power station, a man from the west coast named Saunes, and went to see him. He was more than willing to help and, despite the restrictions then in force, for three days kept the [hydro-electric] power station running without

a break. Rasmussen said that when the manager heard why electricity was so urgently needed, he declared, 'I'll get water, even if I have to pee it myself!'

The updated weather reports were of immense value to the pilots who took off from the aircraft-carriers north-west of Sørøya at 04.15 next morning. The attack was carried out in two waves by a total of forty-two Barracuda bombers and fifty-one covering fighters. When the first wave reached the Kå fjord in perfect weather at 05.30, the *Tirpitz* was about to weigh anchor. The attackers had got there just in time. 'Bombs rained down, exploded and damaged the upper deck, penetrating its light armour and ripping open bulkheads and steam-pipes. Dead and wounded men were everywhere, lying in pools of blood and water [from the spray of near-misses]. Bullets from the fighters' machine-guns swept the decks, killing the wounded. The gun crews were forced to take cover. The ship's control system failed. Surprise was total.'

Operation Tungsten was an Allied success. On board the *Tirpitz* 112 men were killed and 316 wounded, including the ship's Captain, Hans Meyer. Fourteen bombs found their target. They were too light to penetrate the heavy armour of the main deck, however, so nothing vital was destroyed; nevertheless, it would take the Germans a further three months to repair the damage done to the deck and upperworks. Once again the battleship was temporarily out of action. From the scene of the bombing Ida reported: 'The local inhabitants are extremely impressed by the bombing. No civilian casualties and very little civilian damage. More later.'

But the Norwegian agents' part in the drama was to have its price. The *Gestapo* was closing in. As early as November 1943 Torstein and Karl had seen wireless vans in the area:

But later things got worse, because the Germans started to drive round in a long black car which stopped outside all the houses in Elvebakken, standing stationary before each house for a little while. There was of course much greater risk of discovery by this method, since the house where we lived stood only some 20–30 metres from the road. We thought many times of moving, but it would have been just as dangerous anywhere in the neighbourhood since there were Germans everywhere. About the only practicable place was in fact Kronstad, where we lived. The nearest Germans were at least 200 metres away. Also we would have had to explain our reasons to so many people, if we had moved to another house. One day while I was transmitting and Elias was as usual keeping watch, he came running in and told me to stop. Over by the

wall of one of the neighbouring houses stood a German with earphones on his head and a rucksack on his back. Out of the rucksack protruded a steel rod about one metre long. The next day the Germans carried out a razzia [raid] at this nearby house. This happened just after the air attack on the *Tirpitz*. Another difficulty was the question of why I had not registered myself for tax; why I had not registered myself in the local population register, etc., etc. Kalle managed to laugh off all these questions, but everything pointed to the fact that the ice was getting very thin.

Karl Rasmussen retained his optimistic outlook, but his smile was forced. At home on the farm Sigrid could see how frayed his nerves had become:

He used to have nightmares. He'd suddenly sit up in bed and shout for me. But he never said anything until after a party at the office. Because I felt sorry for my mother, who was looking after little Brit, I insisted on leaving early. On the way home Kalle told me for the first time all of what he was doing. I had long had my suspicions, but it was almost too much for me even so. I was absolutely paralysed. It had never occurred to me that they were engaged in such extensive and dangerous espionage activities. I just threw myself to the ground and wept. I begged him to give it up, but he said there was no going back. It was a long and doleful walk home. Both of us cried. He saw me weep only twice that winter. That was the first time.

Torstein Pettersen Råby had already resolved to close down Ida and flee across the border to Sweden. As early as the evening of 4 April he sent a signal to London reading: 'It has been pretty hot here lately and the Germans are in a fury. I must emigrate.' But the British were planning a new air attack against the *Tirpitz* and exhorted him to carry on. 'Both Admiralty and the Intelligence Service fully understand that the situation necessitates your leaving. Nevertheless, we think it right to tell you that reports over the next three weeks would be of very high value.' On three occasions in April and May Torstein and Karl were poised to transmit weather reports. But the attacks were postponed – and German vigilance continued to increase. In the meantime Torstein had found someone to take his place. It was Elias Østvik from Hammerfest, who had long wished to set up a transmitter which, at least in part, would be in a position to take over after Ida. In May 1944 one of the transmitters in the old 'Venus' store on the island of Kalvøya was dug up and transported to Hammerfest. A Norwegian Telegraph Authority wireless operator, Johannes

Ofstad, took charge of the transmitter. Råby accompanied Østvik into Hammerfest and helped him carry the transmitter and generators to a small cabin beside a lake some distance from town. But the transmitter, codenamed Vali, lacked crystals. Despite repeated attempts, Østvik, Ofstad and Råby never succeeded in raising London.

After saying goodbye to Duklæt and Storvik, Råby returned to Alta. On 15 May an attack launched by twenty-seven Barracudas from two aircraft-carriers had to be aborted because of bad weather. Late in the evening of the following day the last report from Ida reached London: 'I am very sorry but I must leave. Vali has begun to transmit – listen according to the agreed plan. I reckon to be in Sweden in eight days.'

Råby and Rasmussen packed the Ida transmitter and sent it to Hammerfest, where it was buried as a spare for Vali. 'I asked Kalle to come with me, but he said he must go back and see how things turned out,' Råby wrote. 'Furthermore, if we had both left at the same time, there would immediately have been a rumpus.'

Karl Rasmussen was not prepared to leave his wife and four-month-old baby daughter unless it was absolutely necessary. She says, 'I said to him, "One day you and Torstein are going to cross over to Sweden without telling me." His answer was, "The day I leave you, I shall tell you. And I shan't leave until I have to." He kept his promise, that's what's so stupid about it all. He should have left with Torstein.'

Instead, Råby set off on the long journey to Sweden together with another member of the Ida Group, Knut Moe from Hammerfest. After a strenuous ski trip of 350 kilometres, the two reached the safety of Karesuando in neutral Sweden on 27 May 1944.

They had got away in the nick of time, but in Porsa transmissions continued as before. Neither Trygve Duklæt nor Rolf Storvik was aware that the net had long since begun to close about them. The high-frequency signals from Lyra had very early on been picked up by the central German D/F station outside Berlin, although the great distance made the bearings uncertain. The closest the Germans could get was that the transmitter had to be located somewhere between Tromsø and the North Cape. Responsibility for counter-espionage activities around the naval bases in the region rested with the *Abwehr*'s main station in Tromsø. From April 1943 onwards the investigation was conducted from a branch office in Alta under the aegis of a former naval pilot from Bremen, *Fregattenkapitän* Claus Kühl. When, that same summer, Kühl was posted to Tromsø, his place was taken by *Kapitänleutnant* Holzabeck.

The Norwegian Nils Bakken from Fægfjord was one of Kühl's agents. According to Bakken's statement to the police after the war, Kühl had ordered him 'to keep his eyes open and report anything that looked suspicious. . . . [His job was] simply to carry out orders, otherwise he would be arrested.' Bakken was fitted up with a wireless transmitter and codebooks and sent to Kvalsund with instructions to report twice a week to Thea in Tromsø.

In the late winter of 1944 Bakken was visited by the local mayor, Rolf Arnt Nygaard, also an *Abwehr* agent, whose cover name was Alf.

Rolf Nygaard said something strange was going on in Porsa and that he had been ordered by Mortensen [an *Abwehr* control officer] to look up the accused [Bakken] in order to have his reports transmitted, as he himself didn't have a transmitter. The accused wrote down Nygaard's report. It was to the effect that he suspected that something illegal was going on in Porsa, as people were always up to date on happenings in the world at large, and he also suspected that several people possessed weapons. . . . Nygaard thought it was time the Germans came to look into things.

A little later, in May 1944, an agitated Nygaard again approached Bakken. Nygaard said that he [Bakken] had to send another signal saying that 'the Germans should come to Porsa, as something very special was afoot. They needed to raid the place as soon as possible. . . . There was traffic there that gave cause for suspicion . . . and a lot of people were passing through the area who had no business there.' Nygaard was convinced that something big was impending, but couldn't say what it was.

One of the strangers who had recently passed through was Torstein Pettersen Råby. This report may therefore have impelled the *Abwehr* to hand the matter over to the *Gestapo* in Tromsø, who in turn brought in the German Security Police in Hammerfest.

Fear was ever present in my home town of Hammerfest during the war. The harbour, in which the mother ship *Black Watch* lay permanently at anchor, was a U-boat base, and the area round about was heavily fortified. But it was the *Gestapo* people feared most. Ever since November 1940 the local detachment had been commanded by 35-year-old *SS-Untersturmführer* Hans Otto Klötzer from Dresden. A miner's son, Klötzer had made hats until, in 1931, he joined Hitler's Nazi party and became a police officer. The police station was a small one, being staffed by only three *Gestapo* men and a handful of local interpreters and secretaries. But both the *Gestapo* and the *Abwehr* had recruited a considerable number of agents and established a network of contacts in the district. Both the mayor, Peder J. Berg, a dedicated member of Quisling's party, and his deputy, Morten J. Tiberg, were in the pay of the *Abwehr*; in fact, the former had been equipped with a wireless transmitter and maintained contact with the *Gestapo* in Tromsø. Klötzer spoke broken Norwegian. He ruled his staff with an iron hand, but was reasonably correct in his dealings with the local population – until the Porsa group was rounded up in the spring of 1944. The British officers who interrogated him after the war summed him up thus: 'He is quite intelligent, but no longer knows the difference between right and wrong. A typical Nazi product, who is a rather stubborn and unpleasant type.'

When Klötzer was charged with tracking down the Porsa and Moen transmitters, as the Germans called them, he seized the opportunity thus offered with both hands. *Abwehr* reports indicated that Porsa was the site of one of the transmitters, but to locate it new and intensive direction-finding measures had to be inaugurated. 'After bearings had been taken by stations elsewhere in Norway, cross-bearings were obtained from stations in the Never fjord area and at Seiland, and they told us that the transmitter simply had to be in Porsa itself. These bearings were obtained by German ships and the work took several weeks,' Klötzer told the Norwegian police after the war.

He was summoned to his superior officer in Tromsø, *SS-Oberhauptsturmführer* Poche, who gave him his instructions. 'It was impressed upon him that the matter was one of vital importance to the success of Germany's naval war and that every means had to be employed to get at the truth. He was ordered always to employ intensive interrogation methods, to ensure that nothing had been missed. A number of professional interrogators from the Tromsø office accompanied him on his return to Hammerfest.'

After further bearings had been taken, on 2 June Klötzer was certain that the object of his search was located in Porsa. He mobilized a force of more than one hundred soldiers, policemen and navy men and gathered them on board a number of guard ships and minesweepers in Hammerfest. He was determined to catch the agents redhanded if he could, so he held his hand until 6 June, when Lyra again went on the air. As the D/F ships sailed slowly through Varg Sound, the strength of the signals increased: Trygve Duklæt and Rolf Storvik were sending two messages to London. One was to say that the Germans were transporting oil south and bringing coal north. The other gave further details of the damage sustained by the *Tirpitz*: 'It is reported from Alta that the hangars and in part the other superstructure on the after deck of the *Tirpitz* will be dismantled.

The materials, which are mainly aluminium, will be sent south. Aircraft parts were observed among the metal residue.'

Klötzer took no chances. He put a patrol ashore in the nearby hamlet of Kvenklubben with orders to make its way across the mountains and strike from the rear. He himself hurried on to Porsa. In a statement made to the police, Rolf Storvik gave a graphic account of what happened next.

On 6 June 1944 two German guard cutters came into Porsa and moored alongside the quay. Duklæt, who had just left the wireless room, was seated beside me. He rushed back to lock the mechanism controlling the entrance to the cellar in case of a house-to-house search. Neither of us thought that the Germans suspected that we had a transmitter. About a hundred soldiers poured from the cutters and surrounded the houses round about. I saw through the window that the head of the German Security Police, Klötzer, was among them and realized at once that we had been discovered.

While the soldiers were busy rounding up all the men and herding them into the ice-store, the *Gestapo* chief made a beeline for Storvik.

He . . . began by asking whether there had been any strangers around of late and who they were. I mentioned a few names, but they didn't seem to be the ones he was looking for. He said that it was someone who had been out of the country. I had received a visit from Arne Pettersen [one of Torstein Råby's cover names] shortly before. He had had something to do with the Alta transmitter and had been in England, so I knew that he was the man Klötzer was after.

Under the direction of Klötzer and his assistants, Rudolf Illing, August Scherer and Alfons Zielinsky from the *Gestapo* in Tromsø, there now began a systematic search of every house in Porsa. The Germans were particularly interested in Trygve Duklæt's flat in what had once been the mine manager's house, where they found some literature on wireless telegraphy. That could be ascribed to Duklæt's having once been a sailor. But it wasn't easy to explain away a scrap of paper with a numerical code that they found in the stove and a pencilled note of a ship's name stuffed into a cupboard in the kitchen.

When Duklæt was brought from the ice-store, Klötzer saw him give his wife a knowing wink. Questioned, Duklæt denied everything, saying that he hadn't the faintest idea of what the figures meant and couldn't imagine how the paper had found its way into his stove.

When the prisoner continued to deny all knowledge of the finds, the *Obersturmführer* went mad. His temper was notorious; even his subordinates feared his rages. He stormed out, to return with a stout stick, with which he began to beat Duklæt. He was methodical in the way he set to work, first striking his victim across the forearms, then proceeding to the shoulders, slowly working his way down Duklæt's back, across his buttocks and finally to his thighs. The beating continued until the prisoner slumped in a heap to the floor. Klötzer then kicked him mercilessly with his highly polished jackboots. At last, no longer able to stand the pain, Duklæt confessed that the transmitter was hidden in the house.

Battered and bleeding, he then showed the Germans how to get into the secret underground chamber. The policemen were amazed: they would never have discovered how to operate the ingeniously contrived mechanism without demolishing the whole house. There in the cellar was the transmitter, and beside it a loaded pistol. But that wasn't the most important thing. The raid had come as such a surprise that Duklæt had not had time to destroy the log containing all the messages that had passed between Lyra and London. Klötzer rubbed his hands in glee. He had made an undreamed-of haul. 'The log and other documents contained full details, complete with sketch maps, of all the German positions in western Finnmark, together with information on garrison strengths, types and numbers of armaments, exercises, U-boat refuelling stations and more. Some papers and messages were signed with a cover name, and these were also in the log.'

Storvik and Duklæt's thoroughness proved their undoing. In regard to German positions around Hammerfest, for example, Klötzer found the following: 'Fortification: Melkoeya position 70° 41' 22" North, 23° 36' East, crew 70 men. Armament 3 × 13 cm. guns, one flame thrower. A.A. unknown. One searchlight.' Another note said 'Fortifications Meridianstotte [a stone marking the meridian] Soeroeysund. Some time ago two field howitzers were set up near the statue but they were removed after representation from the Chief of the Fillet factory. There are now two field guns out on Fuglenes. 70° 40' 36" North, 23° 32' 46" East.'

The volume of evidence was overwhelming. For the first time in his three years' service in Hammerfest Klötzer cast all inhibitions aside. Determined to

extract a full confession, he resorted to torture of the most brutal kind. 'When Klötzer found that most of the messages were signed "Panter" [Panther], he resumed his relentless beating of Duklæt. Blood flowed, but Klötzer refused to let up, until at last the prisoner gasped that Rolf Storvik could give him the answer he was seeking.'

The beatings continued until Klötzer had elicited a further two names from the hapless Duklæt. Panter was Håkon Korsnes Jr, the shopkeeper in Storekorsnes a little further south along the shore of Varg Sound. He had gathered information and charted the German minefields for Lyra. Another source was a forty-year-old engineer at the power station in Hammerfest, Egil Hansen, who had supplied a great deal of information about the U-boat base and the *Black Watch*, as well as details of fortifications in and around the town. Klötzer wirelessed back to tell the police to arrest Hansen.

For the time being he was content with what he had achieved. Armed guards were posted in Porsa, and when the minesweepers left they took with them Trygve Duklæt and his wife Ingeborg, together with Rolf Storvik and his parents, Hans and Hilmar Storvik. The ships put in at Storekorsnes to pick up old Håkon Korsnes and his two sons, Håkon Jr and Victor, but Lyra's contact in the village of Øksfjord, Egil Samuelsberg, managed to make his getaway before the ships docked.

On the night of 7/8 June, thirty-six hours after the raid had begun, Klötzer took his prisoners ashore in Hammerfest. They were lodged in the town's auxiliary prison, to which Egil Hansen had already been taken.

As the night progressed I gathered from various remarks I overheard from the corridor that it was Porsa that was at the root of it all. . . . At my first interrogation Klötzer produced a variety of papers and lists and began to question me about them. I assumed that the Security Police had found these papers in Porsa. Besides, through my window I had talked with Rolf Storvik in the exercise yard, and he told me that the transmitter had been found . . . and also my papers. It later transpired that the Security Police knew just about everything, so there was no point in giving evasive answers. Whenever I tried to cover something up I was struck in the face and told that I was lying.

In Hammerfest news of the round-up spread fear and terror. The *Gestapo* set about their task systematically. Many people had, in one way or another, been involved in resistance activities. No one knew whose door would be broken down that night. Klötzer's threats and brutality came as a shock to most people:

formerly, he had not been viewed as overly brutal. From then on, however, no one was spared, least of all Rolf Storvik.

When I was questioned, Klötzer had with him a wooden club and a rubber hose, with both of which he beat me. He hit me everywhere he could reach and the blows left a lot of ugly weals. Illing used the same improvised weapons and the two joined forces to beat me. They also employed a knotted leather whip. They used all their strength and many a time I was close to fainting. Sometimes they would have a bottle of schnapps and glasses ready to hand, and make good use of them. I could be interrogated for as long as sixteen hours at a stretch. Most of the time I was made to stand. . . . More than once Klötzer laid his pistol on the table and threatened to shoot me unless I told them all I knew.

One of the first to be arrested was a young sergeant from Hammerfest, Sverre Kaarby, who had passed information to Lyra. But Kaarby knew more. Only a couple of weeks or so earlier the Soviet intelligence service had parachuted a wireless operator, Aksel Bogdanoff, into the Torskefjord mountains, some 20 kilometres from Hammerfest. Two young lads out skiing had stumbled on Bogdanoff's camp and declared their willingness to supply him with information; they had also initiated Kaarby into what they were doing.

To start with an *Oberscharführer* (sergeant) set about beating Kaarby with a club until he fainted. Not until a couple of buckets of water were thrown over him to revive him was he asked the first question. After being interrogated for eight hours without a break and tortured at intervals, he was finally dumped back in his cell and left in peace. By then, the Germans knew all they wanted to know.

On the night of 9/10 June Kaarby was made to show the Germans the Soviet agent's hiding-place. That same day the second of the Russian's helpers, 24-year-old Alfred Sundby, was arrested.

I was questioned by Klötzer in his office. He asked whether I had been in the Torskefjord mountains. I said I hadn't, and he hit me in the face with his clenched fist and kept on hitting me until I fell to the floor. . . . He went on beating me (with clubs) to get me to confess, but I continued to deny everything. . . . Klötzer then brought in Bogdanoff, who had been found that same night in the mountains . . . and asked him if he knew me, to which Bogdanoff nodded in affirmation. Bogdanoff looked as though he had been

very badly treated, as two men had to support him between them and he was hanging on them, rather than standing on his own two feet.

Elias Østvik, a key figure in the network, was arrested and after being severely tortured was compelled to lead his captors to the place by Vestfjell lake where the Vali transmitter was hidden. However, the venerable standby transmitter Ida was never found. It had been buried in a garden, but to spare the householder Storvik claimed to have thrown it into the sea. Two more central personalities, both seamen, Captain Øystein Jacobsen and First Officer Paul Johnsen, were also taken, as were eight to ten other more peripheral figures who had rendered assistance; and all this only four days after Lyra had been seized. Although he did not know it at the time, Klötzer had rolled up the whole of the British Secret Service's organization in western Finnmark. The three transmitters, Lyra, Vali and Ida, were no more. Not only that but the Germans were starting to show an interest in Alta, where the Ida organization had dissolved itself three weeks earlier, on 16 May. Torstein Pettersen Råby and Knut Moe had fled to Sweden, but in the Tverrelv valley Karl Rasmussen had on that occasion resolved to stay with his wife to see how things went.

> I remember the day he left. It was a bright summer evening, 11 June. He had been warned. He knew that the Lyra Group had been arrested and had to expect that they [the *Gestapo*] knew his name. He had destroyed his equipment and thrown all the documents he had into the river. I wept softly, for the second time. We sat talking for a long time. He said that he would be thinking of us, of me and little Brit, on Midsummer's Eve. Then he was gone. Never have I felt so alone.

Shortly after Karl's departure the *Gestapo* pounced. They raided the farm and Sigrid was subjected to repeated interrogation. 'They thought I knew where Kalle was. They questioned me day and night, but I knew nothing. He hadn't told me where he was going. They even burst into my bedroom in the middle of the night to see if he was there. In the end I had to sign a document. Then the German said that if I had not told them the truth I had signed my own death warrant.'

Karl Rasmussen had travelled by one of the Highways Department's lorries the long road via Alteidet and on to Lyngen, whence an escape route led to Sweden. 'They drove as far south as they could until they reached the Signaldal valley. There they planned to put up with someone who could guide them on the last short leg to the border. Seeing a woman in a nearby wood waving a white handkerchief, they assumed they had found the right house. But it was a trap. The house was full of German soldiers.'

Rasmussen was taken to *Gestapo* headquarters in Tromsø and tortured. After questioning by Alfons Zielinsky in a second-floor room, the Germans prepared to take him back to his cell in the basement. 'There were two German soldiers holding him, but the door of the room was too narrow for all three to squeeze through at the same time. They had to release their grip. That gave Karl the chance he was waiting for. He sprinted across the landing and threw himself out of the window on to the pavement below. The impact broke his neck. He died on the spot.'

The date was 16 June 1944. Sigrid Rasmussen does not think her husband was attempting to escape. 'I'm sure he chose to end his own life,' she says, 'as the torture was too hard to bear. He had to find a way out before they made him talk. The way he did it was typical of him. He was strong: he was prepared to face the consequences of what he had done.'

The day before Karl Rasmussen's suicide, Harry Pettersen was arrested and taken to Hammerfest, where he was beaten and tortured for three long days.

Scherer continued to beat me with a club and threatened to shoot me and I don't know what. . . . He read out to me a confession purportedly made by Rasmussen in Tromsø to the effect that I had been a member of the organization and had supplied information. I found it hard to believe, as I thought they were bluffing, so I continued to deny everything. I have since learned that it was indeed all a bluff: Rasmussen hadn't said a word.

After her husband's death Sigrid Rasmussen was arrested and taken to Tromsø together with two other Ida contacts, Jonas Kummeneje and Asbjørn Hansen. She denied all knowledge of Ida and was believed. Alfons Zielinsky personally arranged for her release. 'Pastor Tveter accompanied me to the churchyard where Kalle had been buried along with some Russian prisoners of war. It was a fine summer day. We walked quietly over to the grave and stood there for a while without exchanging a word. Then Tveter left, leaving me alone by the grave. I sat down for a while on a slab of stone. I'm sure I shed a few tears.'

The raid had been a triumph for Klötzer and his brutal *Gestapo* henchmen. Over thirty people in western Finnmark were arrested, and about half of them risked the death penalty. But the Germans had other plans. Having now in their possession Bogdanoff and Duklæt's transmitters, and with both operators

under arrest, they began to plan a comprehensive and cunning charade. The two agents were to be 'persuaded' to continue to transmit messages to London and Murmansk – but the information the messages contained would be false, to fool the British and Russians. After much cajoling on Klötzer's part, the head of the *Gestapo* in Norway, *SS-General* Wilhelm Rediess, finally agreed that none of the prisoners would be executed if Duklæt and Bogdanoff were willing to collaborate. It was an offer neither could refuse. During what remained of the summer the rest of the prisoners were transferred to camps further south, while the two wireless operators were kept under close guard in the auxiliary prison in Hammerfest. Nothing is known about the messages concocted by the Germans that Bogdanoff sent to Murmansk, but many of Duklæt's messages have survived. The first is dated as early as 12 June, when the *Gestapo* was still engaged in rounding up suspects. 'Personal observation on the 12th. Three cargo ships passed here at 1030. One ship was about 4,000 and loaded, one ship about 6,000 tons, loaded, one ship about 3,000 tons loaded, escorted by one small warship, course south.'

Duklæt said later:

I was sure that they knew in England that we had been arrested, so I had no qualms about transmitting the Germans' false messages. Moreover, one of the German operators wasn't too careful about how he encoded the signals, so I often managed to slip in an indication that I was transmitting on behalf of the Germans. I was told by England, too, that I shouldn't worry and should continue transmissions. It turned into a farce, but it seemed to me that the Germans really did believe that the station in England had not realized that they were behind it all. They were overjoyed whenever a message came in from England.

The Germans went to great lengths to maintain the deception. Their object was to lure the British into sending over a courier with a new wireless transmitter destined for either Tromsø or Hammerfest. A new network was to be built up under German control. One of the men arrested in connection with the Porsa raid, Finn Hareide, was released and 'induced' to move into a bed-sitter in Hammerfest. Gisle Rinnan, brother of the notorious torturer Henry Oliver Rinnan, to whom reference has been made earlier, journeyed north from Trondheim for the express purpose of overseeing the operation.

On 24 July Duklæt wirelessed to London: 'German specialists, who had been visiting Hammerfest in the course of the investigation, have now left. I have

myself been in Hammerfest and have arranged a new contact. I need more
money immediately. This can be deliverd to Finn Hareide in Hammerfest.
Password OMEGA.' Klötzer had given Hareide strict instructions to obey orders,
otherwise he would 'be shot immediately'. Hareide provided details of his
dilemma in a postwar account.

One day I was on watch when I received a telephone call from the place
where I was staying. The caller presented himself as Larsen [Gisle Rinnan's
cover name]. . . . When I got home, there he was. He said his name was
Sverre Larsen. I could tell by his dialect that he was from the Trondheim
region. . . . He said a British agent was going to bring me the transmitter
and that I had to try to get out of him cover names and information about
other underground organizations and their activities. It was a matter of
finding out as much as possible about such clandestine organizations and the
people and places involved. I understood then what they were after: the
Security Police wanted to try to set up an undercover organization run in
reality by themselves. Once enough people had been implicated, they would
move in and arrest them. . . . I went to see Klötzer and told him that I
wouldn't do it. His answer was simply that matters had by then gone so far
that it was too late to back out and that I would just have to go through
with it.

But Hareide and Rinnan's wait was in vain. No courier came from London, and
after five days Rinnan returned to Trondheim. Some weeks later the Germans
had another try. Again it was a question of money and a new transmitter. The
signal Duklæt sent read: 'Your 12 of 14th. An apparatus like Lyra's will be
O.K. because we have A.C. The telegraphist will be Sverre Larsen, of Tromsoe.
He lives at Storgaten 91, IV Floor. Larsen will go to live with his relation
Hareide as soon as he receives the set. The courier must come to Tromsoe. He
must know the code.' The problem was that there *was* no Sverre Larsen. The
man who had been selected on this occasion to wait for the hoped-for courier
was Nils Bakken, the Norwegian *Abwehr* agent from Fægfjord. But Bakken,
too, was destined to wait in vain. He spent no fewer than five weeks in his
Tromsø flat, but there was no sign of a courier.

The British had seen through the deception, but still the Germans refused to
give up. The tone of their signals grew increasingly desperate. The message sent
on 13 November, for example, read: 'Hammerfest evacuated. Here (Porsa) also,
only men are left. On Thursday (16th), we also must leave. I shall destroy the

W/T apparatus, if I do not receive other instructions. I shall go first to Tromsoe. Can I there get into contact with you?'

The last message, which was dated 6 December 1944, read: 'On December 11th I am leaving Porsa for Tromsoe. Hareide was evacuated three weeks ago. I have no contact with Larsen because of the break-down of post and telegraph services. Is he still in Tromsoe?' No reply was ever received. The masquerade was at an end. By this time the German naval bases in western Finnmark had been evacuated and the occupying forces had retreated westwards. The German plan had ended in failure, but Klötzer kept his word and none of the men under arrest was executed. All – with the notable exception of Karl Rasmussen – survived the war. Torstein Pettersen Råby wrote:

> I hope it will be clear from my report that he [Rasmussen] was the man behind Ida. He took every risk that had to be taken: he was comparatively newly married and had a little daughter now 6 months old. . . . I have never had a better friend than Kalle. When things were at their worst, he used to say, 'This is where we give a horse laugh'. If it is felt that Ida contributed anything to this war, the thanks are due to Kalle. . . . His last act of heroism was to kill himself, when matters had gone so far that he would perhaps be forced to inform against his friends.

Sigrid Rasmussen never remarried.

> For me, there was no one but Kalle. He was a good man, and an honest one too. There was something very special about him. Everyone liked Kalle, and I loved him. Many times, when life has gone against me, I have cursed Torstein for taking Kalle from me. Ever since his death, through all these years, I have missed him; but deep down inside I understand, of course, that at the time our struggle could only be won by those in a position to do their bit. It was a great sacrifice for me, as it was for so many. The war took a heavy toll on both sides of the battlefield. I live on my memories and in the certainty that Kalle's contribution helped to shorten the war. The honour in which he is held post mortem is proof enough. It gives meaning to the meaningless.

On 6 June 1944, the same day that Klötzer struck in Porsa and the Allies landed in Normandy, *Kapitän-zur-See* Rudolf Peters was promoted to Rear-Admiral and appointed to command the Battle Group in the Kå fjord. There he witnessed a succession of bombing attacks on the *Tirpitz*. The last took place on

15 September when twenty-seven Lancasters dropped a number of 5-ton Tallboy bombs on the base. One bomb struck the battleship's bow, putting it out of action for good.

On 7 October the decisive attack on the Litza front was launched, after Finland had been forced to conclude a separate peace with the Soviet Union and abandon their German allies. The Soviet forces broke through and put the *20. Gebirgsarmee* to flight.

Hitler's response was savage in the extreme – the same scorched-earth policy he had so mercilessly employed in the Ukraine and Russia. No heed was to be paid to the civilian population, with the consequence that 50,000 people were driven from their homes and deported southwards. Vast areas of the counties of Finnmark and Nord-Troms were razed and one tiny community after another was left a heap of smoking ruins. Every building was torched, every telegraph pole blown up, every harbour installation demolished.

On 15 October the *Tirpitz* finally left the Kå fjord, limping along at a speed of 7 knots, aided by tugs. Seventeen months earlier she had arrived as the German Battle Group's flagship; now she was leaving as a wreck. On Sunday 12 November she received her death blow in Tromsø. After yet another attack she heeled over and capsized, taking with her over a thousand young sailors.

At about the same time the U-boat base in Hammerfest was abandoned. Under escort, the *Black Watch* and *Admiral Carl Hering* sailed to Kilbotn, near Harstad, where they continued to wage submarine warfare to the very end. But on 4 May 1945 – five days after Hitler's suicide in the bunker in Berlin – forty British bombers mounted an all-out attack on the base. The *Black Watch* was sunk with heavy loss of life. Ironically, *U-711*, the U-boat that never reached *Gruppe Eisenbart* off Bear Island, had completed its final patrol that very morning. When the last air attack of the war in the north began, she was moored alongside the *Black Watch*. *Kapitänleutnant* Hans-Günther Lange, who a few days earlier had been awarded the Knight's Cross of the Iron Cross with Oak Leaves, was standing at the rail of the depot ship when he heard the sound of approaching bombers. 'I had gone on board the *Black Watch* to hand over the war diary. When the attack began I jumped aboard [the U-boat] and cast off. But it was too late. She had been hit and sank quickly. Only a few men were saved. I had kept my men alive for several years. Now, all of a sudden, on the next-to-last day of the war, it was all over.'

As early as 20 October 1944 the 1st Battle Group had been formally dissolved. Peters's closing address constitutes a sad but precise summing-up of the situation. 'As the last Commander of the 1st Battle Group I did not succeed

in leading this well-trained and highly efficient force, eager to fight that it was, against the enemy. This is the tragedy of the Command that I joined on 6 June.'

Since the loss of the *Scharnhorst*, Rolf Johannessen's five destroyers had largely remained inactive, safeguarding the *Tirpitz*. 'At last this guard job is over. Now we can operate freely again,' wrote the Flotilla Commander before setting course for Tana to assist the retreating *Wehrmacht* as it razed Finnmark.

In Honningsvåg Johannessen was relieved by *Kapitän-zur-See* Freiherr von Wangenstein. For that reason he was not involved in the German forces' shameful and brutal conduct as they slowly retreated from northern Norway and the destroyers sailed from one blazing little port to another. The men who manned the destroyers had come to fight. Instead, they were compelled to take part in Hitler's last and most infamous act in Norway, the destruction of a whole region.

On 18 November – while Hans Otto Klötzer was still trying to get London to respond – *Z 29* left Varg Sound and sailed south. Ahead of her lay Porsa, Storekorsnes, Lerres fjord, Kå fjord, Talvik, Isnestoften and Lang fjord. Though little more than scatterings of houses, it had been among them that the fate of the German High Seas Fleet had been sealed. Now there was not a soul to be seen: every humble dwelling had been burned to the ground. In the course of a few short weeks most of the population had been forcibly evacuated. It was perfect autumn weather, mild and without a breath of wind, the sky a deep blue. In the sheltered recesses of the fjords the mountainsides were ablaze with russet and gold. The destroyer took on oil from a tanker in the roads, before putting a patrol ashore to perform one last task. In a simple Garden of Remembrance in Elvebakken a marble monument had been erected in honour of the men lost with the *Scharnhorst*. The stone was dug up and hoisted on board *Z 29*, which then set off south at full speed.

For close on two years western Finnmark had been a key theatre of German and Allied naval strategy. Now it was over. The German Battle Group was no more. Even its memorial had gone; nothing remained to mark its passing but scorched ruins.

Table of Equivalent Ranks

German Navy	Royal Navy
Grossadmiral	Admiral of the Fleet
Generaladmiral	No equivalent
Admiral	Admiral
Vize-Admiral	Vice-Admiral
Konter-Admiral	Rear-Admiral
Kommodore	Commodore (2nd class)
Kapitän-zur-See	Captain
Fregattenkapitän	Commander
Korvettenkapitän	Lieutenant-Commander
Kapitänleutnant	Lieutenant
Oberleutnant-zur-See	Sub-Lieutenant
Leutnant-zur-See	Junior Sub-Lieutenant
Oberfähnrich-zur-See	Midshipman
Fähnrich-zur-See	Junior Midshipman

Notes

CHAPTER ONE

Death off the North Cape

p. 3 *Utterly exhausted* The first-hand accounts in this chapter are based on many long conversations the author had with the following *Scharnhorst* survivors between 1998 and 2002: Helmut Backhaus, Helmut Feifer, Rolf Zanger, Nicolaus Wiebusch, Willi Alsen, Franz Marko and Ernst Reimann. It is not known how many of the thirty-six men who survived the sinking are still alive. Some ended up in East Germany; others settled abroad and have had no contact with the *Scharnhorst* Veterans Association. It is believed that about ten of them are still alive.

p. 4 *Contrary to expectations* Quoted from the *Draft Interrogation Report on Prisoners of War from the Scharnhorst*, Director of Naval Intelligence, 23 February 1944. ADM 199/913, Public Record Office (now the National Archives), London (hereafter PRO).

p. 6 *All hands on deck!* Quartermaster Wilhelm Gödde was the highest-ranking survivor and the one with the longest service. After the war he compiled two accounts of the action. These were quoted in, among other works, *Oberleutnant-zur-See* Karl Peter's exemplary account of the battle published in 1951, *Schlachtkreuzer Scharnhorst: Kampf und Untergang*, pp. 36ff. Gödde's accounts are in the shape of long and detailed letters to the *Scharnhorst*'s one-time First Officer, *Kapitän-zur-See* Helmuth Giessler. Dated 18 July and 12 December 1948, they were written shortly after Gödde's return to Wilhelmshaven following his years of captivity in the USA, which means that, along with Sträter's report and the summary compiled by the British and incorporated in the *Draft Interrogation Report* (see above), they must be regarded as the best available first-hand accounts of the sinking. As far as possible Gödde's descriptions have been cross-checked against the relevant war diaries (KTBs) in the Militärarchiv, Freiburg. The following have been consulted: KTB *SKL*, KTB *FdU*, KTB *Gruppe Nord*, KTB *FdU Norwegen*, KTB *Admirals Nordmeer*, KTB *1. Kampfgruppe*, KTB *Scharnhorst*, KTB *Tirpitz*, KTB *4. Zerstörerflottille*, KTB *Z 29, Z 30, Z 34* and *Z 38*, KTB *5. Räumbootflottille*, KTB *U-277*, KTB *U-354*, KTB *U-387*, KTB *U-601*, KTB *U-636*, KTB *U-711*, KTB *U-716* and KTB *U-957*.

p. 6 *Others elected to remain on board* Able-Seaman Günther Sträter was the only one of the thirty-six prisoners of war from the *Scharnhorst* to benefit from the exchange scheme operated by the Red Cross and to be repatriated in 1944. On his return to Germany he submitted a written report to the *Abwehr* and the German Naval High Command.

Dated 6 October 1944, his account is appended to the *Scharnhorst*'s war diary in RM 92/5199, Militärarchiv, Freiburg (hereafter MA). I spoke to Sträter on the phone in 2002, but he was ill at the time and did not wish to enlarge upon the information contained in his original report.

p. 7 *Nineteen-year-old Ordinary Seaman Helmut Boekhoff* Boekhoff took up residence in England after the war and was interviewed by Ludovic Kennedy in connection with the television film *The Sinking of the Scharnhorst*, which Kennedy made for the BBC in 1971.

p. 7 *'All that could be seen . . .'* Quoted from *Battle Summary No. 24: The Sinking of the Scharnhorst 26th December 1943*, London, February 1944. ADM 234/342, PRO.

CHAPTER TWO

An Unsuccessful Attempt

p. 9 *'Shall we go?'* Stein Inge Riise located the wreck of the *Gaul* in connection with a journalistic investigation into the loss of the trawler undertaken by the independent producer Norman Fenton, Anglia Television and Channel 4 in 1997 in collaboration with the *Brennpunkt* team of the Norwegian Broadcasting Corporation (NRK). Our finding of the wreck attracted considerable international attention, and the public enquiry into the loss of the trawler is still in progress. Norman Fenton's documentary film *Mysteries of Gaul*, which I co-produced for NRK, won the Royal TV Academy Award in London as the best home current affairs documentary of 1998.

p. 10 *The last signal* A collection of wireless signals relevant to the battle is to be found in ADM 223/36, PRO. Among them are signals intercepted by the British Intelligence Service and decrypted at Bletchley Park.

p. 11 *No fishing is more demanding* The articles in question appeared in, among other publications, *Lofotposten*, Svolvær, on 1 April 1977.

CHAPTER THREE

A Time for Dreams

p. 17 *Sigrid had first met* This account is based on conversations and interviews I had with Karl Rasmussen's widow, Sigrid, between 1998 and 2002. She has also written a personal 12-page account of her life with Karl ('Kalle'). See also Harald Riesto's article *Frihetskjemperen Karl Halvdan Rasmussen og etterretningsgruppen Ida*, published by the Municipality of Vadsø in 1995.

p. 19 *Some 2,000 kilometres to the south* I met *Frau* Gertrud Bornmann (née Damaski) at a reunion of *Scharnhorst* veterans in Bad Harzberg in May 2001 and subsequently visited her at her home in Lollar near Giessen. I am deeply indebted to her for allowing me to make use of the letters she exchanged as a young girl in the autumn of 1943 with her boyfriend, Heinrich Mulch, a writer on the Admiral's staff in the Kå fjord. The letters are written in old German script and for that reason I found them very difficult to read. *Frau* Bornmann transcribed some of them for me herself and I have also received help from Bodil K. Nævdal PhD, Oslo, *Fräulein* Henny Schäfer, Giessen, and Jürgen Oemichen of Årjäng, Sweden.

CHAPTER FOUR

Operation Ostfront

p. 25 *Adolf Hitler's rage* This account is based on Michael Salewski: *Die deutsche Seekriegsleitung 1935–1945*, vol. 2, Munich, 1975, pp. 185ff, and Cajus Bekker: *Verdammte See*, Frankfurt am Main (Ullstein), 1975, pp. 268ff.

p. 27 *Hitler chose Dönitz* For a portrait of Dönitz, see Peter Padfield: *Dönitz: The Last Führer*, London, 2001 (new edn), pp. 266ff, and Karl Dönitz: *Memoirs: Ten Years and Twenty Days*, pp. 299ff, first published 1958, new edn London, 2000.

p. 29. *A week or so later* This information is taken from the *Scharnhorst's* war diary (hereafter KTB (*Kriegstagebuch*)), which, with a few exceptions (some days in September are missing), covers the whole of 1943 up to 15 December and is to be found in RM 92/MA. For an account of the *Scharnhorst's* early history, see Heinrich Bredemeier: *Schlachtschiff Scharnhorst*, new edn, Herford, 1999. *Fregattenkapitän* Bredemeier commanded C turret on board the *Scharnhorst* up to the summer of 1943. The book was written in collaboration with two of the battlecruiser's ex-captains, *Vizeadmiral* Curt Caesar Hoffmann and *Vizeadmiral* Friedrich Hüffmaier, together with *Kapitän-zur-See* Helmuth Giessler, who was the battlecruiser's Navigation and First Officer from 1939 to May 1943. (*See* Holger Nauroth: *Schlachtkreuzer Scharnhorst und Gneisenau: Die Bildchronik 1939–1945*, Stuttgart, 2002.) I have also received much valuable information, augmented by letters and photographs, from the families of the battlecruiser's three key officers, *Kapitän-zur-See* Fritz Hintze, Captain; *Fregattenkapitän* Ernst-Dietrich Dominik, First Officer; and *Korvettenkapitän (Ing.)* Otto König, Engineering Officer. In this connection I wish to express my gratitude to Hintze's niece, *Frau* Karin Woltersdorf; Dominik's son and daughter-in-law, *Fregattenkapitän* Wulf and Erika Dominik; and König's brother Thomas, his sister Mrs Elena König Willow and his nephew Mark Willow, both the last-mentioned of whom are resident in the USA. Information on the careers of these three senior officers and others was obtained from Deutsche Dientsstelle, Berlin.

CHAPTER FIVE

The Mystery Deepens

p. 37 *The relentless submarine campaigns* Reports of ships lost in the Barents Sea during the First World War are to be found in ADM 137, PRO. The person who probably knows most about sinkings in Norwegian waters is *Kaptein* Erling Skjold of the Royal Norwegian Air Force, who, on his own initiative, has constructed a unique database, *Norsk Skipsvrakarkiv*, devoted to the subject. Skjold also rendered valuable assistance in the search for the wreck of the *Scharnhorst* by providing relevant documents.

CHAPTER SIX

Empty Days

p. 41 *Dönitz had promised Hitler* The controversial British historian David Irving's

The Destruction of PQ17, rev. edn, London, 1980, is still regarded as the standard work on this tragedy. See also Richard Woodman: *Arctic Convoys 1941–1945*, London, 1994, pp. 185ff. An Icelandic sailor, Ib Arnasson Riis, was recruited by the *Abwehr* in Copenhagen in 1940 and given the code name Edda. He was landed on Iceland by submarine in April 1942, but gave himself up to the British authorities some days later. Having spent some days at the infamous MI5 Camp 020 outside London, he agreed to work as a British double-agent and was sent back to Iceland. His first mission was to inform the Germans that convoy PQ17 was about to assemble and would sail in early July. This formerly unknown operation casts a completely new light upon the PQ17 tragedy and needs further investigation. The Cobweb files were released to the PRO in the spring of 2003, from where the author obtained a set of copies in July 2003. A copy of the Edda/Cobweb telegrams to the *Abwehr* are to be found in the MA, Freiburg.

p. 42 *When the British Defence Committee* Quoted from John Winton: *The Death of the Scharnhorst*, London, 1983, pp. 50ff.

p. 42 *In the Lang fjord* The main source is KTB *Scharnhorst* for 1943, supplemented by the *Draft Interrogation Report* and the war diaries of other ships at the base, among them that of the 4th Destroyer Flotilla. See also Bredemeier and *Oberleutnant-zur-See* Adalbert Brümmer's description of life in the Alta fjord in 'Schlachtschiff Tirpitz im Einsatz: Ein Seeoffizier berichtet' in the journal *Marine-Arsenal*, no. 6/93. Anton Røde has supplied me with much interesting information on the Lang fjord of years gone by. See also *Aftenposten*, Oslo, of 17 October 2000.

p. 46 *When we got there* This account is taken from the *Draft Interrogation Report*, p. 63.

p. 50 *As early as April* See Salewski, pp. 313ff.

CHAPTER SEVEN

London Comes to Life

p. 51 *A few weeks after* A vivid, dramatized account of Torbjørn Johansen's bicycle trip is to be found in Bjørn Rørholt's *Usynlige soldater*, Oslo, 1990, pp. 178ff. For details of intelligence work in northern Norway, see also Gunnar Pedersen: *Militær motstand i nord 1940–45*, Tromsø, 1982, and Berit Nøkleby: *Pass godt på Tirpitz*, Oslo, 1988. The sterling work done by the Johansen family is described in Dag Christensen: *Den skjulte hånd*, Oslo, 1992.

p. 53 *With a few exceptions* See Ragnar Ulstein: *Etterretningstjenesten i Norge 1940–45*, vol. 2, Oslo, 1990, p. 236. The original reports and maps are preserved in the archives of the Home Front Museum in Oslo. The museum has been of inestimable help in extracting information from the files. In this connection I am especially indebted to Mrs Anne-Karin Sønsteby.

p. 53 *Lindberg and Johansen's controller in England* For more information on Welsh, see, e.g., Arnold Kramisch: *Griffen*, Oslo, 1987, pp. 94ff. From 1943 until his death in 1954 Welsh occupied a highly important position in MI6 as head of Atomic Intelligence, in which capacity he often found himself at odds with at least one prominent British scientist. For a more precise, though less flattering, portrait, see Stephen Dorril: *MI6: Inside the Covert World of Her Majesty's Secret Intelligence Service*, London, 2000, pp. 134ff.

p. 53 *The wireless reports from Tromsø* For more on the OIC, see Patrick Beesly: *Very Special Intelligence: The Story of the Admiralty's Operational Intelligence Centre, 1939–45*, new edn, London, 2000.

p. 54 *Some preparations had already* The early history of Lyra is rather complex. The transmitter was first taken to the Bogen fjord, near Narvik, in the autumn of 1942, this fjord being the site of one of the *Kriegsmarine*'s principal bases. It was never operated from there, however, as there was no electricity supply available where it was hidden. For this reason reports on German naval units in and around Narvik were largely sent by courier to Sweden and thence to London. It was not until the winter of 1943, when the German Battle Group moved to Alta, that the transmitter was taken to Porsa and entrusted to Rolf Storvik. This portrayal of events is based on Trygve Duklæt's report of 22 May 1945, his statement to the police of 10 April 1946 and Rolf Storvik's police statement of 8 September 1945. Some of these documents are in the Home Front Museum files, others are in private hands.

CHAPTER EIGHT

Off Bear Island
p. 57 *'There was a special horror'* See Paul Lund and Harry Ludlam: *Trawlers Go to War*, London, 1971, pp. 177ff.

p. 58 *Winston Churchill was* For an account of Churchill and his clashes with the Russians, see, e.g., Woodman, *Arctic Convoys*, pp. 344ff, and Barry Penrose: *Stalin's Gold: The Story of HMS Edinburgh and its Treasure*, London, 1982, pp. 41ff.

p. 60 *The upshot was* The original intention was that each convoy should consist of 35 ships, but in the interests of safety it was later decided to halve the size of convoys to give the escorts fewer ships to safeguard. This explains the designations of the convoys, e.g., JW55A and JW55B.

p. 60 *Early in September* Based on the war diaries of the German Battle Group's ships, primarily the *Scharnhorst* and destroyers.

p. 61 *The naval chiefs were still pondering* For an account of the attack on the Tirpitz by midget submarines, see David Woodward's classic *The Tirpitz and the Battle for the North Atlantic*, New York, 1953, pp. 116ff, Ludovic Kennedy: *Menace: The Life and Death of the Tirpitz*, London, 1981, pp. 98ff and Paul Kemp: *Underwater Warriors*, London, 1996, p. 144.

p. 67 *The only German units* Surprisingly little has been written about the German U-boat bases in Trondheim, Narvik and Hammerfest, which, from 1943 until the spring of 1944, played an increasingly important role in the battle against the convoys. I have received a vast quantity of valuable information from a German expert on the subject, Jürgen Schlemm. Schlemm is one of the enthusiasts behind the website *uboat.net*, which contains a wealth of data on German U-boats. My interview with the former U-boat skipper Hans-Günther Lange took place in Kiel in the summer of 2001. After the war both Lange and Reche helped to build the West German *Bundesmarine*'s Submarine Service in collaboration with, among others, the Norwegian Navy. In 1964 Lange was appointed C-in-C of the *Bundesmarine*'s Submarine Service.

p. 70 *Gruppe Eisenbart* Johann Andreas Eisenbart (1663–1727) was in his day a prominent, though highly controversial, physician. Enjoying as he did royal patronage, he travelled far and wide in what is now Germany together with a large entourage of assistants and entertainers, and boasted unashamedly of his ability to cure people of their ills. After his death he passed into legend, most notably as a braggart and charlatan. A lampoon entitled *Ich bin der Doktor Eisenbart* ironizes over a doctor who took the lives of more people than he cured, but latter-day research has done much to restore Eisenbart's reputation as a medical practitioner whose ideas were well in advance of his time.

CHAPTER NINE

Operation Venus
p. 71 *The time was half-past one* See Rørholt, pp. 236ff, and the logbook of the submarine *Ula* for September 1943 in the Naval Museum, Horten. The curator, *Kommandørkaptein* Ingvar Fosheim, has been most helpful.
p. 72 *It was an ambitious undertaking* Countless stories are told about the deeds of Torstein Petersen Råby, colourful and courageous as he was, many of them with himself as the more or less reliable source. The Home Front Museum files contain many examples. Råby's Ida report is dated 31 July 1944. See also Jostein Nyhamar's in-depth interview with Råby in *Aktuell*, Oslo, no. 40/1958; both this and Råby's Ida report are in the Ida file at the Home Front Museum. After the war Råby achieved international recognition as the wireless operator of the *Kon-Tiki* expedition. He died prematurely of heart failure on an expedition to Greenland under the leadership of Bjørn Staib in 1964 at the age of forty-five.

CHAPTER TEN

An Unexpected Catch
p. 78 *Reports obtained from England* For more on Kenneth Knox, see Keith Jessop: *Goldfinder*, London, 1998, pp. 259ff. Jonathan Davis, a Hull-based freelance journalist, tracked down and spoke to Knox and other witnesses for us.
p. 79 *I had no millionaires* My search was funded by NRK Television and the BBC's *Timewatch* Department in conjunction with my work on the documentary *Scharnhorsts siste reise* ('The *Scharnhorst* Mystery'). The film was produced by me and directed by Norman Fenton. It was shown by NRK and the BBC in the spring of 2001, and in Germany and the USA in 2002.
p. 79 *On 22 November 1993* Interviews with and letters from Reidar Nygård dated 4 May 1999 and the Mine Disposal Unit's report of 16 December 1993.

CHAPTER ELEVEN

Alarums and Excursions
p. 83 *Herrle and I became close friends* Interviews with Lange in June 2001. In other respects this chapter is largely based on the war diaries of *FdU Norwegen* in Narvik and the U-boats concerned, together with KTB *Gruppe Nord*, Kiel, KTB *Admirals Nordmeer*, Narvik, and KTB *1. Kampfgruppe*, Alta, all in MA, Freiburg, and *Das U-boot Archiv*,

Cuxhaven. The more emotive accounts are drawn from the writings of the German war correspondent Horst-Gotthard Ost, who in 1942/43 spent several months on board U-boats in the Barents Sea. His hard-to-find book *U-Boote im Eismeer*, Berlin, 1943, conveys a dramatic and authentic impression of U-boat warfare in the Arctic.

p. 85 *On 1 December at 14.25* Information obtained from KTB *Scharnhorst* and KTB 4th Destroyer Flotilla. The portraits of Hintze and Hüffmaier are largely drawn from the *Draft Interrogation Report*, in which the latter seems to have been rather harshly dealt with. Bredemeier is much more favourably inclined towards Hüffmaier than are the *Scharnhorst*'s survivors.

p. 91 *Most of those in a position* See Salewski, pp. 313ff, and Bekker, p. 328 ff.

p. 93 *Hintze's suspicions* All information from the Ida and Lyra folders in the Home Front Museum's archives and from Sigrid Rasmussen.

CHAPTER TWELVE

Further Setbacks

p. 99 *In mid-September* In the evening of 17 February 1978 the fishing boat *Utvik Senior* sank under mysterious and dramatic circumstances, her crew of nine disappearing without trace. The following year wreckage began to appear in places far distant from where, in the light of the official version of the sinking, it might have been expected. After searching the seabed for four years, in the spring of 2002 I found the ship's main engine at a depth of 36 metres, 4 nautical miles offshore. An account of the search and find was included in the documentary film *Gåten Utvik Senior* ('The Riddle of the *Utvik Senior*'), which was shown on NRK's Channel 1 on 30 April 2002. A more detailed account is to be found in my book *Forlis* ('Shipwreck'), published in Oslo in 2002. The position and state of the wreckage both suggest that the *Utvik Senior* may have been run down by an unidentified submarine. My locating of the engine led to the setting up of an official commission to enquire into every aspect of the tragedy.

CHAPTER THIRTEEN

Studied Indifference

p. 105 *The fast convoy JW558* See Woodman, *Arctic Convoys*, pp. 344ff. Reports on this convoy are to be found in ADM 199/PRO. The Germans' views and surmises are taken from the relevant war diaries, MA, Freiburg.

p. 107 *Only eighty of the ship's officers and men* I wish to thank Wilfred and Oliver Weiss for providing me with information on their brother and uncle, Karl Ernst Weiss, who was the hairdresser on board the *Scharnhorst*.

CHAPTER FOURTEEN

The Mystery of the Logbook

p. 111 *Jamaica, Matchless and Virago were the last* Taken from *Battle Summary No. 24*, ADM 234/PRO.

p. 113 *Only one of the navigation officers* Interview with Rex Chard, 20 February 2001.

CHAPTER FIFTEEN

Admiral Fraser's Plan

p. 117 *Fraser had joined* Information on Fraser and Vice-Admiral Burnett is taken from John Winton: *The Death of the Scharnhorst*, London, 1983, which affords an excellent description of the battle as seen from the British side, and Richard Humble: *Fraser of North Cape*, London, 1987.

p. 119 *After two days of exchanging* Taken from Admiral Arseni Golovko's diary *With the Red Fleet*, New York, 1965, and here quoted from Winton.

p. 120 *One by one the ships* See Skule Storheill's report 'Senkningen av slagskipet Scharnhorst den 26. desember 1943' in *Norsk Tidsskrift for Sjøvæsen*, 1946. Storheill and the *Stord* were ordered to patrol the mouth of the fjord in the evening of 23 December. This meant that Storheill was unable to attend the final conference on board the *Duke of York*, for which reason the account of this conference is taken from *Battle Summary No. 24*.

CHAPTER SIXTEEN

The Dream of Oil

p. 124 *When I saw these wells* Correspondence with the Norwegian Petroleum Directorate May/August 1999. The Directorate's Press Officer, Jan Hagland, was very helpful.

CHAPTER SEVENTEEN

The Report from U-601

p. 127 *The weather is worsening* Quoted from *U-601*'s war diary. Again I am indebted to Jürgen Schlemm and *uboat.net* for assistance in charting *Gruppe Eisenbart*'s movements. Otherwise, my main sources have been the war diaries of Peters, Bey and Schniewind, augmented by Salewski, Bekker and Winton.

p. 131 *It must have been a strange time for Bey* See Dönitz: *Memoirs* and the *Draft Interrogation Report*, as well as Bekker and Fritz-Otto Busch: *Dramaet om Scharnhorst*, Oslo, 1958, pp. 36ff, which provides a highly dramatized, but largely correct, picture of the battle. Captain (later Rear-Admiral) Rolf Johannesson's brusque comments are to be found in the transcript of a talk he gave to the Naval Academy in Kiel on 8 April 1962. His views were further enlarged upon in an article entitled 'Erinnerungen des Chefs der 4. Zerstörerflottille: Der untergang der Scharnhorst am Nordkap' published in *Marineforum*, 12/1984.

p. 134 *At about 18.30 on Christmas Eve* The signals are discussed in various places. See, e.g., Bekker, pp. 334ff, and Patrick Beesly and Jürgen Rohwer's classic study in *Marine Rundschau*, no. 10/77, 'Special Intelligence und die Vernichtung der Scharnhorst'.

p. 135 *When Grossadmiral Karl Dönitz* See Padfield, pp. 339ff.

p. 136 *The Luftwaffe pilots are doing* Quoted from Bekker, p. 335.

p. 137 *The Commander of JW55B's close escort* The reports of the Commander of the escort, Captain J.A. McCoy, and the Commodore, Rear-Admiral M.W.S. Boucher, are to be found in ADM 199, PRO.

CHAPTER EIGHTEEN

The Naval College Simulator

p. 141 *I first met Commander Marcus* See Osen's 1998 article, 'Krigsdramaet utenfor Senja', *Troms Folkeblad*, 1998, and Bjørn Bratbak: *Uskyldige måtte ofte lide*, Stavanger, 2000. *K21*'s killing of unarmed civilian fishermen is one of the few such incidents known from the Second World War. Like Great Britain, in 1943 Norway was allied to the Soviet Union, but neither during nor after the war did the Soviet government apologize for the massacre. It has also proved difficult to obtain documentation on the tragedy from Soviet archives, even after the end of the Cold War. Lunin made a career in the Red Fleet after the war and died as a much admired admiral many years later.

p. 143 *Then sixty-five years of age* The frigate KNM *Oslo* suffered an engine breakdown and sank off Bergen in February 1994 with the loss of one member of her crew. As Inspector-General Prytz shouldered responsibility for the loss of the ship – although, formally, it had nothing to do with him.

CHAPTER NINETEEN

The Scharnhorst *Puts to Sea*

p. 147 *A convoy carrying war materials* Quoted from Dönitz: *Memoirs*, p. 375.

p. 148 *The captain of* R 58 Werner Hauss was interviewed by Fritz-Otto Busch in the 1950s; see *Dramaet om Scharnhorst*, p. 42. See also KTB of the 5th Minesweeper Flotilla. In other respects this chapter is based on interviews with *Scharnhorst* survivors, Gödde and Sträter's reports, and the war diaries of *Admirals Nordmeer*, Fleet Commander Schniewind, the 4th Destroyer Flotilla, *Z 29*, *Z 30* and *Z 38*. See also Bekker and Peter.

p. 153 *Hauss was not the only one* This account is based on interviews with Harry Pettersen and Per Digre in the spring and summer of 1999. Some uncertainty attaches to the true source of the information about the departure of the *Scharnhorst* and destroyers. Pettersen is of the opinion that it was Digre, Torstein Råby says it was Kummeneje, while Sigrid Rasmussen cites a third source, Egil Emaus; all of these men lived on the shores of the Lang fjord. Quite a number of ships sailed in and out of the fjord all that day, and from 12 noon the *Scharnhorst* had steam up. Christmas Day being a public holiday, many people must have been at home and observed the heightened activity, though the coming of darkness would have made it difficult to discern details. However, the Northern Lights would have helped to illuminate the scene when the fleet set sail between seven and eight in the evening. Despite unremitting investigation I have been unable to find any documentation to prove that the signal was actually sent, so reliance must be placed on the recollections of those concerned.

p. 155 *A few nautical miles away* This information is taken from KTB *U-716*, together with letters from, and talks I had in 2002 with, the U-boat's wireless operators, Peder Junker and Josef Rennings, as well as Hans Evert and Heinz Wachsmann, both of whom also served under Dunkelberg in the Battle of the North Cape. *U-716* was the sole *Eisenbart* U-boat to survive the war. Despite thorough investigation I have been unable to solve the riddle surrounding the fateful signal supposedly transmitted by

U-716 at 03.27 the following night (see next chapter), a signal which, it seems, was received only by *Z 29*. None of the U-boat's crew has any recollection of this signal. The explanation may be simply that, although it was indeed sent, it was not recorded in the U-boat's war diary.

p. 159 *On board the* Duke of York For details of the signals that reached Fraser, see F.H. Hinsley: *British Intelligence in the Second World War*, vol. 3, part I, London, 1984, pp. 262ff. See also Beesly and Rohwer, as well as Hugh Sebag-Montefiore: *Enigma: The Battle for the Code*, London, 2000, pp. 249ff.

CHAPTER TWENTY

'I have confidence in your will to fight'
p. 161 Punkt Lucie *(Point Lucie) was* For a description of fortifications in Finnmark, see Thorbein Gamst: *Finnmark under hakekorset*, Oslo, 1984, p. 116. Once again, war diaries are the main source for this chapter, together with reports and interviews with *Scharnhorst* survivors.

p. 163 *At the Admiralty in London* The times given in the German, British and Norwegian reports differ in accordance with the time-zone employed. I have stuck to the times in the originals, which explains why there are some discrepancies. See, e.g., the *Ostfront* signal, in which the Germans used local time (17.00) while the British were one hour later (18.00).

p. 164 *On the* Stord *we follow* Gunnery Officer Nils Owren's account is in the form of an appendix to Busch: *Dramaet om Scharnhorst*, pp. 165ff. Lieutenant Bryce Ramsden's description is taken from his article 'An Eyewitness Account of the Action from the Air Defence Platform', which originally appeared in *Blackwood's Magazine* in 1944.

CHAPTER TWENTY-ONE

What was in the Mind of Konter-Admiral Bey?
p. 171 *At 08.40 the alarm sounded* This chapter is based on the *Draft Interrogation Report* and *Battle Summary No. 24*, the war diaries of the ships engaged in the battle (apart from the *Scharnhorst*'s diary, which was lost with her) and the various Fleet Commands, together with the eye-witness accounts of survivors. See also Bekker, Peter, Busch, Watts and Winton. Contemporary films also contain much unique material. They include sequences taken in Scapa Flow on New Year's Day 1944 by Pathé News, Ludovic Kennedy's 1971 documentary for the BBC, the documentary *Kurs Murmansk* produced by the Press Service of the Norwegian Defence Forces in 1956, and the film of the *Scharnhorst* produced by History Films, Munich.

p. 180 *Despite the storm* For details of Marx's observation, see Bekker, pp. 345 ff. Further information is contained in an article published in *Marineforum* on 7 August 1984 entitled 'Hohentwiel und ES' by Frank de Haan, who on 26 December 1943 was *Gefechtsstandsoffizier* of *1. Staffel* of *Seefernaufklärungsgruppe 130* in Tromsø, and also in an article headed 'Das blinde Schlachtschiff' in *Schleswiger Nachrichten* no. 299 (1959). I wish to thank the editor of this newspaper, Dirk Jennert, for providing me with a copy of this article.

Marx's signals gave rise to many acrimonious discussions between the *Kriegsmarine* and the *Luftwaffe* during the war. When Rolf Johannesson visited Tromsø in the winter of 1944 he met *Generalmajor* Roth, who expressed his astonishment that the Flotilla Commander had been unaware that the presence of Fraser's Force 2 had actually been reported by the *Luftwaffe*. Johannesson recorded in the war diary that it was 'shattering' to learn this from a chance meeting. Johannesson's remark called forth a tart comment from U-boat Commander Peters, who opined that what Roth had said 'in convivial company' was not in accordance with the facts. From the written review of the affair, which the author recently found in Freiburg, it is evident that owing to interference Marx's first signal was picked up by the German radio station at Banak and did not reach Roth at Bardufoss until 12.59. Seven minutes later, at 13.06, the signal was passed on on the joint *Luftwaffe/Kriegsmarine* channel (FVLM). It was recorded by Peters in Narvik as having been received at 13.41. The report also reveals that Marx broke off his shadowing of the unidentified units at 11.35 because of bad weather and the onset of darkness. He did not return to Tromsø, however, but chose to land at the German seaplane base in the Bille fjord, some 100 kilometres south of the North Cape. It was only after he had been debriefed that at 15.50 his second and more detailed report was relayed *by telephone* to *Fliegerführer* Lofoten, whence it was phoned to Peters in Narvik at 16.30. Roth continued to maintain that Peters had received Marx's observation of 'one large and several smaller vessels' *verbally* at this point, although the written report was not transmitted until 08.55 next day, 27 December. Peters, for his part, claimed that the weaknesses of the German radar had been so strongly emphasized that the signal had had to be treated as totally unreliable. Regardless of the truth of the matter, it was already too late. When the phone rang at *Admirals Nordmeer* in Narvik at 16.30 on 26 December 1943, only a quarter of an hour was left until the *Duke of York* opened fire. The trap had already snapped shut.

CHAPTER TWENTY-TWO

Defeat
p. 187 *After the dramatic events of the morning* Sources as above. Parham, Courage and Cox are quoted from Winton.
p. 201 *A moment later heavy shells* The real turning point of the battle was when the *Scharnhorst* reduced speed from about 30 to a bare 20 knots between half-past six and a quarter to seven in the evening. It is no longer possible to determine precisely what caused her to do so; the statements of witnesses are too much at variance. It may have been a shell from the *Duke of York*, but it can also have been engine trouble, as the engines had long been over-taxed. The *Scharnhorst* had had problems with her boilers and turbines on several occasions in the past, one such being during her engagement with the British battleship *Renown* in April 1940; see Bredemeier, pp. 43ff.
p. 214 *The young lieutenant* It is not known how many of the *Scharnhorst*'s officers took their own lives on board. The *Draft Interrogation Report* says that Bey and Hintze shot themselves on the bridge, whereas *Battle Summary No. 24* quotes eye-witnesses on the *Scorpion* who thought they had seen Hintze, at least, in the sea, severely wounded.

My conversations with survivors incline me to believe that many officers chose to go down with their ship, while others shot themselves at their posts. Whatever the truth of the matter, the fact remains that of the eighty officers and cadets on board, not one was saved.

p. 217 *The only destroyer* There is no justification for claiming that, prompted by war's brutal logic that a dead enemy is a good enemy, Fraser simply left the majority of the Germans in the sea to drown. On the other hand, no order was issued to pick up survivors. Only two of the thirteen Allied vessels present took part in the rescue operation, and only one of those, the destroyer *Scorpion*, did so deliberately. Nor were there any U-boats in the neighbourhood. It is true that the cruiser *Belfast* reported an 'unknown radar echo' at 20.10, but this report was cancelled two minutes later. On the other hand, of course, Fraser could not know exactly where the German U-boats were. Wireless traffic between the *Eisenbart* Group and Naval HQ in Narvik had been monitored for some days. As C-in-C he had to assume that there might well have been U-boats in the vicinity and take appropriate action. To have allowed his ships to lie stationary in the water longer than was absolutely necessary would have exposed his own men to a not inconsiderable risk. He had, therefore, sound reasons for ordering the fleet to set a course for Murmansk some three-quarters of an hour after the sinking.

CHAPTER TWENTY-THREE

Found!

p. 223 *The town of my birth* This chapter is based on my own notes and recollections of the expedition undertaken between 26 and 29 September 2000. The TV team consisted of the British director Norman Fenton, Leif Erik Bye as the film cameraman and Einar Bakke, an NRK sound engineer. The Norwegian Defence Forces' Research Institute was represented by its head, Jarl Johnsen, together with the following: Marlow Kristiansen, Kjersti Skreosen, Arnfinn Karlsen and Commander Jan Loennechen. Like the men of the Royal Norwegian Navy to whom reference is made in the text and the crews of the *H.U. Sverdrup II* and KNM *Tyr*, they all deserve credit for help in finding the wreck of the *Scharnhorst*.

CHAPTER TWENTY-FOUR

The Intelligence Riddle

p. 237 *It was a Tromsø man, Egil Lindberg, who first claimed* All primary sources are drawn from the Home Front Museum's archives, i.e., the Ida, Lyra, Venus and Upsilon files.

p. 239 *Not surprisingly, those agents* The idea of a book seems to have been mooted for the first time at a veterans' reunion held on 8 May 1985 to celebrate the fortieth anniversary of the liberation of Norway. That work on the book was accorded great importance is ascribable to the fact that the agents concerned reacted strongly to the Museum's having commissioned Ragnar Ulstein to write the history of wartime intelligence activities in Norway. In the opinion of Bjørn Rørholt and others, Ulstein was a saboteur and 'dynamite man' and as such knew little about the work of the agents who operated wireless transmitters. In consequence, behind the scenes there smouldered a long and bitter conflict over Ulstein's commission. In my own book, *Muldvarpene* ('The Moles'), published in 1986, I made a tentative attempt to discuss the significance of signals intelligence compared with the work done by agents in the field; that was what prompted Rørholt to seek me out. From 1987 onwards he and I had many interesting discussions on the subject. Whatever the truth of the matter, nothing can detract from the achievements of these agents. They risked their lives, and the work they did contributed significantly to the outcome of the war. The men behind Ida, Lyra, Vali and the other transmitters were true heroes.

p. 244 *All the time the* Scharnhorst *remained* A batch of decrypted signals is to be found in ADM 223/36, PRO, London. My investigations revealed that the circumstances surrounding some of these signals are unclear; for one thing, some of them are marked 'CX'. This would normally indicate that the source was Humint (Human Intelligence), i.e., that they were sent by an agent. One signal appears to have been filched from the wastepaper basket of *Fliegerführer Lofoten* at Bardufoss, which would mean that the British had an agent at *Luftwaffe* HQ. If they had, it was not known in Norway. The explanation may be that they 'invented' such an agent to protect Enigma – further proof of how far they were prepared to go to keep the secret of Bletchley Park.

CHAPTER TWENTY-FIVE

Aftermath

p. 250 *Nils Owren, Gunnery Officer* Quoted from Busch: *Dramaet om Scharnhorst*, p. 175. Other primary sources are reports from and interviews with survivors – see above.

p. 253 *On his very first patrol* Basse, one of the U-boat skippers who took part in the search for survivors, reported a strong smell of oil in a position 72.40 N 29.00 E, about twelve hours after the *Scharnhorst* had gone to the bottom. By then the Germans had activated their wireless beacons on the Finnmark coast, which suggests that the positions reported by the U-boats of *Gruppe Eisenbart* were reasonably accurate. In the hope of being able to calculate the position of the wreck from Basse's report, I spent a lot of time charting the U-boats' movements on that dramatic day. Bjørn Åge Hjøllo, a meteorologist at the Marine Forecasting Centre in Bergen, very kindly worked out how far an oil slick would drift under the weather conditions prevailing at the time of the battle, and arrived at a distance of some 12 to 15 nautical miles (see map, p. 114). Our finding the wreck further to the west means that Basse's reported position cannot have been correct.

CHAPTER TWENTY-SIX

The Reckoning

This chapter is based on extensive police interrogations conducted in 1945 and 1946 of Hans Otto Klötzer, Trygve Duklæt, Rolf Storvik, Harry Pettersen, Alfred Sundby, Egil Hansen, Nils Bakken and others involved in the Porsa affair. Central documents are two long articles, 'Oppdagelsesferd på den øde jord' ('A journey of exploration in a desolate landscape') and 'Den skjulte krigen' ('The clandestine war') written in 1993 by a former

MP and government minister, Annemarie Lorentzen, for a Hammerfest magazine devoted to local history, *Øyfolk*. These articles are in turn based on work performed just after the Liberation by the late police inspector Astor Engedal, who, as a young police officer, was assigned the task of investigating the activities of the *Abwehr* in Troms and Finnmark. Engedal was undoubtedly the person who knew most about the German Intelligence Service's network, both in western Finnmark and in northern Norway as a whole, and I am grateful for the information he gave me before his death in 2002. See also the trial of Hans Otto Klötzer in 1948, which resulted in his being sentenced to eighteen years' imprisonment. Weighing heavily against him were the flagrant crimes he committed when, after New Year 1945, he was made head of the *Gestapo* in Drammen. It is no longer possible to say exactly how much the activities of the two *Abwehr* agents Bakken and Nygaard contributed to the rolling up of the Porsa network. My assessment is that the information Klötzer received sufficed to draw his attention to that tiny village and made it easier to obtain the wireless fixes that proved the network's undoing. Nygaard was sentenced to ten years' imprisonment after the war. See also Tore Pryser: *Hitlers hemmelige agenter*, Oslo, 2001, p. 81 and pp. 284ff, as well as Kjell Fjørtoft: *Lille-Moskva*, Oslo, 1983, pp. 176ff. Pryser's knowledge of the subject has been of great assistance. As regards the Germans' attempt to hoodwink the British after the Porsa network had been broken up, copies of the most interesting signals are to be found in the Lyra file in the Norwegian Home Front Museum.

Bibliography

Barnett, Correlli. *Engage the Enemy More Closely*, London, Penguin, 2000

Battle Summary No. 24: Sinking of the Scharnhorst, 26th December 1943, London, Public Record Office, February 1944, ADM 234/342

Beesly, Patrick. *Very Special Intelligence: The Story of the Admiralty's Operational Intelligence Centre 1939–45*, rev. edn, London, Greenhill, 2000

—. *Very Special Admiral: The Life of Admiral J.H. Godfrey CB*, London, Hamish Hamilton, 1980

— and Rohwer, Jürgen. 'Special Intelligence und die Vernichtung der Scharnhorst', *Marine Rundschau* 10/7

Bekker, Cajus. *Verdammte See: Ein Kriegstagebuch der deutschen Marine*, Oldenburg, Ullstein, 1971

—. *Das grosse Bildbuch der deutschen Kriegsmarine 1939–45*, Oldenburg, Ullstein, 1972

Blair, Clay. *Hitler's U-boat War: The Hunted 1942–1945*, London, Cassell, 2000

Bredemeier, Heinrich. 'Schlachtschiff Scharnhorst', Herford, Koehler, 1994

Breyer, Siegfried. 'Schlachtschiff Scharnhorst'. Reprint from *Marine-Arsenal*, Friedberg, 1986

—. 'Schlachtschiff Tirpitz'. Reprint from *Marine-Arsenal*, Friedberg, 1987

Brünner, Adalbert. 'Schlachtschiff Tirpitz im Einsatz: Ein Seeoffizier berichtet', Reprint from *Marine-Arsenal*, Friedberg, 1993

Burn, Alan. *The Fighting Commodores*. Annapolis, Naval Institute Press, 1999

Busch, Fritz-Otto. *Tragödie am Nordkap*, Hanover, Adolph Sponholtz Verlag, 1952

Christensen, Dag. *Den skjulte hånd*, Oslo, Gyldendal, 1990

Der Scheinwerfer. Newsletter of the Tirpitz Veterans Association

Dickens, Peter. *Narvik: Battles in the Fjords,* Annapolis, Naval Institute Press, 1997

Dönitz, Karl. *Memoirs: Ten Years and Twenty Days*, rev. edn, London, Cassell, 2000

'Draft Interrogation Report on Prisoners of War from the Scharnhorst', Director of Naval Intelligence, 23 February 1944, London, Public Record Office, ADM 199/913

Evans, Mark Llewellyn. *Great World War II Battles in the Arctic*, Westport, Greenwood Press, 1999

Fjørtoft, Kjell. *Lille-Moskva*, Oslo, Gyldendal, 1983

Fraser, Bruce. 'The Sinking of the German Battle-Cruiser Scharnhorst on the 26th December 1943', *London Gazette*, 1947

Gray, Edwyn. *Hitler's Battleships*, Barnsley, Leo Cooper, 1999

Hinsley, F.H. *British Intelligence in the Second World War*, 5 vols, London, HMSO, 1979–90

Humble, R. *Fraser of North Cape*, London, Routledge & Kegan Paul, 1983

Irving, David. *The Destruction of PQ17*, London, Panther, 1985

Iversen, Klaus. *100 år med lys og varme. Hammerfest Elektrisitetsverk 1891–1991*, Hammerfest, Hammerfest Elektrisitetsverk, 1991

Jessop, Keith. *Goldfinder*, London, Simon & Schuster UK, 1998

Kemp, Paul. U-boats *Destroyed: German Submarine Losses in the World Wars*, Annapolis, Naval Institute Press, 1997

Kennedy, Ludovic. *Menace: The Life and Death of the Tirpitz*, London, Sphere Books, 1981

Kolyshkin, I. *Russian Submarines in Arctic Waters*, New York, Bantam, 1985

Koop, Gerhard and Schmolke, Klaus-Peter. *Battleships of the Scharnhorst Class*, tr. Geoffrey Brooks, London, Greenhill, 1999

Lund, Paul and Ludlam, Harry. *Trawlers Go to War*, London, New English Library, 1975

Mulligan, Timothy P. *Neither Sharks nor Wolves*, London, Chatham, 1999

Nauroth, Holger. *Schlachtkreuzer Scharnhorst und Gneisenau: Die Bildchronic 1939–1945*, Stuttgart, Motorbuch Verlag, 2002

Ogden, Michael. *Slaget ved Nordkapp*, Stavanger, Stabenfeldt, 1962

Ost, Horst-Gotthard. *U-boote im Eismeer*, Berlin, Franz Schneider Verlag, 1943

Padfield, Peter. *Dönitz: The Last Führer*, New York, 1984

Pearson, Michael. *Red Sky in the Morning: The Battle of the Barents Sea, 31 December 1942*, Shrewsbury, Airlife, 2002

Peillard, Léonce. *Sink the Tirpitz*, London, Jonathan Cape, 1968

Penrose, Barrie. *Stalin's Gold*, London, Granada, 1982

Peter, Karl. *Schlachtkreuzer Scharnhorst: Kampf und Untergang*, Berlin, Mittler, 1951

Pope, Dudley. *Slaget i Barentshavet*, Oslo, Cappelen, 1959

Pryser, Tore. *Hitlers hemmelige agenter*, Oslo, Universitetsforlaget, 2001

Riesto, Harald. *Frihetskjemperen Karl Halvdan Rasmussen og etterretningsgruppen Ida*, Vadsø, Vadsø bibliotek, 1995

Rohwer, J. and Hümmelchen, G. *Chronology of the War at Sea*, New York, Arco, 1971

Rørholt, Bjørn. *Usynlige soldater*, Oslo, Aschehoug, 1990

Roskill, Stephen. *The War at Sea*, London, HMSO, 1961

Ruge, Friedrich. *Der Seekrieg 1939–45*, Stuttgart, Koehler, 1962

Rust, Eric C. *Naval Officers under Hitler: The Story of Crew 34*, New York, Greenwood, 1991

Salewski, Michael. *Die deutsche Seekriegsleitung 1935–1945*, 3 vols, Frankfurt am Main, Munich, Bernard & Graefe, 1970–75

Schoefield, B.B. *The Russian Convoys*, London, Pan Books, 1971

Sebag-Montefiore, Hugh. *Enigma: The Battle for the Code*, London, Weidenfeld & Nicolson, 2000

Showell, Jak P. Mallmann. *German Navy Handbook 1939–45*, Stroud, Sutton Publishing, 1999

Skodvin, Magne (ed.), *Norge i krig*, 8 vols, Oslo, Aschehoug, 1984–87

Smith, Michael. *Station X: The Codebreakers at Bletchley Park*, London, Macmillan, 1998

Storheill, Skule. 'Senkningen av slagskipet Scharnhorst den 26. desember 1943', *Norsk Tidsskrift for Sjøvæsen*, 1946

Ulstein, Ragnar. *Etterretningstjenesten i Norge 1940–45*, 3 vols, Oslo, Cappelen, 1989–92

Watts, A.J. *The Loss of the Scharnhorst*, London, Ian Allen, 1970

Whitley, M.J. *German Capital Ships of World War Two*, London, Cassell, 1989

Winton, John. *The Death of the Scharnhorst*, London, Panther, 1984

Woodman, Richard. *Arctic Convoys*, London, John Murray, 1994

Woodward, David. *The Tirpitz and the Battle for the North Atlantic*, New York, Berkley, 1953

Øyfolk. 'Årbok for lokalhistorie og kultur i Hammerfest' ('Yearbook of Local History and Culture in Hammerfest'), various editions, 1990–99

Index

(Subheadings are arranged in chronological order)

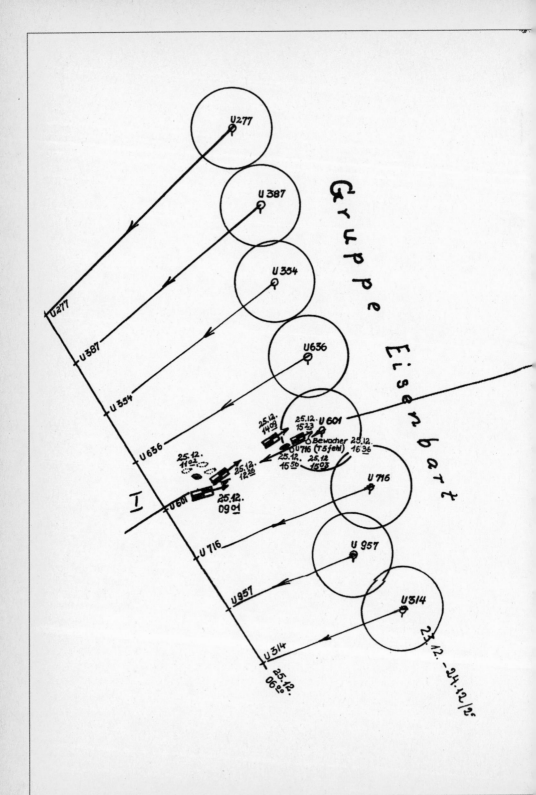